The New Tinsmith's Helper and Pattern Book: A Textbook and Working Guide for the Ambitious Apprentice, Busy Mechanic Or Trade School Student, Giving a Practical Explanation of the Properties of Circles, the Mensuration of Surfaces and Solids, Simple Geome

Hall V. Williams

The New Tinsmith's Helper and Pattern Book

A TEXTBOOK AND WORKING GUIDE for the ambitious apprentice, busy mechanic or trade school student, giving a practical explanation of the properties of circles, the mensuration of surfaces and solids, simple geometrical drawing, the forming of seams, laps and joints, and one hundred problems on the layout and cutting of Conical Vessels, Elbows and Piping, Furnace Fittings, Ducts, Gutters, Leaders and Roofing, Tinclad Fireproof Doors, Cornice and Skylight Work; with ninety-two tables and many shop kinks, recipes, and formulas.

By

Hall V. Williams

Fourth Edition

New York
U. P. C. Book Company
231-249 West 39th Street
Nineteen Hundred and Nineteen

PREFACE

For many years "The Tinsmith's Helper and Pattern Book" has been one of the most popular books on tinsmithing and elementary sheet metal work. It is to be found in the majority of the shops, because it explains the elements of pattern drafting and shows how the rules of mensuration are applied to the problems which come up daily. This New Helper is an outgrowth of that practical guide.

At first it was intended to merely revise the old book, but it soon became apparent that an entirely new treatment of the subject was necessary in order to cover the ground. This book is new with the exception of the chapter on Mensuration, which has been re-arranged and amplified, and possibly some fifty pages of problems and tables which are classified according to the phase of the work they cover.

The present work has 360 pages, 248 figures and 92 tables as against the 120 pages, 53 figures and 24 tables contained in the former work.

The additional matter covers simple geometry and every phase of modern pattern cutting, from the making of every type of seam, lap and joint, to conical problems and tinware, elbows, piping, ducts, gutters, leaders, cornice and skylight work, and furnace fittings. The use of triangulation in the development of pattern problems is simply explained. Information is also included on tin roofing, corrugated iron work, laying metal shingles, tile, slate, etc.

The chapter of tables contains practically all the data the sheet metal worker requires, from the weight of iron and steel, copper, brass and aluminum sheets and bars, to the capacities of cylinders and rectangular tanks in U. S. gallons. Our Canadian and English friends will find complete tables of capacities based on their standard Imperial gallon. The metric equivalents of all our measures are also given.

The chapter on Recipes and Formulas gives the mixtures for all the soft and hard solders, soldering fluxes, cements, putties, inks for making sheet metal work, rust preventives, etc.

It is the belief of the editor and publishers that this handy little volume is the most complete textbook and guide for the apprentice or trade school student, as well as an up-to-date reference book for the mechanic and shop foreman. Anyone who fails to find the information which he thinks ought to be in the book will confer a favor by writing the publishers.

A more comprehensive treatment of the subject is given in "The New Metal Worker Pattern Book," and "The Advanced Tinsmith's Helper, and Pattern Book" just published.

Table of Contents

THE NEW TINSMITH'S HELPER

CHAPTER I

Mensuration

Mensuration is that branch of mathematics which is employed in ascertaining the extension, solidities and capacities of bodies capable of being measured.

Definitions of Arithmetical Signs

$=$	Sign of	Equality, and signifies		as $4 + 6 = 10$.
$+$	"	Addition,	"	as $6 + 6 = 12$, the Sum.
$-$	"	Subtraction,	"	as $6 - 2 = 4$, Remainder.
$\times$	"	Multiplication,	"	as $8 \times 3 = 24$, Product.
$\div$	"	Division,	"	as $24 \div 3 = 8$.
$\surd$	"	Square Root,	"	Extraction of Square Root.
6^2	"	to be squared,	"	thus $8^2 = 64$.
7^3	"	to be cubed,	"	thus $3^3 = 27$.

SURFACE MENSURATION

The Square, Rectangle, Cube, Etc.

1. The side of a square equals the square root of its area.

2. The area of a square equals the square of one of its sides.

3. The diagonal of a square equals the square root of twice the square of its side.

4. The side of a square is equal to the square root of half the square of its diagonal.

5. The side of a square equal to the diagonal of a given square contains double the area of the given square.

6. The area of a rectangle equals its length multiplied by its breadth.

7. The length of a rectangle equals the area divided by the breadth; or the breadth equals the area divided by the length.

To Measure or Ascertain the Quantity of Surface in Any Right Lined Figure Whose Sides are Parallel to Each Other.

Rule: *Multiply the length by the breadth or perpendicular height, and the product will be the area or superficial contents.*

Example: The sides of a square piece of iron are 9⅞ inches in length, required the area of this sheet of iron.

Ans.: Decimal equivalent to the fraction ⅞ = .875, and $9.875 \times 9.875 = 97.5$, etc., square inches, the area.

Example: The length of a roof is 60 feet 4

inches and its width 25 feet 3 inches; required the area of the roof.

Ans.: 4 inches = .333 and 3 inches = .25 (see table of equivalents), hence, 60.333 × 25.25 = 1523.4 square feet, the area; or, to convert back to feet and inches, 1523 square feet and 57⅗ square inches.

Triangles

1. The complement of an angle is its defect from a right angle.

2. The supplement of an angle is its defect from two right angles.

3. The three angles of every triangle are equal to two right angles: hence the oblique angles of a right angled triangle are each other's complements.

4. The sum of the squares of two given sides of a right angled triangle is equal to the square of the hypothenuse.

5. The difference between the squares of the hypothenuse and given side of a right angled triangle is equal to the square of the required side.

6. The area of a triangle equals half the product of the base multiplied by the perpendicular height of the triangle.

To Find the Area of a Triangle When the Base and Perpendicular are Given.

Rule: *Multiply the base by the perpendicular height and half the product is the area.*

Example: The base of the triangle is 3 feet 6 inches in length and the height 1 foot 9 inches; required the area.

Ans.: 6 in. = .5 and 9 in. = .75, hence,

$$\frac{3.5 \times 1.75}{2} = 3.0625$$

square feet, the area.

To Find the Hypothenuse When the Base and Perpendicular are Given.

Rule: *Add the square of the base to the square of the perpendicular and the square root of the sum will be the hypothenuse.*

Example: The base of the triangle is 4 feet and the perpendicular 3 feet; required the hypothenuse.

Ans.: $4^2 + 3^2 = 25$, $\sqrt{25} = 5$ feet, the hypothenuse.

To Find the Perpendicular When the Hypothenuse and Base are Given.

Rule: *From the square of the hypothenuse subtract the square of the base, and the square root of the remainder will be the perpendicular.*

Example: The hypothenuse of the triangle is 5 feet and the base 4 feet; required the perpendicular.

Ans.: $5^2 - 4^2 = 9$, and $\sqrt{9} = 3$, the perpendicular.

To Find the Base When the Hypothenuse and Perpendicular are Given.

Rule: *From the square of the hypothenuse subtract the square of the perpendicular, and the square root of the remainder will be the base.*

Example: The hypothenuse of a triangle is 5 feet and the perpendicular is 3 feet, required the base.

Ans.: $5^2 - 3^2 = 16$ and $\sqrt{16} = 4$, the base.

Polygons

The side of any regular polygon multiplied by its apothem or perpendicular, and by the number of its sides, equals twice the area.

To Find the Area of a Regular Polygon.

Rule: *Multiply the length of a side by half the distance from the side to the center, and that product by the number of sides; the last product will be the area of the figure.*

Example: The side of a regular hexagon is 12 inches, and the distance therefrom to the center of the figure is 10 inches; required the area of the hexagon.

Ans.: $\frac{10}{2} \times 12 \times 6 = 360$ square inches $= 2\frac{1}{2}$ square feet.

To Find the Area of a Regular Polygon When the Side Only is Given.

Rule: *Multiply the square of the side by the multiplier opposite to the name of the polygon in the ninth column of the following table, and the product will be the area.*

Example: A hexagon side is 12 inches, required its area.

Ans.: $12^2 = 144$; $144 \times 2.598076 = 374.1229$ square feet.

Table of Angles

Table of angles relative to the construction of Regular Polygons with the aid of the sector, and of coefficients to facilitate their construction without it; also, of coefficients to aid in finding the area of the figure, the side only being given.

Names.	Number of sides.	Angle at center.	Angle at circum.	Perp'n side being 1.	Length of side rad. being 1.	Rad. of cir. side being 1.	Rad. of cir. per. being 1.	Area side being 1.
Triangle	3	120	60	.28868	1.782	.5773	2.	.433012
Square	4	90	90	.5	1.414	.7071	1.414	1.
Pentagon	5	72	108	.6882	1.175	.8506	1.238	1.720477
Hexagon	6	60	120	.866	1.	1.	1.156	2.598076
Heptagon	7	51 3-7	128 4-7	1.0382	.8672	1.152	1.11	3.633912
Octagon	8	45	135	1.2071	.7654	1.3065	1.08	4.828427
Nonagon	9	40	140	1.3737	.684	1.4619	1.06	6.181824
Decagon	10	36	144	1.5388	.618	1.618	1.05	7.694208
Undecagon	11	32 8-11	147 3-11	1.7028	.5634	1.7747	1.04	9.36564
Dodecagon	12	30	150	1.866	.5176	1.9318	1.037	11.196152

NOTE.—"Angle at center" means the angle of radii passing from the center to the circumference or corners of the figure. "Angle at circumference" means the angle which any two adjoining sides make with each other.

The Circle

1. The radius of a circle is a straight line drawn from the center to the circumference.

2. The diameter of a circle is a straight line drawn through the center and terminating both ways in the circumference.

3. A chord is a straight line joining any two points of the circumference.

4. The versed sine is a straight line joining the chord and the circumference.

5. An arc is any part of the circumference.

6. A semicircle is half the circle cut off by a diameter.

7. A segment is any portion of a circle cut off by a chord.

8. A sector is a part of a circle cut off by two radii.

9. The circle contains a greater area than any other plane figure bounded by an equal perimeter or outline.

10. The areas of circles are to each other as the squares of their diameters. Any circle twice the diameter of another contains four times the area of the other.

11. The circumference of a circle equals its diameter multiplied by 3.1416.

12. The diameter of a circle equals its circumference multiplied by .31831.

13. The area of a circle equals the square of its diameter multiplied by .7854.

14. The square root of the area of a circle multiplied by 1.12837 equals its diameter.

15. The diameter of a circle multiplied by .8862, or the circumference multiplied by .2821, equals the side of a square of equal area.

16. The side of a square multiplied by 1.128 equals the diameter of a circle of equal area.

17. The number of degrees contained in the arc of a circle multiplied by the diameter of the circle and by .008727, the product equals the length of the arc in equal terms of unity.

18. The length of the arc of a sector of a circle multiplied by its radius equals twice the area of the sector.

19. The area of the segment of a circle equals the area of the sector, minus the area of a triangle

whose vertex is the center and whose base equals the chord of the segment.

20. The sum of the diameters of two concentric circles multiplied by their difference and by .7854 equals the area of the ring or space contained between them.

To Find the Circumference of a Circle Whose Diameter is Given.

Rule: *Multiply the diameter by 3.1416.*

Example: The diameter of a circle being 5 feet 6 inches, required its circumference.

Ans.: $5.5 \times 3.1416 = 17.27880$ feet, the circumference, or, converting back to feet and inches, 17 feet and 3 5/16 inches.

To Find the Diameter of a Circle When the Circumference is Given.

Rule: *Multiply the circumference by .31831.*

Example: A straight line or the circumference of a circle being 17.27880 feet, required the circle's diameter corresponding thereto.

Ans.: $17.27880 \times .31831 = 5.5000148280$ feet, diameter, or actually 5½ feet.

To Find the Area of a Circle When the Diameter is Given.

Rule: *Multiply the square of the diameter by .7854.*

Example: The diameter of a circle is 9⅜ inches; what is its area in square inches?

Ans.: $9.375^2 = 87.89$, etc., $\times .7854 = 69.029$, etc., square inches, the area. 0.29 feet equal about ⅓ of a square inch.

To Find the Diameter of a Circle When the Area is Given.

Rule: *Extract the square root and multiply it by 1.12837.*

Example: What must the diameter of a circle be to contain an area equal to 69.029296875 square inches?

Ans: $\sqrt{69.02929}$, etc., $= 8.3091 \times 1.12837 =$ 9.375, etc., or 9⅜ inches, the diameter.

Given the Diameter of a Circle to Find the Side of a Square of Equal Area to the Circle.

Rule: *Multiply the diameter by .8862.*

Example: The diameter of a circle is 15½ inches; what must each side of a square be to be equal in area to the given circle?

Ans.: $15.5 \times .8862 = 13.73$, etc., inches, length of side.

Given the Side of a Square to Find the Diameter of a Circle of Equal Area.

Rule: *Multiply the side of the square by 1.128.*

Example: Each side of a square is 13.736 inches in length; what must the diameter of a circle be to contain an area equal to the given square?

Ans.: $13.736 \times 1.128 = 15.49$, etc., or 15½ inches, the diameter.

To Find the Diameter of a Circle Any Chord and Versed Sine Being Given.

Rule: *Divide the sum of the squares of the versed sine and one-half the chord by the versed sine; the quotient is the diameter of corresponding circle.*

Example: The chord of a circle equals 8 feet and the versed sine equals 1½; required the circle's diameter.

Ans.: $8^2 + 1.5^2 = 66.25 \div 1.5 = 44.16$ feet, the diameter.

Example: In the curve of a railway a stretched line is 80 feet in length and the distance from the line to the curve is found to be 9 inches; required the circle's diameter.

Ans.: $80^2 + .75^2 = 640.5625 \div 2 = 320.28$, etc., feet, the diameter.

To Find the Length of Any Arc of a Circle.

Rule: *From eight times the chord of half the arc subtract the chord of the whole arc, and one-third of the remainder will be the length, nearly.*

Example: Required the length of an arc, the chord of half the arc being 8½ feet and chord of whole arc 16 feet 8 inches.

Ans.: $8.5 \times 8 = 68.0 - 16.666 = \frac{51.334}{3} =$ 17.111⅓ feet, the length of the arc.

To Find the Area of the Sector of a Circle.

Rule: *Multiply the length of the arc by half the length of the radius.*

Example: The length of the arc equals 9½ inches and the radii equal each 7 inches; required the area.

Ans.: $9.5 \times 3.5 = 33.25$ inches, the area.

To Find the Area of a Segment of a Circle.

Rule: *Find the area of a sector by the rule given for sector of a circle, whose arc is equal to that of* *the given segment, and if it be less than a semicircle subtract the area of the triangle formed by the chord of segment and radii of its extremities; but if more than a semicircle add area of triangle to the area of the sector, and the remainder or sum is the area of the segment.*

To Find the Area of the Space Contained Between Two Concentric Circles, that is to say, the Area of a Circular Ring.

Rule 1: *Multiply the sum of the inside and outside diameters by their difference and by .7854; the product is the area.*

Rule 2: *The difference of the area of the two circles will be the area of the ring or space.*

Example: Suppose the external circle equals 4 feet and the internal circle 2½ feet, required the area of space contained between them or area of a ring.

Ans.: $4 + 2.5 = 6.5$ and $4 - 2.5 = 1.5$, hence, $6.5 \times 1.5 \times .7854 = 7.65$ feet, the area; or,

The area of 4 feet is 12.566; the area of 2.5 is 4.9081. (See table of areas of circles.) $12.566 - 4.9081 = 7.6579$, the area.

Cylinders

The circumference of a cylinder multiplied by its length or height equals its convex surface.

To Find the Convex Surface of a Cylinder.

Rule: *Multiply the circumference by the height or length, the product will be the surface.*

Example: The circumference of a cylinder is 6

feet 4 inches and its length 15 feet, required the convex surface.

Ans.: $6.333 \times 15 = 94.995$ square feet, the surface.

Ellipses or Ovals

1. The square root of half the sum of the squares of the two diameters of an ellipse multiplied by 3.1416 equals its circumference.

2. The product of the two axes of an ellipse multiplied by .7854 equals its area.

To Find the Area of an Ellipse or Oval.

Rule: *Multiply the diameters together and their product by .7854.*

Example: An oval is 20 x 15 inches, what are its superficial contents?

Ans.: $20 \times 15 \times .7854 = 235.62$ inches, the area.

To Find the Circumference of an Ellipse or Oval.

Rule: *Multiply half the sum of the two diameters by 3.1416 and the product will be the circumference.*

Example: An oval is 20 x 15 inches, what is the circumference?

Ans.: $\frac{20 + 15}{2} = 17.5 \times 3.1416 = 54.978$ inches, the circumference.

Cones and Pyramids

1. The curve surface of a cone is equal to half the product of the circumference of its base multiplied by its slant side, to which, if the area of the base be added, the sum is the whole surface.

To Find the Convex Surface of a Right Cone or Pyramid.

Rule: *Multiply the circumference of the base by the slant height and half the product is the slant surface; if the surface of the entire figure is required, add the area of the base to the convex surface.*

Example: The base of a cone is 5 feet diameter and the slant height is 7 feet, what is the convex surface?

Ans.: $5 \times 3.1416 = 15.70$ circumference of the base and $\frac{15.70 \times 7}{2} = 54.95$ square feet, the convex surface. Converting feet to inches, .95 square feet equal 136⅘ square inches.

To Find the Convex Surface of a Frustum of a Cone or Pyramid.

Rule: *Multiply the sum of the circumference of the two ends by the slant height and half the product will be the slant surface.*

Example: The diameter of the top of the frustum of a cone is 3 feet, the base 5 feet, the slant height 7 feet 3 inches; required the slant surface.

Ans.: $9.42 + 15.7 = \frac{25.12 \times 7.25}{2} = 91.06$ square feet, slant surface. To change to square inches, .06 square feet equal 10¾ square inches.

Spheres

1. The square of the diameter of a sphere multiplied by 3.1416 equals its convex surface.

2. The height of any spherical segment or zone, multiplied by the diameter of the sphere of which

it is a part and by 3.1416, equals the area or convex surface of the segment; or,

3. The height of the segment muliplied by the circumference of the sphere of which it is a part equals the area.

To Find the Convex Surface of a Sphere or Globe.

Rule 1: *Multiply the diameter of the sphere by its circumference and the product is its surface; or,*

Rule 2: *Multiply the square of the diameter by 3.1416; the product is the surface.*

Example: What is the convex surface of a globe 6½ feet in diameter?

Ans.: $6.5 \times 3.1416 \times 6.5 = 132.73$ square feet; or, $6.5^2 = 42.25 \times 3.1416 = 132.73$ square feet, the convex surface.

MENSURATION OF SOLIDS AND CAPACITIES OF BODIES

1. The solidity of a cube equals the area of one of its sides multiplied by the length or breadth of one of its sides.

2. The length of a side of a cube equals the cube root of its solidity.

To Find the Solidity or Capacity of Any Figures in the Cubical Form.

Rule: *Multiply the length of any one side by its breadth and by the depth or distance to its opposite side, and the product is the solidity in equal terms of measurement.*

Example: The side of a cube is 20 inches; what is its solidity?

Ans.: $20 \times 20 \times 20 = 8000$ cubic inches, or 4.6296 cubic feet.

Example: A rectangular tank is in length 6 feet, in breadth 4½ feet and its depth 3 feet; required its capacity in cubic feet; also its capacity in United States standard gallons.

Ans: $6 \times 4.5 \times 3 = 81$ cubic feet; $81 \times 1728 = 139{,}968 \div 231 = 605.92$ gallons.

Cylinders

1. The area of the end of a cylinder multiplied by its length equals its solid contents.

2. The area of the internal diameter of a cylinder multiplied by its depth equals its cubical capacity.

3. The square of the diameter of a cylinder multiplied by its length and divided by any other required length, the square root of the quotient equals the diameter of the other cylinder of equal contents or capacity.

4. The capacity of a cylinder, 1 inch in diameter and 1 inch in length, equals .0034 United States gallon.

5. The capacity of a cylinder, 1 inch in diameter and 1 foot in length, equals .0408 United States gallon.

6. The capacity of a cylinder, 1 foot in diameter and 1 foot in length, equals 5.875 United States gallons.

7. The capacity of any other cylinder in United States gallons is obtained by multiplying the square of its diameter by its length, or the capacity of any other sphere by the cube of its diameter and by the

number of United States gallons contained as above in the unity of its measurement.

To Find the Solidity of Cylinders.

Rule: *Multiply the area of the base by the height and the product is its solidity.*

Example: The base of a cylinder is 18 inches and height 40 inches. What is its capacity?

Ans.: $18^2 \times .7854 \times 40 = 10,178.7840$ cubic inches.

To Find the Contents in Gallons of Cylindrical Vessels.

Rule: *Take the dimensions in inches and decimal parts of an inch. Square the diameter, multiply it by the height, then multiply the product by .0034 for wine gallons, or by .002785 for beer gallons.*

Example: How many United States gallons will a cylinder contain whose diameter is 18 inches and length 30 inches?

Ans.: $18^2 \times 30 = 9720 \times .0034 = 33.04$, etc., gallons.

Cones and Pyramids

1. The solidity of a cone equals one-third the product of its base multiplied by its height.

2. The square of the diameters of the two ends of the frustum of a cone added to the product of the two diameters, and that sum multiplied by its height and by .2618, equals its solidity.

Nearly all appliances for measuring liquids are frustums of cones in shape, rather than cylinders; so it might be well to pay particular attention to gallon capacities in the examples for frustums.

To Find the Solidity of a Cone or a Pyramid.

Rule: *Multiply the area of the base by the perpendicular height and one-third the product will be the solidity.*

Example: The base of a cone is 2¼ feet and the height is 3¾ feet, what is the solidity?

Ans.: $\frac{2.25^2 \times .7854 \times 3.75}{3} = 4.97$ cubic feet, the solidity.

To Find the Solidity of the Frustum of a Cone.

Rule: *To the product of the diameters of the ends add one-third the square of the difference of the diameters; multiply the sum by .7854 and the product will be the mean area between the ends, which multiplied by the perpendicular height of frustum gives the solidity.*

Example: The diameter of the large end of a frustum of a cone is 10 feet, that of the smaller end is 6 feet and the perpendicular height 12 feet, what is its solidity?

Ans.: $10 - 6 = 4^2 = 16 \div 3 = 5.333$ square of difference of ends; and $10 \times 6 + 5.333 = 65.333 \times .7854 \times 12 = 615.75$ cubic feet, the solidity.

To Find the Contents in U. S. Standard Gallons of the Frustum of a Cone.

Rule: *To the product of the diameters, in inches and decimal parts of an inch, of the ends, add one-third the square of the difference of the diameters. Multiply the sum by the perpendicular height in inches and decimal parts of an inch and multiply* *that product by .0034 for wine gallons, and by .002785 for beer gallons.*

Example: The diameter of the large end of a frustum of a cone is 8 feet, that of the smaller end is 4 feet and the perpendicular height 10 feet; what are the contents in United States standard gallons?

Ans.: $96 - 48 = 48^2 = 2304 \div 3 = 768; 96 \times 48 + 768 = 5376 \times 120 \times .0034 = 2193.4$ gallons.

To Find the Solidity of the Frustum of a Pyramid.

Rule: *Add to the areas of the two ends of the frustum the square root of their product, and this sum multiplied by one-third of the perpendicular height will give the solidity.*

Example: What is the solidity of a hexagonal pyramid, a side of the large end being 12 feet, one of the smaller ends 6 feet and the perpendicular height 8 feet?

Ans.: $374.122 \times 93.53 = \sqrt{34{,}991.63} = 187.06$.

$$374.122 + 93.53 + 187.06 = \frac{654.712 \times 8}{3} =$$

1745.898 cubic feet, solidity.

Spheres

1. The cube of the diameter of a sphere multiplied by .5236 equals its solid contents.

2. The capacity of a sphere 1 inch in diameter equals .002266 United States gallon.

3. The capacity of a sphere 1 foot in diameter equals 3.9168 United States gallons.

4. The solidity of any spherical segment is equal to three times the square of the radius of its base,

plus the square of its height, multiplied by its height and by .5236.

5. The solidity of a spherical zone equals the sum of the squares of the radii of its two ends and one-third the square of its height, multiplied by the height and by 1.5708.

To Find the Solidity of a Sphere.

Rule: *Multiply the cube of the diameter by .5236 and the product is the solidity.*

Example: What is the solidity of a sphere, the diameter being 20 inches?

Ans.: $20^3 = 8000 \times .5236 = 4188.8$ cubic inches, the solidity.

The oblate spheroid, the prolate spheroid and a few other shapes have not been discussed because they are not generally used in the shop, and this manual has been boiled down so as to give the greatest amount of usable material in the space available herein.

Further information on the practical application of mensuration to shop and outside problems is given in Neubecker's "Mensuration for Sheet Metal Workers."

CHAPTER II

Simple Geometrical Problems

A knowledge of geometry is very useful, and while some of the mechanics who read this chapter may feel that they can do all that is required of them by rule of thumb, it is recommended that they study the methods given in these simple problems. No one who hopes to become an expert pattern drafter should fail to study geometry, for it is the foundation on which all the principles of pattern cutting are based.

The problems presented in this chapter have been selected for their importance, and a more comprehensive treatment of the subject is given in "The New Metal Worker Pattern Book."

To Erect a Perpendicular to a Straight Line

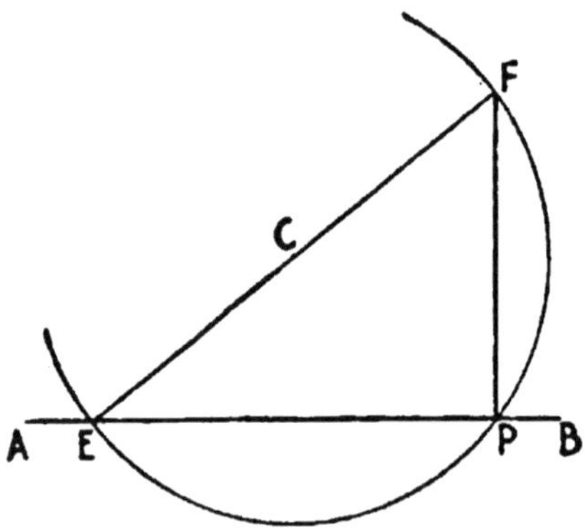

FIG. 1.—Erecting a Perpendicular.

In Fig. 1 A B is the straight line, and P the point at which perpendicular is to be erected. Take any point, C, outside of line A B as center, and with radius C to P strike an arc. Draw a line from where arc cuts line A B through C to arc again, thus establishing point F. A line drawn from F to P is the required perpendicular.

To Erect a Perpendicular to an Arc

In Fig. 2, A D B is the given arc. With A and then B as centers, with a radius greater than half the length of the arc A B, describe arcs X X and Y Y. Then draw a line, F D E, through the points where the arcs X X and Y Y cross each other and the result is the perpendicular required; always use extreme care in the operations.

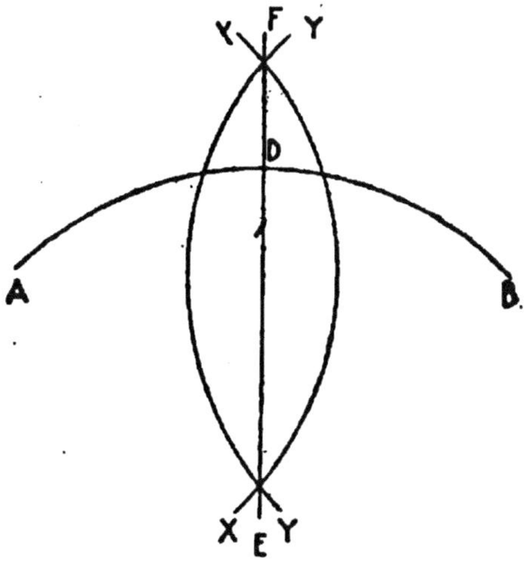

FIG. 2.—To Erect a Perpendicular to an Arc.

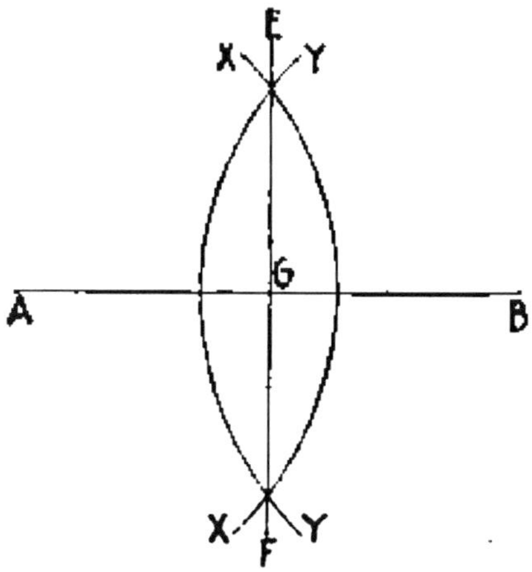

FIG. 3.—To Divide a Straight Line

To Divide a Straight Line into Equal Parts

In Fig. 3, A B is the given line. With the points A and B as centers and with radius greater than one-half the length of A B, draw arcs X X and Y Y as shown. Then draw a line E F through the points where these arcs cross each other, thus dividing line A B into two equal parts at G. Incidentally E G or F G are perpendiculars to A B, so that this method will do for erecting perpendiculars, at G, to A B.

To Find the Center of an Arc

Let H K in Fig, 4 represent the given arc. Span dividers any convenient radius and describe small arcs, as at V and O, being sure to have the point of the dividers on the arc H K. Draw lines through them, as shown by dotted lines, and the intersection, S, will be the center sought. Arc B from V and O, bisects angle V S O.

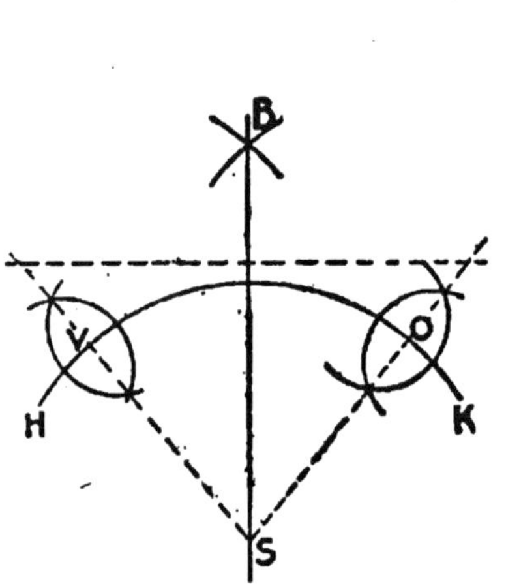

Fig. 4.—Finding the Center of an Arc.

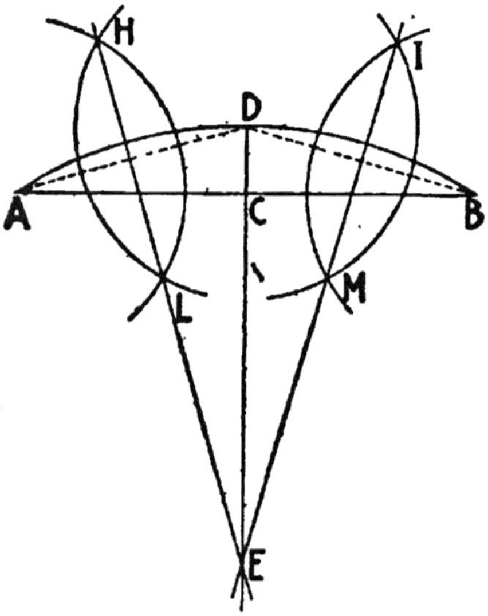

Fig. 5.—Finding the Center of the Arc.

Having Chord and Height of Segment to Find Center of the Arc

In Fig. 5 let A B be the chord and C D the height of the segment, then draw lines A D and B D. Bisect these lines as shown and extend the lines H L and I M until they intersect each other as at point E, then E is the center sought. Continuing line D C until it cuts either H L or I M is another method in which but one bisecting line, either H L or I M, is used.

To Bisect an Angle

In Fig. 6 A C B is the given angle, and to bisect it strike an arc, to any convenient radius, using B as center and establishing points D and E. With the compass set to a radius more than half the distance from D to E and with these points as centers strike intersecting arcs, thus producing point H. A line from H to B bisects the given angle A B C; in part, a similar procedure to that of Fig. 4.

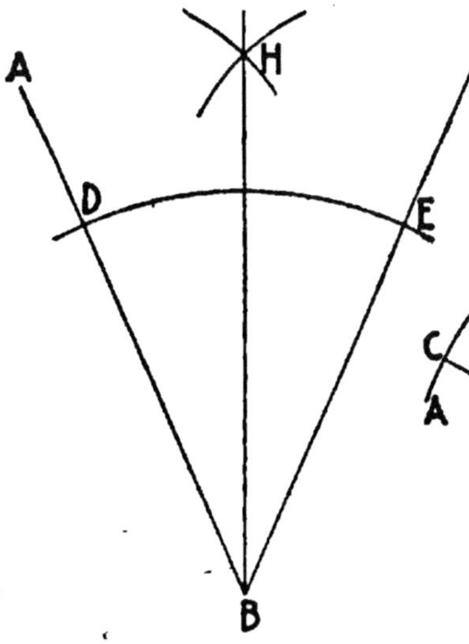

FIG. 6.—Bisecting an Angle.

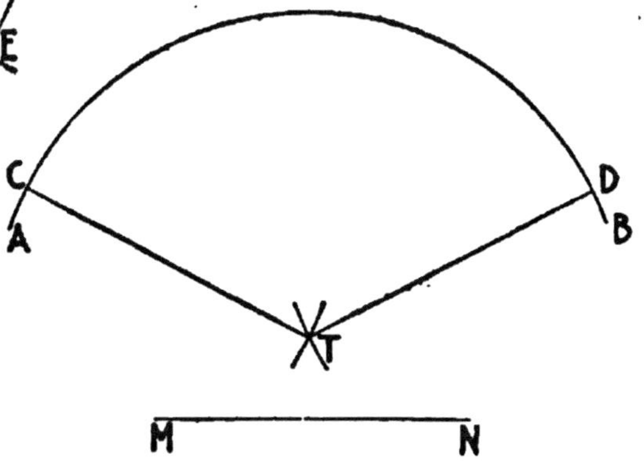

FIG. 7.—Locating the Center.

Arc and Radius Given, to Locate the Center

In Fig. 7, assume that A B is the given arc and line M N the radius. Set the compass to radius M N and with any point on arc, say C, as center, describe a short arc. With any other point on arc A B, as D, for center describe another arc cutting the first one at T, which is the center of the given arc A B.

To Draw a Straight Line Parallel to Another

In Fig. 8, let A B be the given line. Select any two points on line A B as C and D and with compass set to radius equal to distance the parallel lines are to be apart, strike short arcs using points C and D for centers as shown. Then draw a line touching these arcs as E F, and that line, E F, will be parallel to, and the required distance from line A B.

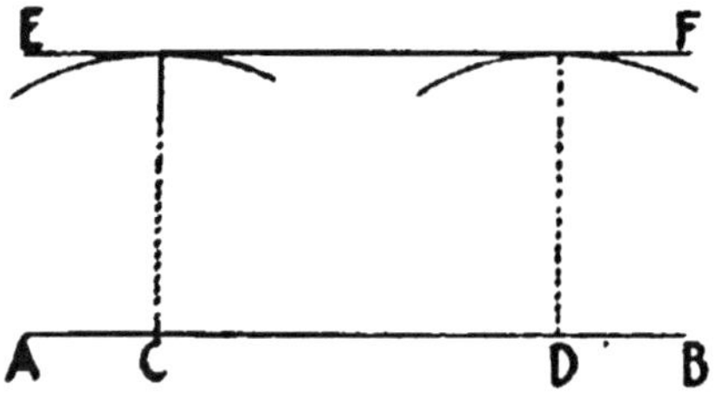

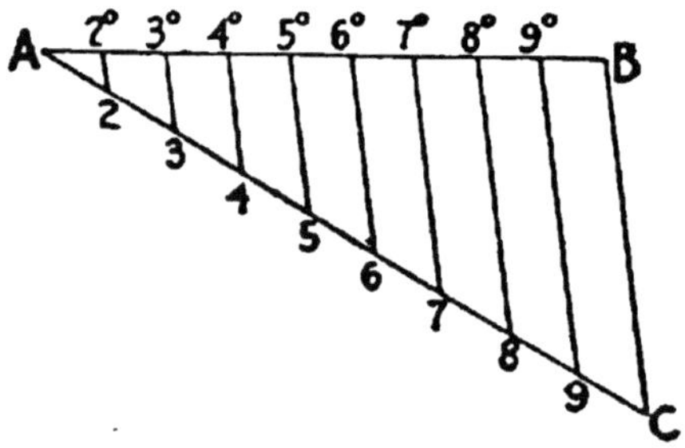

FIG. 8.—Drawing Parallel Lines. FIG. 9.—Dividing a Line Equally.

To Divide a Straight Line into a Number of Equal Parts

In Fig. 9, assume that line A B is to be divided into nine equal spaces. From A draw another line, at any convenient angle. Step this line off into nine equal spaces as shown on line A C by setting the dividers at will, but trying to arrange it so the last swing will come near the end of the line A C. From C draw a line to B and then draw lines, parallel to line C B, from the points on line A C to intersect the line A B, giving points A 2°, 3°, 4°, 5°, 6°, 7°, 8°, 9° and B. These spaces on A B are all equal and divide A B into nine spaces. Both problems on this page are very useful and the reader will do well to memorize them.

To Draw a Tangent to a Circle or Arc

In Fig. 10, let M D N be the given arc of the circle and to draw a tangent at D set the compass to a convenient radius and with D as center describe arc cutting M D N at A B. Join points A and B. Then set compass to radius equal to distance between D and the line A B. With this radius and with B as center describe an arc above line A B. Then draw a line extending through point D and touching the second arc as shown by E D H, which is the tangent.

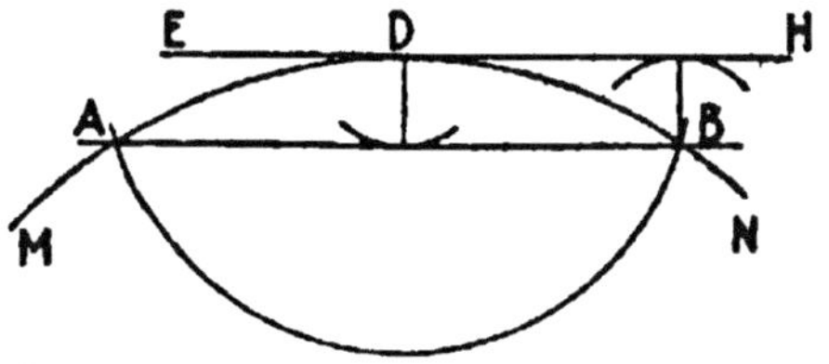

FIG. 10.—Drawing the Tangent.

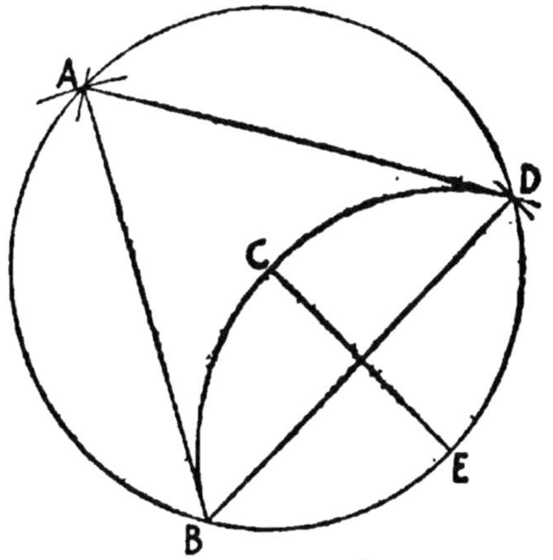

FIG. 11.—A Triangle in a Circle.

To Inscribe an Equilateral Triangle in a Circle

In Fig. 11, let A D B be given circle, then with compass set to radius of the circle and from any point on it at will as E describe arc B C D cutting circle at points B and D and naturally passing through center of circle C. Draw line B D, which is one side of the triangle. With the compass set to a radius equal to space B D and with B and then D as centers describe arcs giving point A. Draw lines from A to D and A to B completing the triangle. The same method of drawing a triangle may be followed when one side is given, as B D.

To Inscribe a Square in a Circle

In Fig. 12, let T be given circle. Through its center A draw two diameter lines at right angles to each other as C D and E F. To be sure you have a square set your dividers to the distance between points C E and using that as a guide check the length of the other sides. Drawing lines from F to D, D to E, E to C and C to F completes the square.

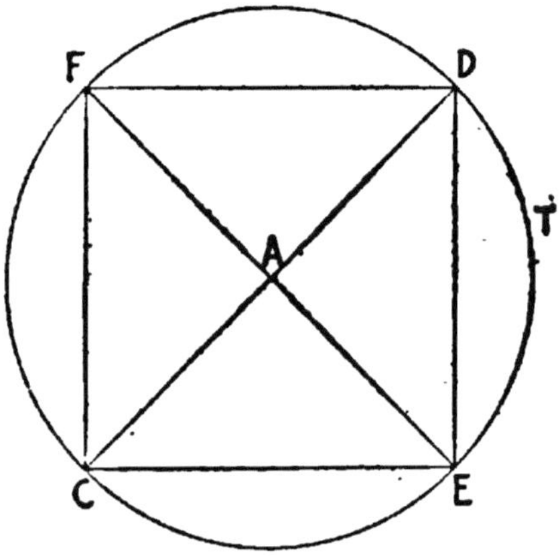

FIG. 12.—A Square in a Circle.

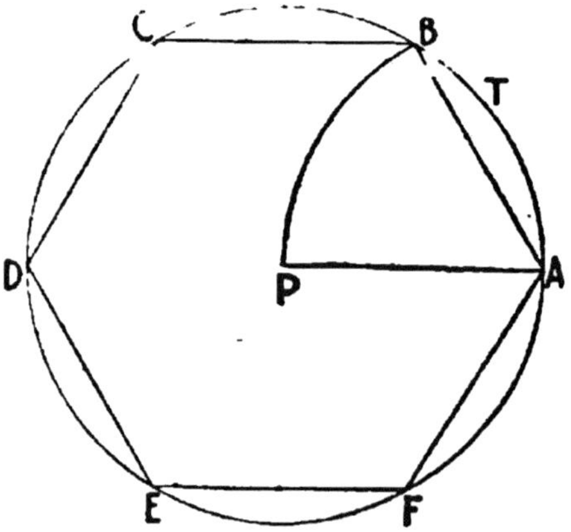

FIG. 13.—A Hexagon in a Circle.

To Inscribe a Hexagon in a Circle

In Fig. 13, let T be the given circle; choose any point for center, as A, on the circle and with a radius equal to that of the circle describe arc P B, P of course being the center of the circle T. Set dividers to space A B and step around circle as B C, C D and so on. In other words, the radius of the given circle equals one side of the hexagon, so all that is necessary to get the other five sides is to step off the length of the radius as often as possible on the circumference, beginning at A. The sixth point should be A.

To Inscribe an Octagon within a Given Square

Draw diagonal lines from corner to corner and the intersection is the center H, as shown in Fig. 14. With the compasses set to a radius from center to corner, and one foot set successively at each corner, describe arcs, as shown. The points at which they cut the square, as K V, will be the corners of the octagon. Draw lines from point to point to complete the figure.

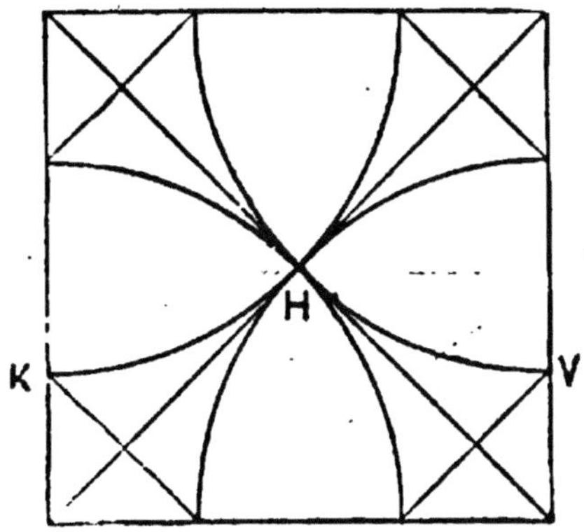

FIG. 14.—An Octagon Within a Square.

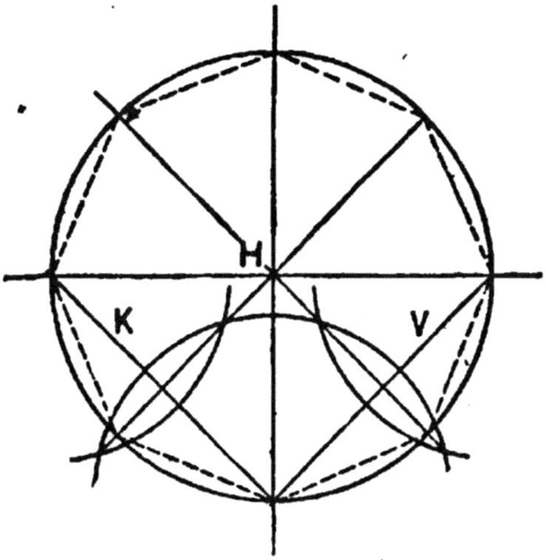

FIG. 15.—An Octagon Within a Circle.

To Inscribe an Octagon within a Given Circle

Draw lines at right angles passing through center H as in Fig. 15. This divides the circle into four parts, which need only to be subdivided into equal parts again to form the corners for the octagon. This may be easily done by drawing the lines K V, and bisecting them, as shown, and drawing lines to the circle through the bisecting arcs locates desired points.

Heart with Square and Compass

Draw line H K the breadth of the heart and describe two semicircles on it as shown in Fig. 16. These semicircles should be of the same size and radius. About the best way to do this would be to divide line H K into four equal parts and then use the first space point from H, and also from K, as centers describe a semicircle from H and then K. Span dividers from H to K and with H as center make sweep K to V. Then with same radius and K as center, make sweep H to V.

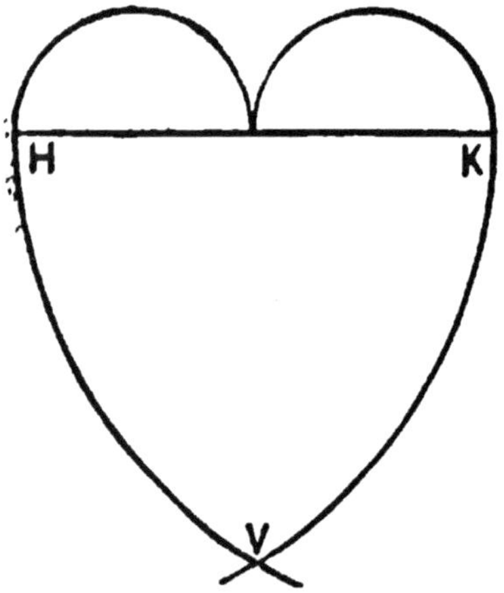

FIG. 16.—A Geometrical Heart.

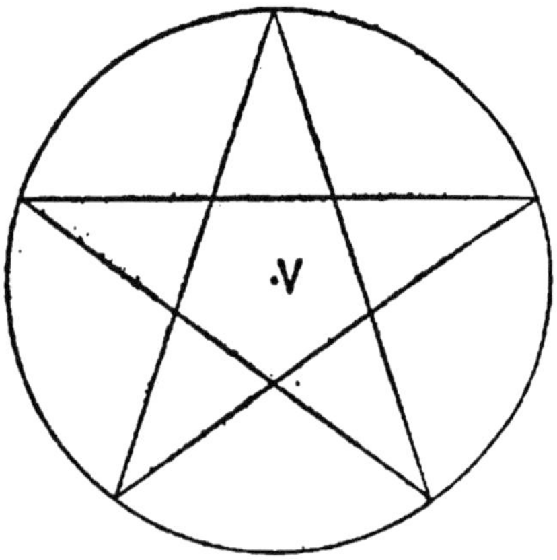

FIG. 17.—A Five Pointed Star.

To Describe a Star

With V in Fig. 17 as center strike circle size of star desired. Divide circle in five parts and draw lines to points.

There is a rule for finding the points of a star other than stepping, but it is not given here because it has been found that this mode is the quickest and most accurate; in fact, it is about the quickest way to draw any polygon.

To Describe an Oval or Ellipse with a Compass

Draw horizontal line F K the length of the oval desired, as shown in Fig. 18, then span the dividers one-third the required major diameter F K, and from V and O as centers describe circles, as shown; then span dividers two-thirds entire length V to K,

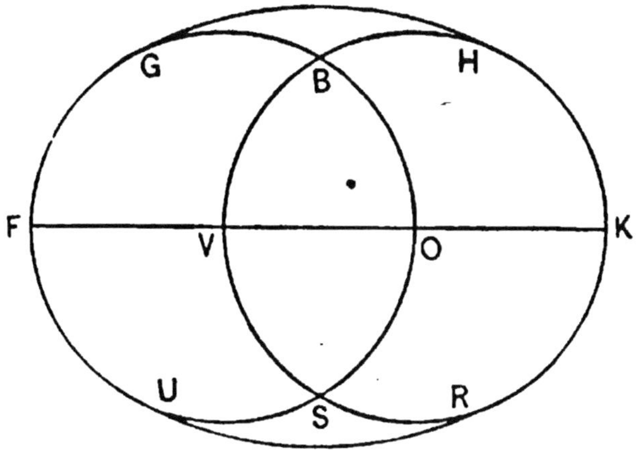

FIG. 18.—Quick Way to Draw an Oval.

and, with one foot at the intersection of the circles, as S and B, draw the arcs G H and U R, stopping them where they touch the circles drawn with O and V as centers, which of course is G H U and R, which completes the oval.

The proportion of the diameters is about as three to four, and makes an oval—or, strictly speaking, an ellipse, that is satisfactory for all ordinary purposes. Drawing straight lines from G to H and from U to R describes an oval that is quite popular for furnace pipes. Or, draw a rectangle as wide as the required oval and as long as the distance from center to center of semicircular ends. Strike half-circles from the centers of the ends of the rectangle.

To Describe an Oval Having Diameters as Five to Eight with a Square and Compass

Draw horizontal line H K the length desired as shown in Fig. 19. Span compasses one-quarter

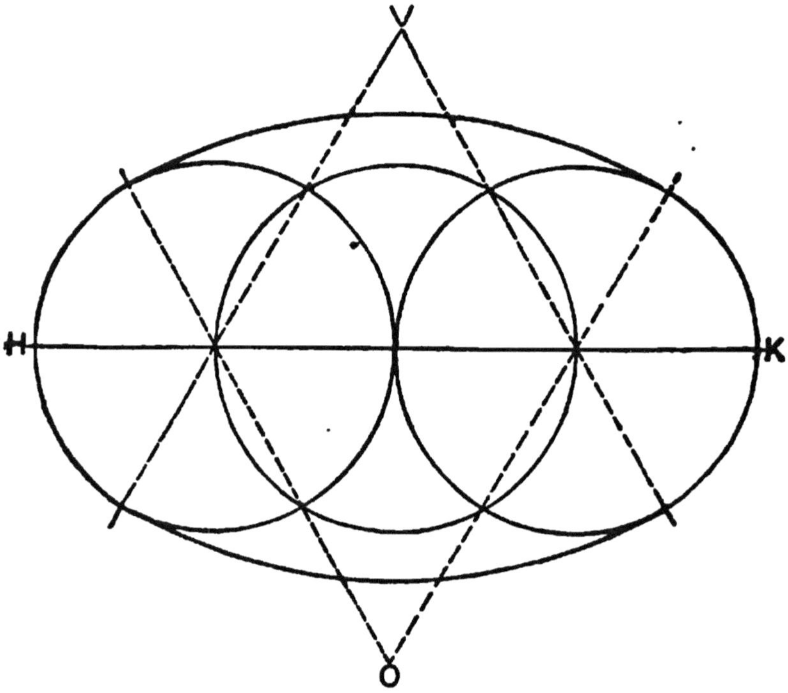

FIG. 19.—Another Method of Drawing an Oval or Ellipse.

the long diameter and describe three circles with that radius, as shown by diagram. Then draw lines through centers of outer circles and their intersections with the inner circle as shown. The oval is completed by drawing the arcs, connecting the outer circles, from points V and O as centers; the dotted lines being the terminus points.

By comparing the diagram, Fig. 19, with the other diagram, Fig. 18, it will be seen that this method gives a more accurate ellipse.

To Describe an Oval with a Square and Compass. Third Method

Draw horizontal line H K and erect line V O perpendicular to it as shown in Fig. 20.

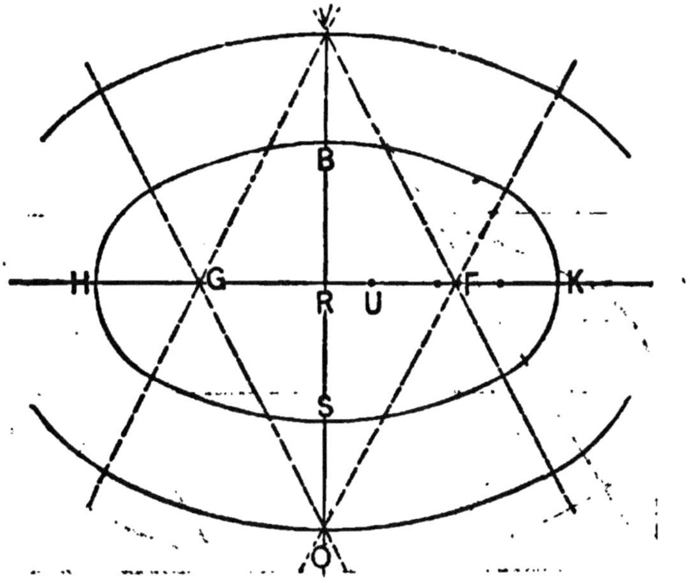

FIG. 20.—A Third Method of Drawing an Oval or Ellipse.

Let H K equal the long or transverse diameter, and S B the short or conjugate. Lay off the distance S B on the line H K, as from H to U. Divide the distance U K into three equal parts. From R, the center, set off two of the parts each side, as G F. On the line V O set off the distance G F from R, as R V and R O. From V and O draw lines passing through G and F, as shown. From the points V, O, G, F as centers describe the arcs that complete the ellipse.

As may be observed, the foregoing procedure more nearly approaches the usual prescribed geometrical procedure.

To Describe an Oval with a Square and Compass. Fourth Method

Construct the parallelogram equal in length and width to the long and short diameters of the oval

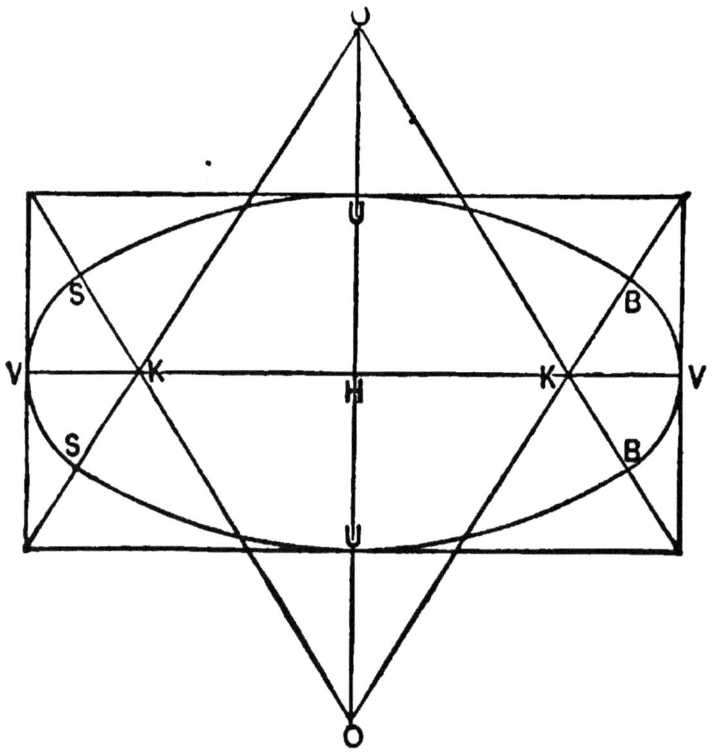

FIG. 21.—A Fourth Method of Drawing an Oval or Ellipse.

desired, as shown in Fig. 21. Divide it into four equal parts by drawing lines through the center, crossing at H. Mark the points K and K one-third the distance from V to H, and draw lines from the corners through these points until they intersect, as shown at O. Then from O and O as centers describe the arcs S U B and S U B; from K and K as centers the segments B V B and S V S; thus completing the required figure.

To Describe Oval with String, Pins and Pencil

Erect perpendicular line H K equal to short diameter and at right angles to it V O, as shown in

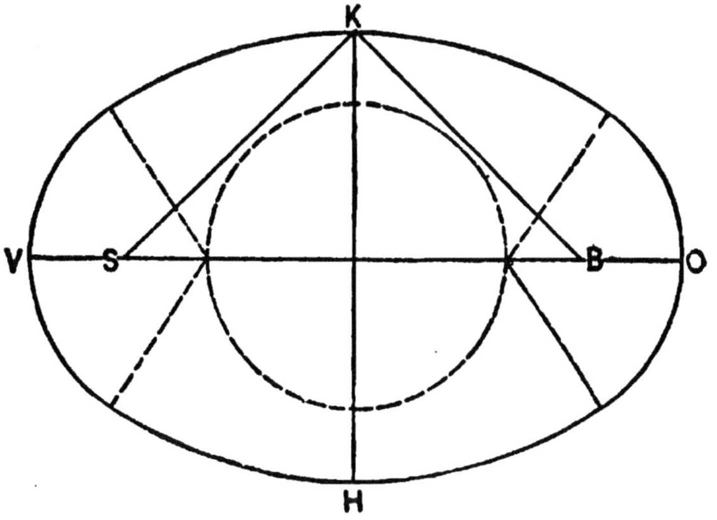

FIG. 22.—Drawing Oval with a String.

Fig. 22. Span dividers one-half the length of the oval, and with H and K as centers describe the arcs S and B. Set pins at these points, and, with a string (one that will not stretch) tied around them so that the loop when drawn tight will reach H or K, as shown, draw the figure with pencil, keeping string equally tense while going around. The various rules for drawing ovals, or rather ellipses, by the use of dividers and other means have been given in this work for the benefit of the student and so the mechanic may select and use the one that seems easiest to him.

This is a mechanical process and there are many other mechanical devices for drawing ellipses. There are also numerous other geometrical processes like developing the oblique section of a cylinder.

To Draw a True Oval

Strictly speaking the foregoing problems are not ovals, but ellipses. A true oval is egg-shaped, and

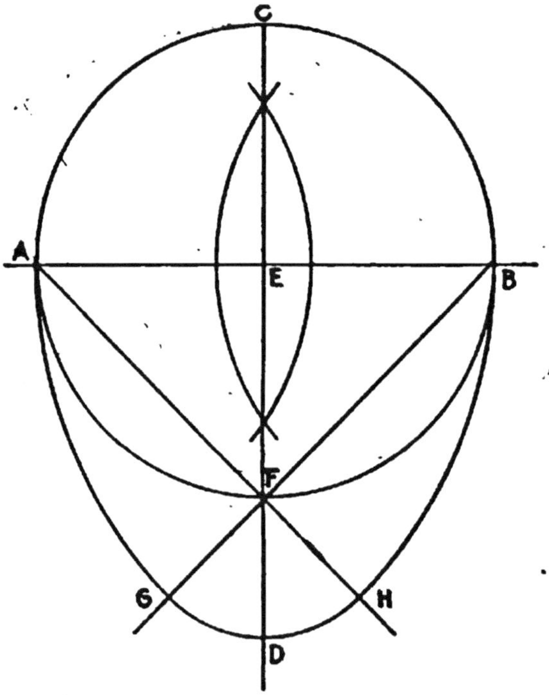

FIG. 23.—Drawing a True Oval.

in Fig. 23 is shown a geometrical method of drawing such a figure. Draw a horizontal line A B the length of the narrowest dimension of the figure. Draw a vertical line C D the length of the longest dimension of the oval; line C D is to pass exactly in the center of line A B by method of Fig. 3, giving point E. With E as center and radius A describe full circle. Draw lines from A and B through F indefinitely. With A and then B as centers describe arcs A G and B H. With F as center and a radius equal to F G describe arc G D H, which will complete the oval.

To Draw a Simple Spiral or Scroll

The scroll or spiral is a typical geometrical problem and, of the many different methods, the following one is recommended for its simplicity. Draw any polygon, for example a hexagon as in Fig. 13. Continue the various sides as shown in Fig. 24. Then with 2 as center and 2 to 1 as radius describe arc 1 A. With 3 as center and A to 3 as radius, describe arc A B. With 4 as center and B to 4 as radius, describe arc B C. With 5 as center and C to 5 as radius, describe arc C D. With 6 as center and D to 6 as radius, describe arc D E. With 1 as center and E to 1 as radius, describe arc E F, completing revolution. As many revolutions as desired may be drawn by just continuing in this wise, as shown in the diagram.

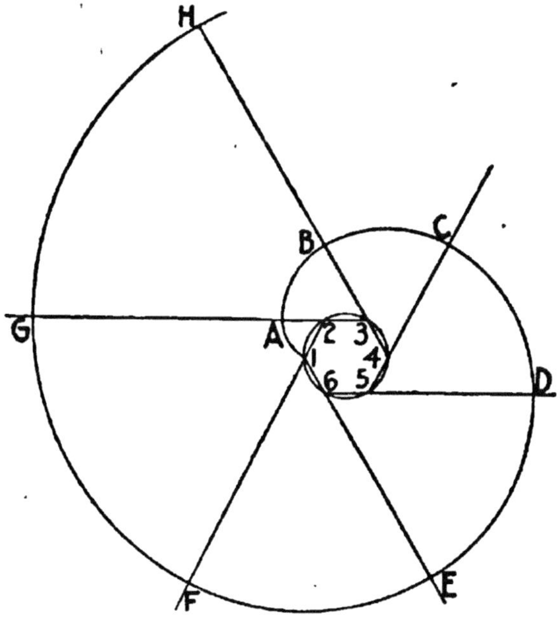

FIG. 24.—A Simple Spiral.

Practical Application of Mensuration and Geometry

This problem is presented in concluding the chapter on geometry to show the practical application of mensuration and geometry to actual shop problems. Fig. 25 illustrates an ordinary hip roof with a flat deck to be covered with tin. In handling work of this character the sheet metal worker is required to calculate the areas of flat surface for the tin, the length of the hips, etc.

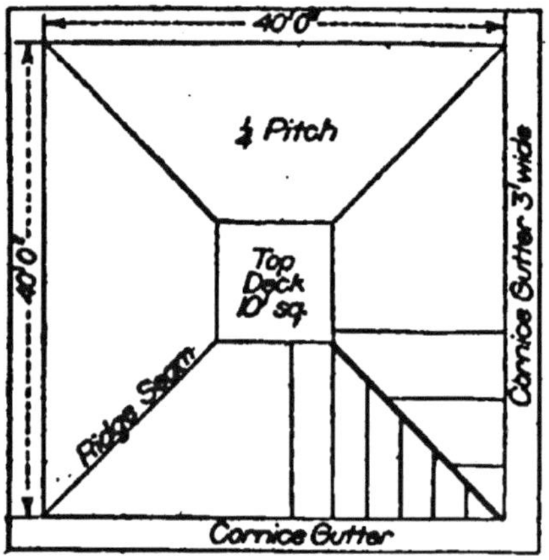

FIG. 25.—Sketch of Practical Problem.

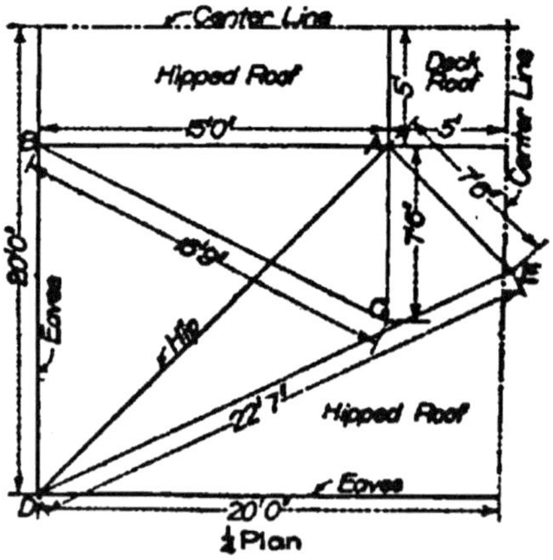

FIG. 26.—Method of Measuring Roof.

Fig. 26 shows the steps followed in determining the area of the roof. This is one quarter of the plan with the cornice gutter omitted. The length is 40 feet on the eaves line for each side, or 40 feet 6 inches over all for each side.

The deck is 10 x 10 feet or 100 square feet of area. Now, the pitch of the roof, as usually figured, is 6 inches to 1 foot of horizontal line, that is to say, one-quarter of the span of the roof. Should this differ though from the reader's idea of pitch, it is to be said that the mathematical operations as herewith expounded would be the same, simply a substituting of his rise per foot for that given here. As it is 15 feet on the horizontal lines from eaves to deck, the rise of the deck above the eaves would be 15 x 6 inches or 7 feet 6 inches.

Draw the quarter plan to a convenient scale as in Fig. 26 which may be made 3/8 inches to the foot. Continue deck line to eaves as A B. At right angles to A B draw line A C, 7 feet 6 inches by scale. Connect B and C and scale, learning thereby that the line is 16 feet 9 inches, which is the slant measurement of the roof from eaves to deck. Determine the area of the roof by the rules given in the chapter on mensuration, viz.: Add the length of the deck to the length of the eaves, divide into one-half and multiply the result by the slant length of the roof, which in turn is multiplied by 4 (the number of sides of the roof). That is, $10 + 40 = 50$; $50 \div 2 = 25$; 25×16 feet 9 inches $= 418$ feet 9 inches; 418 feet 9 inches $\times 4 = 1675$ square feet as the area of the hipped roof.

The length of the hip A D is ascertained by drawing a line from A, at right angles to it, and seven feet six inches long, to scale, thus locating point E. Connect E and D. Scale and it will be found that the slant of the hips measures twenty-two feet seven inches from the eaves to the deck.

CHAPTER III

Conical Problems and Tinware

Pattern for Cone

In Fig. 27, H K V represents a cone for which an envelope is wanted. And by envelope is meant the surface of the cone, for pattern cutting is the science of the developing the surface of solids.

Span the dividers from V to H and describe the arc O S. Set off the arc equal in length to the cir-

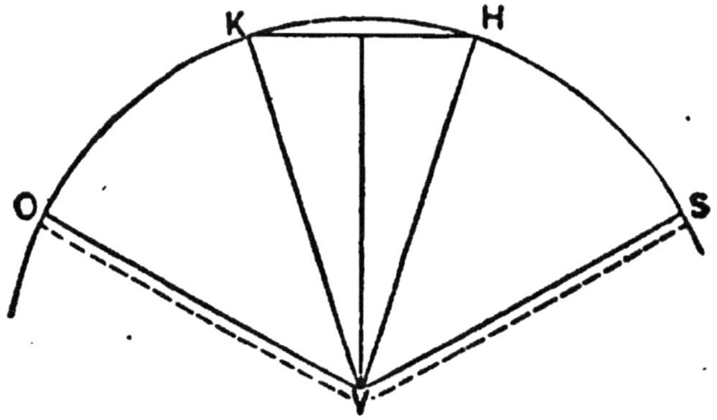

FIG. 27.—Cutting a Cone Pattern.

cumference of the required cone. Draw the lines V O and V S, allowing for locks or laps, as shown by the dotted lines.

For the circumference, refer to the tables in Chapter XII or obtain by some of the rules given in Chapter I. By using the rules familiarity with them is obtained. which is desirable. Of course, stepping around a circle of the required diameter would also do.

The Old German Rule for Developing the Patterns for the Cone

Take the slant height of the cone H K, in Fig. 28, as a radius, and describe a circle. Divide the diam-

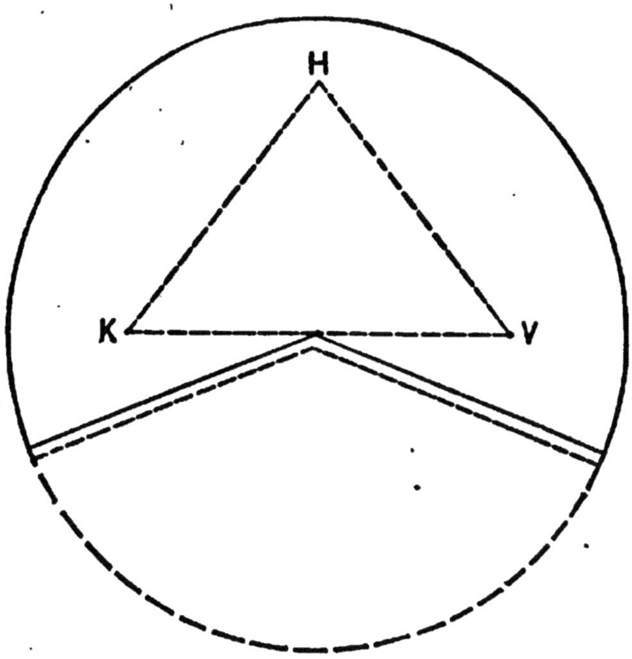

FIG. 28.—A German Rule for Cones.

eter of the base of the cone K V into seven equal parts and set off a space equal to twenty-two of these parts on the circle already struck. From the extremities thus measured off draw lines to the center.

The dotted lines shown parallel to the solid lines from the center, represent allowances for locks for seaming after forming the metal into shape. Of course, these laps are allowed in accordance with the method used for making the seam and a lap should be allowed on the outer circle if required.

Steamer or Pitched Cover

Strike circle 1 inch larger than rim burred. Draw line through center H, as shown in Fig. 29, and from either side cut 1 inch on circle to 1 inch from center K. Draw lines and cut out. Or, strike circle the same or larger. Draw line through center and cut on it to center. After burring put in rim; draw up and mark, cut out triangular piece and solder. The latter method is much quicker and equally as good as the first.

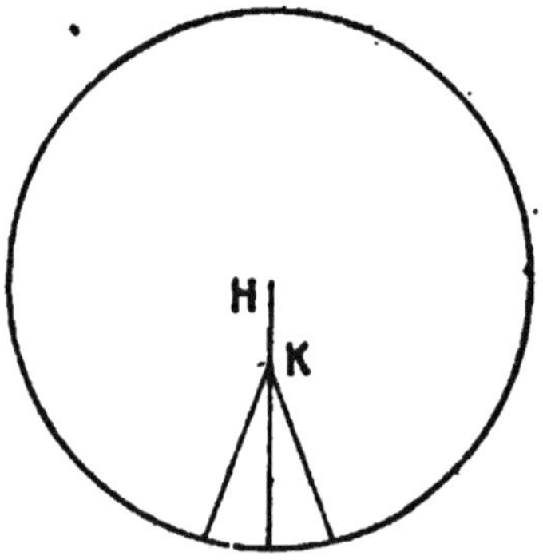

FIG. 29.—A Pitched Cover.

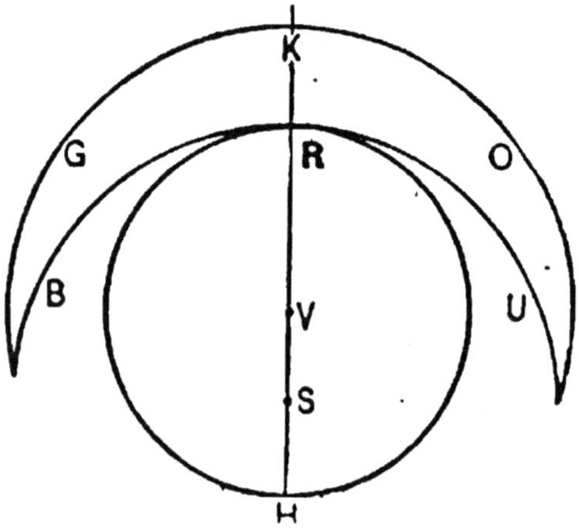

FIG. 30.—Measure Lip Pattern.

A Measure Lip

Draw line H K as shown in Fig. 30, and upon it, with V as center, describe a circle the size of measure. With S, half the distance from V to H, as center, describe semicircle B U. Make R K the desired width. With V as center and the compass set to the radius V K, describe the arc G O; continuing the arc to both sides, until it intersects arc B U. Cut on arcs B U and G O to obtain the required lip pattern.

Flaring Vessel in Three Pieces

Draw line H K; then locate points V and O as far apart as the height of the vessel, as shown in Fig. 31. With the intersections V and O for centers, describe circles equal in size to the top and the bottom of vessel. These circles, or rather arcs, are

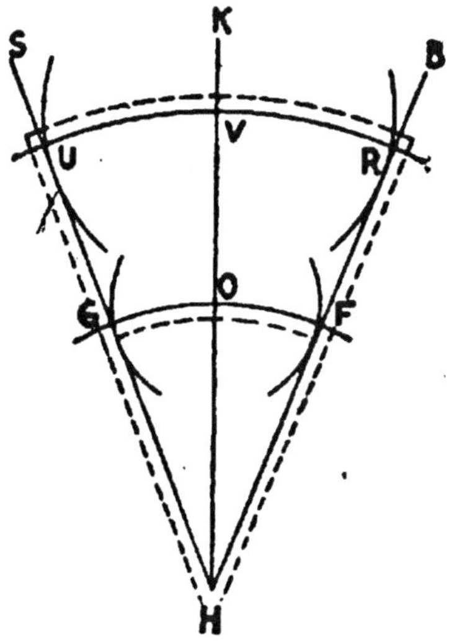

Fig. 31.—Pattern in Three Pieces.

to be described on both sides of line K H as shown in the diagram. Draw lines S H and B H touching on or, more properly speaking, tangent to these arcs or circles. With intersection H as center and with the radius H V, describe the segment U R. Then with the radius H O describe the segment G F.

Allow for locks, as shown by dotted lines. It is to be understood, of course, that it takes three of these to make the girth or entire pattern; meaning, that for an entire pattern, arcs U V R and G O F are continued to both sides and made the same length as U to R, and G to F. Then lines are drawn to H.

Pattern for Frustum of a Cone

Lay the square on your sheet and construct the right angle H K V, as shown in Fig. 32. Draw line O S parallel to K V, making the distance K O

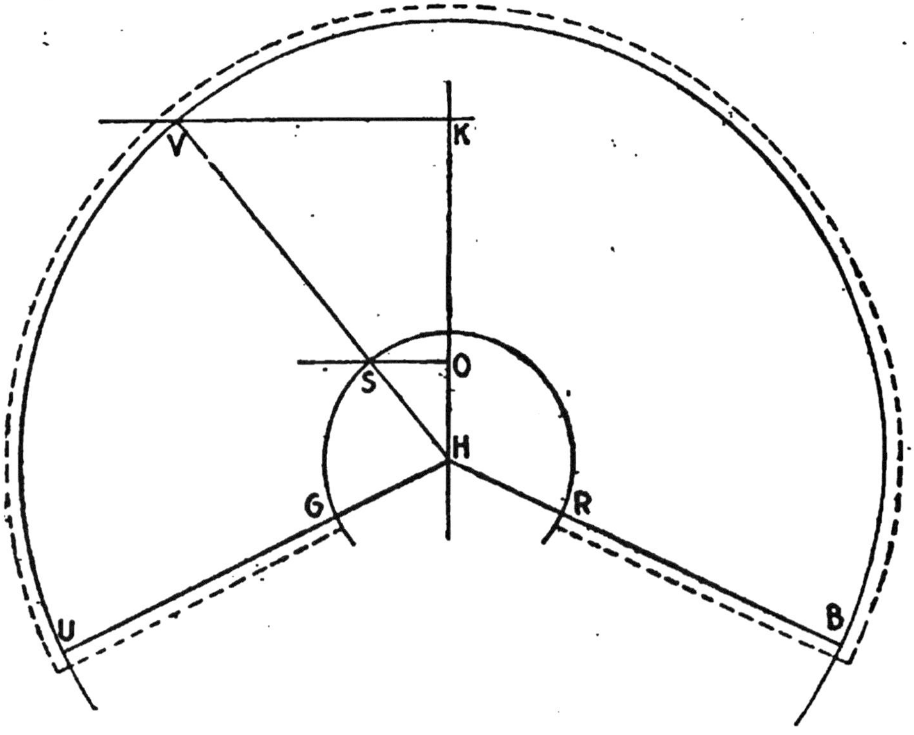

FIG. 32.—One Method for Frustums.

the altitude. On these lines lay off one-half the diameter of the large and small ends. Draw a line through points V and S to the intersection at H. Then, with H as the center, describe the semicircles B U, R G. Lay off circumference of large end on line B U and draw lines to center H. Allow for all edges. For two sections take one-half of the piece, allowing edges on piece used for pattern.

Another Method of Developing the Pattern of a Frustum of a Cone

Draw perpendicular line H K, as shown in Fig. 33, and from K lay off diameter of large end, as V O. On the line H K lay off the height of frustum, as K S. Draw line parallel to V O, and on it lay off small diameter, as B U. Draw lines through

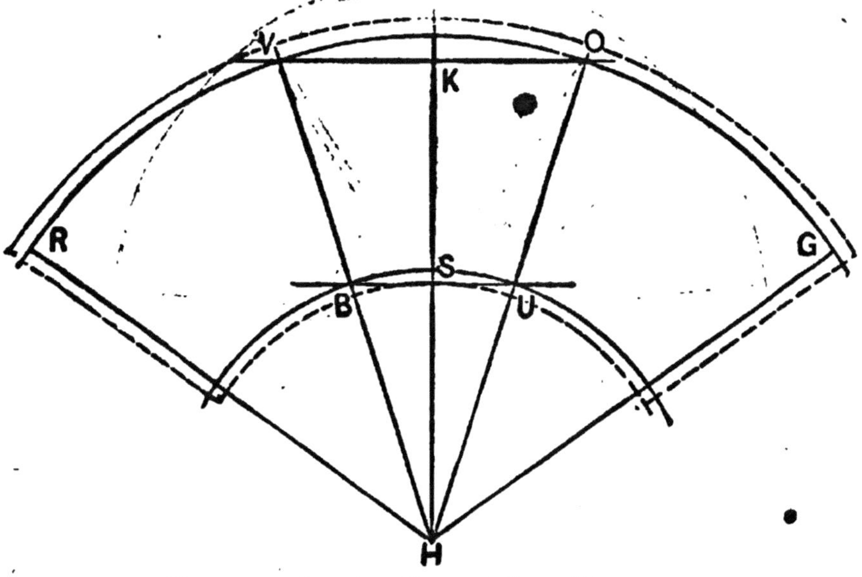

FIG. 33.—Another Case of Cone Frustums.

points V B and O U until they intersect at H. With H V as radius draw large arc R G; and with H B as radius describe small arc. Make arc R G equal to the circumference of the large end and draw lines from R and G to center H. To find this circumference refer to the tables, Chapter XII, or draw a circle with V O as diameter and step it with the dividers.

Allow for all edges, wire, burr and locks as shown by the dotted lines. This forms a pattern in one piece.

To Describe Pattern for Flaring Vessels

For example, it is desired to describe pattern for pail 12 inches in diameter at top, 9 inches at bottom and 9 inches deep, which is a very common article in tinsmithing and the dimensions are the usual ones.

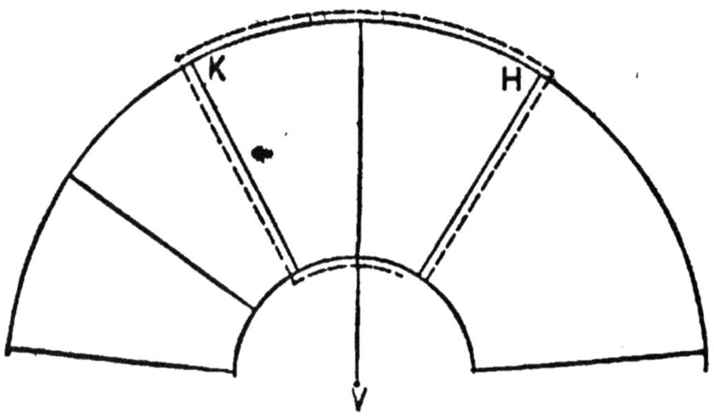

FIG. 34.—Flaring Vessels.

Take the difference between large and small diameters (3 inches) for the first term, the height for the second and the large diameter for the third, thus, 3 : 9 : : 12.

12 x 9 ÷ 3, this gives radius by which the pattern may be described. Span the dividers (or use beam compasses, piece of wire, straight edge or any convenient device) 36 inches and strike large circle as in Fig. 34. With radius less the slant height of pail strike small circle. Ascertain the circumference required and divide by the number of pieces to be used. Lay off on outer circle and draw lines to center, as H K V.

Allow for locks, burr and wire as may be required according to the process of making pails.

To Describe Patterns for Flaring Tinware

In Fig. 35 is given a popular rule for flaring tinware. Let H K V O represent the elevation of an ordinary tin pan, constructed in four pieces, 15½ inches in diameter at the top. Below the elevation is shown the same in plan. The pan is a

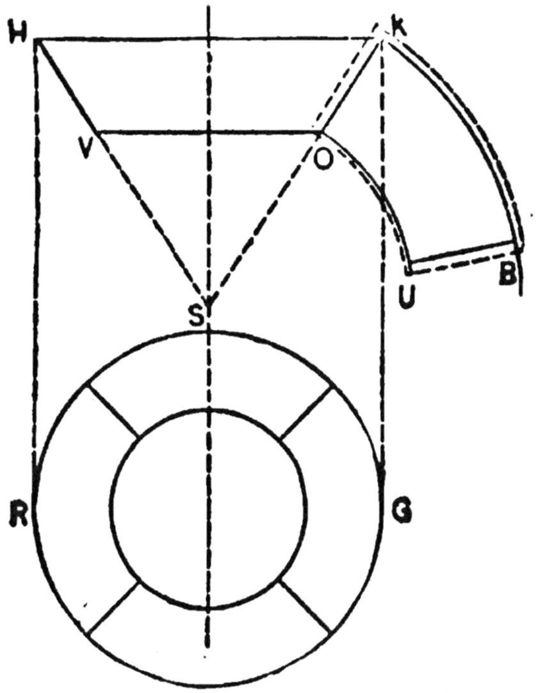

FIG. 35.—A Popular Rule for Flaring Tinware.

frustum of a cone, and if the sides of the pan were continued down until they intersected at S, as shown, the cone would be complete. The radius of the envelope of the cone must be either S H or S K. To describe the section of the frustum which is required, place one foot of the dividers at the center S, and with the radius S H describe the arc K B. With the radius S V describe O U. This gives the width of the pattern and the proper sweep.

To get the length of the piece, refer to the table of circumferences or find, by the rules given, the circumference of the article, which in this case is 48⅝ inches. There being four pieces, divide by four, which gives 12 5-32 inches. Span the dividers 1 inch, step off the 12 and add the fraction. Draw line from the center S to the point last ascertained; which is S to B.

Allow for locks, wire edge and burr; all as indicated on the pattern by the dotted lines.

The pattern for the bottom is the smaller circle with edges allowed for seaming.

Strainer Pail or Watering Pot Breast

Strike a circle the size of the pail or pot desired as in Fig. 36. With the radius V K 1¾ inches

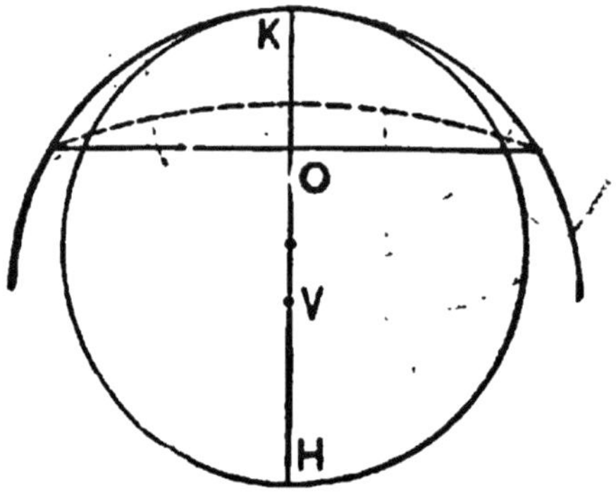

FIG. 36.—Pail Breast Pattern.

more or less than radius of circle described according to the pitch desired and with point V as center describe an arc. Draw the chord, making the segment K O which is the pattern of the desired width. The breast may be cut out if preferred, as shown by dotted lines.

Can Breasts—First Case

Draw horizontal line H K and, parallel to it, at a distance equal to the height of breast, draw line V O, as shown in Fig. 37. On H K lay off diameter of can, as S B. On V O lay off the size of opening, as U R. Then extend lines B R, S U, until they cross G. With G as center and G S as radius, describe outer circle. G to U as radius and G as center, de-

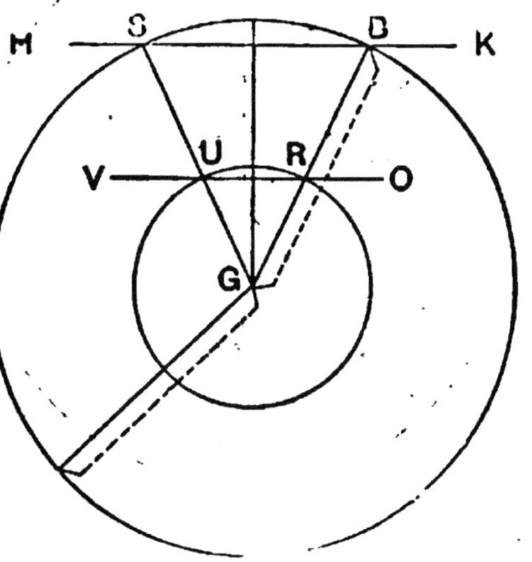

FIG. 37.—First Case of Breasts for Cans.

scribe inner circle. Starting at B set off the outer circle, by stepping with the dividers, the length of the circumference of a circle having a diameter equal to space S to B. Of course, this circumference can be readily found by referring to the circumference table herein.

This is the usual procedure for all flaring articles and follows the general principles of all previous cone problems. The various laps and locks are provided on the pattern as shown by the dotted lines on the pattern.

Can Breasts—Second Case

Can breasts, as a rule, mean the sloping tops of cylindrical cans. The small opening is usually fitted with a screw cap spun from zinc or brass; or else, a small inverted frustum of a cone is soldered on, and an ordinary cork is thrust into it for a stopper.

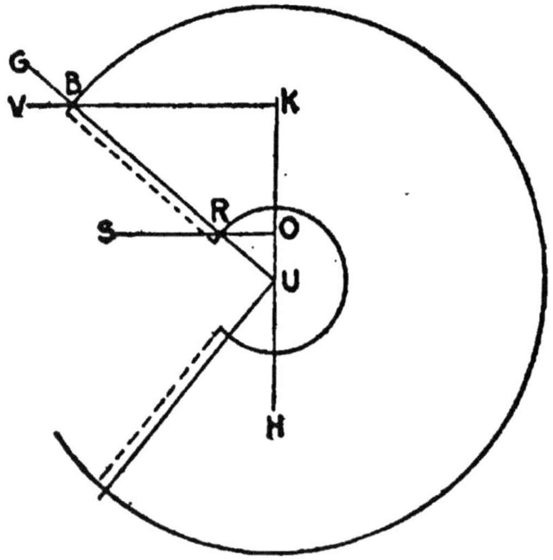

Fig. 38.—Second Case of Breasts for Cans.

Draw the two horizontal lines, K V and O S, and perpendicular to them the line K H, as in Fig. 38. Set off on line K V from the point K one-half the diameter of the can. On O S the point R is one-half the diameter of the opening. Produce the line U G, touching the points B and R, until it intersects H K. With U as center and the radius U B, describe the outer circle. With the same center and the radius U R, describe the inner. Then span from K to B and step six times on large circle to obtain size of breast. Draw line to center and allow for locks, as shown by dotted lines.

Can Breasts—Third Case

Describe a circle the size of can desired, as indicated by medium sized circle in Fig. 39. Draw line through center and mark point H at three-fourths of diameter. Then with the three-fourths of diameter as radius and with H as center strike circle K V. Span to diameter of can and step three times on large circle.

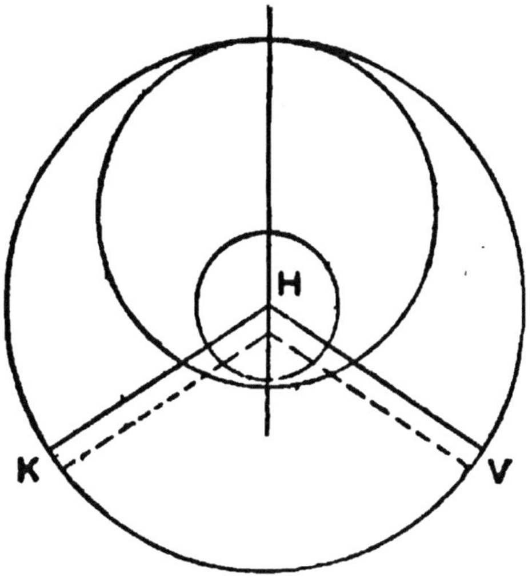

FIG. 39.—Third Case of Breasts for Cans.

Draw line from center to point K V, allowing for edges and locks as may be required by the process of making the can. For more or less pitch make circle K V larger or smaller.

Small circle in center for opening in top. Hoods and pitched covers may be cut by same rule inasmuch as they are like bodies.

These problems are based on the principles of cone envelopes. The years of success of this treatise attest the usefulness of these problems and they are again presented for this reason.

Rectangular Funnel

Draw side of the rectangular funnel, as shown by H K V in Fig. 40. Continue side lines, as shown by dots. From point of intersection as center, describe arc and chord K V and H. Draw end O K S, producing lines to intersect at B. From B

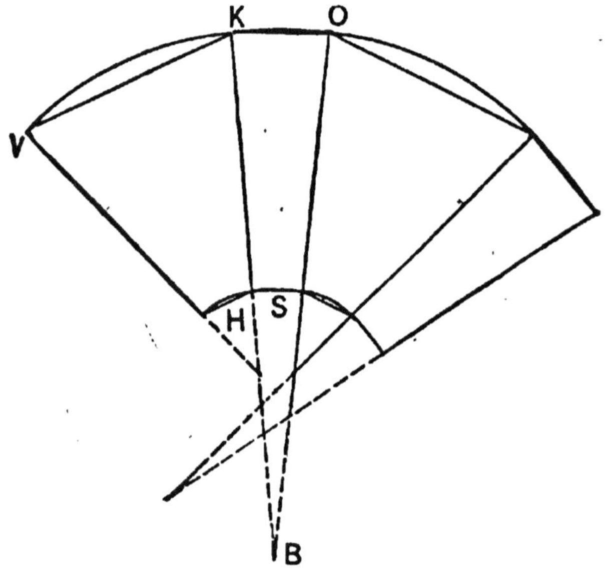

Fig. 40.—Pattern Process for Square Funnels.

as center describe arc and chord O K and S. The other side and end obtained in the same manner, as shown in cut. Can be made in two or more pieces by dividing the pattern. It is to be understood that this funnel has sides of different dimensions. Should a square funnel be wanted the same procedure would apply.

All locks and edges must be allowed for on the pattern piece, which are not, however, shown in the diagram. The provision for these depends on how the seam is to be made.

Flaring Square Vessel or Frustum of a Pyramid

In Fig. 41 let K V and B U represent the width of the bottom and top of one of the sides, respectively, the distance between them being the slant height. Continue lines until they intersect at R. With radius R B strike circle U B G. With R as

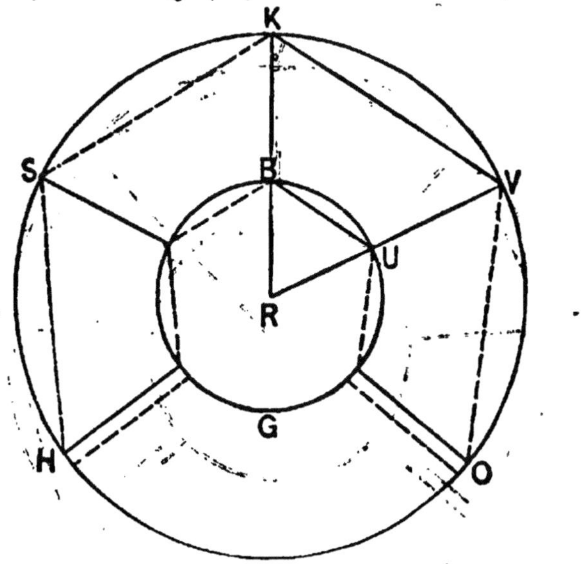

FIG. 41.—Pattern for Square Vessel.

center and R K as radius describe the outer circle. Span dividers from K to V and set off on outer circle the distance, as V O, K S, etc.; draw lines through these points tending toward the center R, also the chords, as shown by dotted lines. Allow for edges. Can be made in two pieces by dividing and allowing for extra lock or seam at the place of division in the pattern.

All three problems are interesting, as they show how cone developments can be employed for objects of rectangular or square shape.

Flaring Hexagon Article or Frustum of a Hexagonal Pyramid

Let V O represent width of the bottom of one side and R G the width of the top of one side, the distance between the slant height. Produce side lines until they cross in the center, as shown by dotted lines. Span dividers from center to O, and

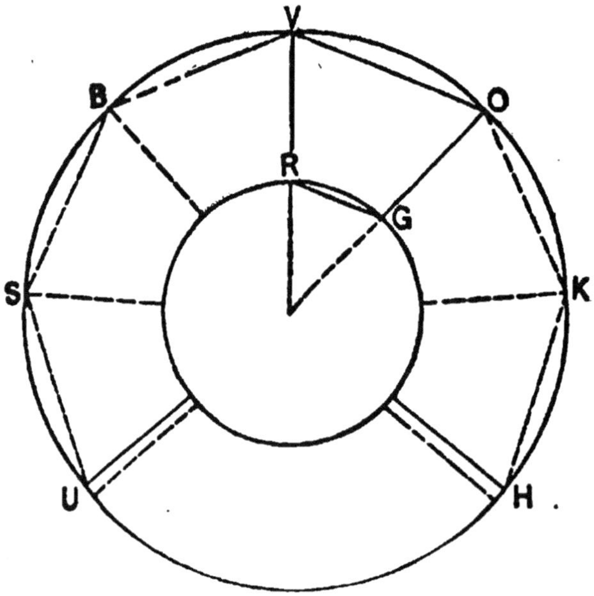

Fig. 42.—Pattern of Hexagon Article.

describe circle H O U; span to G and describe inner circle; span again from V to O and step on the outer circle three spaces each side from O, as K, H, B, S, U. Draw lines from these points tending toward center, and connect by chords as H K, K O, etc., as shown.

Cut out piece H U, allowing for the locks, as shown in Fig. 42. Pattern for a pentagon article may be described by the same rule, in which case the pattern would have five parts.

Tapering Octagon Article or Frustum of an Octagonal Pyramid

Draw bottom K H and top V of one side, with distance between the slant height, and continue side lines until they intersect at O. With O as a center and the radii O V and O H, describe inner and

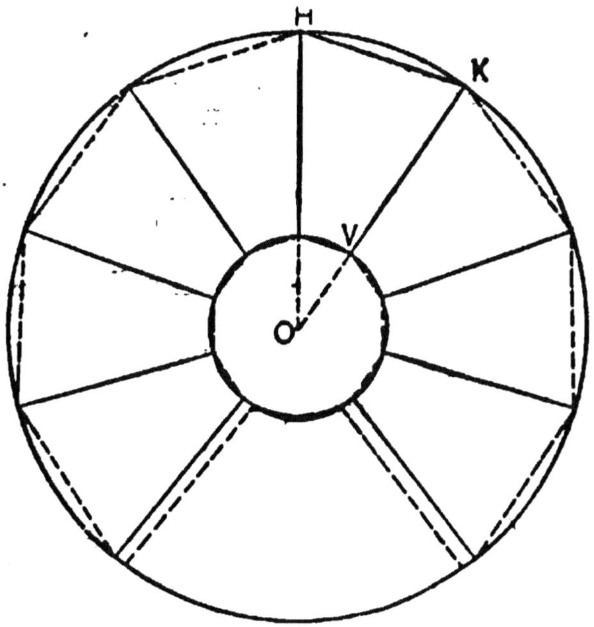

FIG. 43.—Pattern of Octagon Article.

outer circles. Set off on them distances equal to H K and V, and connect by chords, shown dotted.

Allow for locks and edges as in Fig. 43, and as stated in the other problems preceding this, the pattern can be subdivided along such lines as V K to suit requirements.

All the foregoing problems like this one are of exceptional value in the tinsmith trade and the principles embodied therein are applicable to innumerable cases.

Flaring Article with Square Top and Base a Rectangle. Two or Four Pieces

Draw rectangular base H K and square top V in center of base. Draw perpendiculars O S and R U. Also place the height of the article O B and

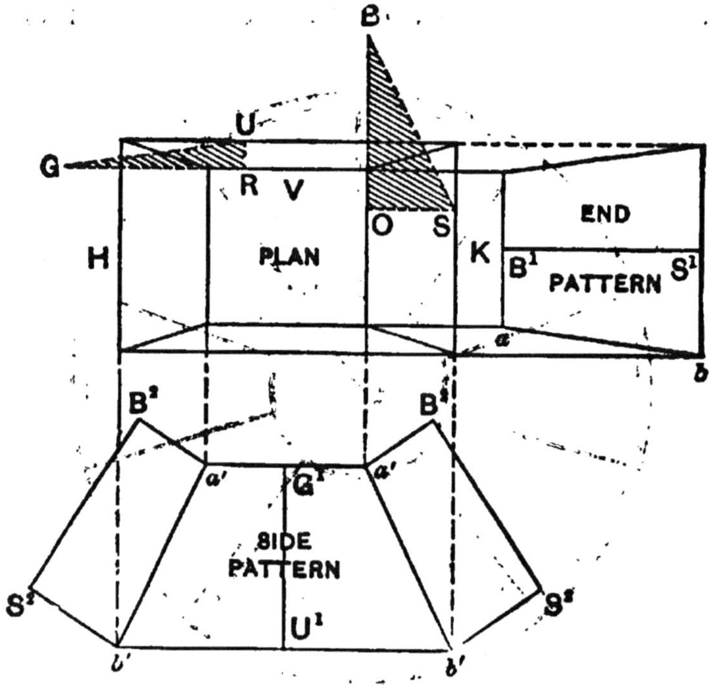

FIG. 44.—Pattern of a Square Flaring Article.

R G. Place the slant height B S on B¹ S¹ and draw lines *a* and *b* which intersect as shown, which gives pattern for end. Place G U on G¹ U¹, draw lines *a′* and *b′* which intersect as shown, which gives pattern for side. Join half of end pattern to either side of side pattern as shown by similar letters, which gives half pattern as shown in Fig. 44. Naturally, if it was so required, the half of pattern G¹ U¹ *a′ b′* could be attached to the end pattern B¹ S¹ *a* and *b*.

To Find Length of Sheet Required for Oval Boiler. Common Method

The diagram, Fig. 45, represents the contour of the universal type of oval clothes boiler or like articles. First describe bottom, length and width desired, cut it out of the metal, then burr and from H as a starting point, first making a mark on the

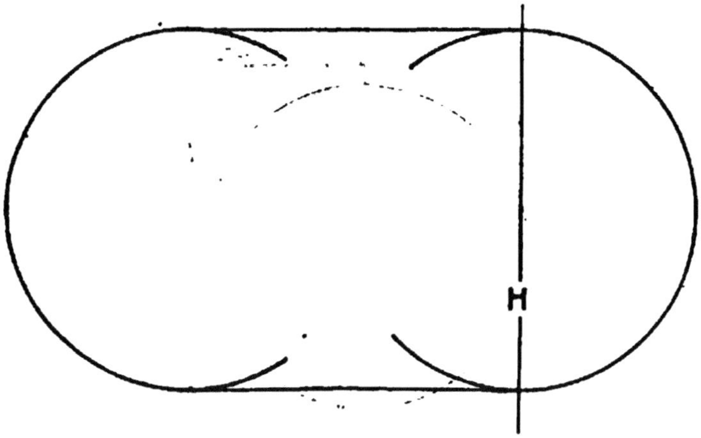

FIG. 45.—Oval Boiler Bottom.

bench where H was, roll on the bench to obtain the circumference.

Some tinsmiths, however, do not first burr the metal but find the circumference by working a thin strip of tin around the bottom and then deduct from this the amount of take-up of the double-seam. If three pieces are to be used for the body of the boiler divide the circumference into three parts and allow edges; if made in two pieces, divide by two. Always divide the circumference by the number of pieces desired. Cut the cover the same size as the bottom, providing it is to be a flat cover; if pitched cover is wanted see the following problems.

Rapid Method of Laying Out an Oval Boiler Cover

In Fig. 46 is shown a rapid method for developing the pattern of an oval boiler cover. First draw line A K, and from R as center describe circle G U, size of boiler outside of rod. Make A K equal to one-half of entire length of boiler, and K S three-

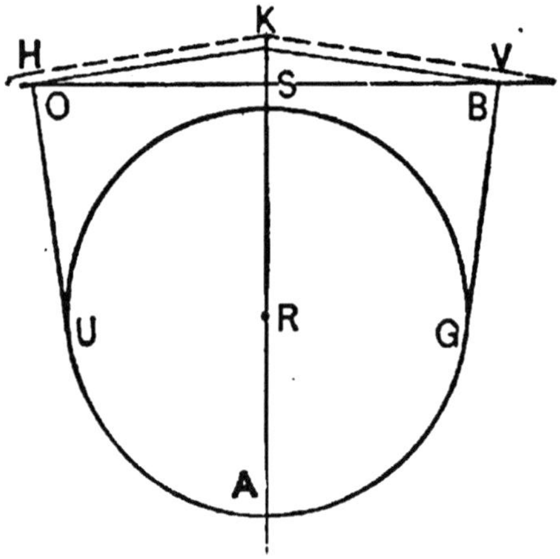

Fig. 46.—Pattern for Oval Boiler Cover.

eighths of an inch, or more if more pitch is desired. Through S draw the perpendicular line H V. Lay corner of square on line H, one blade at K, the other touching circle, describe lines U H K; in similar manner obtain K V G, completing the half pattern.

In the diagram, the dotted lines at H K and K V are allowances for the groove seam to join the two halves of the cover. A double allowance along the line B G A U O should be made for the clinch edge by which the rim of the cover is fastened on. As a rule the cover is formed to shape by making slight bends on lines K A U to K and G to K, and rounding up between bends before joining the halves.

To Describe Pattern for Oval Flaring Vessel. Four Pieces

Describe bottom as by Fig. 21. Obtain length of arcs S U B and S V S of that diagram, also length of corresponding arcs at the top of vessel. Now, in Fig. 47, draw horizontal lines H K and V O, making the distance between the desired slant height.

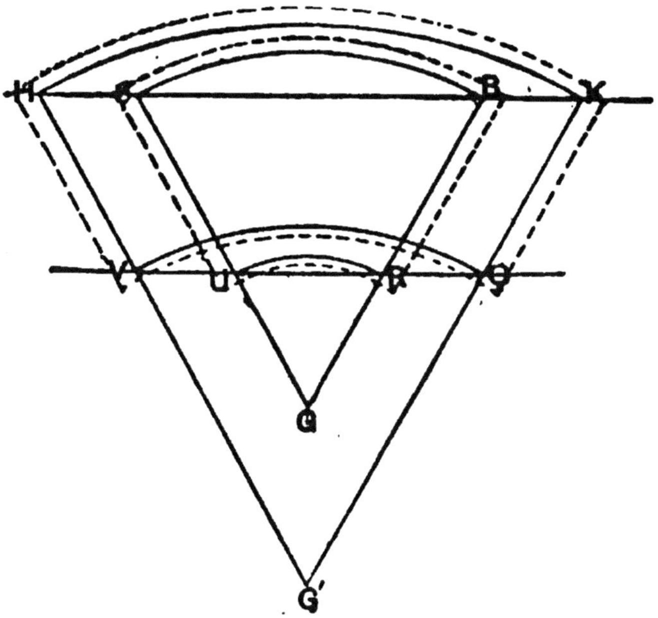

Fig. 47.—Pattern of Oval Vessel.

Make H K equal in length to that of the piece at the top, and V O to that of the bottom, for the sides. S B and U R for the end pieces. Produce lines through these points to intersect at G and G′. Describe the arcs from these points.

Allow for all edges, locks, wire and burr, as indicated by the dotted lines: also carefully lay out the various notches, as poor or careless notching spoils otherwise good work.

To Describe Pattern for Flaring Article with Straight Sides and Round Ends. Two Pieces

Draw the outline of the bottom and side, as in Fig. 48. Erect two perpendicular lines, H V, K O, distance between the length of sides A B; at right angles to these, two lines, distance between the slant

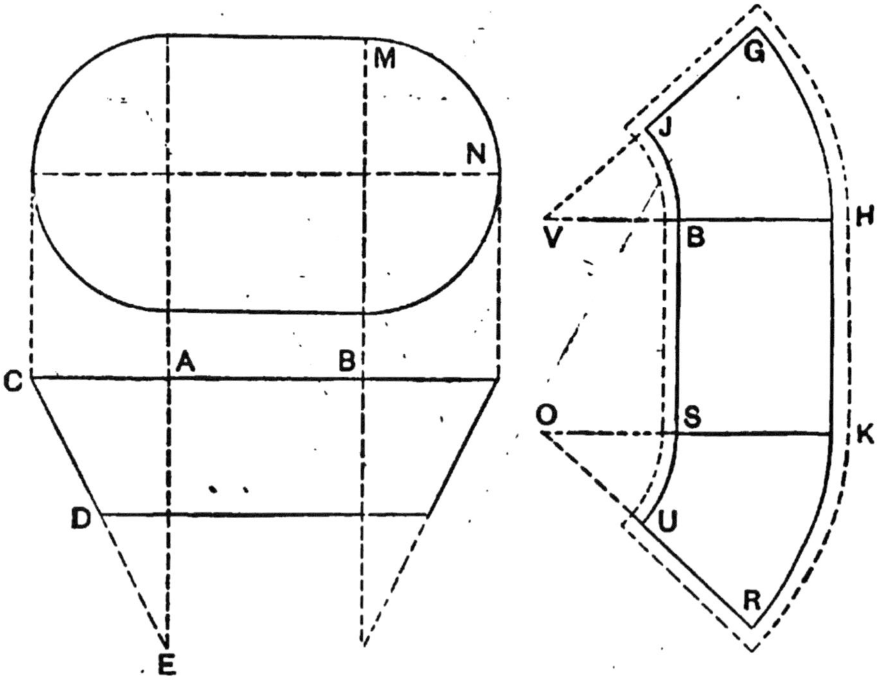

FIG. 48.—Pattern of Article with Round Ends.

height of article C D. On H V and K O set off the radius C E as V and O. From V and O as centers, with radii V B, V H and O S, O K, draw the arcs B J, H G and S U, K R. Make the arcs H G and K R equal to one-half the circumference of the ends M N and draw lines to V and O. Allow for all edges, locks, wire and burr, as shown in the pattern at the right of the diagrams.

To Describe Pattern for Flaring Oval Vessel. Two Pieces

Draw plan according to rule given in Fig. 18, or any other method. Construct right angle triangle T H^1 S^1 in Fig. 49, and parallel to H^1 S^1, draw H^1 O^1, the distance between height of article. Lay off on H^1 S^1 the distances H S and V S in plan and on H^1 O^1 the distances H O and V O in plan. Draw lines through these points to intersect the line R^1 T at U and T. Using T as center draw the arcs O^1 K^1 and S^1 R^1, making the distance along the arc S^1 R^1 equal to U R in plan. Draw line from R^1 to T. Take radius V^1 U on the lines R^1 T and S^1 T and obtain centers B and C, with which describe the arcs R^1 G^1 and S^1 G^1, which make equal in length to G R or U B in plan. Draw lines to centers B and C.

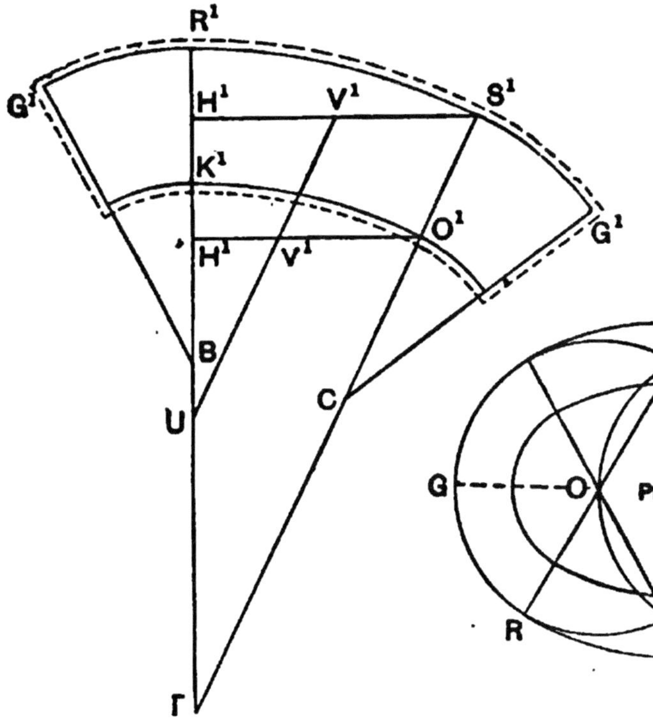

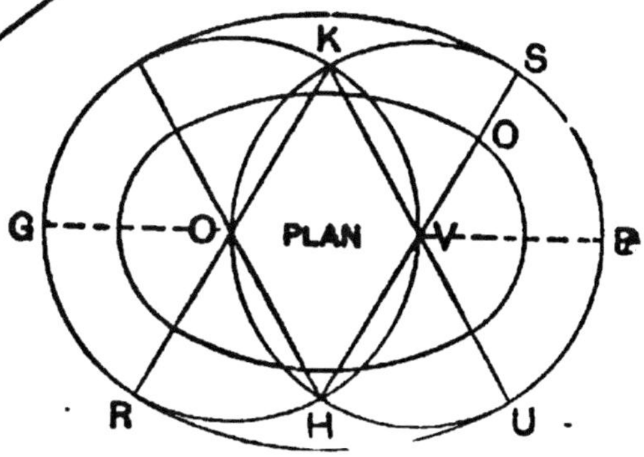

FIG. 49.—Pattern for Flaring Oval Article.

Flaring Article, Top and Base a Rectangle. Two Pieces

Draw side elevation in Fig. 50, as H K, V O, of the longest side. Span dividers the difference between the shortest side of the base and longest side of top. From V and O as centers describe arcs S and S. With blade of square resting on arcs and the corner at H and K, draw lines H B and K G. Set off H B and K G equal one-half of shortest

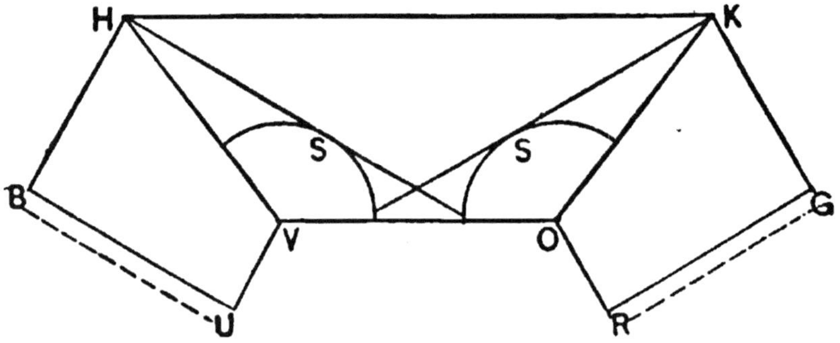

FIG. 50.—Pattern of Transition Article.

sides of base and draw lines B U and G R at right angles to H B and K G; also lines U V and R O at right angles to U B and G R.

Allow for all edges, locks, wire and burr, as shown in the pattern at B U, R G of Fig. 50, by the dotted lines; notching, of course, is governed by the widths of locks, machines used and in general method followed in the particular shop; careful notching bespeaks the careful mechanic and enhances the looks of the finished article.

It is to be understood that this is a quick method, a more strictly accurate method is as shown by Fig. 44.

Round Base and Square Top Article. Two Pieces

Referring to Fig. 51 for the procedure, first erect perpendicular line. Span dividers to three-quarters diameter of base and describe semicircle H K V. Make K V and K H each equal to one-quarter the circumference of the round base and draw lines to center. Span dividers to three-quar-

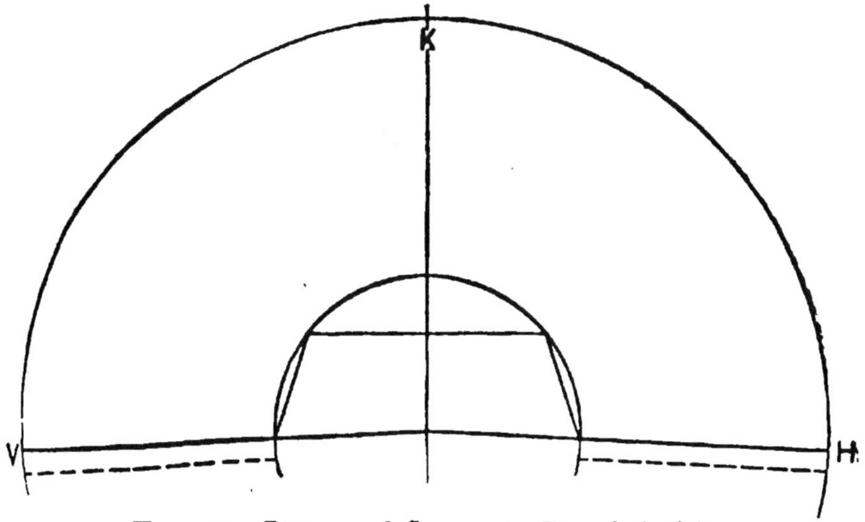

FIG. 51.—Pattern of Square to Round Article.

ters size of top from corner to corner and describe inner circle. Lay out sides of top, size required, on circle, as shown.

Allow laps as shown by the dotted lines which are for the seam to join the two halves; other edges are to be provided in accord with the requirements of the article. This procedure is a quick rule, the more accurate method would be by the modern system of triangulation. Triangulation is a science of pattern cutting that is fast becoming the only method used for developing patterns for bodies of irregular shapes, and should therefore be studied.

Rectangular Base and Round Top Article. Two Pieces

Referring to Fig. 52 for the procedure, first draw horizontal lines H K, V O. Make H K equal to the longest side of base, V O equal to one-fourth the circumference of the top, the distance between slant height; draw side lines through these points. With radii one-half the difference between

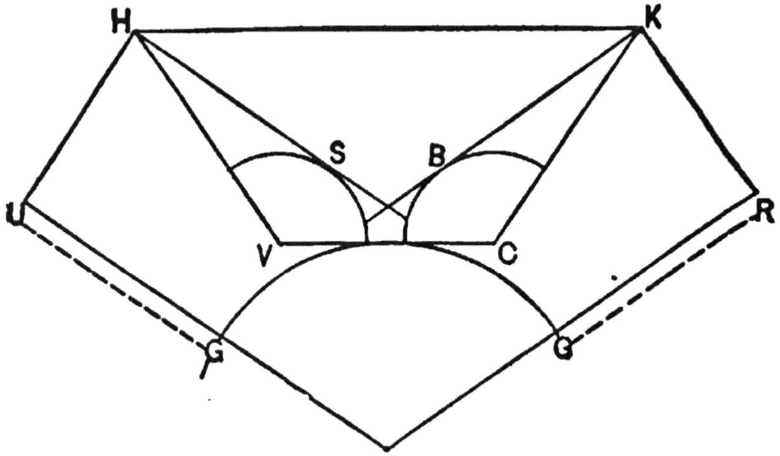

Fig. 52.—Rectangular Base to Round Top Pattern.

V O and the shortest side of the base, describe the arcs S, B; with blade of square resting on arcs, and corner at H and K, draw lines K R, H U, equal to one-half the short side; at right angles to K R, H U, draw lines R G and U G; U G and R G produced will intersect; from this point span dividers to line V O and describe the arc.

Allow for locks and edges, as shown in the diagram, other edges depending on requirements. These methods are a rapid substitute for triangulation.

Square Base and Round Top Article. Two Pieces

Referring to Fig. 53 for the procedure, first draw horizontal lines H K, V O; H K equal to the length of one side of the base, V O equal to one-fourth the circumference of the top, the distance between the slant height; draw lines through

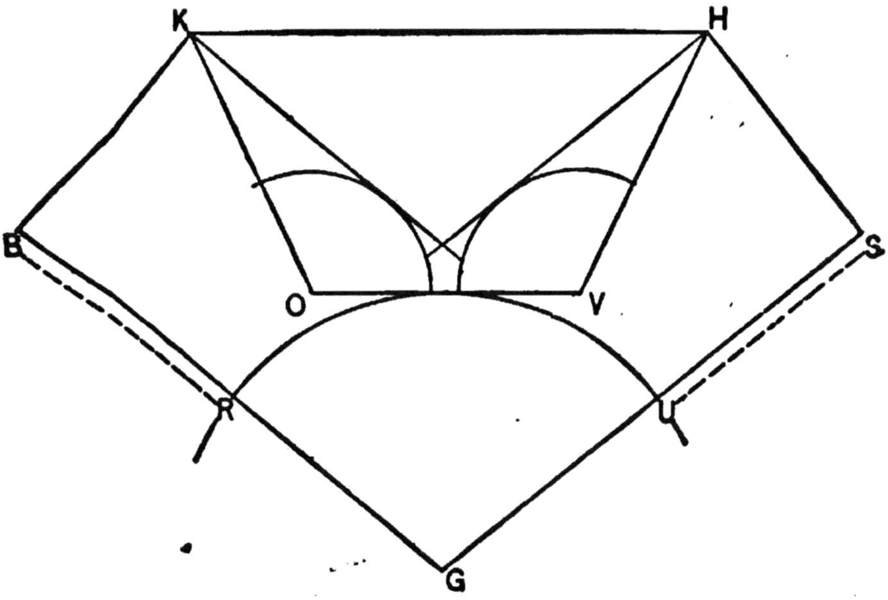

FIG. 53.—Pattern for Article of Square Base and Round Top.

these points. With radii one-half the difference between K H and O V, describe arcs; with blade of square resting on arcs and the corner at H and K, draw lines H S and K B, equal to one-half the base; at right angles to H S and K B draw S U and B R, produced to intersect at G. Span dividers from G to line V O and describe the arc.

The providing of edges for seams and other essentials can only be prescribed in a general way owing to conditions being different in each case. The dotted lines at B R and U S show laps.

Scale Tray or Scoop

A sketch of the finished article is shown in Fig. 54, it being made in two pieces with a seam at its cross center. As may be noticed, the problem em-

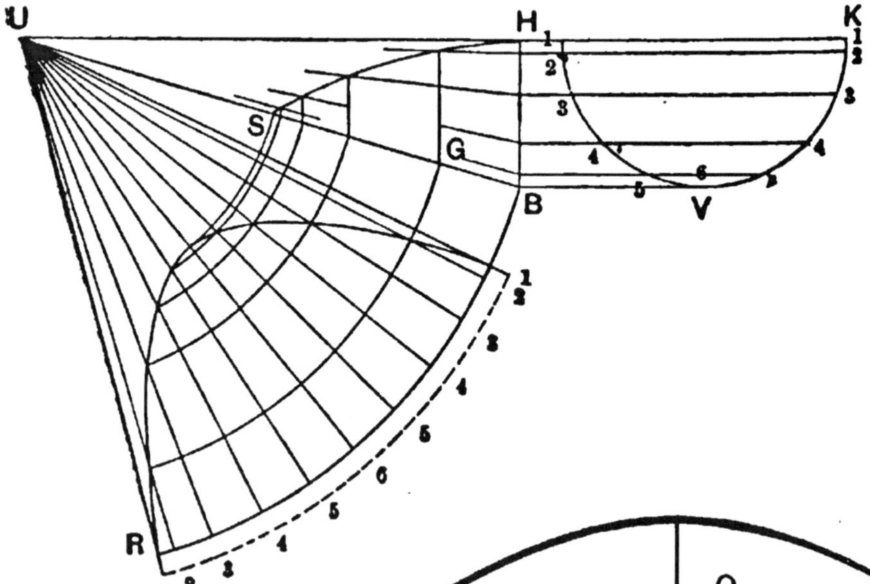

Fig. 55.—Pattern of Scale Scoop.

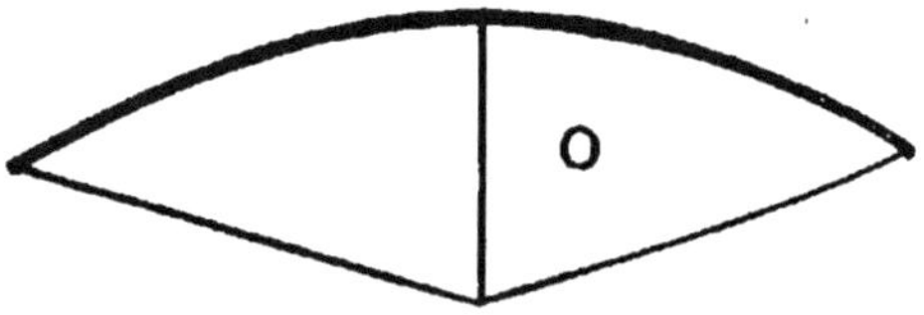

Fig. 54.—Sketch of Finished Article.

braces the conical or flaring method of developing patterns, technically known as developing the surface of solids by radial lines.

To develop the pattern but one section, O, Fig. 54, need be drawn; so, as in Fig. 55, construct a sectional view as H K V and let H S B represent one-half elevation of it, or O in Fig. 54. Continue lines B S and K H until they cross at U. Divide H K V into any given number of spaces, continuing the same to the line H B, as shown by short lines.

Draw lines from the division points on H B to the point U, thus obtaining the intersections on the line S H. With the T square at right angles with H U, drop the points thus obtained on H S, onto the line B S.

With U as center and U B as a radius describe the arc B R. Step off upon this arc spaces equal to those in H K V, using dividers, which gives the length B R. Draw radial lines from U to space marks on line B R, as shown.

With U as center and the various points on S B as radii, describe arcs, intersecting similar radial lines as shown. Then a line traced through the points thus obtained, together with the arc B R, will be the outline of the required pattern. Allow for edges, as shown by dotted lines.

It is to be understood, of course, that the dotted lines show allowed edge for the groove seam at the cross-section center line of the scoop, as shown by the vertical line in Fig. 54. As a rule, a wire is curled into the outer edge of such articles, and in that case an edge should be provided for the wire along the outer line of the pattern. This edge to be of a size suitable for the thickness of wire used; some mechanics allow three times the diameter of the wire, that depending on the mode of wiring.

Using the design of Fig. 54, scoops could also be treated as parts of cylinders and the patterns developed by the parallel line system. Some have part O of Fig. 54 as shown, but the other part has its nose continued around to form a bag filling funnel, the pattern of which is cut by the same methods.

Funnel Pattern by Short Rule

As the usual way of making funnels requires no fixed proportions, advantage can be taken of a geometrical coincidence for the rapid development of the flaring body.

By proportions is meant the diameter of the circle at the top of the body proper, that is, the width

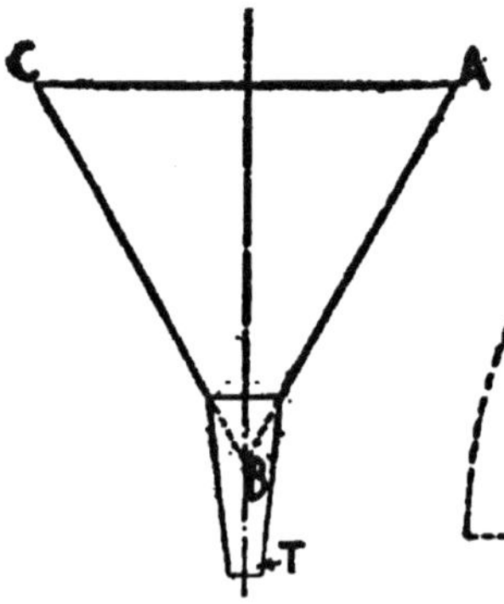

FIG. 56.—Elevation of Object.

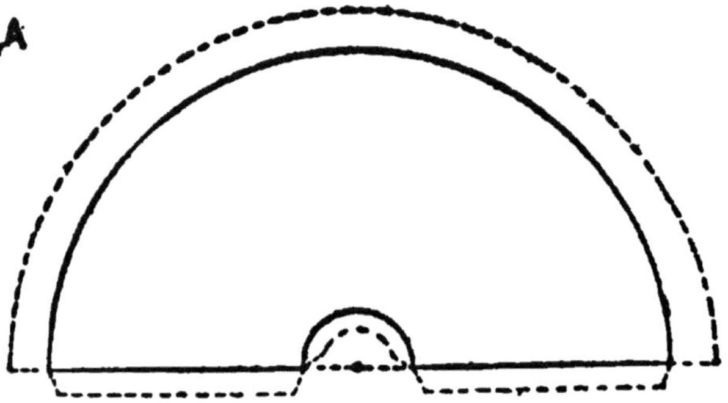

FIG. 57.—Pattern of Object.

across as C A in Fig. 56 and the depth of the body or slant height C B, so that the body forms an equilateral triangle as shown by A B C.

In Fig. 56 is shown an ordinary funnel and if the distance A B is the same as A C no elevation is required; simply span the compasses to the diameter of what is wanted for the large end and strike a half-circle as in Fig. 57. Now set the compasses to the diameter of the small end and strike the half-circle shown. The spout T of Fig. 56 is laid out as in Fig. 33.

Allow edges for seams and wire, as shown by the dotted lines in Fig. 57.

To Obtain Length of Piece for Tea Kettle Body

The old-time tinsmith had many well tried methods like this; however, modern ideas are more along strictly scientific lines.

Tea kettles like these are mostly made by coppersmiths and in the book "Art of Coppersmithing" there is a detailed discussion on the making of tea kettles.

The way in general practice is to roll the bottom after burring on the bench to obtain circumference,

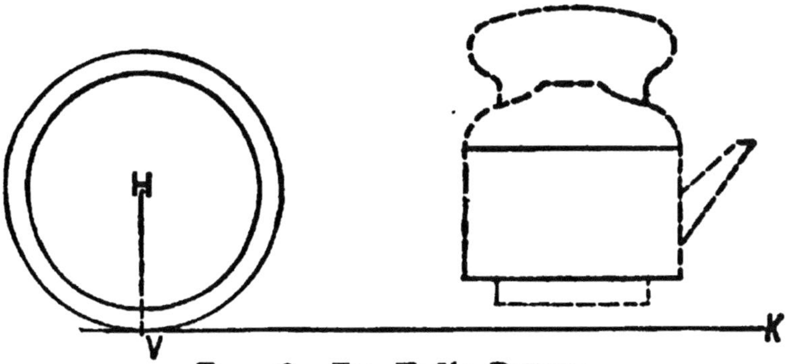

FIG. 58.—Tea Kettle Pattern.

and use strip 3/4 inch less in length, as shown by figure. H represents the pit; K V the length of the strip or sheet, these remarks naturally referring to Fig. 58.

Of course, the length of the body could be found by reference to the table of circumferences herein. The pattern of the spout and breast, also cover, is governed by the design, methods employed in the particular shops and so on. As they are usually raised or hammered to shape, the patterns, no matter how obtained, although most likely the radial line method could be used, would only be approximate.

Mode of Stringing Together a Number of Patterns

Fig. 59 represents the three pieces of a 6-quart pan usually cut from one sheet of 10 x 14 tin. Instead of using one piece for pattern and placing it three times, three pieces are fastened together by soldering on two strips of tin with a heavy hem on each side, and all placed at once, thus saving time

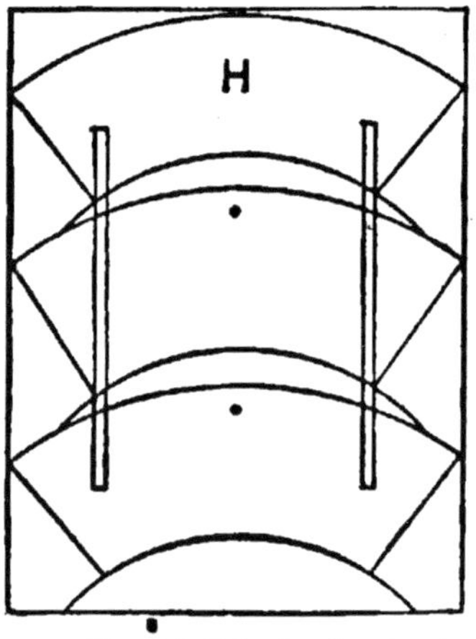

FIG. 59.—Rapid Method of Marking Out Blanks.

and vexation. To use to advantage begin at the bottom of the string pattern and mark around on the outside first, and then mark in the centers right across.

If the strips of tin with the hem edges are not stiff enough; why, light band iron could be substituted. These should be riveted on instead of soldered as for the tin strips.

The lines curving beyond the patterns show how the sheet is first cut into. The bands being narrow no attention need be paid to the part of the sheet not marked under them.

Another Mode of Stringing Patterns

Fig. 60 represents a string of rim or hoop patterns, fastened as shown in the same manner as described in Fig. 59. Rims of any width can be put together in this manner and a great saving of time is the result when once properly done. Patterns for all articles of tinware should be strung in this way, when more than one piece is obtained from a sheet, that the marking out may be expedited and less tedious. A space should be left between each pattern for the scratch-awl.

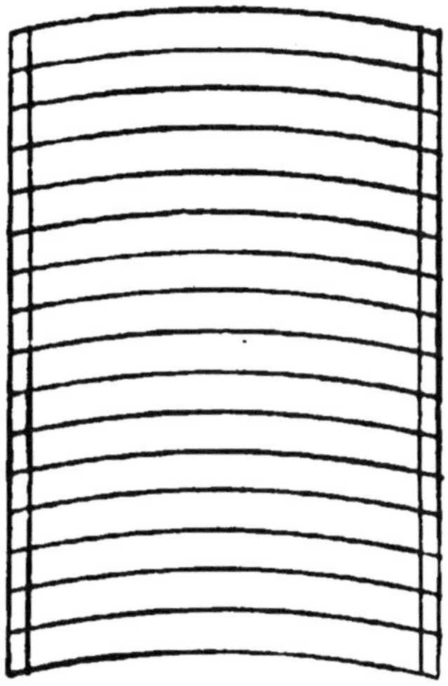

FIG. 60.—Another Rapid Method.

If the material to be cut is of light weight, two or more sheets can be cut at one time by pinning together; for instance, mark out one sheet, lay it evenly on two more sheets, notch in along the edges about an inch and on a slant and, say, six inches apart. Bend notches over with the pliers and flatten down with the mallet. In this case the notches could be at the top and bottom of sheets.

Description of Boiler Block, for Shaping or Truing the Bodies of Oval Articles

By Fig. 61 is represented a block for truing up boilers after they are formed up in the rollers and locked together. Many mechanics depend upon the stake and the accuracy of the eye, but after using

FIG. 61.—Elevation of Block.

this method would not abandon it, as better results are obtained and in much less time. The block is made of 2-inch plank, by placing one on another and securing with four long bolts passing completely through them. The proper dimensions are as follows:

Bottom,	13	inches wide,	25	inches long.
Top,	10	" "	19	" "
Height,	12	"		

As the shaping of the boiler bodies are dependent on this block it follows that extreme care is requisite when shaping the block especially as it tapers.

The procedure, in using the block, is to force the boiler body down on the block as far as it will go and then to tap on the wired edge of the boiler body with a mallet.

Pattern for a Drip or Roasting Pan

In Fig. 62, A is the elevation of the pan; now, draw a rectangle B C D E. Draw the sides of the pan to this; that is, B F equals B′ F′ of the elevation. Distance F G equals H J, as the flare is equal

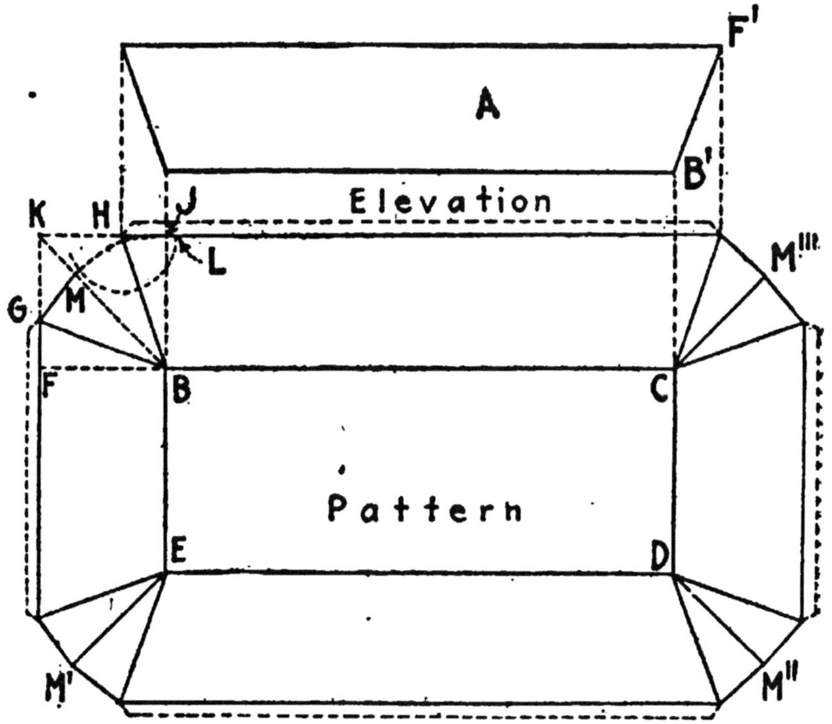

Fig. 62.—Drip Pan Pattern.

all around. Bisect angle G H B by drawing line to K.

With the compass at H and set to almost touch line K B, as shown, swing around to L. With B as center swing an arc from L to line K B, locating point M. Point M shows amount of fold or material for each corner, so that pan can be made in one piece with water-tight corners. Complete each corner the same way, M′ M″ and M‴ being the point M just mentioned. Provide edge, as shown dotted for the wire.

Pattern for a Chimney Cap

To design and develop patterns of the object shown in Fig. 63 it is to be said that the pattern problem comprises developing the surface of a cone. In the sketch, which is for an 8-inch pipe and drawn one-twelfth full size. A is simply a short joint pipe, which, of course, can also be a square-to-round chimney base. C and C are the braces and D the cap. Inasmuch as there are no fixed rules for proportioning the cap, and as most mechanics have a 30-deg. triangle, and as that amount of pitch for the cap would seem pleasing to the eye, the lines *a b* and *b c* are so drawn, as shown. The length of these lines may be as wanted, only it should be remembered that the

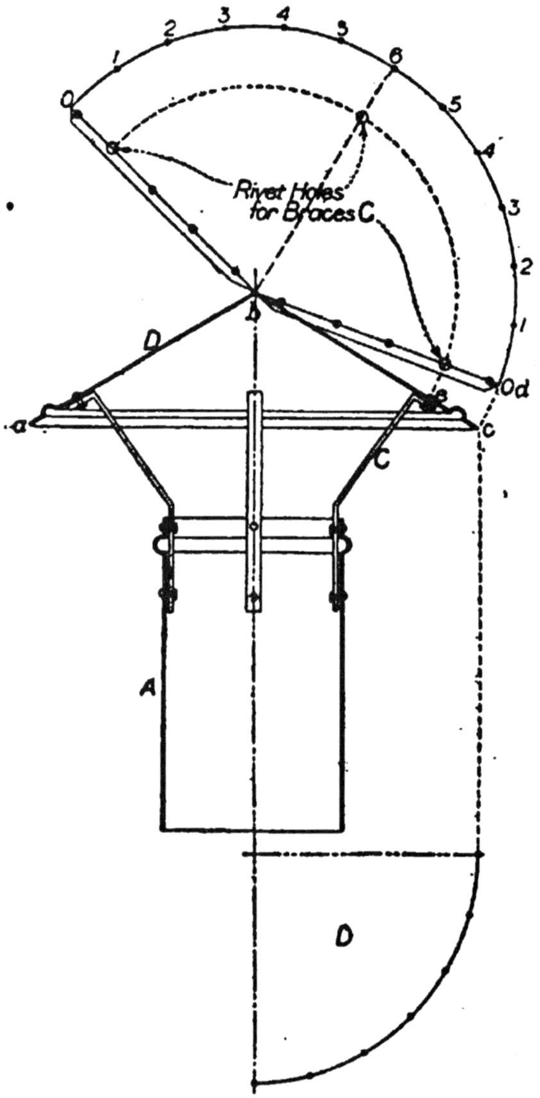

Fig. 63.—Pattern for Chimney Cap.

cap must be of a sufficient height above the pipe to allow a free passage of the smoke. It is better to err by making the space between the cap and pipe too great rather than too small. It is also to be remembered that the longer the lines *a b* and *b c* are, or which is the same thing, the larger the cap the more storm-proof it is, and as it naturally covers a larger area it can be raised so much more above the pipe.

For the pattern of the cap the leg of the compasses is set at *b* and the other leg at *c* and a long arc drawn. On this arc a point is chosen as *d* and from this point the half-circumference of the base of the cap or cone which is shown as a quarter-section at *d* is set off; that is, from 0 to 6 is set off twice in the arc as shown. If a full pattern is desired this is doubled.

The braces C are made from 1/8- and 1-inch tinned straps which bind the bundles of sheet iron, and after they are punched and formed to shape, as indicated in the drawing, they are first riveted to the cap and then to the pipe. The holes for the rivets are accurately spaced on the pattern for the pipe and punched with a solid punch before the pipe is rolled up. The holes in the cap can best be spaced by swinging an arc from *e* with *b* as center and then intersecting with a line drawn from *b* to 6. The holes together with those of the seams are punched before the cap is formed to shape, the forming being done by coaxing it over a blown horn stake. As shown in the sketch, a bead can be swadged on the cap and the pipe to stiffen them.

CHAPTER IV

Elbows and Piping

To Describe a Tapering Elbow

Draw elevation of elbow at any angle desired and draw miter line H K as shown. Establish height and diameter of small end as V O and extend the lines 1-V and 7-O until they meet at B. Draw half profile S, which space into equal parts and draw vertical lines to 1-7, from which draw radial lines to the apex B, which will cross the miter line H K as shown. From these intersections draw horizontal lines to the side B-7 as shown from 1 to 7. With B-7 as radius, draw the arc 7′-7′ equal to the circumference of the circle S. From the points on 7′-7′ draw radial lines to the apex B, which intersect by arcs struck from B as center, with radii equal to the points between 1 and 7. U R G O is the pattern for the upper arm and R G 7′-7′ pattern for the lower arm. See Fig. 64 on opposite page for the diagram referred to.

It is to be understood that the smaller piece is to be turned half way around when joining the two pieces. That is to say, the seam for the largest or first piece is at the throat, while the seam for the smaller or second piece will be at the heel; throat and heel being the common terms of the trade.

Edges should be allowed for along the miter line for seaming, also along the sides, depending on the method of seaming used.

These methods are the basic principles for the system of developing tapering elbows of three or more pieces. The system must only conform to the rule that all the pieces are to be parts of one cone, or its frustum. That is to say, the various pieces

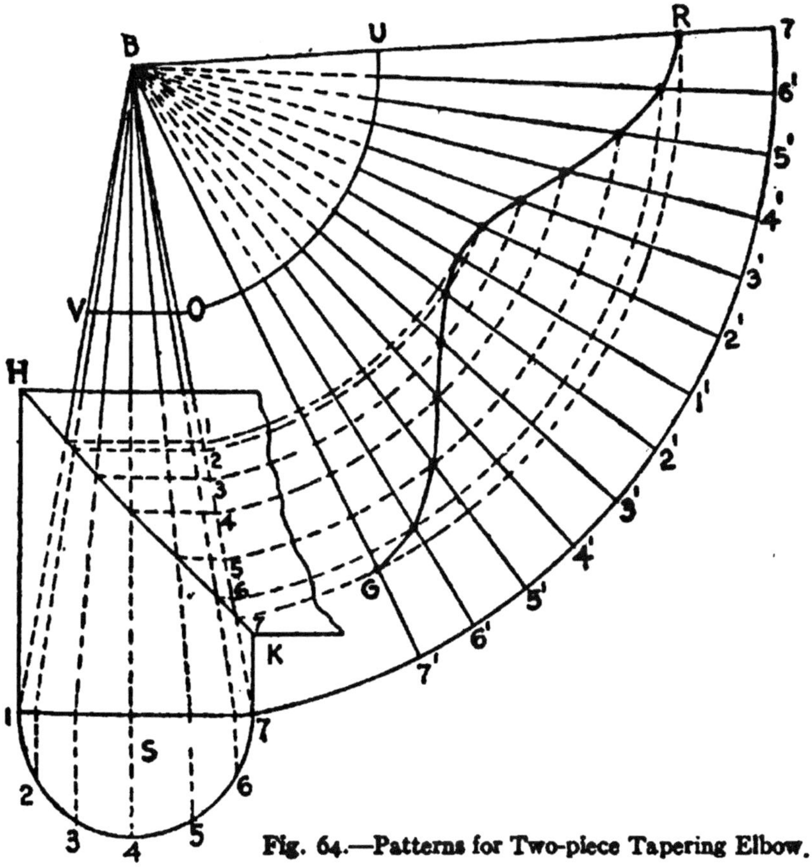

Fig. 64.—Patterns for Two-piece Tapering Elbow.

are turned on their axes so that they constitute a cone, as was done with the two pieces in Fig. 64.

A better system for three or more pieces would be to have the pieces at each end of the elbow straight and the taper provided for in the intermediate pieces; which means that the end pieces would be cut by the parallel line system and the others by triangulation.

A Square or Right Angle Elbow, in Two Pieces

Draw the elevation of the elbow, as B S, O V, K H. Draw line from V to O. Divide one-half of the plan into a convenient number of equal parts, as shown by dotted lines; erect lines to intersect O V. Make the line B R equal in length to the circumference of the elbow. Set off on this line spaces cor-

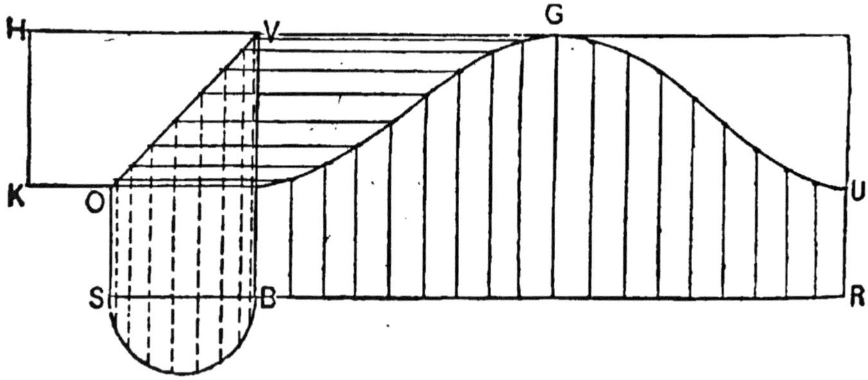

Fig. 65.—Two-piece Elbow Pattern.

responding to those in the plan, the same number each side of the center line; then draw lines parallel to the arm of the elbow, cutting the corresponding lines as indicated. By tracing through these points the irregular line U G the pattern is obtained, referring to Fig. 65. Allow edges for lock and provide lap for the rivets.

The general principle for cutting elbow patterns is the same throughout, and to understand the principle is to be able to describe pattern for any elbow, at any angle and of any number of pieces. It is the design of this work to make the principle clear to the readers.

Quick Method for Cutting Two-piece Elbow

In Fig. 65 is shown the strictly scientific method, according to orthographic projection, of developing two-piece elbow patterns. Now, in Fig. 66 is given a method based on a geometrical coincidence which is employed to save time in developing such patterns.

As may be seen, no elevation, plan or other view

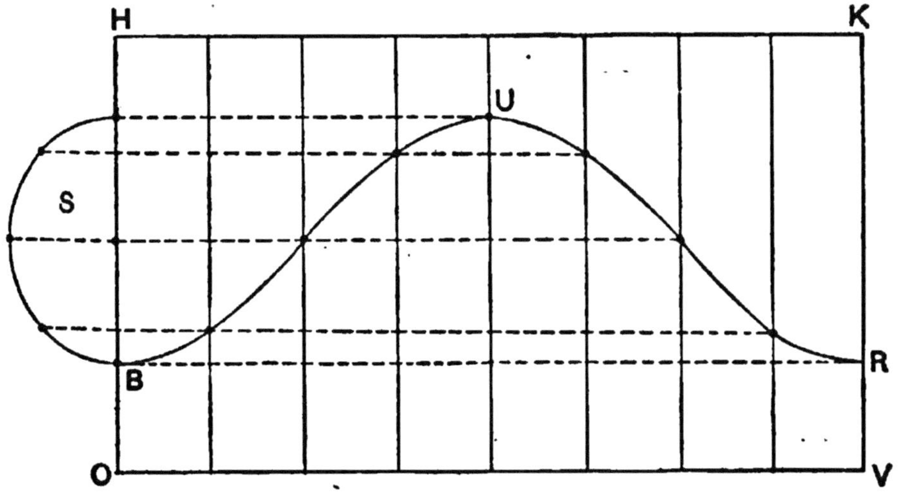

FIG. 66.—Quick Method for Elbow Pattern.

or views of the elbow need be drawn; no preliminary drawings whatsoever.

Lay out on sheet length required for elbow, as H K V O. Describe semicircle S the desired size of pipe, which divide into four parts. Space the length of the sheet into twice the number of squares in S, and draw vertical and horizontal lines until they intersect. O B U R V is then the pattern.

Allow for flanges for seaming the two parts together, also edges for locks or rivet flange for vertical seams of the two pieces.

A Square Three-piece Elbow

This is a complete demonstration, as shown in Figs. 67 and 68, of the method of developing patterns for a three-piece elbow. It is not the shortest way of proceeding, nevertheless it is strictly correct

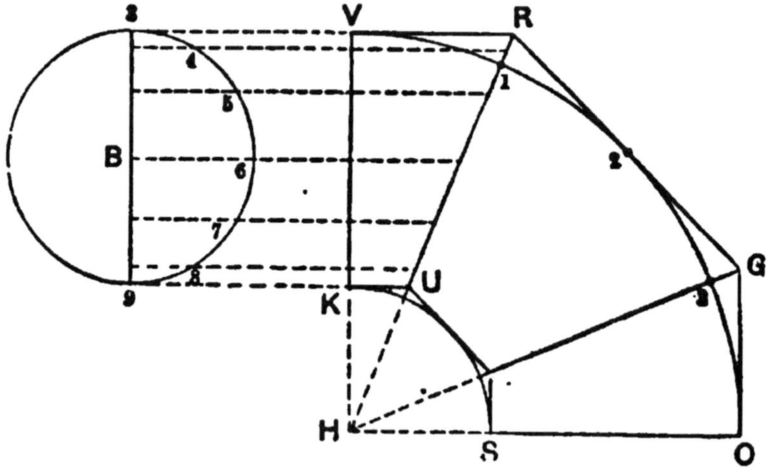

FIG. 67.—Elevation of Elbow.

and based on the principles of orthographic projection.

Let H K be the throat and K V the diameter of the elbow. Draw the quadrant V O, which divide into four equal parts, as shown by 1, 2, 3. Draw miter lines through 1 and 3 as H R and H G. Draw the circle B equal to diameter of elbow and divide one-half of B in equal parts, as shown; draw lines to intersect miter line R U, as directed by the diagram in Fig. 67.

Referring now to Fig. 68, which is the complete set of patterns, and referring to Fig. 67 when required by reference letters in the text, continue as follows:

Construct parallelogram H K V O equal in length to the circumference of B. Through the spaces on H K draw parallel lines as shown. Measuring from V K, take the various distances to the miter line R U and place them on similar lines measuring from H K. H S B K is then the pattern for the end. Double the distance from 3 to R′ and place it from

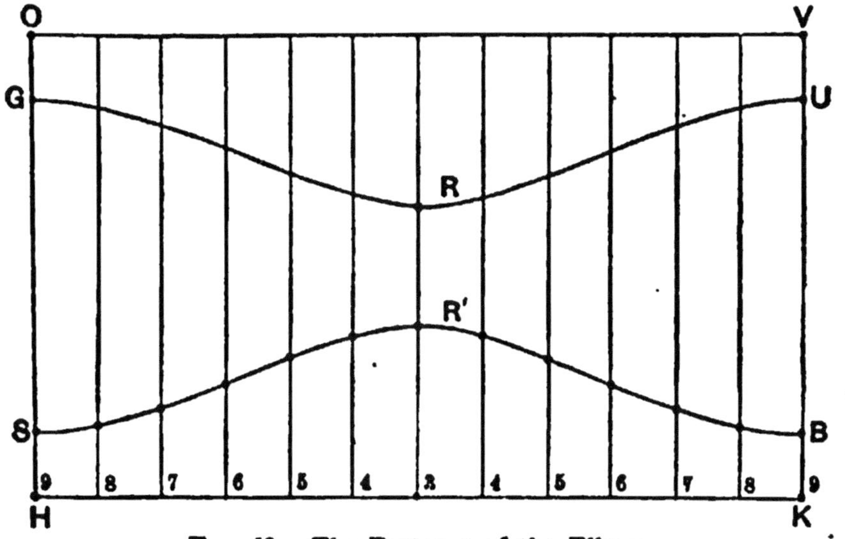

Fig. 68.—The Patterns of the Elbow.

S to G and B to U and transfer the miter line S R′ B to G R U. Place H S as shown by G O and U V and draw O V, which completes the three patterns.

Allow for seams and so forth in accordance with the scheme used for making elbows.

Attention is called to the grouping of the three patterns to form a rectangle; the idea being to cut the three pieces from a sheet without waste. This is the customary shop procedure and patterns for preservation should be bound together in the manner of stringing patterns given in Fig. 59.

A Four-piece Right Angle Elbow

As for the three-piece elbow, this is a complete demonstration of the exact method of cutting four-piece elbows, as shown in Figs. 69 and 70.

As was stated in the previous problems, this method is not the quickest but it is the truly scientific procedure and a good one for demonstrations.

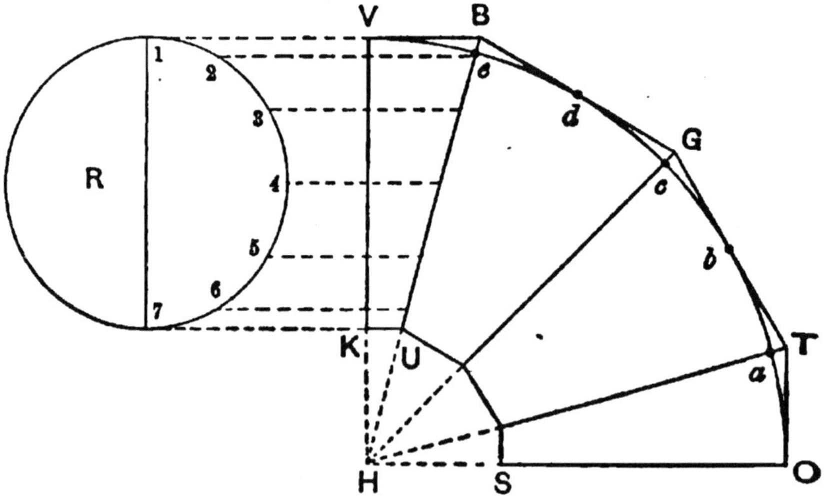

FIG. 69.—Elevation of Four-piece Elbow.

It may be of interest to state that elbows of any shape are developed by the method explained in connection with these problems of pieced elbows; for instance, profile R could be elliptical.

Let H K be the throat and K V the diameter of the elbow. Draw the quarter circle V O, which divide into six equal parts, as shown by *a b c d e*. Draw miter lines through *a, c* and *e,* as shown by H B, H G and H T. Draw the circle R, which space as shown, and draw lines to intersect the miter line B U, as in Fig. 69; which is the preliminary drawing.

Referring now to Fig. 70, which is the complete set of patterns and referring to Fig. 69 when so directed by the reference letters in the text, proceed as follows:

Construct parallelogram H K V O, equal in length to the circle R, as shown by similar figures on H K, through which draw parallel lines as shown.

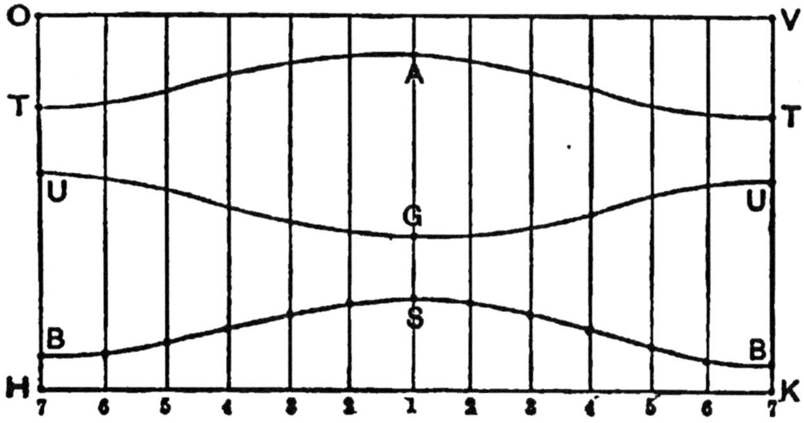

Fig. 70.—Complete Set of Patterns.

Measuring from V K, take the various distances to the miter line B U and place them on similar lines in the pattern, measuring from H K, and obtain B S B. Double 1 S and place at B U and B U and trace the miter cut B S B as shown by U G U. Place S G at U T and U T and trace U G U as shown by T A T. Make T O and T V equal to S 1 and draw line O V, which completes the four patterns.

Allow for locks for the various seams for joining the pieces together and the rivet or lock edges for the vertical seam of each piece.

A Five-piece Right Angle Elbow

As with the foregoing problems of this nature, the following is a demonstration of the complete steps of developing patterns for a five-piece elbow as shown in Figs. 71 and 72.

The principles embodied in the procedure exemplified in these four or five problems should make

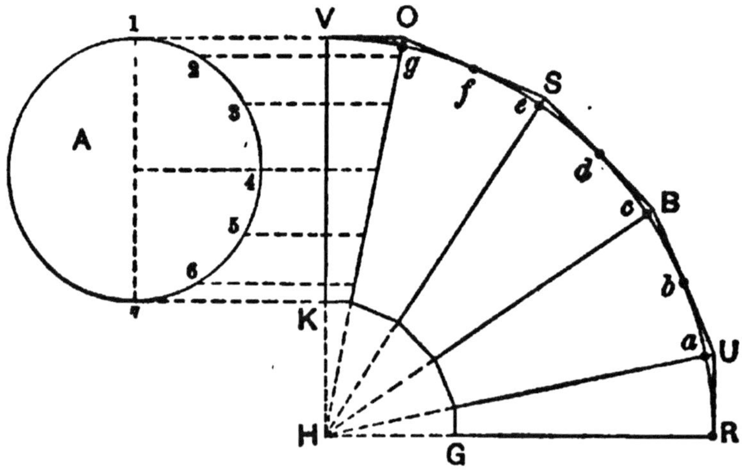

FIG. 71.—Elevation of a Five-piece Elbow.

the procedure quite clear for the developing of elbows of any number of pieces and indeed, at other than a right angle.

Draw throat H K and diameter K V. Draw quadrant H V R, which divide into eight parts as shown from *a* to *g*; draw miter lines H U, H B, H S and H O. Divide profile A into equal spaces, and draw lines from these points to miter line H O, as shown in Fig. 71.

Referring now to Fig. 72, which is the complete set of patterns, and referring to Fig. 71 when so directed by the reference letters in the text, proceed as follows:

Make 1 1 equal to circumference of profile A. Draw parallel lines as shown in pattern. Use dividers and measure various distances from V K to miter line H O, which transfer to similar lines measuring from 1 1, and obtain miter cut H K V.

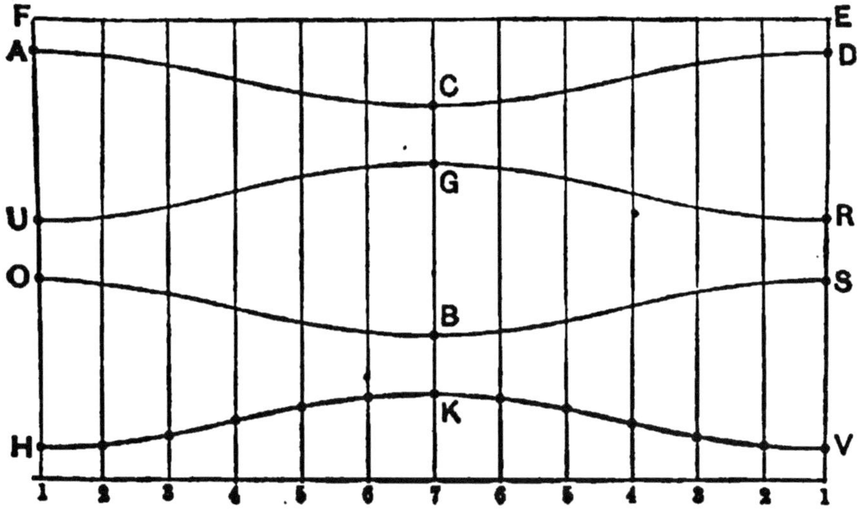

FIG. 72.—Complete Set of Patterns for Five-piece Elbow.

Double 7 K and place at H O and V S and draw miter cut O B S. Place K B at O U and S R and draw miter cut U G R. Make U A and R D equal to H O and draw miter cut A C D. Make A F and D E equal to H 1 and draw F E, which completes the five patterns. It is to be understood that this system of grouping the patterns causes the seams to come opposite each other in adjoining pieces, which is a decidedly good feature.

Allow for locks and so on as previously directed, inasmuch as these problems are all similar.

An Offsetting or Obtuse Elbow

When the pattern for an obtuse or rather an elbow offsetting, as shown in Fig. 73, is desired it is only necessary to draw a cor-

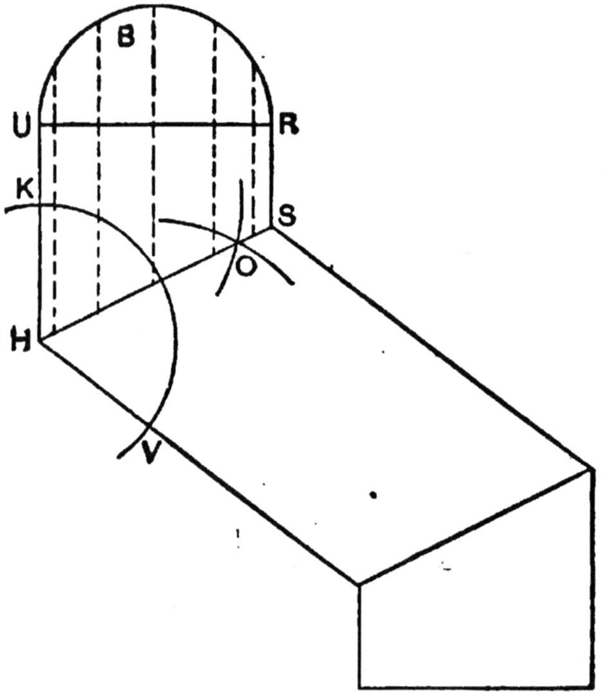

FIG. 73.—Rise of Miter Line in Elbows.

rect representation of the elbow and obtain the miter line, as follows: With H as center, draw the arc K V. With any desired radius, and using K and V as centers, intersect arcs at O. Draw the miter line H O S. Place the half profile B in position as shown, which space, and draw parallel lines to the miter line H S. Then proceed as by the rules already given in the four or five foregoing problems of like problems.

Rises for Elbow Miter Lines

The rise in an elbow is equal to the difference in length between the longest side and the shortest side of an end piece. In Fig. 74, showing a three-piece elbow, the distance A B is the rise. The following are the rises of elbows of from 3 to 10 pieces, the diameters of which are 1 inch:

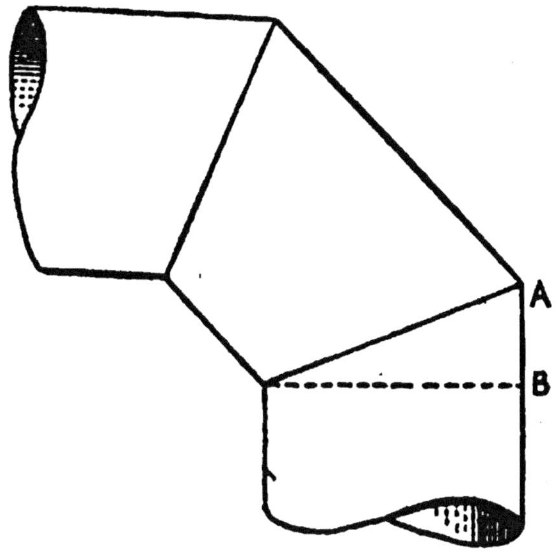

FIG. 74.—Rise of Miter Line in Elbows.

Table of Rises

3 piece,	0.414 or, 13-32	inch	rise	7 piece,	0.132 or, 9-64	inch	rise
4 "	0.268 or, 17-64	"	"	8 "	0.113 or, 7-64	"	"
5 "	0.199 or, 3-16	"	"	9 "	0.098 or, 3-32	"	"
6 "	0.158 or, 5-32	"	"	10 "	0.087 or, 5-64	"	"

To Find the Miter Line Rise for an Elbow of Any Number of Pieces and of Any Diameter

Rule: *Multiply the rise given in the above table by the diameter in inches of the desired elbow and the result will be the rise in inches for the miter line of the desired elbow.*

Example: Find the rise for a seven-piece elbow the diameter of which is 11 inches.

Answer: Table gives rise as 0.132; then, $0.132 \times 11 = 1.452$ or 1 15/32 inches, the desired rise.

Gray's Practical Elbow Chart

There are many devices to cut elbow patterns. Also charts have been prepared for figuring the number of pieces to use in making up an elbow of angle from the standard elbow patterns, as in Fig. 75, on the opposite page.

Although useful in many other ways, the main purpose of this chart is to instantly tell how to make offsetting elbows from the patterns of right-angled elbows of different number of pieces.

The regular elbow patterns can be developed for right-angled elbows, to full size, by following the instructions given herein for right-angled elbows of various number of pieces. Those who do not want to bother laying out their own patterns may purchase full size sets on heavy paper, all ready to lay on the metal. They are known as "Gray's Perfect Elbow Patterns," sets A and B.

Supposing you have a set of patterns at hand and, as per the example given in the chart, you have an offsetting angle in a run of piping that is 45 degrees from the original line of run. In fact, you do not know what degree the angle is but are able to set a bevel to the angle.

Now, this bevel is laid on the chart as shown, and it points to 45 degrees. Reading up the dotted line to the box tail of the arrow pointer on that degree, three combinations will be found in the box.

Deciding that, as in the example on the chart, a three-piece angle elbow will do, you select the first piece pattern of a right-angled five-piece elbow and cut out two pieces like the pattern. You also cut out one piece of any one of the middle sections of this five-piece right-angled elbow and, joining the

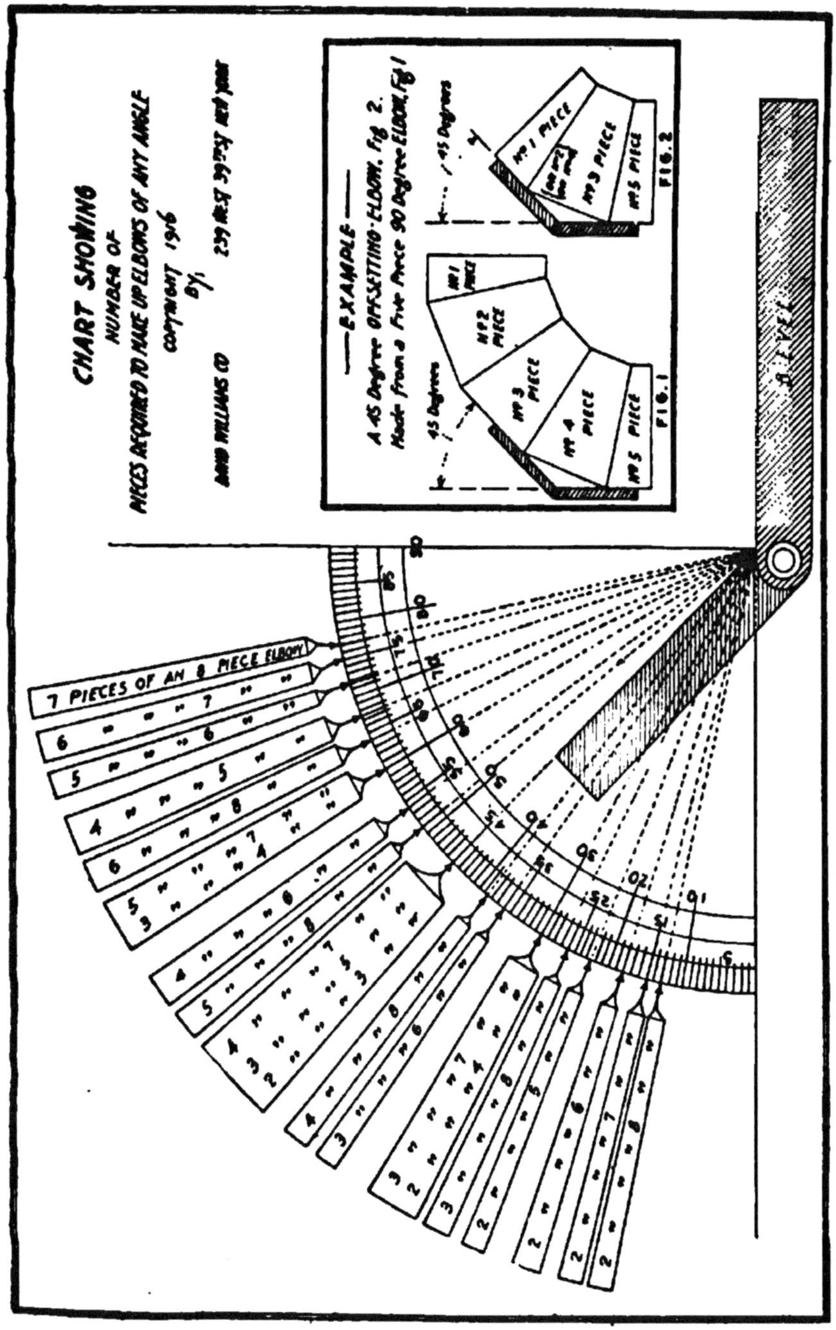

Fig. 75.—A Useful Elbow Chart.

three pieces as in the chart, you obtain the required angle elbow.

Ideal Rule for Elbow Patterns

One of the nicest, most accurate and rapid methods of cutting elbow patterns is in this manner. Make a small memorandum chart—it even need not be drawn to scale—of the rises per foot of elbow miter lines as in Fig. 76. The rises here shown were found by drawing elbow elevations, as in Fig. 71, for instance, and, of course, could be carried up to any number of pieces.

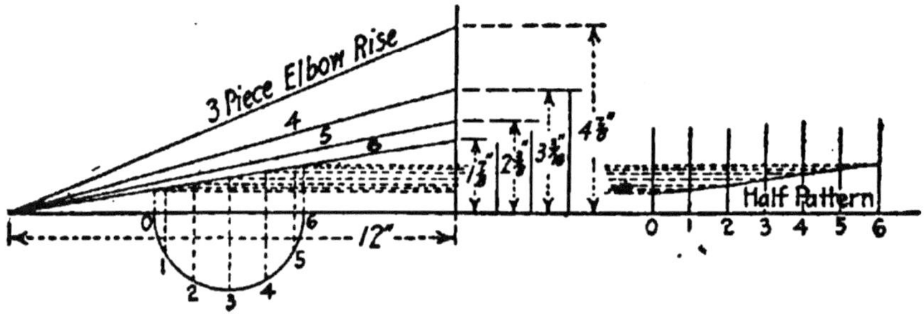

FIG. 76.—Cutting Elbow Patterns.

Now, supposing a six-piece elbow 4 inches in diameter is wanted. Simply draw a straight line 12 inches long and at one end erect a perpendicular line 1⅞ inches high. Draw a line completing the triangle, as shown in Fig. 76, this line being the required miter line.

Anywhere on this line locate a center and scribe a 4-inch half-circle, as shown. Divide into a number of spaces. Place these spaces on the extended 12-inch line, as shown at the right of Fig. 76. Erect perpendicular lines, which in turn are intersected by lines projected from the miter line, which gives the half-pattern, the set being complete as in, say, Fig. 72.

Rectangular Elbows—First Case

Rectangular elbows are common fittings. To cut the pattern for an elbow in which the turn is on the wide side of the pipe, first lay out a full-size side elevation (the profile really is not necessary) in this manner: Draw horizontal line A 7 and ver-

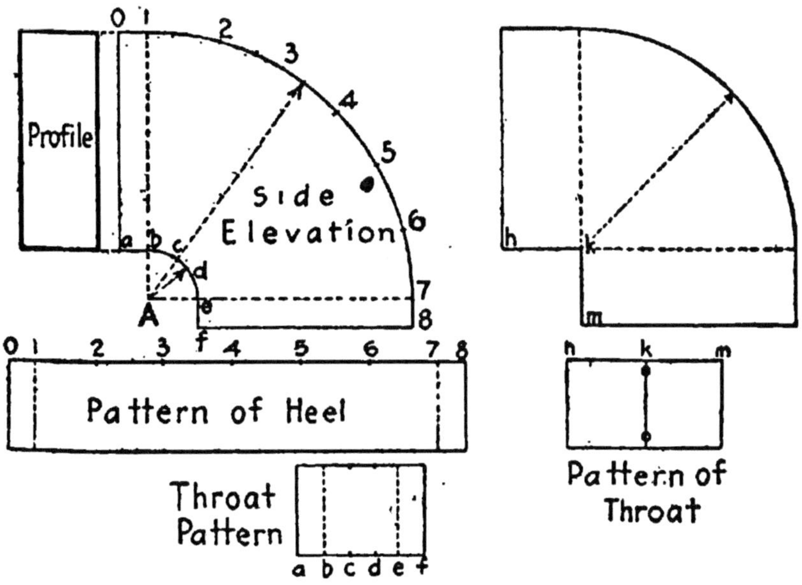

FIG. 77.—Elevation and Patterns of Rectangular Elbows.

tical line A 1. A is the center, and scribe throat to required radius as *b* to *e*. Scribe heel the distance away from throat equal to widest dimension of pipe. Add the straight parts 0 1 *a b* and *e f* 7 8.

The pattern for the heel is just a rectangular piece the width of narrowest dimensions of pipe and the length of the stretchout in elevation 0 to 8. The same is true for the throat pattern. Sometimes the throat is made as in the diagram at the right of Fig. 77, in which case the pattern is as shown below the diagram; a square bend is made along line *k*.

Rectangular Elbows—Second Case

The making of rectangular piping, or as some call it, duct work, is an important part of the sheet metal trade. Wall stacks for heating and ventilating, often of huge dimensions, are made this shape. And, too, the wall risers in furnace heating are frequently made rectangular as well as other fittings in this line, like cold air boxes for furnaces.

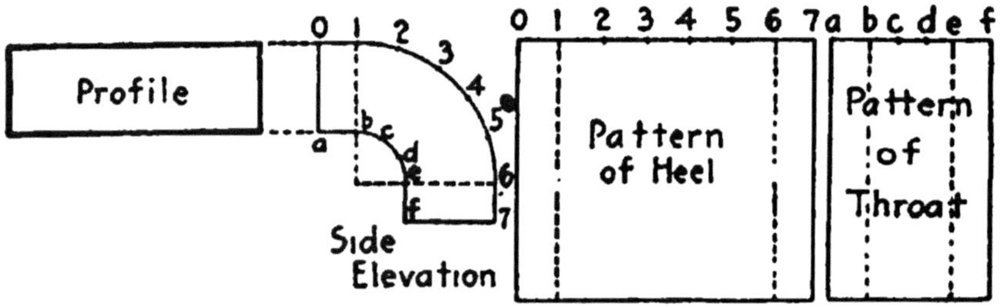

Fig. 78.—Elevation and Patterns of Rectangular Elbows.

The problems in rectangular elbows discussed here are those of frequent occurrences and lead up to complicated designs in unusual cases.

The turn, as in Fig. 78, can be on the narrowest side of the pipe or rectangle, just the opposite of the case of Fig. 77, and especial care must be exercised in laying out these types of elbows to be sure and have the turn on the right side. With rectangles of the proportions here shown the chance of error, while possible, is not as great as when the dimensions are almost equal.

As was directed for the other elbow, first draw side elevation, then take stretchouts of the heel and throat and cut out sheets the length of these stretchouts and to the width of the widest dimension of the rectangle. Provide for laps, etc.

Compound Elbows in Rectangular Piping—First Case

First draw where convenient, an outline of the rectangular duct as 8 A B C, which will represent the end of the horizontal duct. The correct distance below this and also as far to the right as it should be, draw the horizontal line 21 D to represent

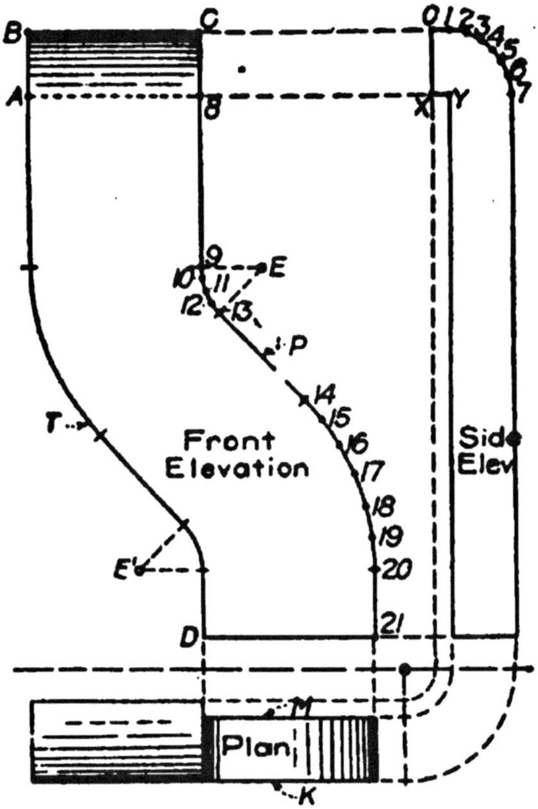

FIG. 79.—Shows Procedure in Making Elbow.

the wide side of the end of the vertical duct. As can be seen, there is ample room between these two ducts to make an easy connecting offset and square elbow, as shown by this front elevation. Note that this is the regulation method of making elbow offsets in pipe work, which is merely the choosing of convenient points like E and E′, as centers and scribing throat and heel sweeps of the turn.

Although not absolutely necessary, a plan is drawn as directed by Fig. 79, as it will help indicate the relative positions of the two duct ends. From the front elevation and plan a side elevation is projected which will indicate the regulation

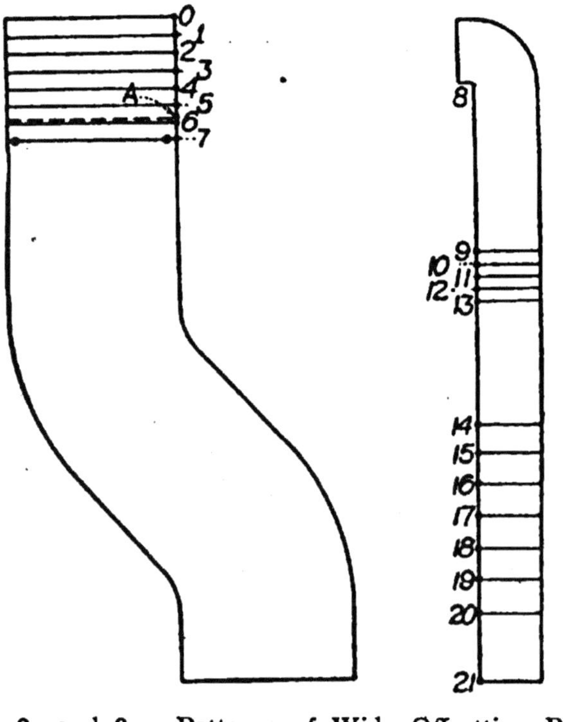

FIGS. 80 and 81.—Patterns of Wide Offsetting Part.

square elbow O X Y 7 required to make the turn from vertical to horizontal. Observe that the throat has a square bend which is customary when, owing to restricted space, a throat of a sweep like the heel is impossible.

Now then, Fig. 79 shows that the scheme in mind is to make the connection between the two ducts by a composite elbow, two offsetting elbows, the turn being made on the widest side of the pipe, as shown by the front elevation and a square elbow, the turn or cheeks being on the narrowest side.

If this is duct work, the three elbows would be made separately and joined by the usual method of slips or angle irons. However, the patterns as here shown are all in one. To make more clear Fig. 80 is given and is just a reproduction of the offsetting elbows of the front elevation of Fig. 79 up to point 8. Point 8 is called 7 in Fig. 80 and from 7 up is nothing more than the stretchout 0 to 7 of the heel of the square elbow of the side elevation of Fig. 79. This pattern is for the side nearest the observer of the front elevation of Fig. 79 or K in the plan. The opposite side, M in the plan, has the same pattern as Fig. 80 except that above 7 the throat stretchout, X Y of Fig. 79, is placed which would mean that the pattern stops there or as at A.

After having cut the two patterns from the metal it is to be noted that the piece terminating at A would have a square bend at 7, while the other piece would be rounded to the shape of the side elevation, starting the rounding at 7.

The pattern of the narrowest sides is given in Fig. 81, the cheeks of the square elbow, shown in the side elevation, Fig. 79, are reproduced and then from point 8 down is the stretchout 8 to 21 of the front elevation, Fig. 79. Of course, this pattern is for side P of the front elevation, Fig. 79, but the stretchout for side T is the same. The only difference is that the smaller curve is toward the bottom of the pattern instead of towards the top.

Compound Elbows in Rectangular Piping—Second Case

The discussion herein of these two cases of compound elbows in rectangular piping is based on actual work. They were originally prepared in response to a query on how to make fittings for these situations. Many solutions of compound elbows

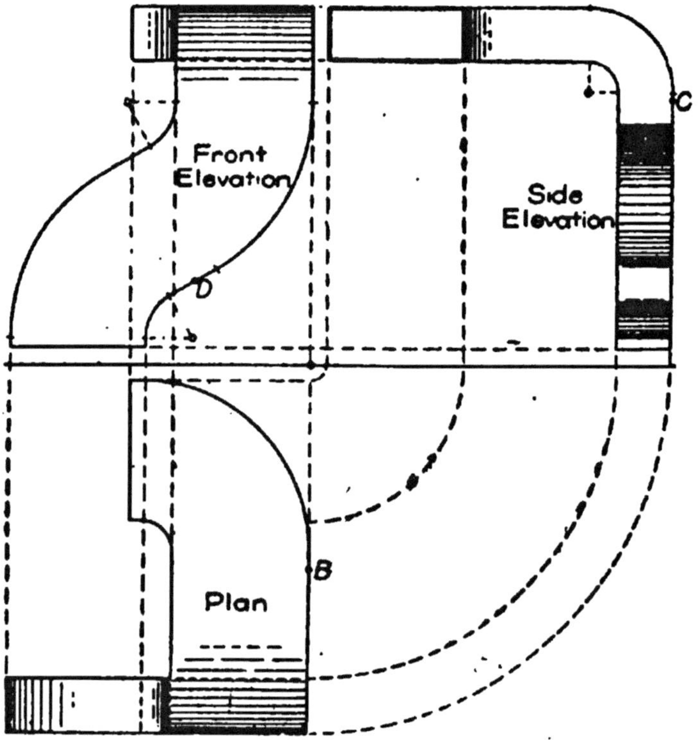

FIG. 82.—Projected View of Second Problem.

treat of a twisting elbow throughout which might be all right in certain cases but principally good problems for technical pattern drafting rather than actual shop practice like these solutions.

The second problem seemingly is more complicated, but an inspection of Fig. 82 will reveal that nothing more is needed than an additional elbow so that the composition consists of double offsetting elbows shown in the front elevation, a square elbow with cheeks on narrow sides as shown in the side elevation and the additional elbow to make the quarter turn horizontally which has its cheeks on the wide sides, as indicated by the plan of the diagrams, Fig. 82.

From the description of the method of developing the patterns for the first problem, it is assumed that the method of obtaining the patterns for the second case requires no explanation; attention is called, though, to the throats, which are all rounded; the patterns of which are obtained by taking the girth of the throat quadrant as explained before.

It should be understood that in the foregoing an attempt was made to describe how such problems would be studied and solved in actual practice. For, assuming that the pipe is 3 x 8 feet, it will be seen that no more extraordinary situation occurs, in either case, than arises on most every job of heating, ventilation or kindred work, and it is common practice, when space is available as it was in these problems, to use just such combinations of common elbows because these fittings are all easily made and erected. It is to be remembered, too, that the slip joints are used so as to cut out the material with the least waste; generally they would be at, say, B in plan, C in side elevation, and D in the front elevation; as shown in Fig. 82.

Full information on the development of compound elbows by the "twist" method are given in the book, "Piping and Heavy Sheet Metal Work."

CHAPTER V

Furnace Fittings

Patterns for an "A" Smoke Jack

This problem is introduced not only because it is a good design for a chimney top, but also because two problems occurring quite frequently in furnace smoke pipe work are involved, namely, a

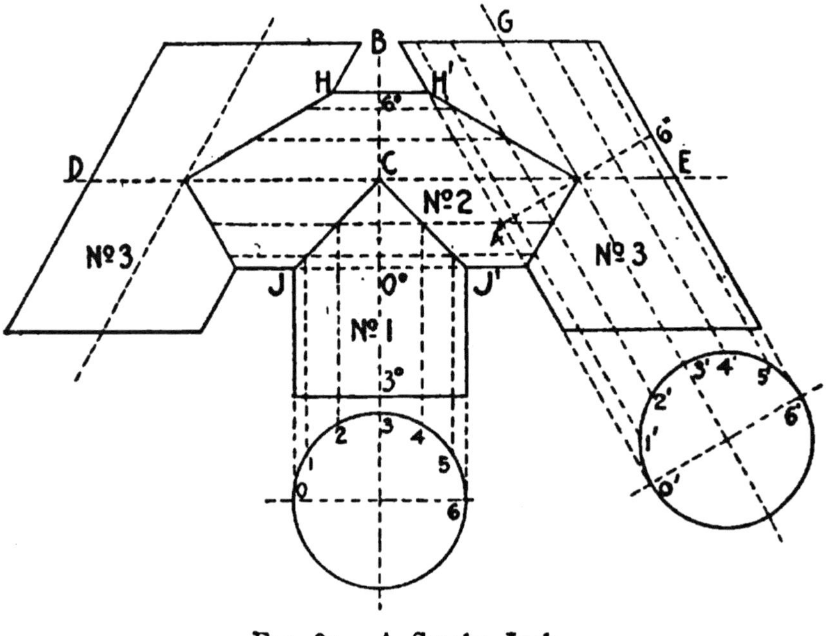

FIG. 83.—A Smoke Jack.

tee joint at a square angle and a tee joint at other than a right angle. Arms No. 1 and No. 2—square tee joint and No. 2 and No. 3 angle tee joint.

As in Fig. 83, draw a vertical line 3 B; also a horizontal line crossing this at C, as D E. Again, axes lines of inclined arms to suit desired proportions. Draw the two profiles of the parts, as 0 to 6 and 0′ to 6′ and divide into equal spaces as shown. Draw the dotted lines from these spaces, also line 4″ 6″ at right angles to line 3′ G.

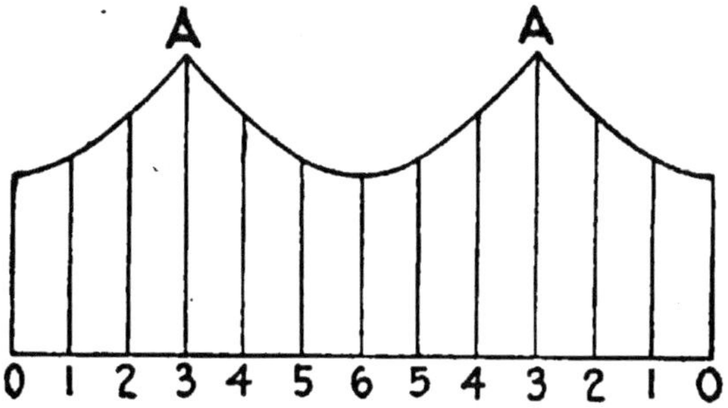

Fig. 84.—Pattern of No. 1 Piece.

Many designers do not cut the tops and bottoms of arms, No. 3, on a horizontal line as shown, but leave the arms straight, that is, on a line parallel to line 4″ 6″. As may be imagined, this does not look as well as the design of Fig. 83, but it saves considerable cutting, which might be quite a factor when figuring for a low cost, especially as the operating of the jack would be the same in either case.

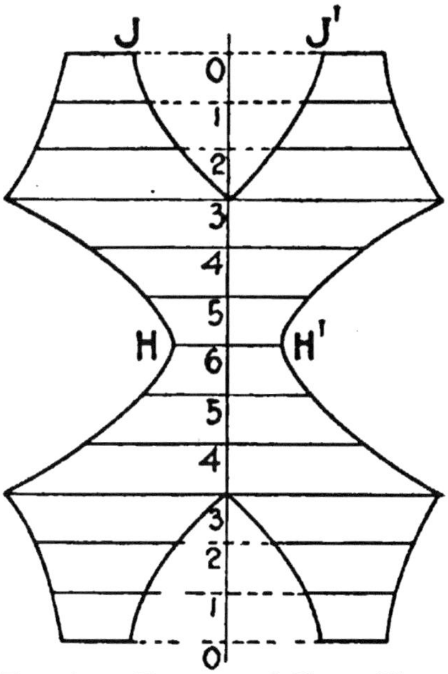

Fig. 85.—Pattern of No. 2 Piece.

For the pattern of the upright piece No. 1 draw a line as 0 to 0 in Fig. 84, with the spaces 0 to 6 to 0 of the profile in Fig. 83. Draw the right angled lines from these spaces. Then carry distances from like lines in Fig. 83 to Fig. 84; thus, line 3° C in Fig. 83 equals line 3 A in Fig. 84, and so on.

For the pattern of piece No. 2 place stretchout on a line as shown in Fig. 85, also right angle lines. Carry the lengths from both sides of line 3° B in

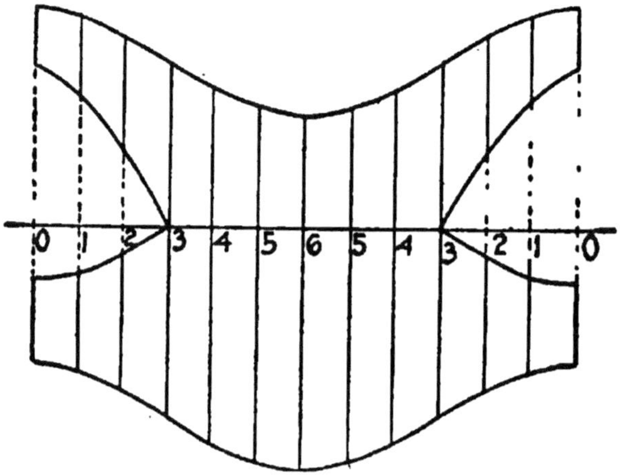

FIG. 86.—Pattern of No. 3 Pieces.

Fig. 83 to both sides of line 0 to 0 in Fig. 85. Thus, spaces 6 H 6 H′ in Fig. 85 is 6° H and 6° H′ of Fig. 83. Also for the cut-out or hole; for instance, 0 J and 0 J′ of Fig. 85 is 0° J and 0° J′ of Fig. 83, and so on.

For the arm pieces, in No. 3, Fig. 83, place stretchout on line 0 to 0 as in Fig. 86 and continue as explained before, measuring from the line 4″ 6″ in Fig. 83; that is to say, the lengths are taken from line 4″ 6″, in Fig. 83, to the top of the arm and are placed above the stretchout line of Fig. 86. Then, lengths taken below line 4″ 6″, of Fig. 83 to the bottom, are placed below stretchout line in Fig. 86.

Laying Out a Chimney Base

Proceed as in Fig. 87, in which 1, 2, 3, 4 is the outline of the bottom of the base and A the size of the round pipe. From the corners of the rectangu-

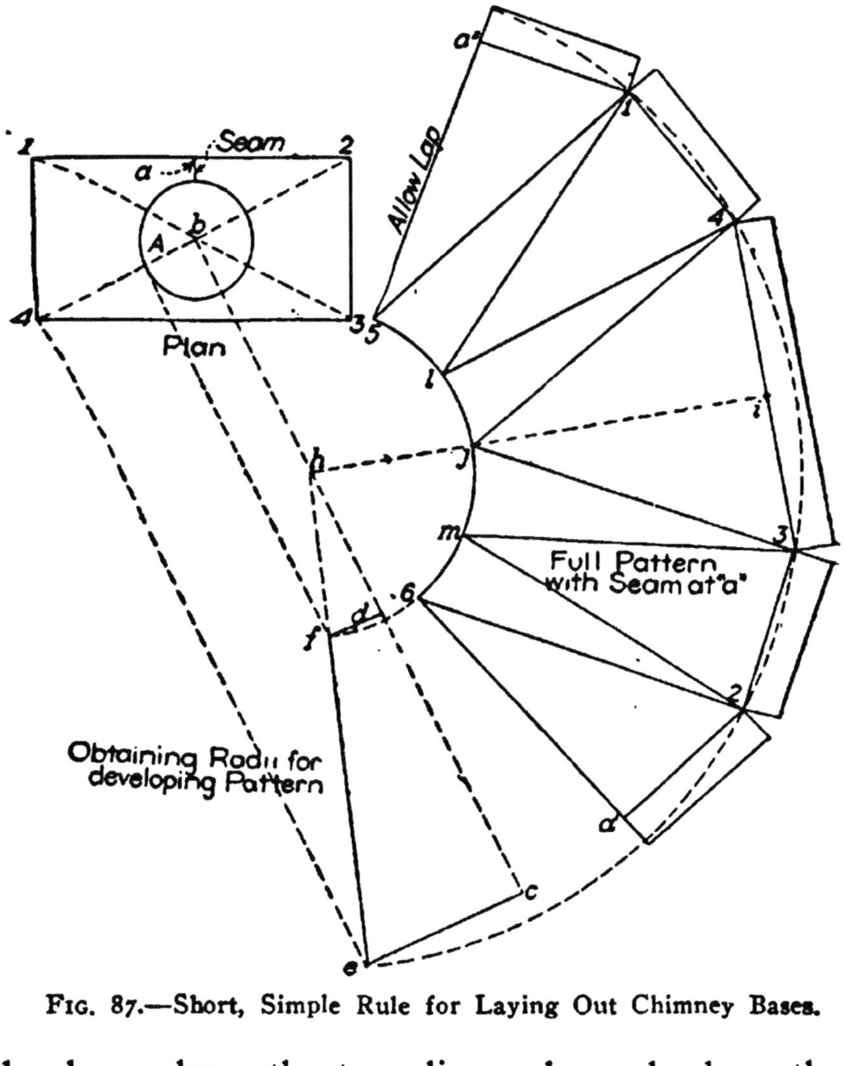

FIG. 87.—Short, Simple Rule for Laying Out Chimney Bases.

lar base, draw the two diagonals, and where they intersect will be the center *b* used for striking the desired size of the smoke pipe A. Now, at right angles to either one of the diagonal lines, in this case 4 *b*, draw lines indefinitely from points 4, A and *b* as shown. Now draw any line as *c e* parallel to 4 *b* and make the height *c d* equal to the desired height of the base. From *d* draw the line *d f* parallel to *c e* until it intersects the perpendicular line drawn from A parallel to 4 *e* at *f*. Draw a line from *e* through *f* until it intersects the center line at *h*; *h f* and *h e* then become the radii for striking the pattern. Now, using these radii, with *h* as center, describe the arcs *f* 5 and *e* 1. Set the dividers equal to 1-4, 4-3 and 3-2 in plan, and place these distances on the outer arc as shown in the pattern from 1 to 4, 4 to 3, and 3 to 2. Now draw lines from 1 to 4, 4 to 3 and 3 to 2 and bisect the side 3-4, thus obtaining the point *i*, from which draw a radial line to *h*, cutting the inner arc at *j*.

Take the girth of full circle A, and place one-half of it on either side of the inner arc, as shown from *j* to 5 and *j* to 6. Bisect *j* 5 and *j* 6 and obtain points *l* and *m*, respectively. Now, draw lines from point 1 on the outer arc to 5 and *b*; from point 4 to *l* and *j*; from point 3 to *j* and *m* and from point 2 to *m* and 6. These lines indicate where slight bends would be made, so as to obtain the transition from square corners to round top. As the seam in this case is to come between 1 and 2 in plan or in the center of the long side at *a*, then to obtain this joint line in the pattern, use *j i* in the pattern as radius, and, with 5 and 6 as centers, draw the arcs *a''* and *a'*, respectively; then using 3 *i* or 4 *i* as radius and 1 and 2 as centers, intersect arcs previously drawn at *a''* and *a'*. Draw lines from 1 to *a''* to 5, and from 2 to *a'* to 6, which completes the pattern.

Pattern for a Furnace Center Boot

Of all the fittings that are made for furnace work, boots or shoes or starters, etc., as they are called, according to the different localities in which they are made, form one of the most important problems. They have offsets one way or two ways.

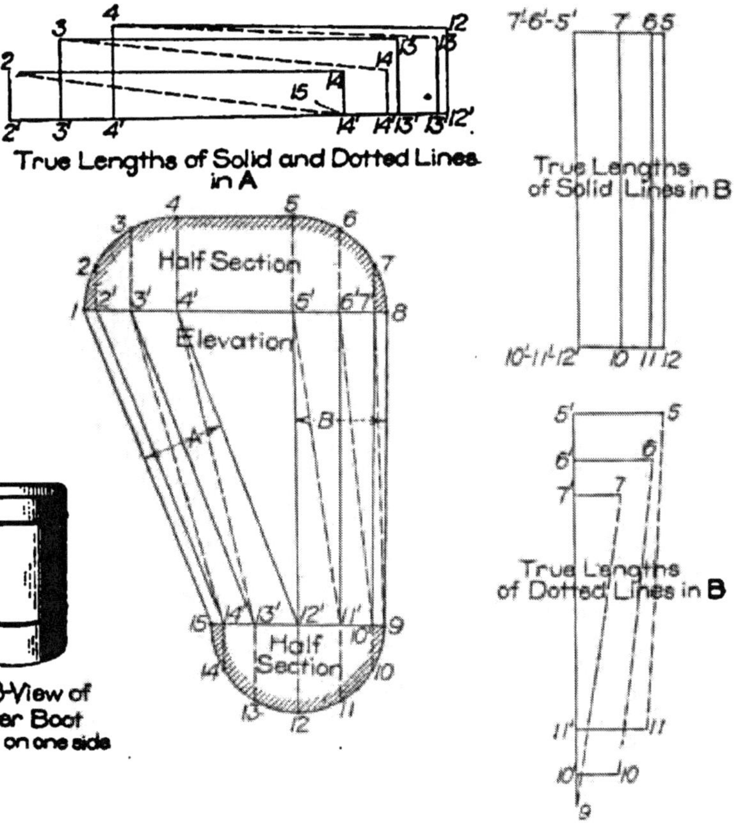

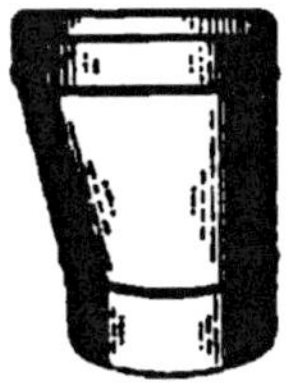

Fig. 88-View of Center Boot Vertical on one side

FIG. 89.—Elevation and True Lengths.

They have their collars at various angles to each other and, in fact, are so diverse in designs that quite a number of articles could be written about them; the style shown in Fig. 88 is a common one and the pattern procedure is as shown in Figs. 89 and 90.

Divide the quarter circles of elliptical section, in the same number of divisions as the quarter circles in the half section and number the points from 1 to 4, 5 to 8 and 9 to 15 as shown. From the divisions in the elliptical section 1 to 8 at right angles to the line 1-8 draw lines intersecting the line 1-8 at 2′, 3′, 4′, 5′, 6′ and 7′. In a similar manner, at right angles to the line 9-15 from the intersections

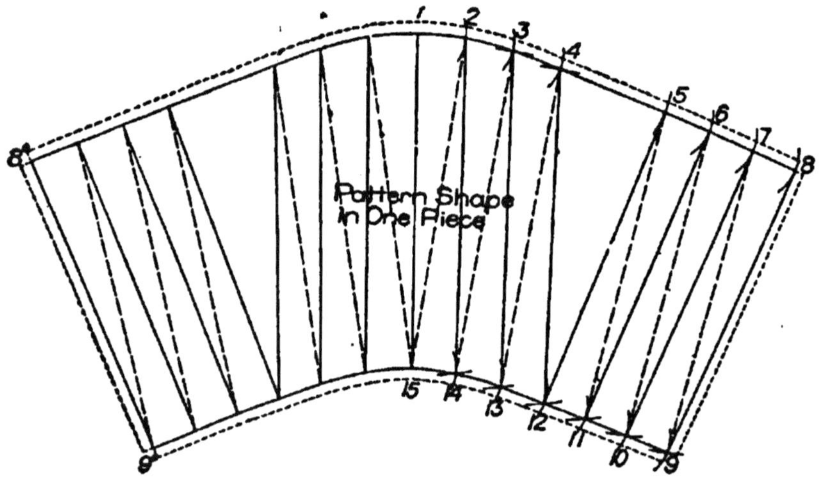

FIG. 90.—Pattern of the Center Boot.

10 to 14, draw lines cutting the line 9-15 at 10′, 11′, 12′, 13′ and 14′. Connect solid lines in elevation as shown, and connect the opposite points by dotted lines all as indicated in the parts marked A and B.

To obtain the true length of the solid lines in A in elevation proceed as follows: Take the various lengths of the solid lines 4′ to 12′, 3′ to 13′ and 2′ to 14′, and place them as shown by similar numbers in the diagram of true lengths in A. From these various points perpendiculars are erected equal to the various heights in the semi-sections in elevation.

For example, the heights of 4'-4 in the semi-elliptical section and 12'-12 in the semi-circle are placed on the proper perpendiculars in diagram for true lengths in A, as indicated by 4'-4 and 12'-12. A line drawn from 4 to 12 is the true length of the line 4'-12' in elevation. Similarly, obtain the true lengths of the dotted lines in A in elevation, also the true lengths of the solid and dotted lines in B.

Cut the pattern as follows. Assuming that the seam is to come along 8-9 in elevation then take the length of 1-15, which shows its true length, and place it as shown by 1-15 in the pattern. Now with 1-2 in the half section as radius, and 1 in pattern as center, describe the arc 2, which intersect by an arc struck from 15 as center and 15-2 in the true lengths in A as radius. Now using 15-14 in the half section as radius, and 15 in pattern as center, describe the arc 14, which intersect by another arc struck from 2 as center and 2-14 in the true lengths in A as radius.

Proceed in this manner, using alternately first the proper division in the semi-elliptical section, then the proper true length of the dotted lines; then the proper division of the semi-circular section, and the proper true length of the solid lines, always following the dotted and solid lines in elevation as a guide, until the seam line 8-9 in pattern is obtained, which equals 8-9 (its true length) in elevation. Trace a line through points thus obtained, as shown by 1-8-9-15 in the pattern, which shows the half pattern. If a full pattern is desired, trace this half opposite the line 1-15, as shown by 8°-9°.

Round to Rectangle Furnace Boot

The problem is an object having a round base and transforms to a rectangular form at the top. This rectangle is so situated in respect to the round base, as to have what is termed a straight back, which is to say, the long center line of the rectangle does not lie in the same vertical plane as does the cross diameter of the round; however, the short center line of the rectangle does lie in the same vertical plane as a diameter, at right angles to the one mentioned, of the round. This then makes a problem of symmetrical halves so that the pattern for one-half will answer for the other half.

First, divide the circle into quarters. Then divide the two quarters represented by E H G into equal divisions, and, from the points in the section E H, draw lines to the corner of the top, represented by B, in Fig. 93, and, from the divisions in section H G, draw lines to the corner of the top represented by C, Fig. 93. It will be necessary to construct the two diagrams of triangles, one for each corner, shown in Fig. 93, so as to obtain the true length of each line. Lay off the line, R J, in Fig. 94, equal to the height of the fitting made to suit the work on which it is to be used. From the point J, and at right angles to the line R J, set off the length of lines in the section E to H, making J 1 equal to B 1, J 2 equal to B 2, etc. From the points thus established in the line J W, Fig. 94, draw lines to R.

To obtain triangles for the section H G, draw lines as shown in Fig. 95, the same as in Fig. 94.

Make V S the same height as R J, Fig. 94; draw S T at right angles to V S, and, on the line S T set off the lengths of the lines in section H G, making S 1′ equal to C 1′, S 2′ equal to C 2′, etc.; from the points thus established in S T, Fig. 95, draw lines

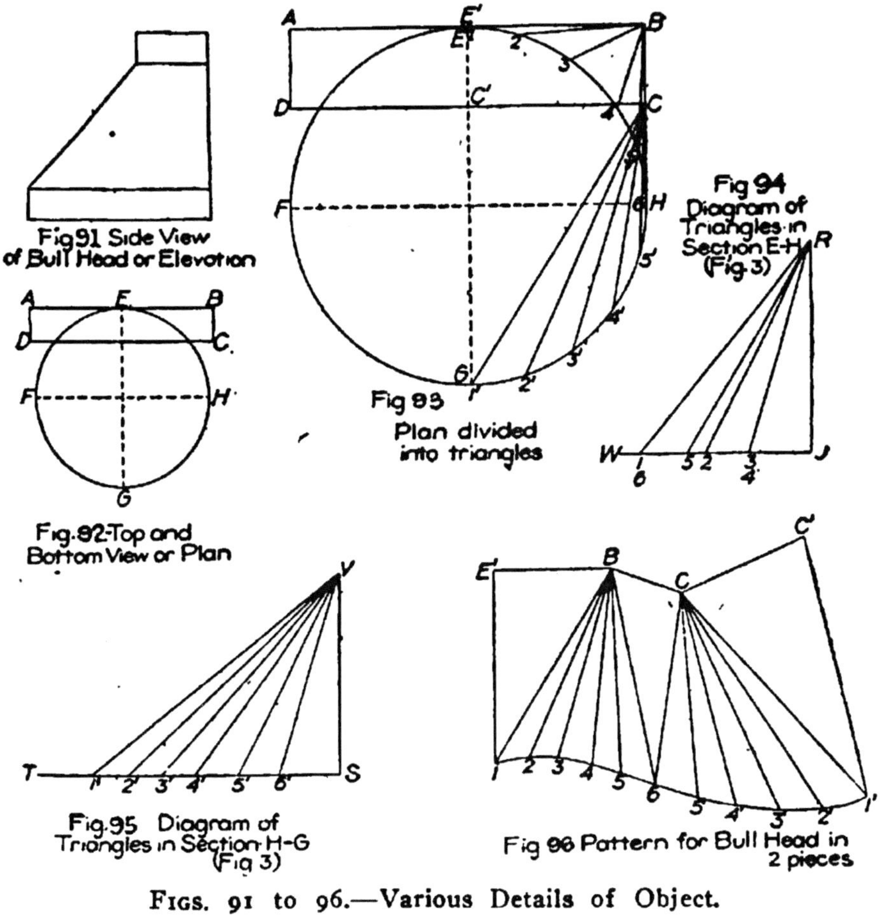

FIGS. 91 to 96.—Various Details of Object.

to V, as shown. To obtain the pattern, lay off line 1 E′ in Fig. 96, and from point E′, and at right angles to 1 E′, draw line E′ B equal in length to E′ B of plan Fig. 93, which is the same as half the length of the long side of the top. Set the dividers to R 1, Fig. 94, and with B of pattern as center, strike an arc cutting the line E′ 1 at 1. Then join 1-B, Fig.

96. With B as center and R 2 in Fig. 94 as radius, describe an arc. With 1, of pattern as center, and 1'-2' of plan as radius, strike a small arc intersecting at 2 with the arc previously drawn. With B, Fig. 96, as center, and R 3, Fig. 94, as radius, describe an arc, and with the dividers set to same space used in stepping off the plan, strike small arc intersecting at 3 of the pattern. Proceed in the same way to lay off the lines 4, 5 and 6. Then, to obtain the point C, of pattern, set the dividers to B C of plan, Fig. 93, and, with B of pattern as center, and B C of plan as radius, describe an arc. Now, with V 6', Fig. 95, as radius, and 6, of the pattern, as center, strike an arc, intersecting with the arc already drawn. This will give the point C of the pattern. With C of the pattern as center and V 5', Fig. 95, as radius, describe an arc. Now, with the dividers set to same space used in stepping off plan at 6-5', using 6 of the pattern as center, strike a small arc intersecting the other at 5'. The remaining lines, 4', 3', 2' and 1' are established in the same way as the preceding one. To complete the pattern, set the dividers to C'-C, and, with C of pattern as center, strike a small arc. Now, from 1' of pattern as center, and the slant height of bullhead Fig. 91, as radius, strike an arc intersecting at C'. Lines traced through the points thus obtained will give the pattern required minus laps.

Drafting the pattern for boot with an offset is done in exactly the same way, only be sure to draw the right amount of offset in the plan and elevation and then proceed as previously explained.

Pattern for an Angular Furnace Boot

A sketch of the fitting is given in Fig. 97 and it is to be understood that this procedure will apply for any combination of sizes, position and dimensions of rectangular collar. The methods and design here explained are scientifically correct and a much better method than the so-called channel boot, which is merely a square box with collars let into it.

By position and dimensions of rectangular collar and combination of sizes in respect to the round collar, is meant that if, for instance, the rectangle collar was turned one-quarter around in relation to its present position an ordinary offset boot would result. Such boots are commonly used when the wall pipe is in a partition over a girder and it is necessary to offset over this girder to make the connection to collar pipe and transition in shape at this place, from the round collar pipe to the rectangular shape of the wall pipe or riser.

Also, if the wall pipe had a shape of what is commonly called "oval," that is to say, a rectangle with semi-circular ends, the procedure here outlined would be in a measure, similar; that is, very little adjusting of the methods would be required.

Now, even if the round collar was situated at a different angle, as say, somewhat off the vertical line in which it is now, so that the boot could be connected to the pitched collar pipe without using an angle elbow, the procedure would be identical to that herein explained.

The first step is to draw the side elevation, as

shown by 1′-2′-3′-9 in Fig. 98. On the line 1′-2′ place the half section of the 3½ x 10-inch pipe, as shown, and on the line 3-9 place the half section of the 9-inch pipe, also shown.

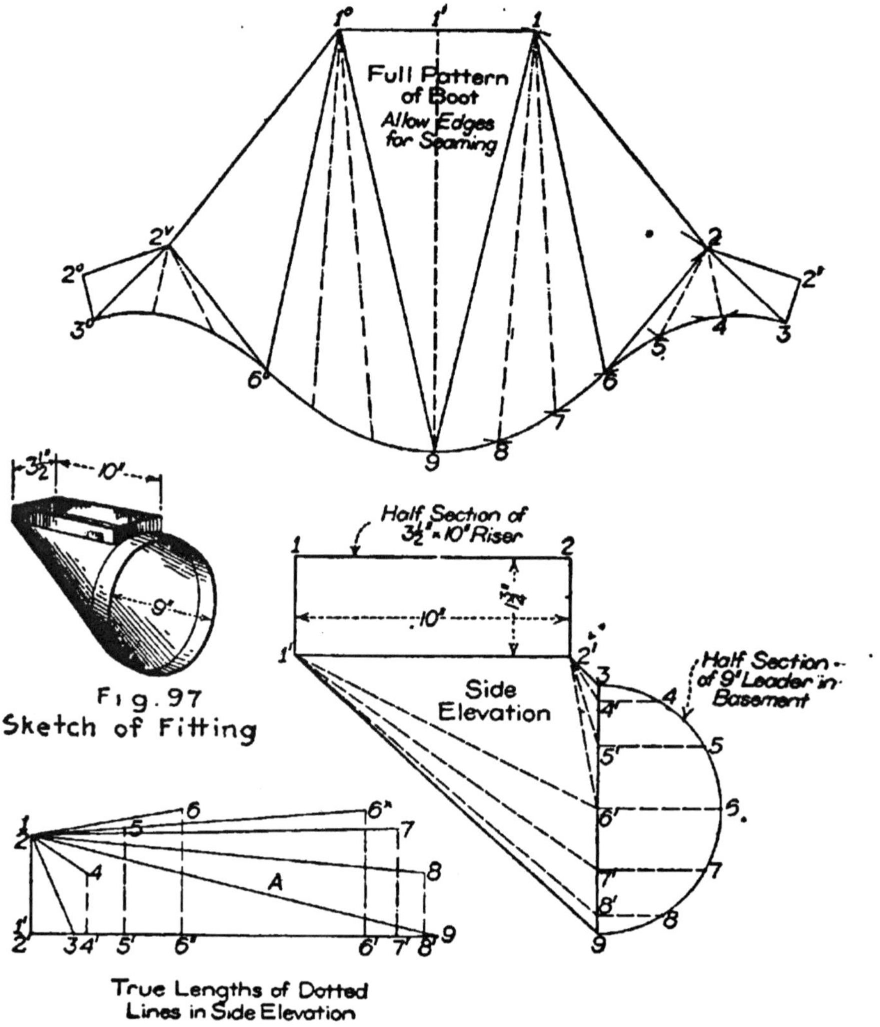

FIG. 98.—Various Details of the Object.

Divide the semi-circle in any number of equal spaces; in this case 6, as indicated by the small figures, 4, 5, 6, 7 and 8. From these points at right angles to 3-9 draw lines intersecting, 3-9 at 4′, 5′,

6′, 7′ and 8′. From the intersections 3, 4′, 5′ and 6′ draw lines to the corner 2′; and from the intersections 6′, 7′, 8′ and 9 draw lines to the corner 1′. These lines represent the bases of sections which will be constructed whose altitudes will equal the various heights in the half sections. For an example: To find the true length of the line 1′-6′ in side elevation, take this distance and place it as shown from 1′ to 6′ in diagram A. From the points 1′ and 6′ at right angles to 1′-6′, erect the lines 1′-1 and 6′-6^x, equal in height to 1′-1 and 6′-6 in the half sections. A line drawn from 1 to 6^x in A is the desired length. In similar manner take the various lengths 1′ to 7′, 1′ to 8′ and 1′ to 9 in the side elevation and place them as shown by similar numbers in diagram A and erect perpendicular lines equal to the proper height in the half sections. Also, take the lengths 2′ to 3, 2′ to 4′, 2′ to 5′ and 2′ to 6′ in the side elevation and place them in diagram A, as shown by similar numbers, and obtain the heights from the half sections.

It will be noticed that the height of the sections at 1′ and 2′ in the side elevation is equal to 1′-1 and 2′-2 respectively, both heights being similar, as shown in diagram A, while the heights at 4′, 5′, 6′, 7′ and 8′ in the side elevation vary, as shown in the semi-circle at 4, 5, 6, 7 and 8, respectively.

Having obtained the true lengths in A, the pattern is now in order, and is developed as follows: Take the length of 1′-9 in the side elevation which shows its true length and place it on the vertical line in the pattern, shown by 1′-9. Now with a radius equal to 1'-1 in the half section in the side elevation, and 1' in the pattern as center, describe the arc 1, which intersects by an arc, struck from 9 as center and 9-1 in the true length A as radius. Now with radii equal to 1-8, 1-7 and 1-6 in diagram A and using 1 in the pattern as center, describe the short arcs 8, 7 and 6. Set the dividers equal to the divisions 9-8, 8-7 and 7-6 in the semi-circular section in the side elevation, and starting from 9 in the pattern step to arc 8, 7 and 6 respectively, and draw a line from 6 to 1 and 1 to 9 and trace the curve from 9 to 6.

Now with a radius equal to 2-6 in diagram A and with 6 in the pattern as center, describe the arc 2, which intersect by an arc struck from 1 as center, and 1-2 of the half section in the side elevation as radius. With radii equal to 2-5, 2-4 and 2-3 in diagram A and 2 in the pattern as center, describe the arcs 5, 4 and 3. Again set the dividers equal to the divisions 6 to 5, 5 to 5 and 4 to 3 in the semi-circular section in the side elevation and starting from 6 in the pattern, step to arc 5, 4 and 3. Draw a line from 3 to 2 and 2 to 6.

Now with radius equal to 3-2' in the side elevation, which shows its true length, and 3 in pattern as center, draw the arc 2', which intersect by an arc struck from 2 as center and 2-2' in the semi-rectangular section in the side elevation as radius. Connect points in the pattern by tracing the curve from 6 to 3, and draw lines from 3 to 2', 2' to 2, 2 to 1 and 1 to 1'. 1'-9-3-2'-2-1-1' is the half pattern; and, 1°-2°-2°-3°-6°-9 added is the full pattern.

Pattern for a Y Fitting

Trunk line systems in furnace heating are becoming quite popular and require special fittings as, for instance, the Y branch. The principles as explained for this case can be applied to any size fitting, no matter what angle the fitting may have, providing the two forks are symmetrical when viewed in plan as shown in diagram X in Fig. 99. As the angles of the forks in this case are the same as shown in the elevation, the one pattern will answer for both. If, however, the angle of the one fork was 45 deg. and the other 30 deg., a separate pattern would have to be developed for each, using the same method as will now be described.

The first step in this procedure is to draw any line as 8-10° equal to 14 inches, which bisect and obtain *a*. From *a* erect the perpendicular *a* 14, equal to one-half of 14 inches, or 7 inches. From *a* draw the angles desired, as *a e* and *a d*. Make these two lines of the desired length and through *e* and *d*, perpendicular to the lines just drawn, draw the line 1-7 the desired diameter, or 10 in. Using *e* as center, with *e* 1 as radius, draw the half section of the pipe. In similar manner, using *a* as center, with radius equal to *a* 8, draw the half section of the large pipe, also the half section of the intersection between the two forks on line *a* 14. It may be of interest to state that the profile *a* 14 11° could be arbitrarily drawn if the conditions required it.

Thus 1-4-7 is the half section of the 10-inch pipe; 8-11-11° the half section of the 14-inch pipe and

a-11°-14 the half section of the joint line between the two forks. Now divide the half sections into equal parts, as shown by the small figures, from which draw perpendicular lines to their respective base lines as shown. Draw solid and dotted lines

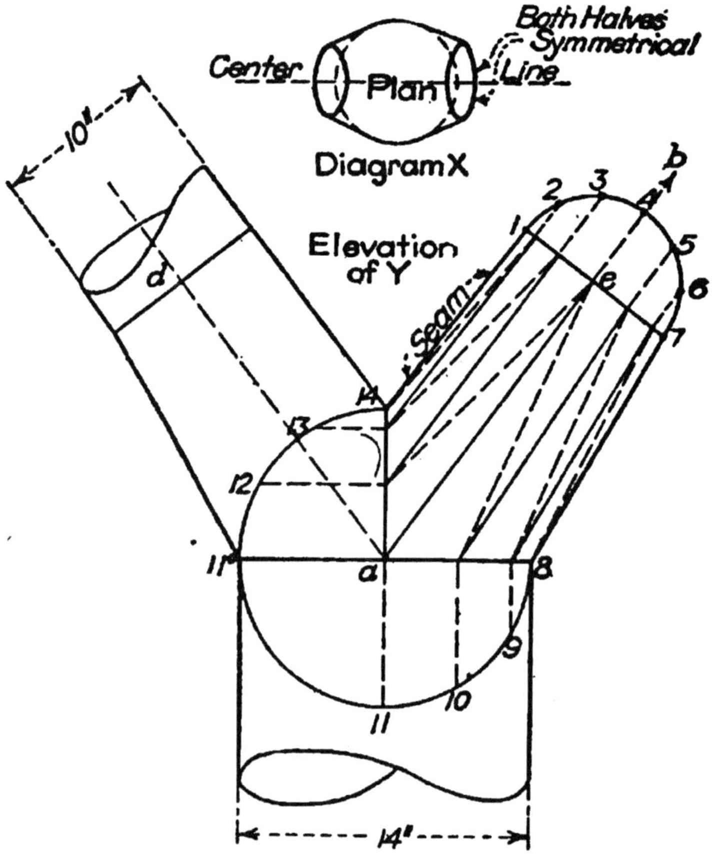

FIG. 99.—First Steps for Developing the Pattern.

as indicated, which will represent the base lines of sections which will be constructed whose altitudes are equal to their respective heights in the various sections. Thus to find the true length of the solid line 12 to 3 in the elevation of the left fork, take that distance and set it on the line A B as shown in Fig. 100. From 12 and 3 erect perpendicular lines equal to the heights to 12 and 3 in the sections, measuring from their respective base lines. The heavy line in the diagram 12-3 will be the true length. In similar manner are the balance of the true lengths for solid and dotted lines found, as shown by similar numbers on the horizontal lines A B of Fig. 100 and C D in Fig. 101.

The next steps are for the pattern shape, so

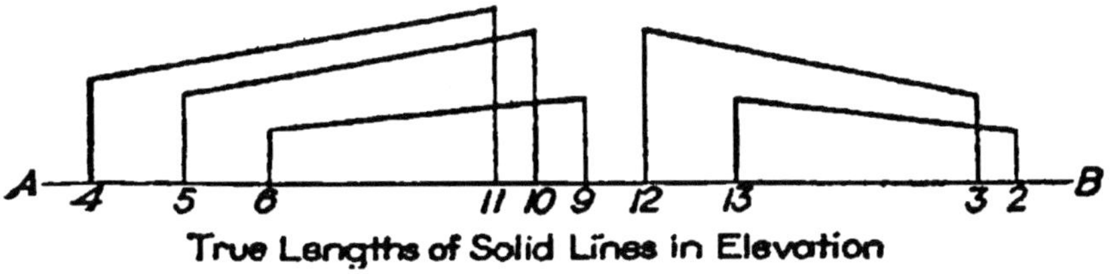

FIG. 100.—Triangulating the Solid Lines.

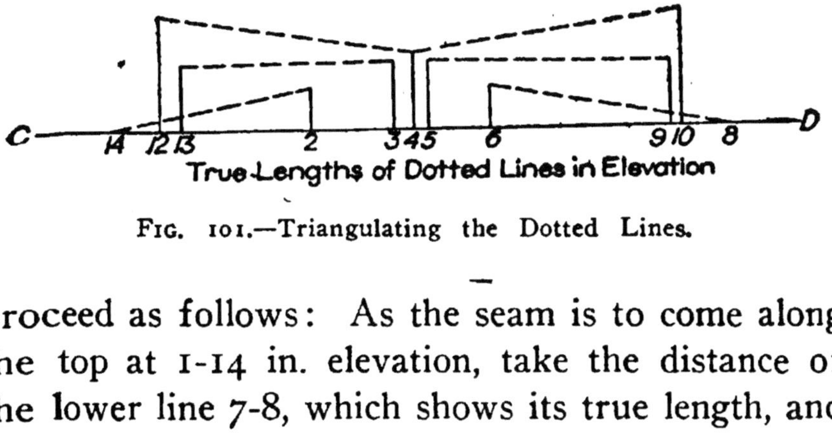

FIG. 101.—Triangulating the Dotted Lines.

proceed as follows: As the seam is to come along the top at 1-14 in. elevation, take the distance of the lower line 7-8, which shows its true length, and place it as indicated by 7-8 in the pattern, Fig. 102. Now with 7-6 in the half section as radius and 7 in the pattern as center, describe the arc 6, which intersect by an arc struck from 8 as center and 8-6 in the dotted true lengths as radius. Now using 8-9 in the lower half section as radius and 8 in the pattern as center, describe the arc 9, which intersect by an arc struck from 6 as center and 6-9 in the solid true lengths as radius. Proceed in this manner, using alternately first the divisions in the top section, then the proper dotted length; again the proper division in the lower section, then the proper true solid length, all as indicated by similar numbers in the pattern, the length of 1-14 being obtained from 1-14 in elevation. Trace a line through points thus obtained as shown, which will be the

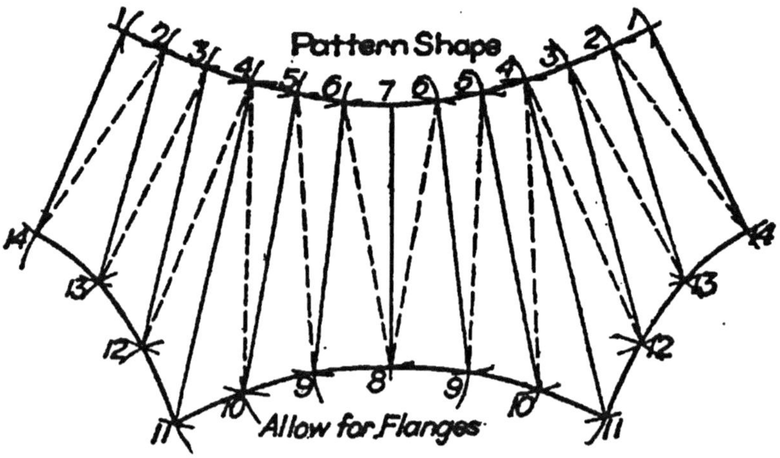

FIG. 102.—The Procedure for the Pattern.

desired pattern for both forks, to which edges must be allowed for seaming, or riveting, inasmuch as the two arms are most always joined by riveting, although by using extreme care they could be double-seamed together.

Forks or Y branches have had the close attention of many draftsmen, and no doubt a book of this size could be written about them alone; however, the fundamental principles embodied in this problem are really involved in all and merely require an adjusting in applying these principles to the case at hand.

Pattern for a Furnace Collar

As stated farther on in the exposition of this subject, the opening in the conical top, or, as it is called in some shops, a furnace bonnet, would be marked by scribing around the collar. Should it be desired to cut it out on the flat, one would proceed to do so by developing the pattern of the top by the radial line method as explained in conical problems, like the scoop problem of Fig. 55. Points 2'-3' and 4' are carried across parallel to the base line A (referring to Fig. 104) to the line where points 1' and 5' are; thence swung radially around to like element line in the pattern just as was done in the scoop problem, thus obtaining the opening in the top for the collar.

In Fig. 104 are shown the true principles for developing a collar intersecting a conical furnace top, which can be applied to any angle, no matter what size the top or collar may have. The diameter of the furnace collar in this case has been made larger and is out of proportion, so that the points of intersections may be more clearly shown.

Referring first to Fig. 104 on next page, A B C D represent the one-half elevation of the conical top, below which in its proper position is drawn the one-quarter plan shown by F B A. Establish at pleasure any two points on the outline of the plan as *a* and *b*, from which points draw radial lines to the center F. From these points *a* and *b* in plan, erect vertical lines intersecting the base line A B of the cone in elevation as is also indicated by *a* and *b*, from which points radial lines are drawn, toward the apex E as shown. Establish the angle which the collar is to have as shown by the center line 3° 3 and with any point on this line as *d* as

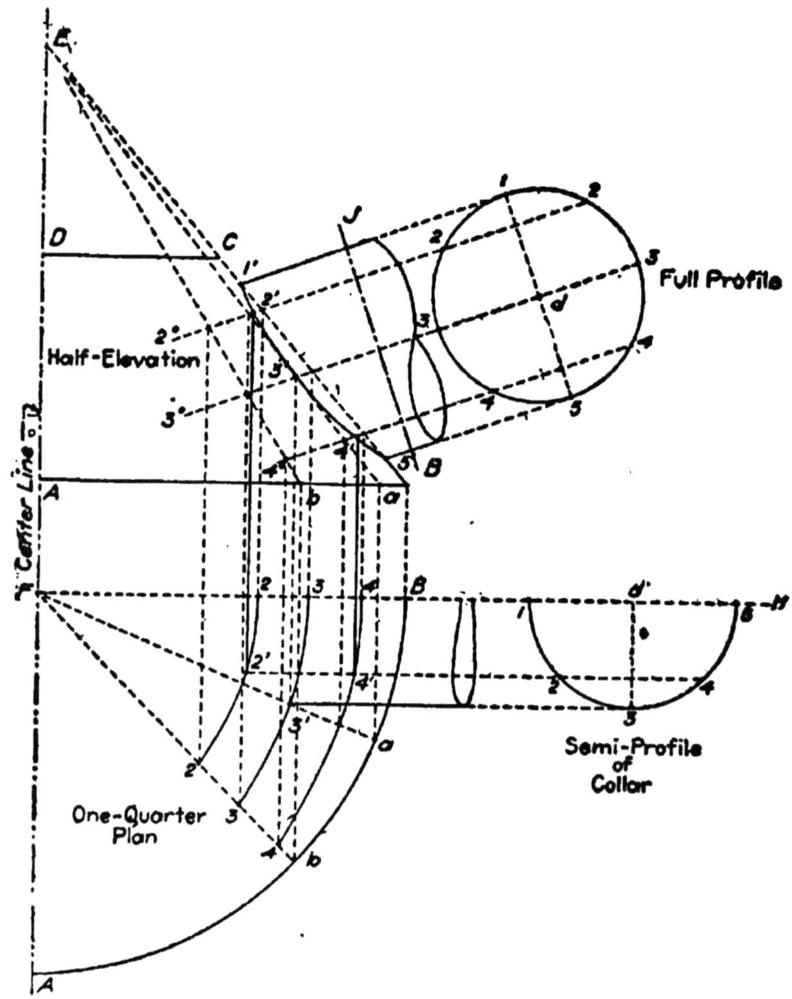

FIG. 104.—Geometrical Procedure for Acquiring Collar Pattern.

center, describe the profile of the collar as shown. Divide this profile into an equal number of spaces, in this case eight, as shown by the small figures 1 to 5 to 1, through which points draw lines parallel to 3 3°, extending them partly in the elevation as shown by 2 2°, 3 3° and 4 4°. The lines drawn from points 1 and 5 in the full profile show their true points of intersection with the furnace top at 1′ and 5′.

Where the planes or lines 2 2°, 3 3° and 4 4° intersect the radial lines drawn from B *a* and *b* in elevation, drop vertical lines to the plan, intersecting similar radial lines also drawn from B *a* and *b* in plan; as will be clearly understood by following the dotted lines. Through the points of intersections thus obtained trace the curves 2 2, 3 3 and 4 4. Then will these curves 2 2, 3 3 and 4 4 in plan represent the horizontal sections on the lines shown in elevation by 2 2°, 3 3° and 4 4°, respectively.

Extend the line F B in plan as F H and with any point on same as *d′* draw the semi-profile of the collar as shown. Divide this into one-half the number of spaces contained in the full profile as shown. Parallel to F H through the point 3 in the semi-profile draw a line until it intersects the horizontal section 3 3 in plan at 3′. In a similar manner through the points 4 and 2 in the semi-profile draw a line until it intersects the horizontal sections 4 4 and 2 2 in plan at 4′ and 2′, respectively. From these intersections 2′, 3′ and 4′ in plan, erect vertical lines, intersecting similar numbered planes or lines in elevation as 2 2°, 3 3° and 4 4° at 2′, 3′ and 4′, respectively. Through the intersections 1′, 2′, 3′, 4′ and 5′ in elevation trace the intersecting line between the collar and conical top as shown in Fig. 104 on the opposite page.

The line of intersection, or miter line, having been obtained the pattern is now in order. As in Fig. 104, at pleasure draw any line as J B in elevation at right angles to 3 3° as shown. Draw any vertical line as J° B°, Fig. 105, upon which place the girth of the full profile as shown by similar numbers. From these points 1 to 5 to 1, at right angles to J° B° draw lines indefinitely. Measuring in each instance from the line J B in the half elevation, take the various distances to points 1′, 2′, 3′, 4′ and 5′ and place them on similar numbered lines in the pattern, measuring in each instance from the line J° B°. Trace a line through points thus obtained; then will L M 1 1 be the pattern for the desired furnace collar, to which flanges must be allowed for seaming.

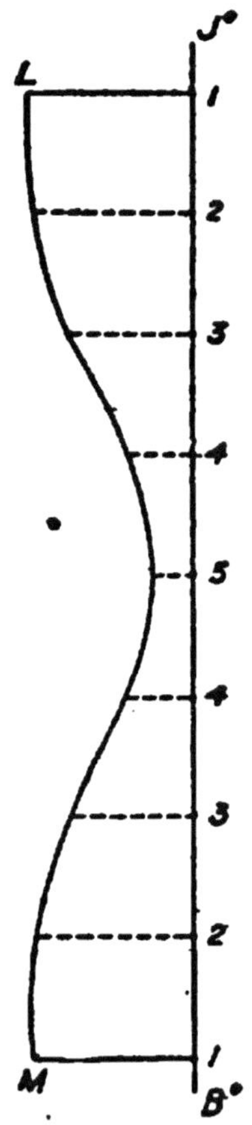

FIG. 105.—Net Pattern for Furnace Collar.

The opening in the conical top has not been developed as this is not necessary, because after the collar is developed, rolled up and seamed it may be held in its desired position on the conical top and the opening scribed around the collar with a lead pencil. The opening may then be cut out partly with a small chisel, after which it is correctly trimmed with the circular shears. Practical methods for joining the collars to the bonnets are explained at length in Chapter IX.

CHAPTER VI

Leaders and Gutters

Making Offsets in Leader Pipes

The following is a description of the method whereby offsets or elbows are made in square leader pipe; a method always found eminently practical and expeditious and for an example a case where the leader passes over the water table of the usual type of frame building is shown, as illustrated in Fig. 106.

The usual procedure when following this method is to send out to the job full lengths of leader, say 10 feet in length, and all offsets and elbows or the like are made there by the mechanic, and in this case measurements would be taken of the water table and in some convenient place, like the cement or stone walk or inside on the floor of one of the rooms of the building if it is not as yet finished, the offset would be drawn full size as shown at A of Fig. 107; a good idea being to use chalk and a line in a way known to all workmen. Now, as all the cuts, or miters, it should be said, would be obtained in identically the same manner, that for the upper one only will be here elucidated to avoid repetition of explanations.

Therefore, at *a* draw a line as *a b* at right angles to *a c*, as shown, employing a small square for the purpose. Many mechanics do not carry a small carpenter's square in their kit of tools. Before proceeding farther it is well to explain how a square

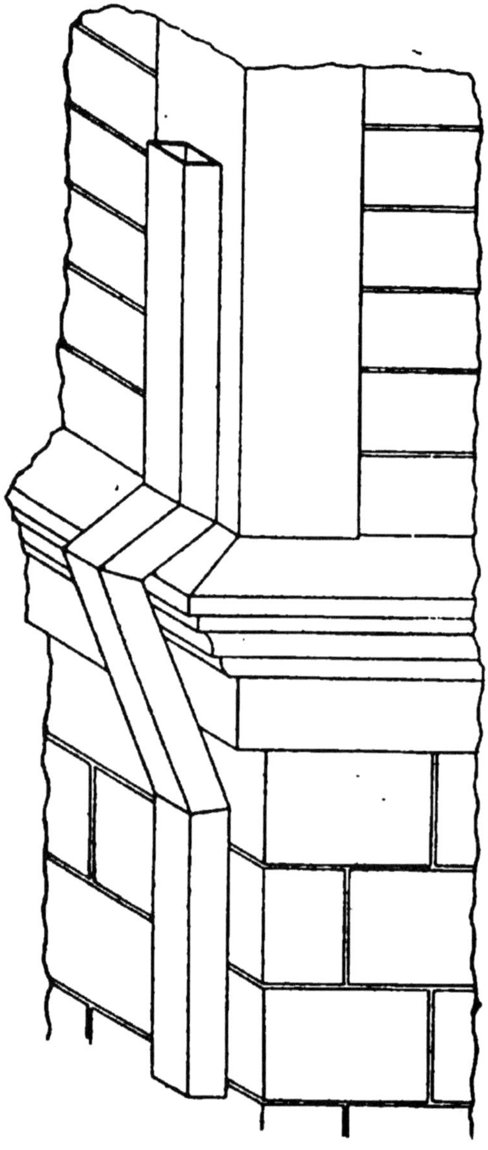

FIG. 106.—Perspective of Typical Case.

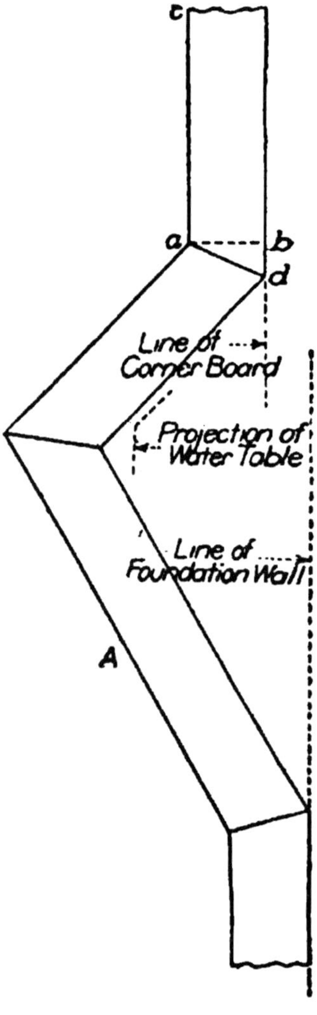

FIG. 107.—Layout of Offset.

can be cut from a piece of sheet metal. As in B of Fig. 108, draw a line *a b* 8 inches long; with the compasses set to span 6 inches and with one leg set at *a* describe an arc toward *c*. Then set the compasses again to 10 inches, and with one leg at *b* describe an arc intersecting the one previously drawn at *c*. A line drawn from *c* to *a* will give a right angle, the basis for a piece of sheet metal cut like B. Stiffen as may be required.

Taking a full length of leader, a point *a* (of C, Fig. 109) is marked on it at the right distance from

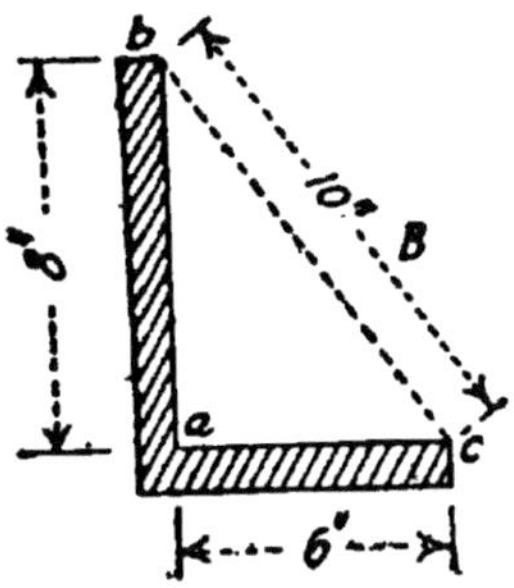

FIG. 108.—Layout of a Square.

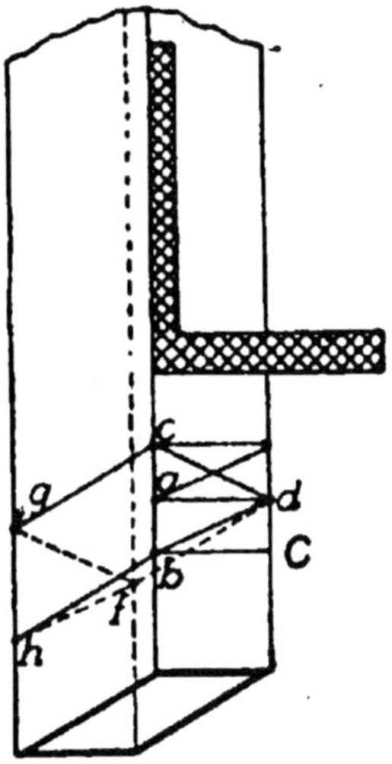

FIG. 109.—Obtaining Cuts.

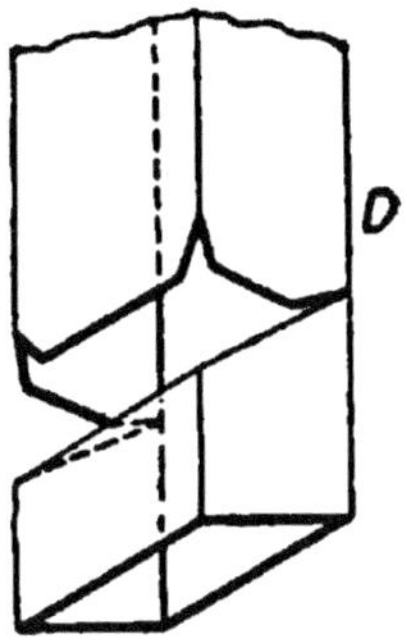

FIG. 110.—Finished Cut for Offset Elbow.

the end of the length of leader in relation to the distance point *a* is from the soil pipe connection (if the leader is connected to the plumbing system, the discharging shoe otherwise), providing the mechanic is working from the bottom up, or if from the top down, the relation point *a* is in the matter of distance from the last length of leader erected, for it is to be understood that good judgment is to be exercised in placing this point to obviate the need of cutting off some of the leader at the ends or, worse still, adding some leader to the ends which would make the job look piecy and decidedly unworkmanlike.

The distance *b d* of A is now placed to both sides of point *a* in C, as indicated by the points *b* and *c*. Holding one leg of the aforementioned square in line with the side of the leader pipe as shown in C, lines are drawn across the pipe from these three points as shown, though only the middle one is required, the idea being to prove accuracy by seeing that all three lines are parallel; from *d* to *c* and *b* lines are drawn as shown, and then from *d* square across the back to *f*, and from *c* and *b* square across the front to the other side, as shown by *g* and *h*; connect these with *b* and the space between *f, g, c, d, b* and *h* is then to be cut out of the pipe, allowing laps at the top, so that the water will not flow against but with the seam, after which the leader pipe at that place will look like at D, Fig. 110 of the group of diagrams.

The lap shown at the front of the pipe is bent outward with the pliers, and then by carefully coaxing the pipe, it is caused to bend along the line *d f* of C until point *h* touches *g* or *b* touches *c* and the joint well soaked with solder. Like everything else, the work is to be done right to be of any value, and it should be obvious that the method outlined in the foregoing is superior to chopping off two pieces of the leader and trimming the ends to a miter and thereby making individual elbows for each bend in the offset, necessitating two joints to each bend which certainly will make the job appear patchy and require more time, solder and pipe.

An Oblique Leader Elbow

A leader pipe elbow pattern 2-inch by 3-inch is to be developed. The elbow is to reach around the corner of a building, the angle of which is 90 deg., as shown in Fig. 111, at an incline or rake of 45 deg. The flat or 3-inch side of the conductor is to face the building on both sides. In Fig. 112 is shown a simple method of finding the miter lock between two similarly sized pipes by means of simple projections. Using this method it will not be necessary to go through the operations of raking or changing of profiles, and the same area of the pipes is maintained. Where the intersection between the two pipes takes place there will not be a true miter line, but rather an intersecting lock, similar to that shown in the perspective in Fig. 113, which, however, is perfectly practical, and this method can be used, no matter what size the pipe may be, or at what angle or rake they incline.

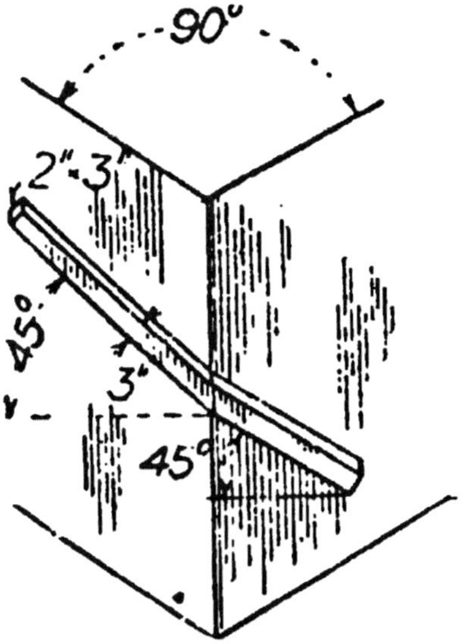

Fig. 111.—Perspective View of Problem.

The method of finding the joint line and developing the pattern is shown in detail in Fig. 112. First draw the wall line represented by F C in the elevation and from any point on it, as 6, draw the desired rake of the pipe, in this case 45 deg., as shown by 6-B. Draw the perpendicular B E equal to 3 inches on the wide side, and from E draw a line indefinitely parallel to B-6. At right angles to the wall line F C draw the line C D equal to 2 inches on the narrow side, and from D, parallel to C F, draw a line until it intersects the line previously drawn from E at 2. From intersection 2 draw the dotted horizontal line, cutting the line of the pipe C-6 extended at 1. Also, from 6 draw the solid horizontal line cutting the outside line of the pipe erected from D, at 4. These are all the projecting points required previous to developing the pattern.

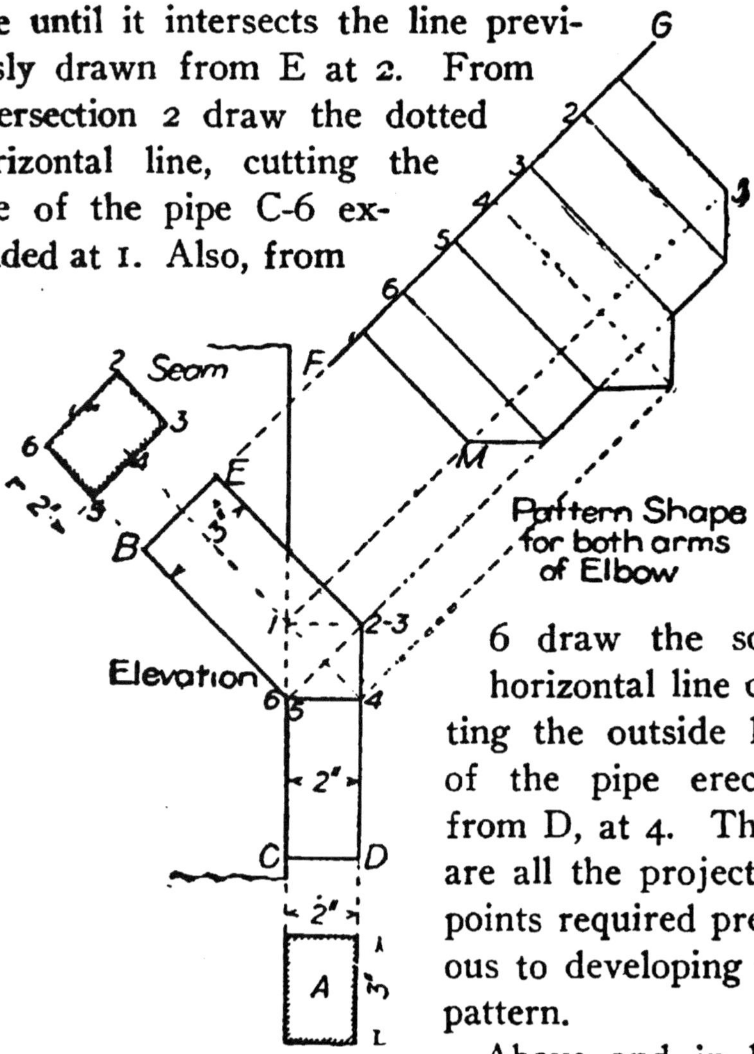

Fig. 112.—Developing Pattern Shape.

Above and in line with B E draw the section of the rectangular pipe and from point 1 in the elevation, which represents the seam line in the rear flat side of the pipe, draw a line parallel to 6-B, cutting the section at 1. In a similar manner project back to the section the corner indicated by 4 in the elevation, which in this case happens to fall on the same line projected from the corner 1 in the elevation. These points, 1 and 4 in the section, are used when laying out the girth or stretch-out of the pipe. Below the line C D in the elevation place a duplicate of the section in its proper position by A. For the pattern extend the line B E, which was drawn at right angles to B-6, as shown by F G. Upon this place the girth of the section from 1 to 6 to 1, as shown by similar numbers on F G. Through these small figures, at right angles to F G, draw the usual measuring lines which are intersected by lines drawn at right angles to B-6 in the elevation from similarly numbered intersections in the joint line in the elevation. Trace a line through the points thus obtained, as shown by J L M, then will 1, J, L, M, 1 be the desired pattern of which two will be required both formed the same way, allowing laps for seaming, riveting and soldering.

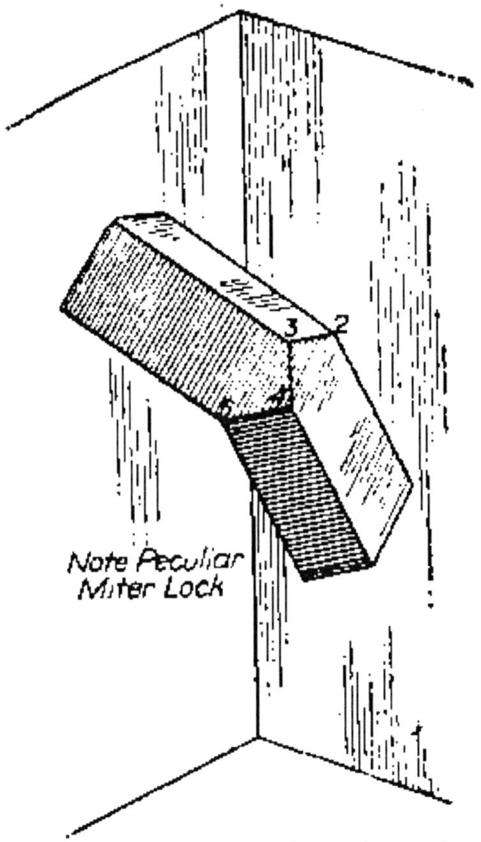

FIG. 113.—Perspective View of Finished Elbow.

True Angle of an Oblique Leader Elbow

This is an interesting problem in leader work and herewith is the solution of the problem as taught in the Gray's Correspondence School of Sheet Metal Pattern Drafting, New York City.

First draw a plan of the corner of the building shown in Fig. 114; establish two points an equal distance from the corner of the building, designated A and B;

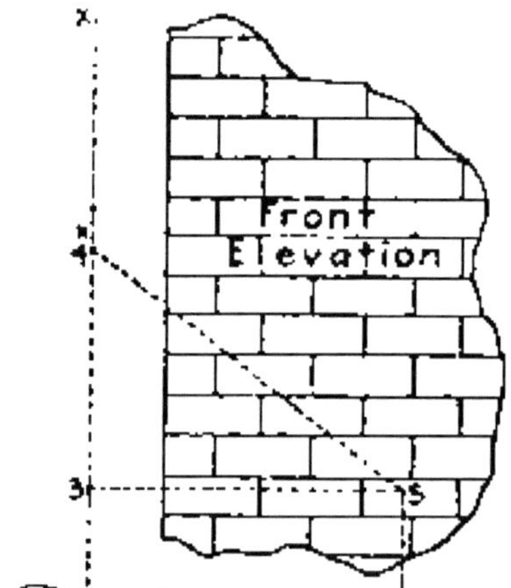

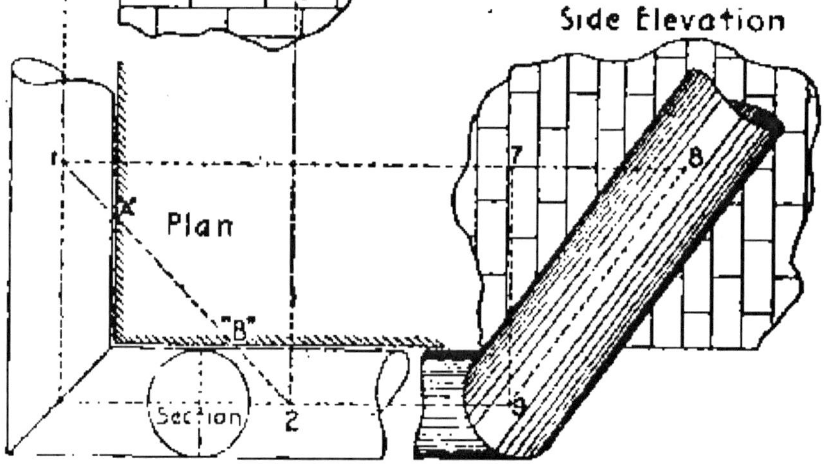

FIG. 114.—The First Steps in the Procedure.

draw a line through these two points, intersecting the center line of both arms of the elbow at 1 and 2. The next operation is to draw the front elevation, the center line of the elbow is all that is wanted as shown by line 4^x 3 and 3 5. Connect 4^x and 5, this line will represent the pitch of the elbow. Now, draw the side elevation to the right of the plan, as shown; distance 7 8 is the same as 3 4^x in the front elevation in this case, but may be otherwise, and line 8 9 is the pitch of the center line of the elbow in this view.

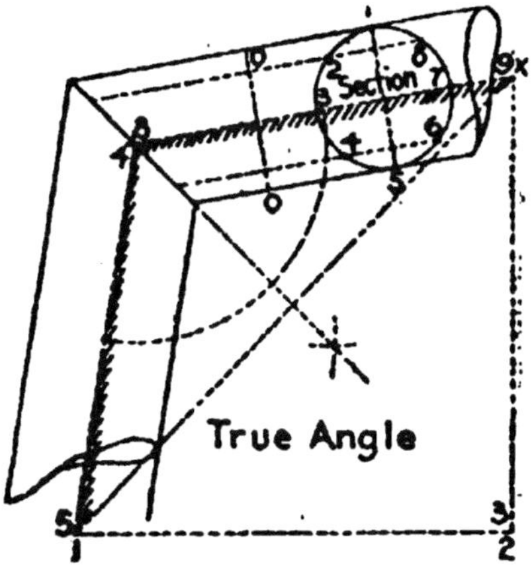

FIG. 115.—The Desired Elbow.

The true angle of the elbow is now found by taking the distance of line 7 to 8 of the side elevation and placing it on line 3 4^x, measuring from 4^x, giving point X, in the front elevation. Now take the full length of line 3 to X and place in the true angle diagram.

Again, take the distance of line 1 2 in the plan, Fig. 114, and place at right angles to line 3 X in Fig. 115. Take the distance 4 to 5 in the front elevation and place it at 4 5 in the true angle diagram by swinging a small arc of this radius as shown. Do the same with distance of line 8 9 of side elevation getting the point of intersection of the two arcs as 4 8. Then 5 4 8 9 X is the true angle sought for.

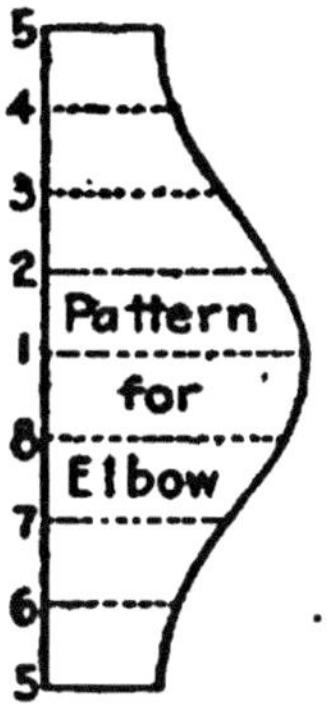

FIG. 116.—The Pattern of Elbow.

Bisect this angle. Draw the rest of the elbow as shown and develop the pattern in Fig. 116 as previously directed in the other chapters. The pattern being the same for both arms of the elbow; it can be of any desired length.

Sizes and Other Facts About Leaders

A good rule to follow for quickly computing the size to be allowed for a leader is to figure up to eighteen hundred square feet of roof area for a three-inch round leader or its equivalent in area for a square-shaped leader. From eighteen hundred to two thousand two hundred and fifty square feet for a three and one-half inch round leader or its equivalent in square leader. From two thousand two hundred and fifty to three thousand square feet for a four-inch round leader or its equivalent in square leader. From three thousand to five thousand square feet for a five-inch round leader or its equivalent in square leader. From five thousand to seven thousand square feet for a six-inch round leader or its equivalent in square leader. Horizontal leaders should be larger and should be set with as much inclination as possible from the horizontal.

It is to be understood that judgment should tell what size leader to use when the roof area passes from one size or factor to another. For it is more economical to use, say, a four-inch leader for three thousand square feet of roof area; but, however, a five-inch leader would give a greater factor of safety in case of an unusual rainfall.

It is not considered good practice to use leaders less than three inches in diameter because of the danger of stoppage or freezing. Two-inch leaders, however, are often used for small porch roofs or the gutters on turret skylights. In corrugated leader, the corrugations are not figured but the smallest diameter of the pipe is called the size of the leader.

A Plain Leader Head

Where just utility and not appearance is requisite the leader head shown in Fig. 117 is ideal, inasmuch

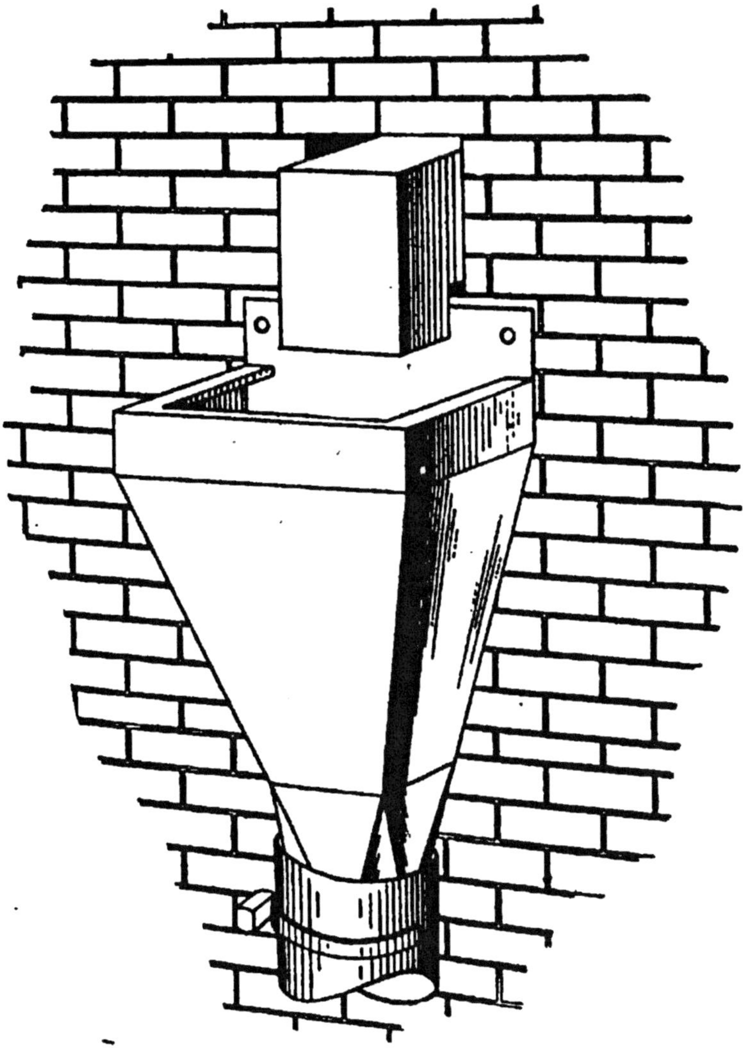

FIG. 117.—View of Leader Head, Leader and Roof Outlet.

as there are no members forming ledges on which damp dirt would accumulate, which naturally would hasten the decay of the head. This is especially true of the tube connection and attention is called to the manner of making this connection so that the flow of water is not retarded and all shelves in the leader are eliminated.

The pattern is obtained, as in Fig. 118, by drawing the side elevation, the front elevation and the inverted plan, as shown. The patterns are developed by placing stretchout adjoining the various views and projecting the points in like position in various views to pattern, as shown.

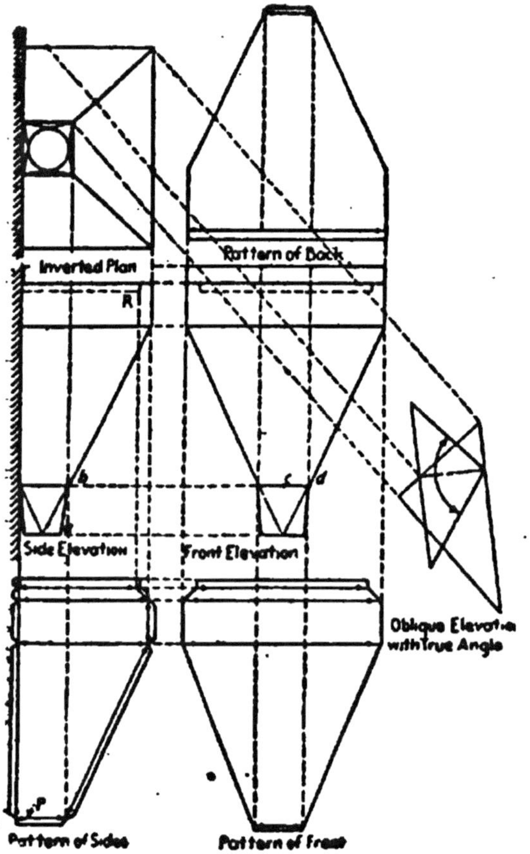

FIG. 118.—Developing the Pattern and Finding True Angle of Hips.

The true angle along the hip, or miter, of the front with the side — the back and side naturally being a right angle — is found by projecting an oblique elevation. Assume any two points on the side and front of head as indicated in the inverted plan. Project these to base line of oblique elevation. Project a line at right angle to hip line from the point in base line to touch the hip line and through the point in the base line, parallel to hip line, draw line as shown; on one side of the line place a point equaling the distance to one side of hip in the inverted plan and the other side equaling the other; complete the triangle, which gives

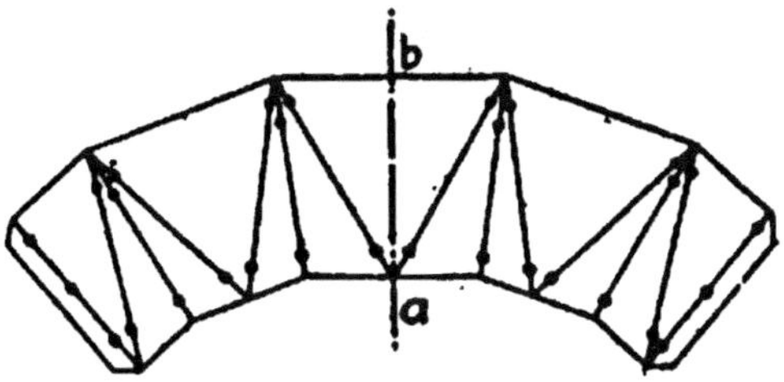

FIG. 119.—Pattern of Tube.

the true angle as indicated by arrow points.

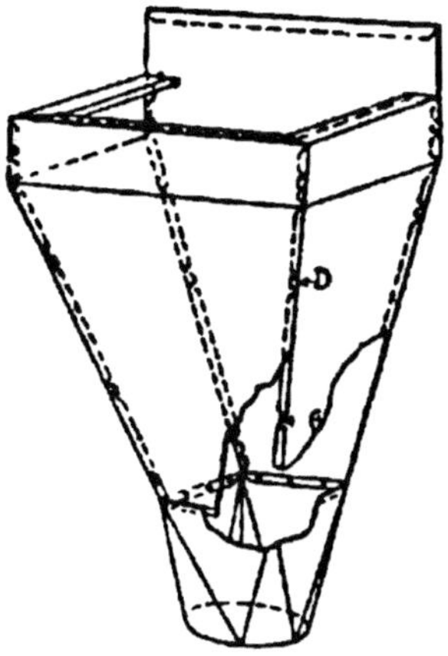

FIG. 120.—Method of Joining the Parts.

The tube pattern is obtained differently from the ordinary methods and in this way:

Any vertical line is drawn as *a b* in Fig. 119, which is the same length as *a b* in Fig. 118. At right angles to this line and through *b* a line is drawn so that to each side of *a b* there is one-half of the top of the tube as *c d* in Fig. 118. Another line is drawn at right angles to *a b* and through *b*, with one-eighth of the stretchout of the bottom or circular part of the tube to either side of *a b*. The pattern is completed as shown, and, although the bottom line should be a curve, this method is accurate enough for that part of the tube is cov-

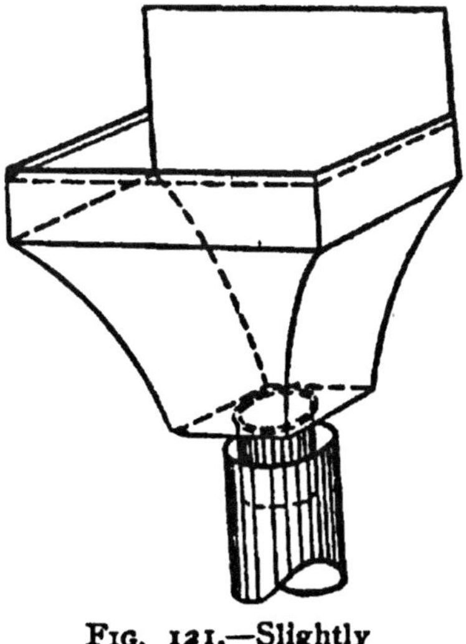

FIG. 121.—Slightly Different Design.

ered by the leader and to develop by triangulation would take too long.

Fig. 120 shows how the various parts are joined in the assembling operations, altogether making the most substantial leader head imaginable. Should, however, it be desired that the head be somewhat less plain in appearance the large straight part could be slightly curved which would give a more ornamental effect, as shown in Fig. 121. This diagram portrays the old style method of joining the tube which could be easily altered to the method described in the foregoing. Naturally the pattern developing procedure is similar.

Heavy Sheet Iron Gutter for Gravel Roof

If it is assumed that the section given in Fig. 122 is at the high end, a fall to the outlet would be obtained by allowing for a pitch at *b* and *c d* in the usual manner. The gravel guard *e* is bent, as shown, as this shape has been proved to be effective for preventing the gravel from being washed or blown into the gutter and was the easiest shape to form. The material being so heavy there is no danger of this guard being crushed by any one treading on it.

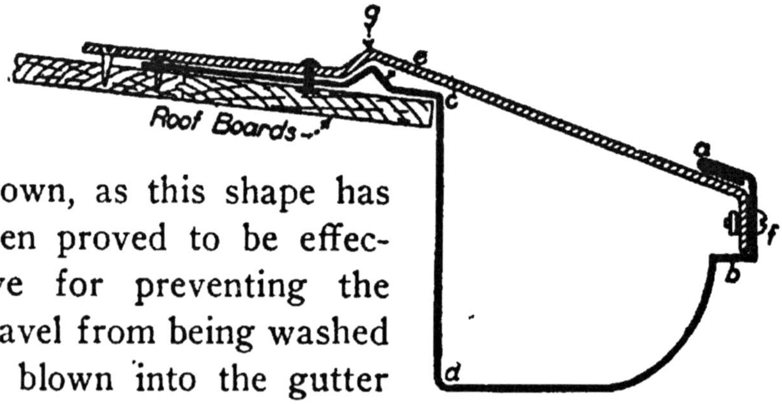

FIG. 122.—Heavy Sheet Iron Gutter on a Gravel Roof.

Rather than cut this guard to allow the ⅛ x 1-inch galvanized band iron braces to pass through, the braces are bent as indicated, for at a test it was found that they had sufficient rigidity at the bend *g* to resist all strains. All braces are formed and punched exactly alike, and when handable lengths of the gutter are assembled in the shop these braces are riveted on, as shown, and by simply keeping the bend *g* against the gravel guard, when drawing the rivet through the gutter flange, the front of the gutter naturally will be straight, when bolt *f* is put in. The rivet is soldered to the underside of the gutter flange to make it watertight, although there would be little danger of a leak at this point for there would be plenty of tar around the brace. The gutter being so heavy the braces are for this reason spaced 2 ft. apart. Obviously by placing the braces in position before the lengths of gutter left the shop, the gutter is not forced out of shape in shipping, and they materially assist in handling and hoisting. The threads of the bolts, holding the braces, should be upset to prevent loosening of the nuts.

When the gravel roofer has run on all his felt the gutter lengths are set in place, the flange nailed every 3 inches with roofing nails and a heavy wood screw driven through the hole in the other end of the brace, as shown. All seams are now riveted where access would allow, and heavily soldered; likewise outlets are soldered in and connected to the leaders. The gravel roofer, prior to spreading his hot tar and pushing in the gravel, swabs a generous quantity of hot tar along the gutter flange and around the braces and before the tar is cool a heavy strip of felt is placed so as to cover the gutter flange down to the gravel guard and up to the roof a few inches. This felt strip also covers the braces. As this would be the weak point of the roof, especial care should be used to thoroughly tar in here.

Developing the Square and Angle Miter Patterns for Plain Gutter

The methods used to make a square miter for a plain gutter are shown in Fig. 123. It is to be understood that although slightly different in design, the methods here explained can be used to cut the patterns for a gutter shown in the last problem. A profile is first laid out full size, as shown at *a*, 1, 9, 10 and 11, Fig. 123. The angles 9, 10, 11, represent the angle made by the pitch of the roof, that is, if the roof pitch is 9 inches in 12 inches, then the rise from 10, 11 should be so laid out. *a* is the bead for which 1½-inch of stock is allowed when wired with a ½-inch rod. The front side of the gutter being

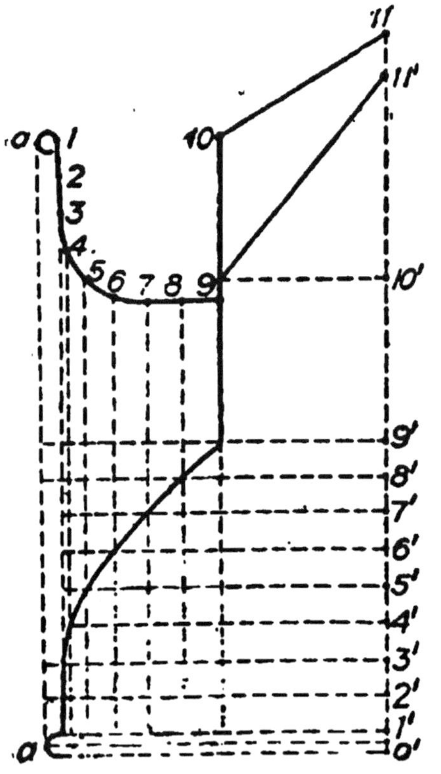

FIG. 123.—Square Miter for Plain Gutter.

curved, is spaced into any number of equal spaces, as shown by 1, 2, 3, 4 to 9. Of course, 7 to 9 is really flat and number 8 could be omitted but number 8 is used here to better explain the procedure, in case it was round.

The line 9 to 10 is the back of the gutter and is straight. The line 10 to 11 is also straight and represents the roof angle. Draw vertical lines as shown from the numbered points, lay out the stretchout line as shown by *a'*, 10', 11', in Fig. 123, making the spaces on the line marked 1', 2' to 10', 11' in each instance equal to the spaces 1, 2 and 10, 11 on the profile. Now, through these points, on the vertical stretchout line, draw horizontal line to intersect the vertical lines from the profile. Thus, horizontal line from say, 3' on stretchout line is to intersect vertical line dropped from point 3 on the profile, and so on.

Then a line drawn through the points of intersection will be the pattern. It will be noticed that at *a* the diameter of the rod is laid off, *a* representing a point in the center of the bead directly opposite 1. In laying out the stretchout 1½ inches are allowed for the bead miter drawn as shown. Also notice that the points 1 to 3 are in a straight line, hence the points of intersection as, 1, 2, 3, 1', 2', 3' are on the same line, making the straight section on the top of the front side of the gutter. The line 9 to 10 is also straight and is placed as shown in Fig. 123. The line 10 to 11 is the pitch of the roof, and a vertical line is drawn through these points as shown, intersecting the horizontal line 10', 11', which represents the points 10 and 11 on the stretchout line. Then the line drawn from the intersection points 10, 10′ and 11, 11′, as shown, gives the proper bevel for the pattern. It probably would have been better to have the pattern placed much more below the profile so that the pattern would not touch the profile, however, the outline of the pattern is easily distinguished from the profile.

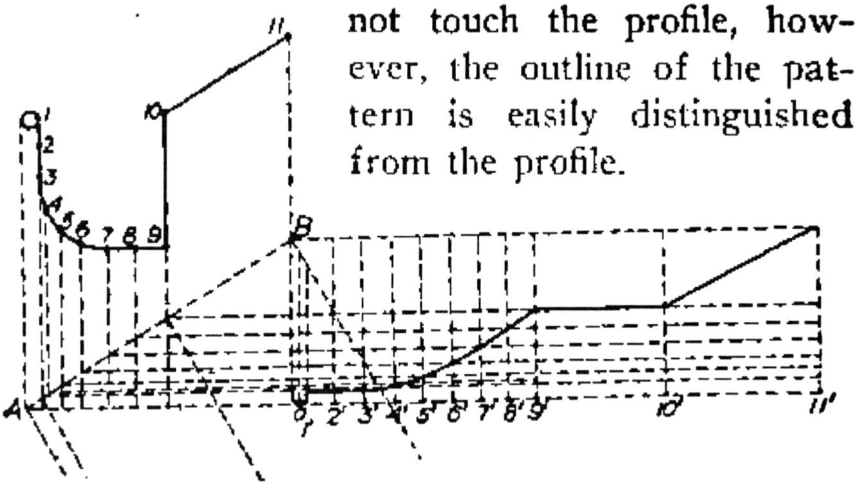

Fig. 124.—Angle Miter for a Plain Gutter.

The method used when the miter is to be other than a right angle is shown in Fig. 124. Let A B be the miter line on the angle required. Then place the stretchout as shown. Draw vertical lines from points in the profile to the angle line and draw the stretchout lines *a* 11′ at right angles to the vertical lines on the profile, also vertical lines from points on the stretchout line from *a* to 11′, placed at distances equal to the spaces in the profile, as shown. Draw horizontal lines from the several points of intersection on miter line as shown, then a line drawn through the intersection will be the pattern required. This method can also be used for a right angle by placing the miter line at an angle of 45 deg.

Straight Eaves Trough Tube Pattern and Opening in Trough

With most mechanics the usual procedure would be to roll up and seam a straight tube small enough to slip easily into the leader. They would then lay a length of the trough upside down on the bench and, while holding the tube in position against the bottom of the trough with one hand, they would scribe around the tube with a compass. The compass would be held steadily against the trough bottom so that the correct varying line would be marked on the tube.

The tube would then be trimmed on this line with the tinner's snips. A quarter inch line would now be scribed along the irregular cut of the tube for a guide line in flanging. This flanging would be done by holding the tube to the mark against any sharp block of iron or bench stake. Then, with the peen of the hammer a flange would be thrown off the irregularly cut end of the tube.

The tube is again held to the bottom of the trough as before, only this time at the correct place on the trough. A line is then scribed around the inside of the tube onto the bottom of the trough. Now, while the helper holds a block of wood or a lead cake against the part of the trough to be cut out, the mechanic chisels along the scribed line. Or else, a small hole is first cut within the scribed line and the balance cut out with a tinner's circular snips. The tube would then be inserted in the hole in the trough and the flange heavily soldered.

A better way is to draw a section of trough and the tube, as in Fig. 125; also the half profile of the tube. One-half of this profile is divided into spaces, and lines are projected from the points 1 to 4 up to the trough. A horizontal stretchout line is now drawn and twelve spaces of the half profile placed thereon as 4 to 4. Vertical lines are erected from these points and are in turn intersected by lines projected across from the section of the trough, which completes the pattern for the tube.

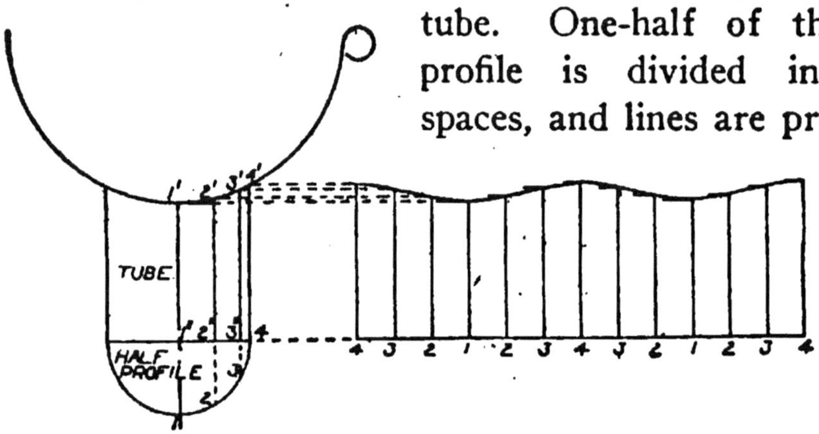

FIG. 125.—Pattern of Tube.

FIG. 126.—Opening in Trough.

To develop the opening in the trough, draw a line as 4′-4′ in Fig. 126, and beginning at some point near the middle set off each way the spaces 1′-4′ in the half profile and through the points draw indefinite perpendiculars, on each of which set off, measuring from and on each side of 4′-4′, the half distances through the tube at these points taken from the half profile. As from 1′ set off to 1″, in Fig. 125, and from 2′ set off 2 to 2″ and etc. Connecting the points thus located will produce the net pattern for the opening.

Flaring Eaves Trough Tube

The problem, as presented in Fig. 127, which shows an end view of the trough with the flaring tube, is for a geometrical proposition of a frustum of a right cone, intersecting a cylinder their axes being at right angles. Draw the elevation and continue the outlines of the tube until they intersect the center line as at A. Bisect the line that represents the base of the cone or *d'*-d and with this point as center and radius to *d* describe a half profile of the base. Space half this semi-circle into a number of equal spaces and project the points, parallel with the center line, to the base of the cone, as *a'*, *b'*, and etc., and from the points on the base draw lines to apex A, and where these lines or elements cross the trough as *g, f, e, d,* will be miter points between the two pieces. The miter points are all, excepting *d,* located on fore-shortened lines or those that do not show their true lengths. To find the true lengths or distances the points are from the apex, the points are revolved around the cone by projecting them at right angles to the center line in elevation, to one of the outlines which is a true length. As *g* is projected to A-*d* and then A-g° is the true length of A-*g; f* is similarly projected and then A-f° will be the true length of A-*f,* and etc.

With A as center and radius to *d,* describe an indefinite arc on which place four times the lengths of the spaces in the quarter profile and from the points draw lines to the apex, and these lines will correspond to the elements of the cone, as shown.

With A as center, radially transfer or radially project the points on the outline A-*d* to lines of corresponding letters. Connect the intersections and then will d-d^v-x-x' be the net pattern of the flaring tube. At the ends material is added for a groove seam and to x-x' material for a joint to

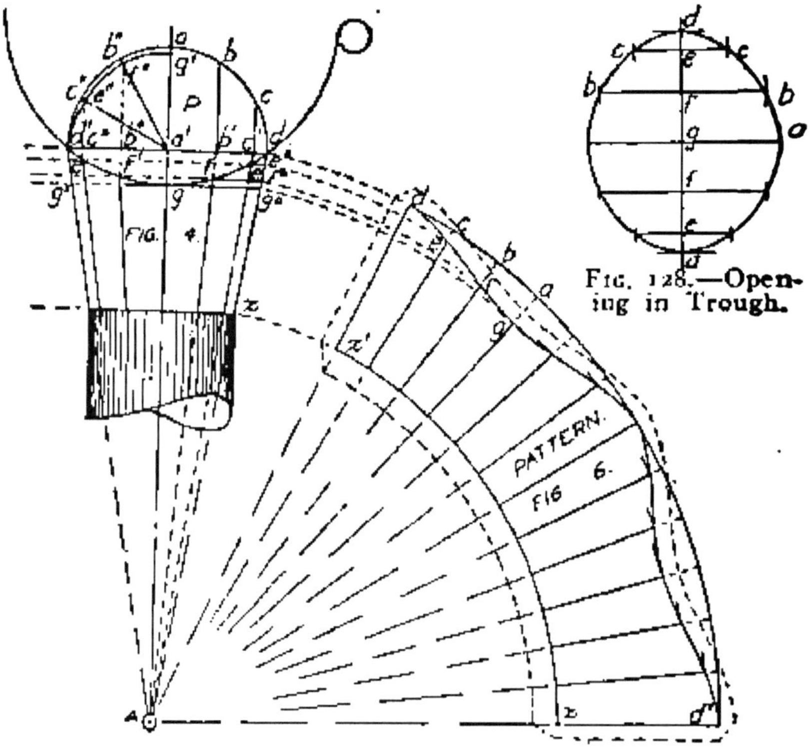

FIG. 128.—Opening in Trough.

FIG. 127.—Pattern of Flaring Tube.

the leader. To d-d^v an allowance is made for a flange to rivet the tube to the trough; all these allowances are shown by dotted lines in the pattern, which, of course, can vary according to conditions.

To develop the opening in the trough it is first necessary to find the half distance through the miter points on the intersection and a part plan of this intersection is requisite. To avoid confusion of lines the left half of P is used and corresponding points lettered the same. From *a'* draw lines to the points on the profile of the base as *a'-a, a'-b"*, *a'-c'* and, etc., and these lines will be the plans of the elements of corresponding lines in the elevation. By projecting the miter points, parallel with the center line, to their corresponding plan elements will locate the miter points in the plan. As *f'* is located on A-*b°*, it is projected to the corresponding line *a-b"* and its location will be *f"* in the plan and the distance *b°-f"* will be the half distance through the cone, front to back through the point *f'* and etc. The distance through *g* will be *g-g"*.

In Fig. 128 draw a line and from some point near the middle begin to set off, each way, the spaces *g-f, f-e,* and *e-d* in Fig. 127. *g* to *d* being the amount in length on the trough that half the tube intersects, and through the points draw indefinite perpendiculars. Measuring on each side of and from the intersections on *d-g-d* transfer the half distances through the cone on similarly lettered points to perpendiculars of the same letters. As from *e,* set off *e"-c°*, from *f* set off *f"-b°* and etc. Connecting the points obtained in this manner will result in the net pattern for the opening in the trough for the tube.

The straight part of tube is just a rectangular piece, its width to be equal to the height required and its length or girth equal to the distance from X' to X of the pattern in Fig. 127. There would be no lap allowed where this straight tube joins the flaring tube as the pattern in Fig. 127 has the lap.

Developing the Patterns and Making Right-Angle Eave Trough Miters

Eave troughs are usually made half round or semicircular with a bead on the front edge, there being two kinds of right angle miters. An outside miter to fit an exterior or external angle, as Fig. 129, and

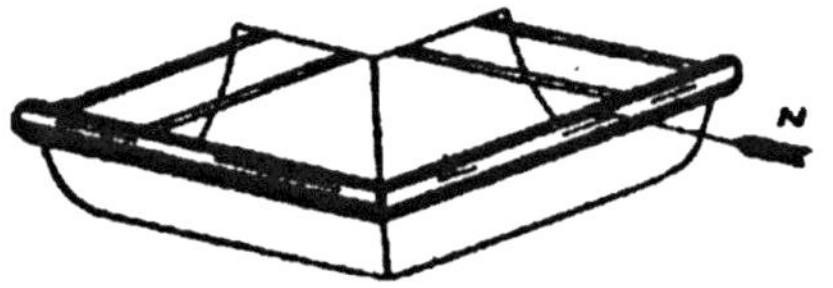

Fig. 129.—Outside miter.

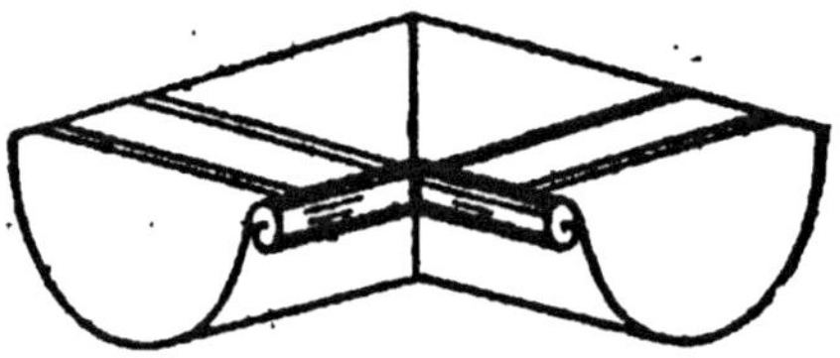

Fig. 130.—Inside Miter.

an inside miter to fit an interior or internal angle, as Fig. 130. Naturally, these remarks refer also to miters at other than a right angle.

When the pattern for either is developed the pattern for the other naturally results from the same process, being simply the reverse cut or the piece cut away from the one.

The method here used is the short method in which the patterns are said to be produced directly from the profile. Technically, this statement is not correct, but as error cannot occur it probably is just as well to continue describing the method or process in that manner. By this it is meant that according to the strict geometrical method, the lines from the profile should be first dropped to a miter line, thence to the pattern stretchout; instead of directly to the pattern from the profile.

As in Fig. 131, draw the profile so that the top edge will be horizontal or level and the back at 19 be as high as the head at 8. If there is enough material it will make a better trough if the back is as high as *c*. To strengthen the edge an angle is sometimes turned as at *b*. The circular part of the trough

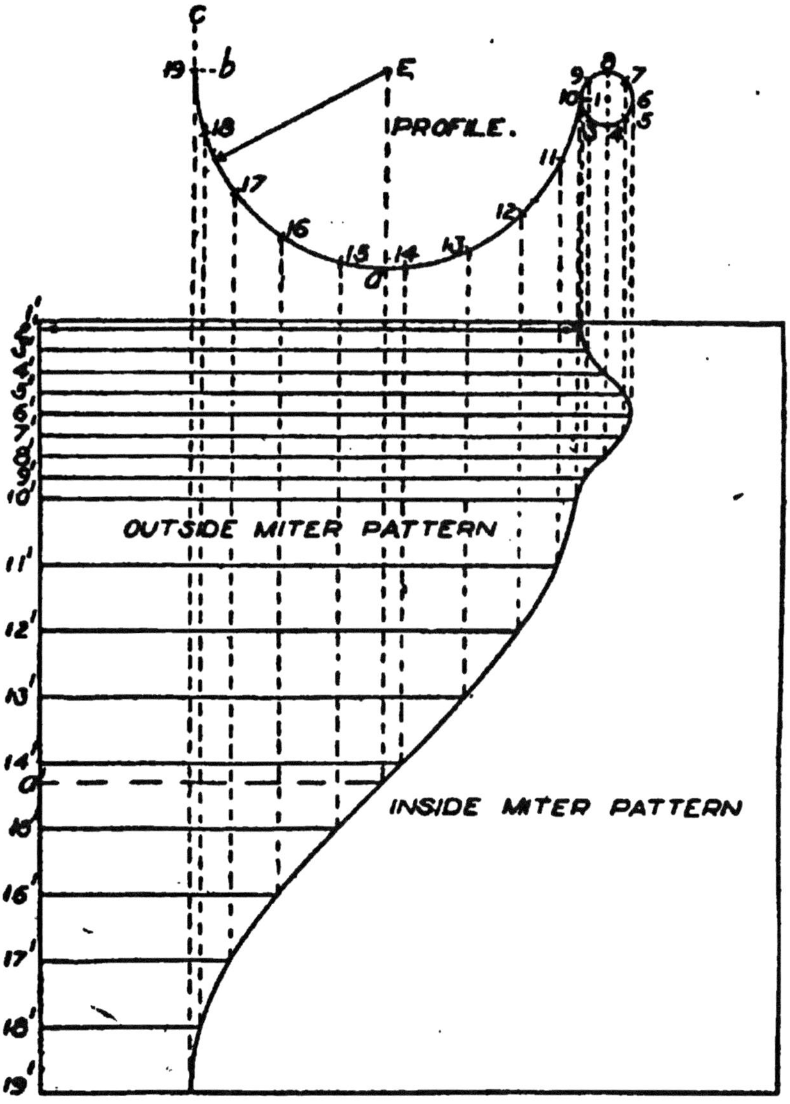

FIG. 131.—The Pattern Developing Process.

will intersect the bead at the point 10, and from 10 the profile of the trough is spaced into a number of equal spaces. Also space the bead into equal spaces in which 2 will be opposite or touch 10.

At right angles to the top of the profile draw a line as 1′-19′ and transfer to this line all the spaces in the profile, including a division between 14 and 15, as *a*, which has been projected from E to locate the bottom center and will be the point on the pattern edge where a convex curve will join a concave curve. From all the points on 1′-19′ draw parallel lines that are at right angles to 1′-19′ and

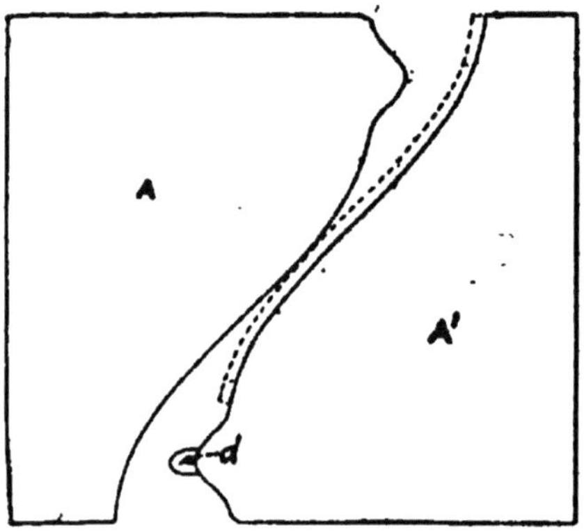

FIG. 132.—Nesting Outside Miter Pattern.

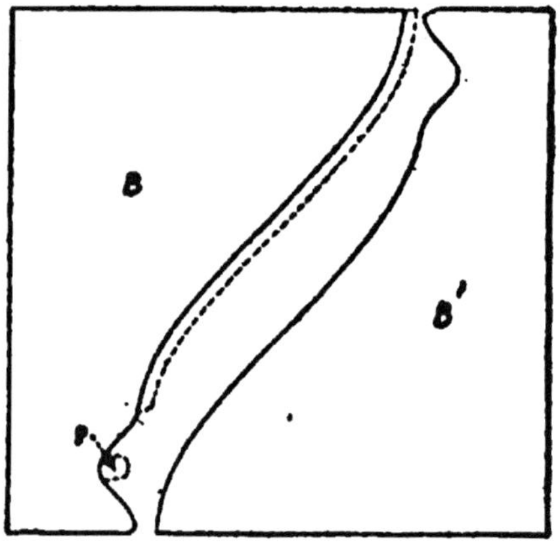

FIG. 133.—Nesting Inside Miter Patterns.

are parallel to the top of the trough. Project at right angles and to these parallel lines the points in the profile having the same numbers. As to line 2′ project point 2, to line 3′ point 3, to line 12′ point 12, etc. Connecting these intersections will produce the net patterns as shown by the inside and outside miter patterns.

There are several ways to put the parts together, one of which is to cut both parts on the net lines as A, Fig. 132, and B′, Fig. 133, butt them together and solder a seam strip or butt strap over the joint. Another way is to leave a lap on one piece as in A′ and B in which the bead is cut on the net edge and butted, sometimes leaving a lip as *d* and *e* to bend onto the adjoining bead and then be soldered. The lap allowed must be turned, half in and half out, to fit the adjoining piece.

A third way to join the pieces is by a double seam, and when this is done the amount of lap or seam allowance on one piece is twice that on the other piece, and the two parts are put together in a manner similar to an elbow, but with the seam flattened. The laps or edges must in this case be turned full or the beads will gap and not come together.

To save material outside miters are cut from sheets as at A and A′ and inside miters as at B and B′, and are formed right and left if formed before beading, or beaded right and left if beaded before forming.

The material for trough miters should always be trimmed so that opposite edges are parallel, and after beading and forming, temporary braces should be soldered in them so they will retain their shapes free from twists, and the edges 8 and 19 must be parallel and in line with each other when viewed along the arrow pointer N, Fig. 129. The pieces are to be formed to profile as nearly as possible, for a trough miter should be true to shape, and if not true it will result in high, low and twisted joints or joints with the front or back, that are high or low where it joins the main trough in spite of all a workman can do to prevent such conditions when out on a job.

It may be well to state that should a roof flange be required, as in Fig. 124, the procedure would not vary in the least from the foregoing.

CHAPTER VII

Cornice Problems

Describing an Ogee and Cove Molding

It is not intended to include expositions on architectural subjects in this treatise, nevertheless the sheet metal worker is called upon to do quite some designing and drafting when engaged in making sheet metal work for the ornamentation of building, and he should, therefore, read good books on architecture. One of the subjects of importance is the designing of moldings and, as with all things, authorities differ as to what is correct; however a good book giving the various designs should be at hand.

The system best suited for sheet metal working is that in which all rounds and the like are composed of parts of circles which allows greater ease and accuracy in bending on the usual machines. Now, the ogee and cove are the most common members and indeed the basis of the other types; so in Fig. 134 is detailed one method of drafting a molding composed of such members as well as straight members like fillets and fascias. Just what proportions to give these members depends a good deal on what authority is consulted or other factors.

The first thing to do is to draw a vertical line, generally called the wall line, as A B, and place thereon the vertical dimensions of the members. Draw horizontal lines through these points and, measuring from A B on the topmost line, place thereon the desired projection of the molding, as C. Draw line C D and continue downward dotted to E. Draw diagonal line E F at 45 deg. Line F G is now drawn and diagonal line G D. Draw horizontal line H I

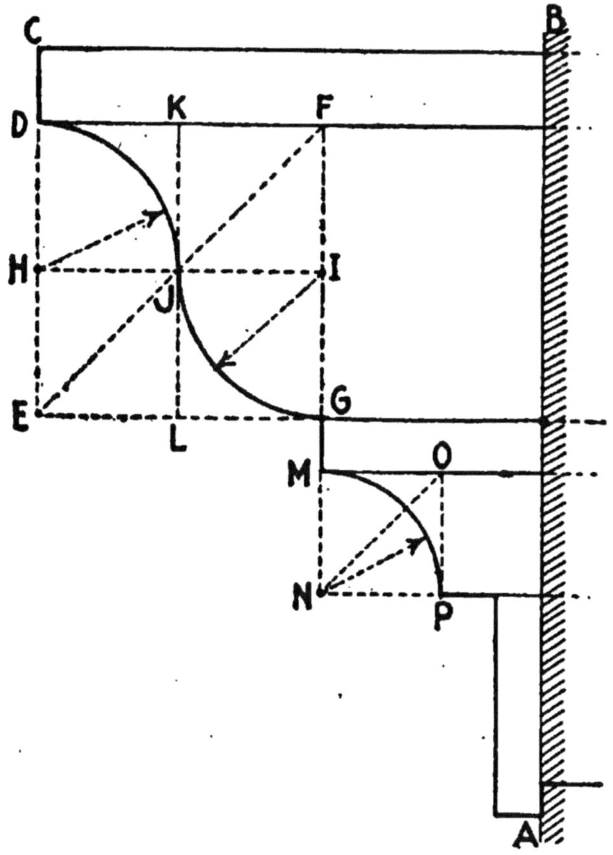

FIG. 134.—An Ogee and Cove Molding.

and vertical line K L. Using H as center, describe quarter-circle D J; using I as center, describe quarter-circle J G, completing the ogee member.

Continue line from G to M and dotted to N. Draw 45 deg. diagonal N O. Draw O P, and now using N as center, describe quarter-round M P. Finish the other members as shown.

A Square Miter

One of the most important miters in cornice work is the square return miter, and Figs. 135A and 135B show how that kind of a miter may be laid out. Of course, line A B of Fig. 135A could be extended downward and the pattern stretchout, A B of Fig. 135B, placed thereon and the points in the profile projected downward about as is explained in the gutter problems of the preceding chapter. The method here expounded is very useful, as the chances are always about even that this scheme must be employed to the other; especially as many mechanics first draw the profile on paper and then develop the pattern directly on the sheet metal with a steel square and scratch awl.

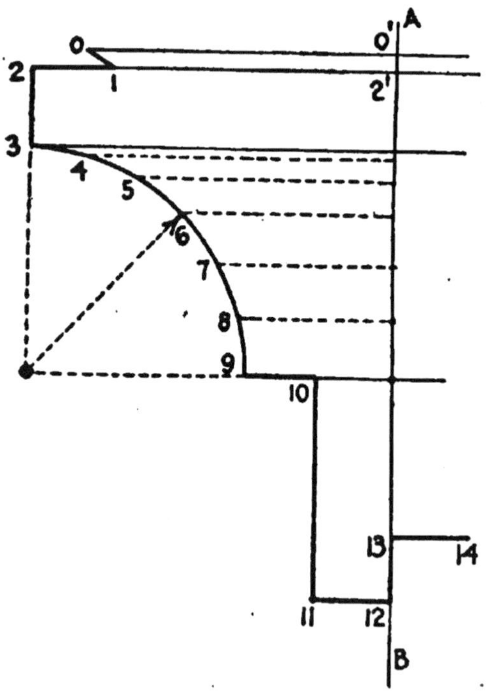

FIG. 135A.—Profile of the Problem.

Another good reason for using this system of carrying the distances rather than projecting them to the parallel lines of the stretchout is, in cornice work often the detail is exceedingly large and composed of many profiles and members, and by this system each profile and member could be developed separately and where convenient.

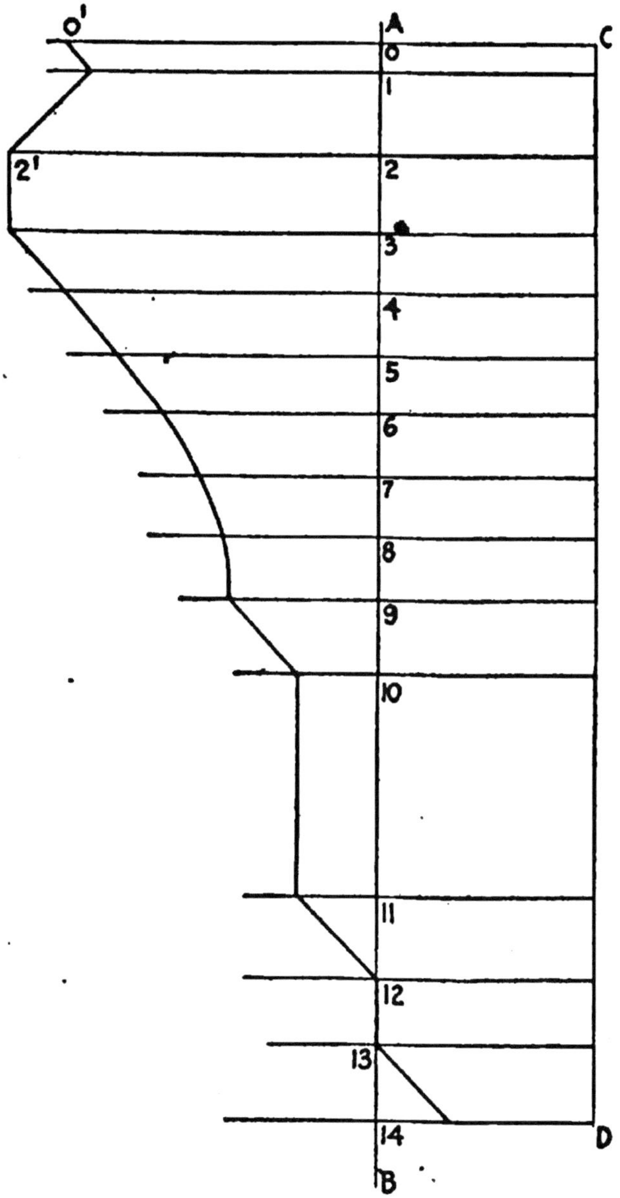

FIG. 135B.—The Pattern of the Profile.

As the system applies, no matter how elaborate the design of the profile may be, a simple contour was adopted to better explain the procedure. Draw line A B in Fig. 135A and place thereon the heights of the members and complete the profile as directed by the diagram. Divide the quarter round or cove into equal spaces and number all points as shown in Fig. 135A.

Now, in Fig. 135B, draw the vertical line A B and place thereon the stretchout, from 0 to 14 of the profile in Fig. 135A. Draw horizontal lines through these points indefinitely, always measuring from line A B, in Fig. 135A, to numbered points, carry the various horizontal distances to like horizontal lines in Fig. 135B. For instance—0 0′ of Fig. 135A is 0 0′ of Fig. 135B, and 2 2′ of Fig. 135A is 2 2′ of Fig. 135B. Note, however, that point 14 is on the other side of line A B in both Fig. 135A and Fig. 135B.

Having obtained these points in this manner, a line is traced through them which is the outline of the miter cut. The length of pattern can be as desired, as shown by line C D of Fig. 135B. Note also how small circles are placed on those horizontal lines which are bending lines, so that there is some sort of a guide to indicate these lines when dotting out on the metal; and, naturally, it is to be understood that if so desired the process of Fig. 135B can be done direct on the sheet metal after Fig. 135B was drawn precisely as explained, and where convenient, as aforementioned.

As explained in connection with the eaves trough problem, an inside miter would be the reverse cut to the right of Fig. 135B.

A Butt Miter Against a Curved Surface.

The problem discussed here, Fig. 136, is exactly like the angle-face miter following. It is intended that this problem will show that the plane or miter line against which the parallel measuring lines of miter problems butt, need not be a straight line or surface, but can be a curve or, indeed, another molding. This problem is also intended to show the measuring lines projected direct to the parallel lines of the stretchout, as discussed in the preceding problem.

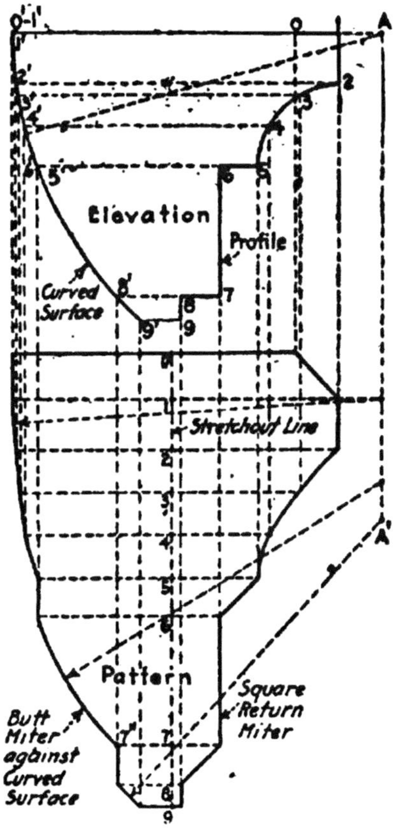

Fig. 136.—A Curved Surface Miter.

The curved surface is described with A as center. Note, also, that members in the pattern, as, 1 to 2, 6 to 7 and 8 to 9, have curved outlines at the butt miter of equal radius to the curved surface and the center for the radius of each is found, for instance, by using 7″ as center and striking an arc on line dropped from A, giving center A′.

Miter at an Angle in Plan

Next in importance to the square return miter is that of a miter at an angle in plan, other than a right angle or square return. The principles explained in connection with this problem and delineated in Fig. 137 and Fig. 138 not only apply to a case like this, but also to many other situations.

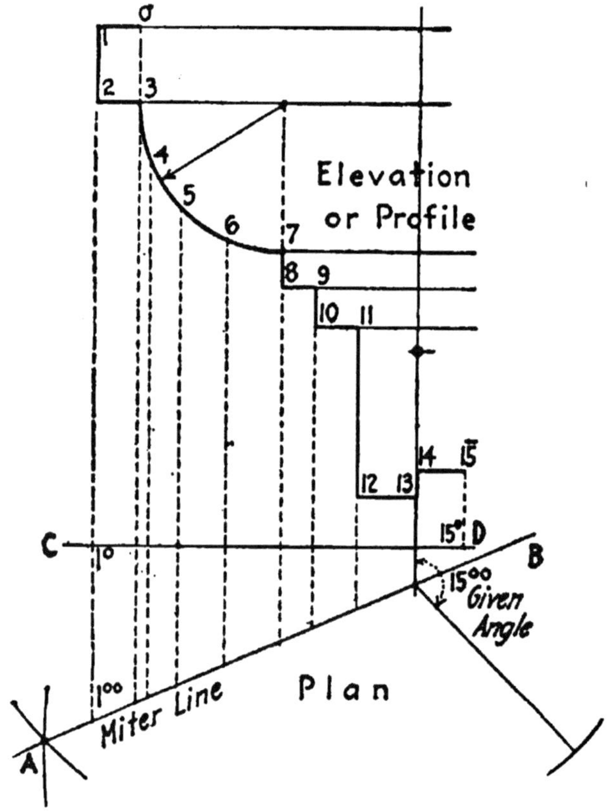

FIG. 137.—Elevation of Molding and Miter Line.

For instance, a butt miter at an angle in plan; as, if this profile was the horizontal molding of a bay window butting against a wall, the miter line A B, in Fig. 137, would represent the wall line. And again, in butt miter cases, miter line A B might be curved just the reverse of the preceding problem, or another molding, or many other diverse objects.

As for the square return miter, the pattern of Fig. 138 could be developed by projecting lines from the miter line direct to the stretchout line, as was done in one of the preceding problems. However, it was the intention of the original author to explain a common shop practice of carrying distances, as he explains in the elbow problems.

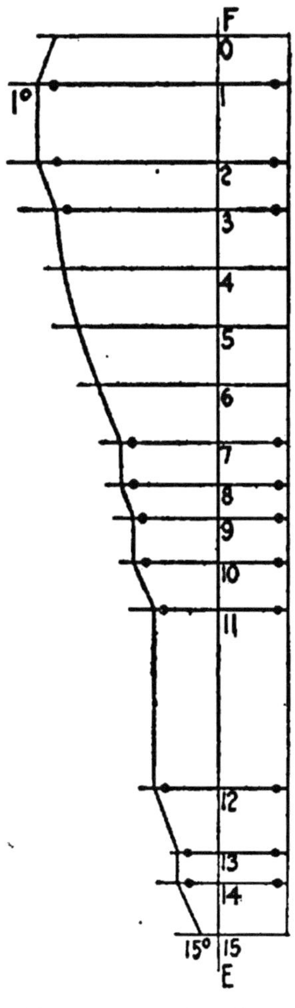

FIG. 138.—The Net Pattern.

Therefore, draw the required profile, as in Fig. 137, and also the given angle, which in the diagram is an octagon angle, as shown. Bisect this angle and obtain the miter line A B. Divide the round of the profile into equal spaces and number the entire profile and drop lines to miter line. Establish any horizontal line as C D.

Now, as in Fig. 138, draw a vertical line E F with the stretchout on it of the profile, then measuring always from this line C D, in Fig. 138, carry the distances from the plan in Fig. 137 to like numbered lines of Fig. 138. To explain: 1° 1°° of Fig. 137 is 1 1° in Fig. 138; also, 15° 15°° in Fig. 137 is 15 15° of Fig. 138 and so on. The small circles on certain lines indicate where square or angle bends are to be made.

A Square Face Miter

In Fig. 139 is given a profile often employed in panel work, and if the pattern for the face miter was to be developed by projecting lines from the profile to the parallel lines of the stretchout line, the stretchout line would then be drawn at right angles to line A B of Fig. 139 and the projecting lines would be a continuance of those lines like o o′.

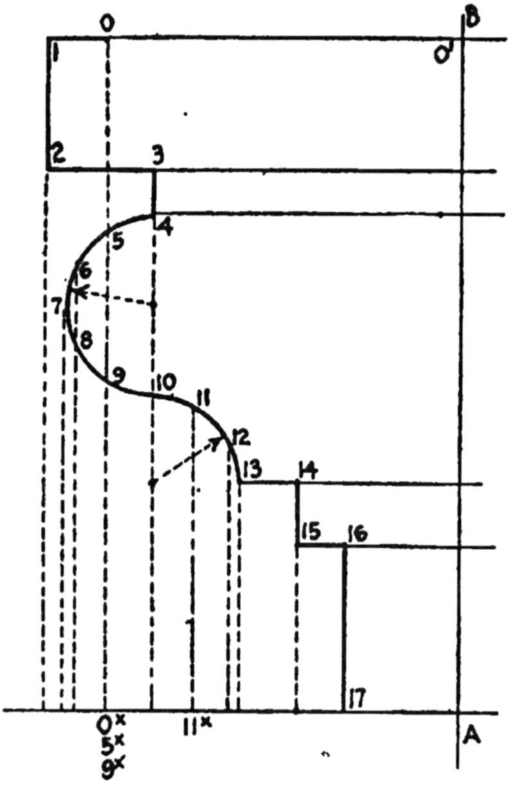

FIG. 139.—The Profile and Lengths.

That is to say, the parallel lines through the stretchout line points would be parallel to the dotted lines in Fig. 139. So, then, to carry the distances, simply take the lengths of these dotted lines. In Fig. 140, line A B is the stretchout line, with the parallel lines at right angles to it and through the stretchout points, as shown by o to 17 Fig. 140.

Carry the lengths from like numbered lines in Fig. 139 to Fig. 140; thus, o o^x Fig. 139 is o o^x Fig. 140, 11 11^x Fig. 139 is 11 11^x Fig. 140, etc.

Note the small circles to indicate the bending lines, and it might be said that some cutters indicate

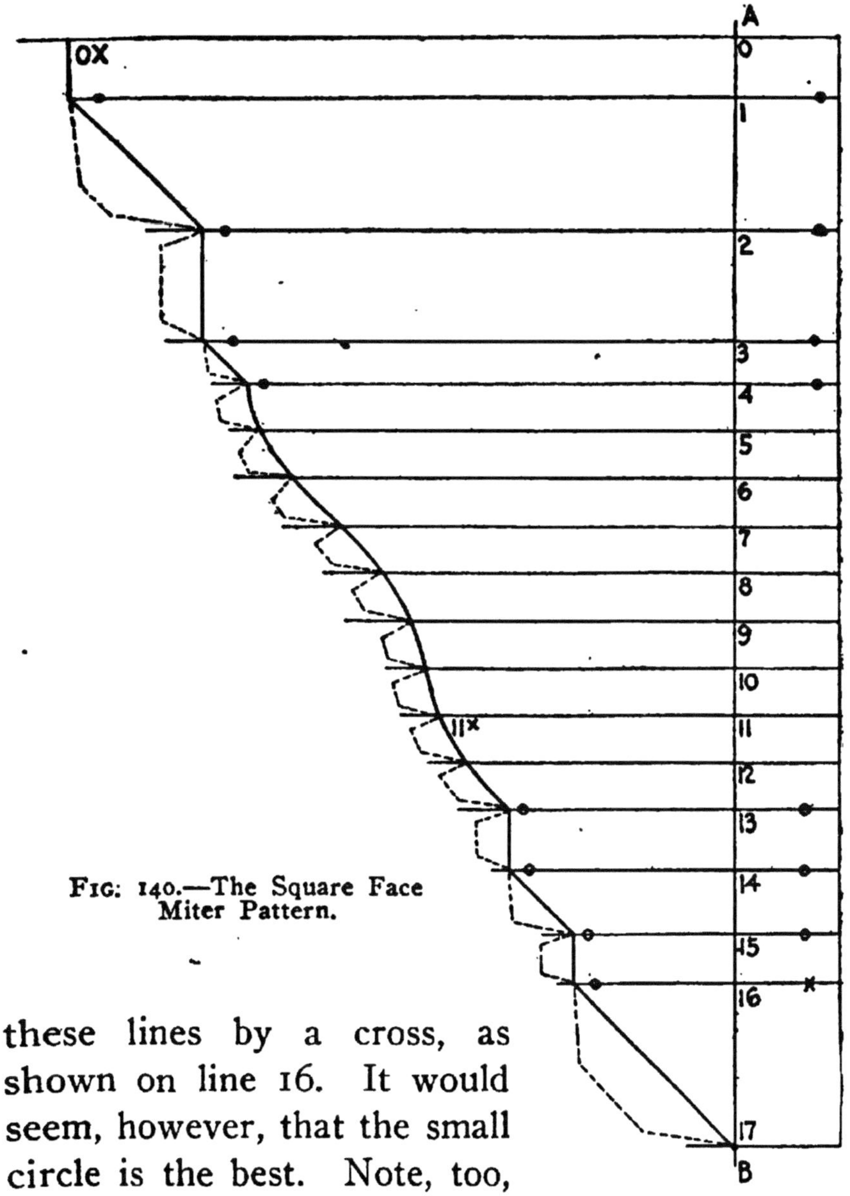

FIG. 140.—The Square Face Miter Pattern.

these lines by a cross, as shown on line 16. It would seem, however, that the small circle is the best. Note, too, how laps would be provided, as shown by the dotted lines. Laps cut so will not interfere with the bending or soldering operations, but give the best assistance.

Angle-Face Miter

The cutting of pattern, or rather the developing of the surfaces of solids, is merely the manipulating of certain geometrical principles and the application of the science of orthographic projection to accomplish desired results. In the preceding problem advantage was taken of a situation, so to speak, in

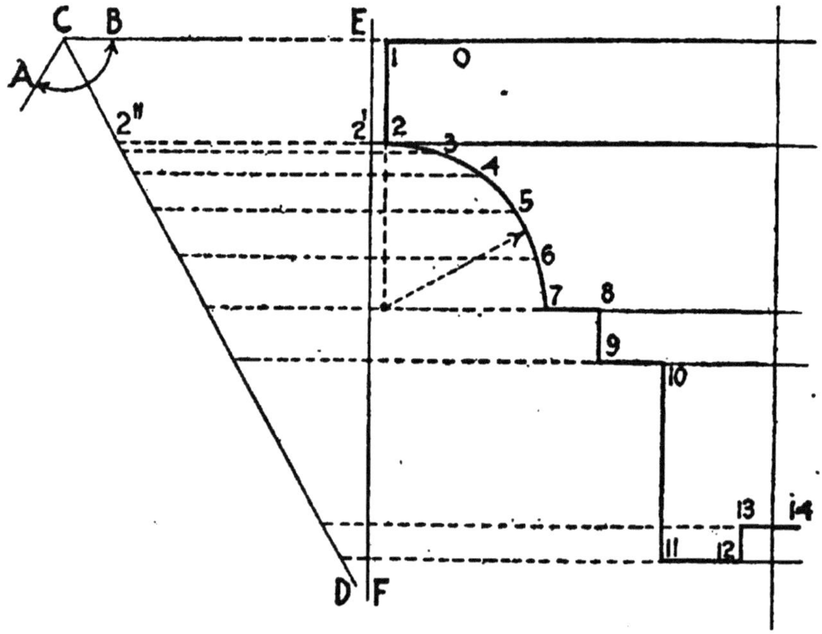

FIG. 141.—Profile and Miter Line of an Angle-Face Miter.

projection, which allows of using shorter methods to arrive at desired results. Now, strictly speaking, and as mentioned elsewhere in this book in connection with such problems, that method is not absolutely in accord with true projection, which might also be said of the square return miter, although a strictly correct pattern is obtained in both cases by this procedure.

The correct method is to use a miter line, and in

face miter problems the line is situated as shown in Fig. 141. In that diagram A B is the given angle, which is bisected to get the miter line C D. The given profile is shown at the right of this line with

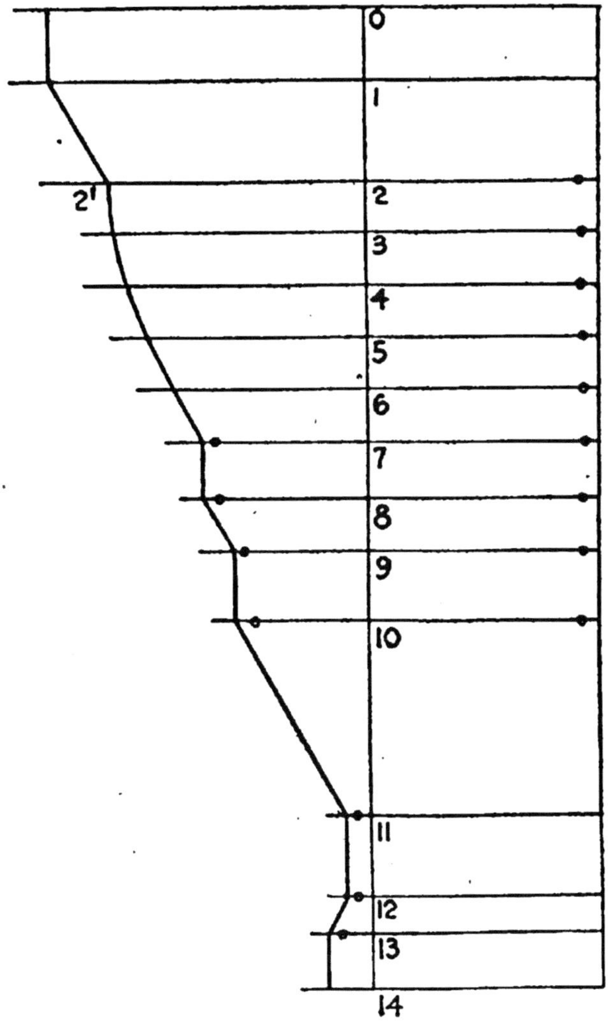

Fig. 142.—Pattern of Angle-Face Miter.

its division points 1 to 14, which are projected across horizontally to the miter line. The angle A C B is bisected according to the method given in Fig. 6, in the chapter on geometry.

Assume any measuring line which would be vertical and established, as indicated by line E F. For the pattern draw where convenient a vertical line on which is placed the stretchout of the profile 1 to 14, in Fig. 141, as shown by line with 0 to 14 division points, in Fig. 142. Draw indefinite horizontal lines, and, measuring from line E F to miter line C D of Fig. 141, carry the distances to Fig. 142, measuring from the vertical stretchout line. Like this, point 2 in Fig. 141 is measured from 2′ to 2″ and placed from 2 to 2′ in Fig. 142, and so forth.

It is to be understood that this problem is the basis of numerous other miter cuts—the apex of a gable molding, the bottom cut of a gable molding finishing on a horizontal line, the cut of a horizontal dormer window molding against a pitch roof and many other like miters.

There are three distinct methods of cutting patterns, or rather, developing the surfaces of solids, to wit: Parallel line system, radial line system and triangulating system. The few foregoing problems were in the category of parallel line problems or miter cutting. Now, the parallel line system can be divided into several divisions. One division in which these problems enter, a simple elevation or plan of the joint gave the miter line and its relation to the profile—if no miter was used a series of measuring lines would be employed.

A considerable number of problems would be comprehended in another division in which quite some preliminary work is requisite before cutting the pattern and a few are to follow.

Raking Miter

One of the best courses in sheet metal pattern drafting is that of Gray's School of Correspondence, and among the one hundred and twenty-five or more plates are several teaching the cutting of different cases of raking miters, one of which is that of Fig. 143A. This is a typical case of such miters and applies when the normal profile is placed in the inclined molding, thus raking or changing, or as some call it, modifying the profile of the horizontal molding.

Quite a number of problems are in the class of raking miters; however, the underlying principles are practically the same in all raking problems. That is, conditions perforce certain requirements as, say, the inclination of the gable and whether the given or normal profile is to be in the gable or horizontal molding, and so forth. Or again, the horizontal molding can miter at other than a right angle, or there is to be a raked return at the apex of the gable and so on.

First draw profile and elevation of foot mold and erect center line. Next draw line C, the angle required intersecting 8 in modified profile, and continue line to center line. Place normal profile A on line C so that point 8 intersects line C. Space profile A into any convenient number of equal spaces, as shown by 1 to 16; place T square parallel with line C; draw lines through all spaces intersecting center line and foot mold, drawing lines from 8 to 16 indefinitely for modified profile. Next draw plan, placing normal profile A on line D, as shown; draw miter line in plan the angle required, draw lines

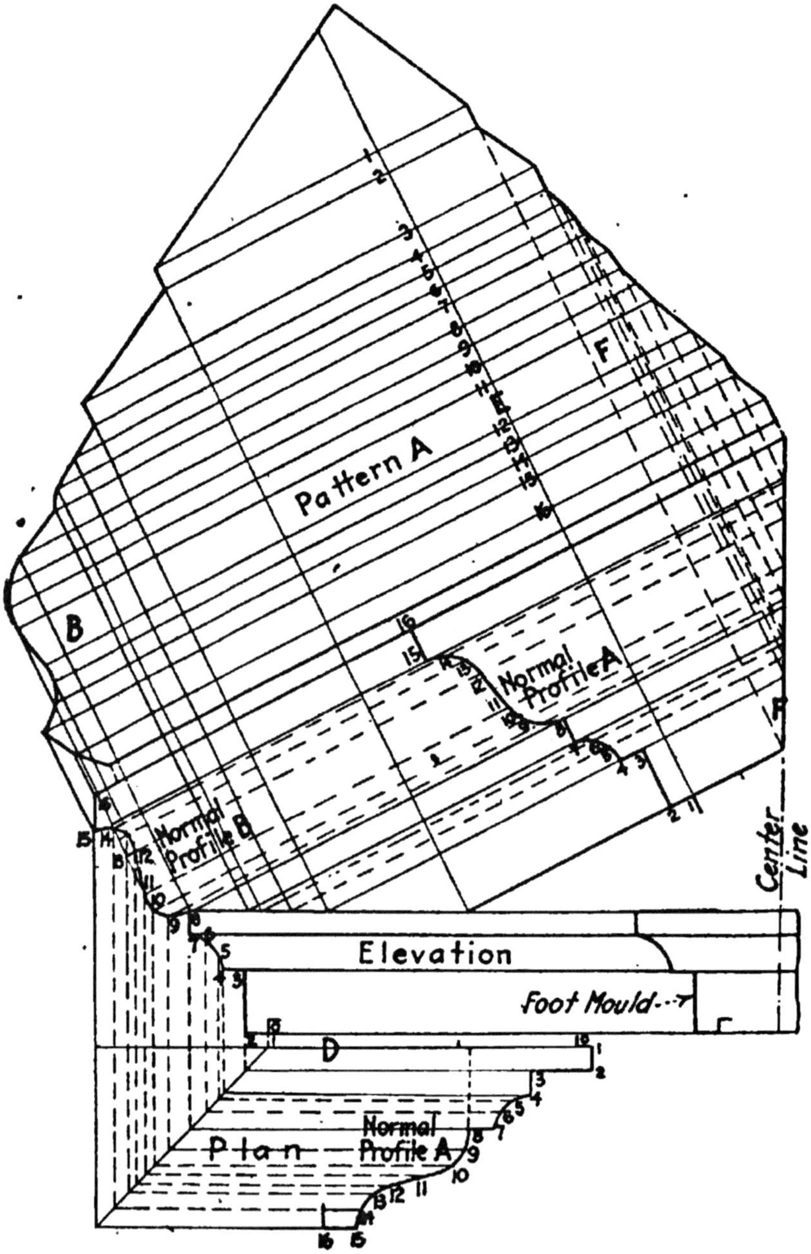

FIG. 143A.—Developing the Pattern for a Raking Miter.

from spacings in profile 8 to 16 intersecting miter line; place T square at right angles to line D; draw lines from intersections in miter line of plan, also intersecting lines of corresponding numbers drawn from normal profile A in elevation. Drawing lines through the intersecting points will give modified profile B. Draw stretchout line E and place spacings on same 1 to 16 from normal profile A. Draw lines through all spacings in stretchout line at right angles to line E indefinitely. Place T square parallel with line E; draw lines from all points in modified profile intersecting lines of corresponding numbers in stretchout B, also draw lines from all points in miter line F to lines of corresponding numbers in stretchout. Drawing lines through the intersecting points will give the patterns B and F, as shown in pattern A, just above the elevation, Fig. 143A.

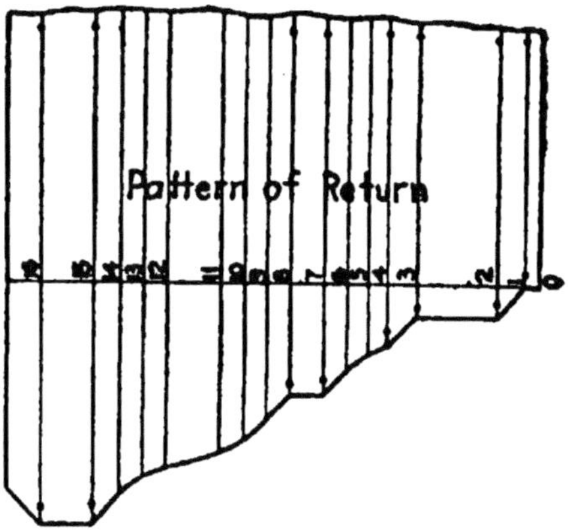

Fig. 143B.—Developing the Horizontal Molding Pattern.

To develop the pattern of the horizontal molding, draw a horizontal line, as in Fig. 143B, and place thereon spacings of modified profile B, as 0 to 16. Draw the vertical lines shown and then taking the various distances from the line D to the miter line in the plan of Fig. 143A, place them on the stretchout line of Fig. 143B.

From 0 to 8 of Fig. 143B is the foot mold pattern; shown from number 0 to the dotted line in the plan, Fig. 143A.

Gable Molding on Square Tower

As was stated in the foregoing article, Gray's School of Sheet Metal Pattern Drafting teaches by numerous specimen plates of the highest possible order that it is possible to make, and in Fig. 144, herewith, is presented the school's lesson on an interesting problem in gable molding cases. Note that the miter at the apex, or rather ridge, bears out the statement made in connection with the problem in angle face miters that face miter cutting, as explained in that problem, would apply to the miter in this case at the ridge.

First draw elevation the pitch required, placing profile A on line C, as shown; space the curved parts of profile A in any convenient number of equal parts and draw lines through all points parallel with line C intersecting miter line E, and extend them indefinitely at D. Next draw profile B, as shown, spacing the curved part of file the same as profile A. Extend lines from all points in profile B intersecting lines of same numbers just drawn from profile A. Drawing lines through intersecting points will give miter line D. Draw stretchout line for pattern at right angles to line C and place spacings on same from profile A. Draw parallel lines indefinitely through all points in stretchout. Place T square at right angles to line C; draw lines from all points in miter lines E and D intersecting lines of corresponding numbers in stretchout. Drawing lines through the intersecting points will give pattern required.

The foregoing explanation had to do with the molding only for this problem. Should a pattern be wanted for the lower or tower proper, the pat-

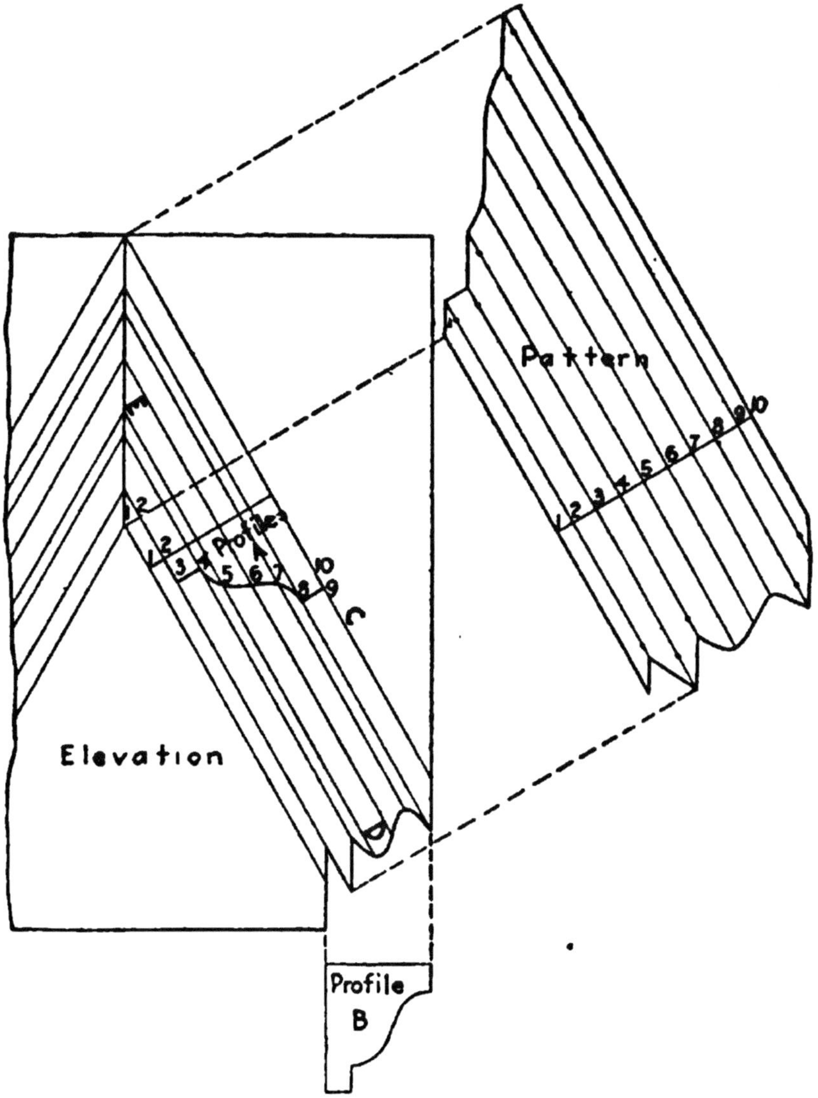

Fig. 144.—Developing the Pattern for a Gable Molding on a Square Tower.

tern would be a duplication of the part of Fig. 144 marked elevation. The triangular roof part can be added to the pattern on line 9.

Hip Finials

Only such drawings are used as will make clear the method of obtaining the patterns. Even though the design is simple, the patterns should be laid out with great care so that the finial will be true and firm when assembled.

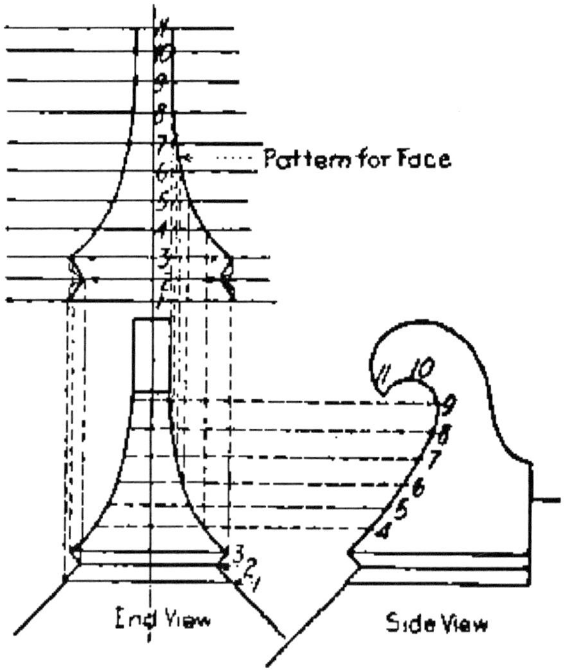

FIG. 145.—Obtaining Face Pattern.

The end and side views of the finial are shown in Fig. 145, also the pattern of the face. As will be noted, the side elevation is stepped off as indicated by the points from 4 to 11. Lines are projected from these points to the front elevation, as shown, then the lines are run up or down as the case may be to the stretchout, as shown from point 9. From point 9 up, the side of the finial is straight. The reason for stepping off the side is to get a true elevation of the face. The lines are then projected to the end view, which shows the miter lines at the corners of the end elevation.

The pattern for the side is developed, as shown in Fig. 146, in which the treatment is reversed from the foregoing. The points are stepped off on the end elevation. Then lines are projected to the side elevation and thence to the stretchout shown above the side view.

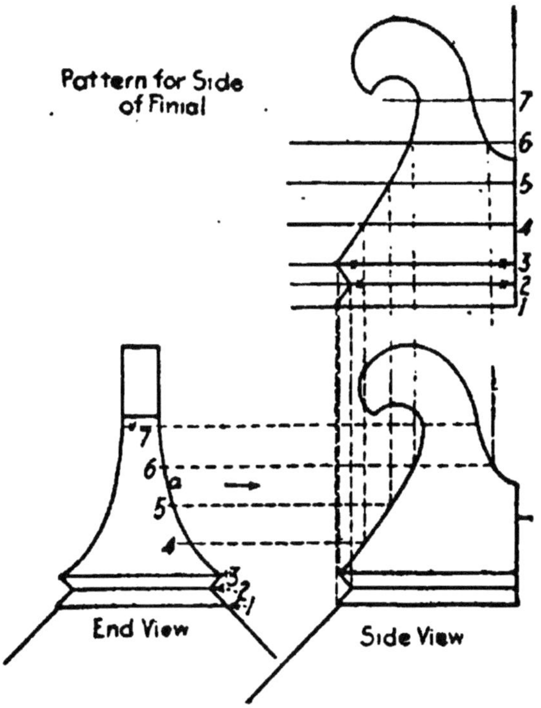

FIG. 146.—Obtaining Side Pattern.

The pattern for the rear of the finial is as shown in Fig. 147. The pattern is shown with laps on the top and bottom. The top strip is developed as shown at A2 in Fig. 147, and to get the point the side elevation is stepped off, as shown from 1 to 9, then projected over to the end elevation and from there to the stretchout. Only 1, 2 and 3 need be projected to the face as that is the length of the flare. The rest is straight and can be struck off with a pencil and straight edge.

To form up this finial the side pieces can be nicely shaped by running through rolls set lightly.

After the parts are all set together and are tacked with solder and the finial is found to be true, it can be more securely soldered and, if of large size, the finial should be riveted together and bosses the full length of the inside of the corners should be soldered in. These bosses not only strengthen the

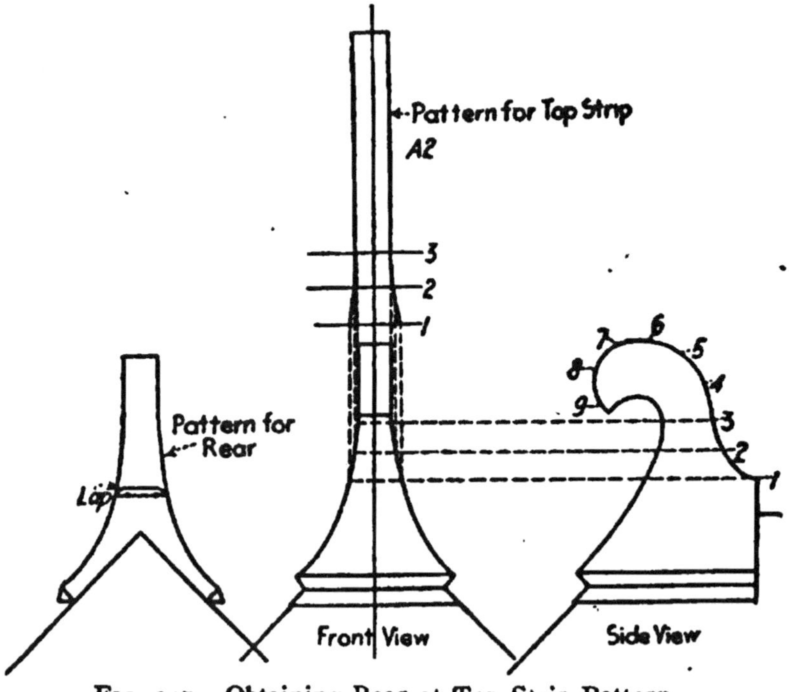

FIG. 147.—Obtaining Rear at Top Strip Pattern.

finial, but if the corner should ever spring a leak, they would throw the water off on the roof. For small finials under 18 inch in height, this bracing and bossing is not necessary, but for larger sizes they should be even more heavily braced, as more surface is exposed to the wind and storm.

Finials are useful for ornamenting ridges, towers or other such parts of buildings and any number of designs can be thought of like crosses or other insignias for religious buildings, weather vanes, etc.

The Gore Pattern for Balls

The method given in Fig. 148 is the old-time tinsmith's procedure. Another method would be by the parallel system of projecting lines from a gore.

Erect perpendicular line H K equal to one-half the circumference of the ball; divide this line into one-half the number of pieces required in full ball;

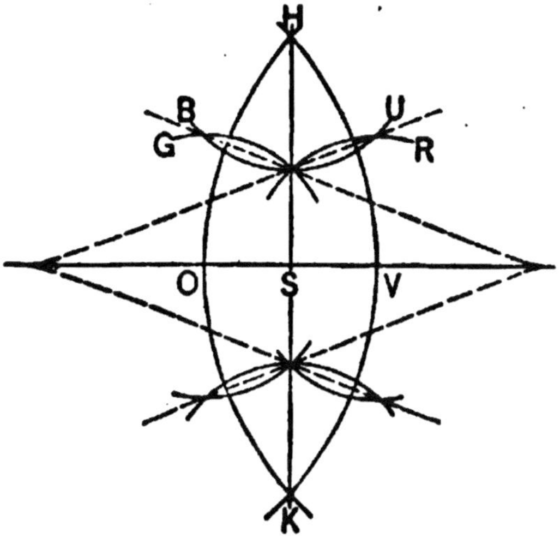

FIG. 148.—Pattern.

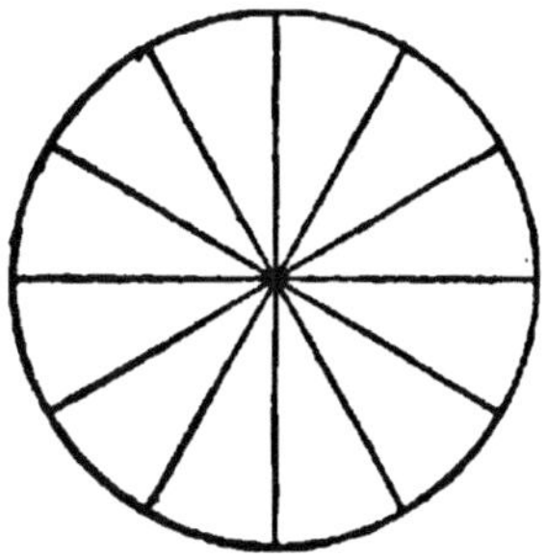

FIG. 149.—Elevation.

make the line V O equal to one of these pieces, cutting H K through the center at right angles; then with H and K as centers, with radius greater than one-half the distance K S, describe the two arcs B U; with V and O as centers, arcs R G; draw lines through these points, as shown by dotted lines. From points of intersection describe arcs H V K and H O K, and so obtain pattern for one piece. Allow for laps or seams. The more pieces used the better globe produced. Good results are obtained by slightly raising the pieces. Fig. 148 is the pattern and Fig. 149 shows the gores.

CHAPTER VIII

Skylights

Single Pitch Skylight

A number of very interesting and practical problems on skylight work are given in the correspondence course offered by Gray's School of Sheet Metal Pattern Drafting, and they have been good enough to grant permission to reproduce two or three of these in the following pages. Those who wish to get a more extended exposition of skylight pattern problems than is given in this little treatise will do well to look into Gray's School, and Volume VIII of the series entitled "Practical Sheet Metal Work and Demonstrated Patterns."

From the time saving standpoint, every one interested in skylight work should have the Full Sized Sheet Metal Patterns prepared by G. L. Gray, as they cover hip, gable and single pitch skylights with various stretchouts of profile, so that they may be made up in any size. Turrets, Louvres and Ventilator patterns are also included. The patterns are all full size and all the sheet metal worker has to do is lay them on the metal, make the proper allowance for distances between his measuring points, prick off the pattern with his awl, and cut out the patterns.

Another timesaver is Smith's Skylight and Roof Tables. This gives the lengths of hip and jack bars at any of the standard pitches for any size skylight. All you have to do is, turn to the table containing the curb dimensions and you will get the length of either the common, jack or hip bar at a glance.

Fig. 150 is a view of a single pitch skylight. In these problems the important part of the work is to make the sections and profiles properly and then

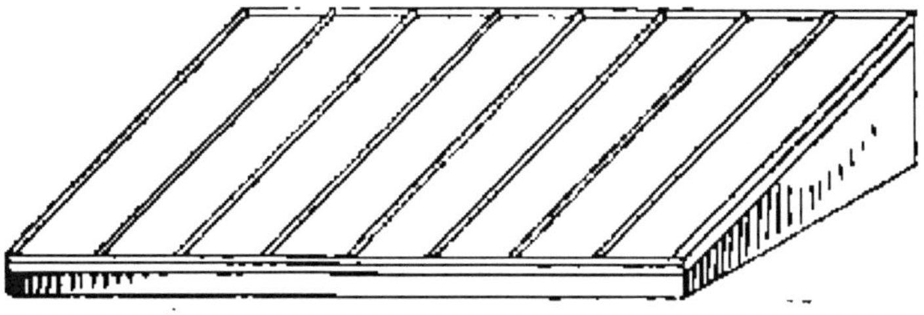

FIG. 150.—Perspective of a Flat or Single Pitch Skylight.

to make a plan showing the correct miter lines, as in Fig. 151. Although single pitch, or rather, flat skylights, involve the elementary constructive characteristics of the entire category of skylights, they are nevertheless the fundamentals in the matter of constructive features, and much time and thought have been expended in experiments to simplify the design and learn a mode of expeditious handling.

The cardinal principles to remember when designing any type of skylight are: To design it of ample strength to resist imposed stresses or loads; sections or profiles of curbs, bars and the like must be as simple as consistent with required strength to allow of rapid forming into shape on the brake and the girth to be such that they will cut out of sheets without waste.

There are several kinds of flat skylights, and the one presented herewith is the most common style, that which is set on a raised curb of sufficient height above the roof to insure imperviousness to storms; the necessary pitch being in the roof proper. The dimensions and shapes of this design are ample for skylights of say eight feet in width, and it is to be

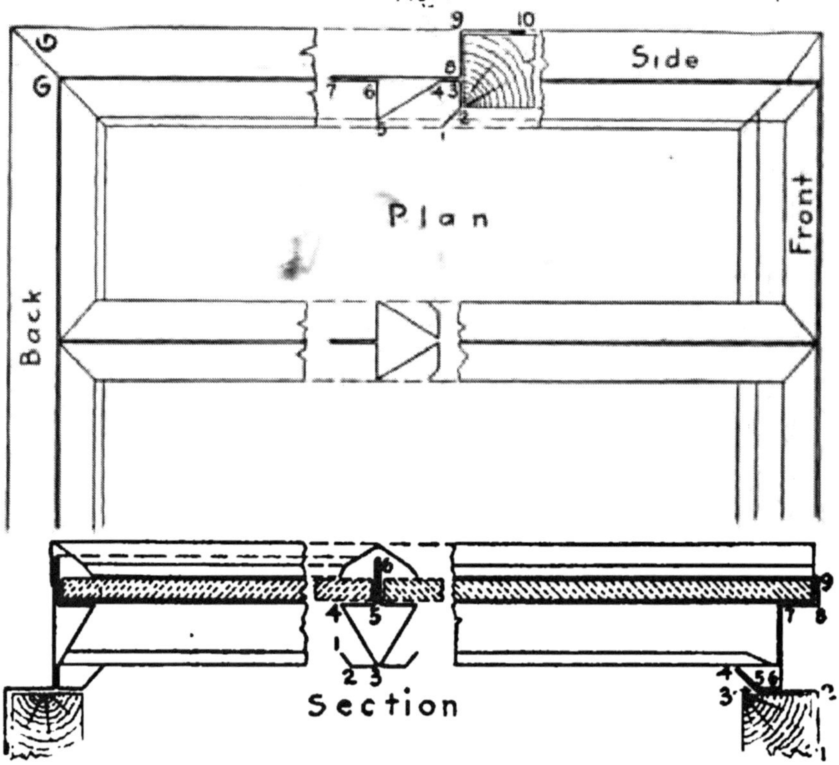

FIG. 151.—Design of a Flat or Single Pitch Skylight.

understood that any length of the skylight is possible for the construction of the roof proper governs this factor, for with proper anchoring of the bottom curb of skylight to the roof curb the length is unlimited. The drainage of the roof back of the skylight, however, must be considered, for with ordinary widths a roof saddle would shed the water to either side of the skylight, whereas with a very long skylight it is best to employ the built-in type, so that the water would flow directly over it. As for the width, naturally, by reinforcing the bar with a core plate, as shown in the large section of a bar, a long bar can be used so that the skylight width could be increased up to at least three-fold possible with the plain bar. A diagram, or section of such bars is given in Fig. 152. Note the core plate of band iron, which should be thick enough to withstand imposed stresses.

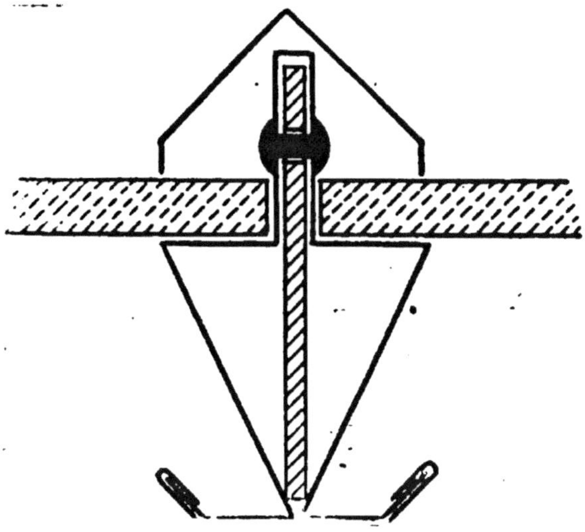

FIG. 152.—Reinforced Bar for Excessive Lengths.

Once it has been definitely decided how to design the constructive features of a skylight, to suit the peculiar conditions of the place where the skylight is to be installed, the pattern cutting can follow prescribed courses, for that is the least of the difficulties.

Now, for the skylight shown in Fig. 151, let it be supposed that the sections as shown are as wanted. Then, the first pattern to be developed would be for the front, as given in Fig. 153. The stretchout of the front section is placed on a line as shown from 1 to 9, the usual parallel lines drawn through these and the miter cut, as shown at the left of the pattern, can be developed either by pro-

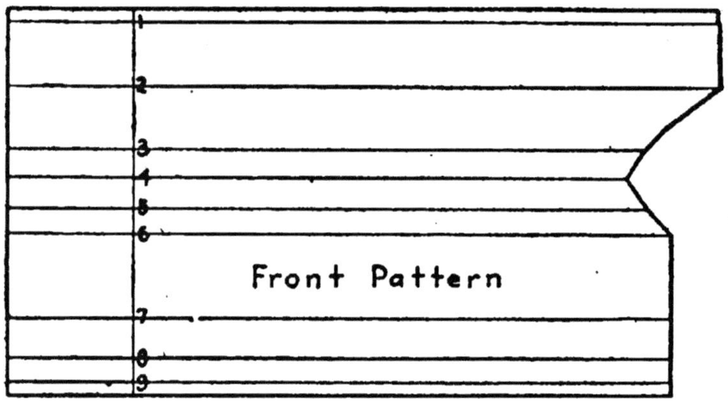

FIG. 153.—One of the Patterns.

jecting lines direct to the pattern from the plan of the miter cut, as directed by like preceding problems, or distances could be carried from the miter plan of Fig. 151 to Fig. 153 as directed in the elbow

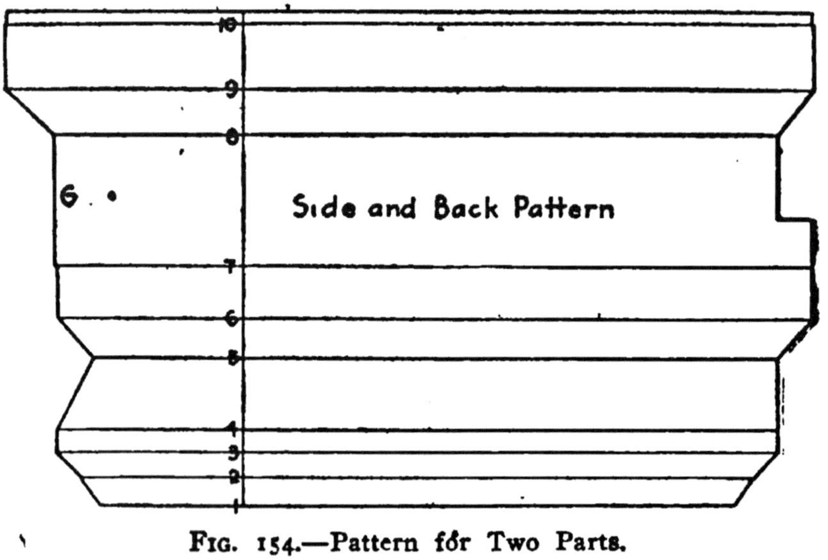

FIG. 154.—Pattern for Two Parts.

or cornice problems. Note that the cut would be the same at each bottom corner of the skylight, so that the miter cut will be the same at each end of the pattern.

For the pattern of the side and back—both have the same profile or section—the stretchout is placed on a line, as in Fig. 154, and the process repeated as directed for the front pattern. If the reader wishes to check up the development he can set his dividers to the length of each of the lines in Fig.

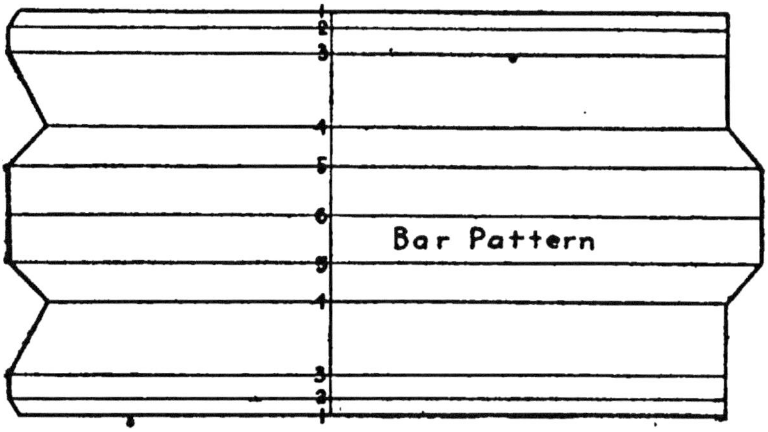

FIG. 155.—The Last Pattern.

154 and try the dividers on like lines in the plan, Fig. 151, making allowances, of course, for discrepancies due to the small size of the diagrams. Observe that there are two different cuts on this pattern, because the miter at the bottom is to fit to the miter of the front, while the other miter is to fit, at G Fig. 151, to the back. This means that when cutting out the back pattern, miter cut G Fig. 154, is to be placed at both ends of the pattern. Two sides like Fig. 154 are required for each skylight and are to be bent right and left.

The pattern for the bar is developed likewise and would appear as shown in Fig. 155. The cap pattern, too, not given herewith, is developed in the same manner. Laps are to be provided on all patterns as experience may dictate and by adding a triangle piece to the pattern at line 8, Fig. 154, from a flat to a single pitch skylight is obtained.

Gable Skylight.

A perspective view of the gable skylight, or as it is often called, a double pitch skylight, is presented as Fig. 156. The same remarks in the introduction to the skylight chapter anent constructions and so forth, are just as pertinent to this type as they are to the single pitch type.

The design and patterns for a gable skylight, Fig. 156, given in Fig. 157, are of an ideal construction, and it may be said that a single pitch skylight can be made from these patterns by simply forming just a half ridge bar and carrying a straight back down from the ridge and forming a curb of like contour to the others.

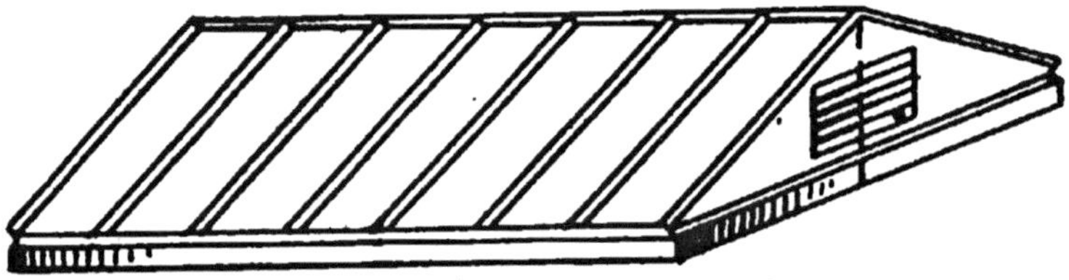

FIG. 156.—Perspective of a Gable Skylight.

When ventilation is required it is customary to place a louvre frame in the sides, or gable ends, as shown in the sketch, or else an elbow can be turned out of each end and a ventilator top placed thereon. As may be seen, the gable end can be made in one

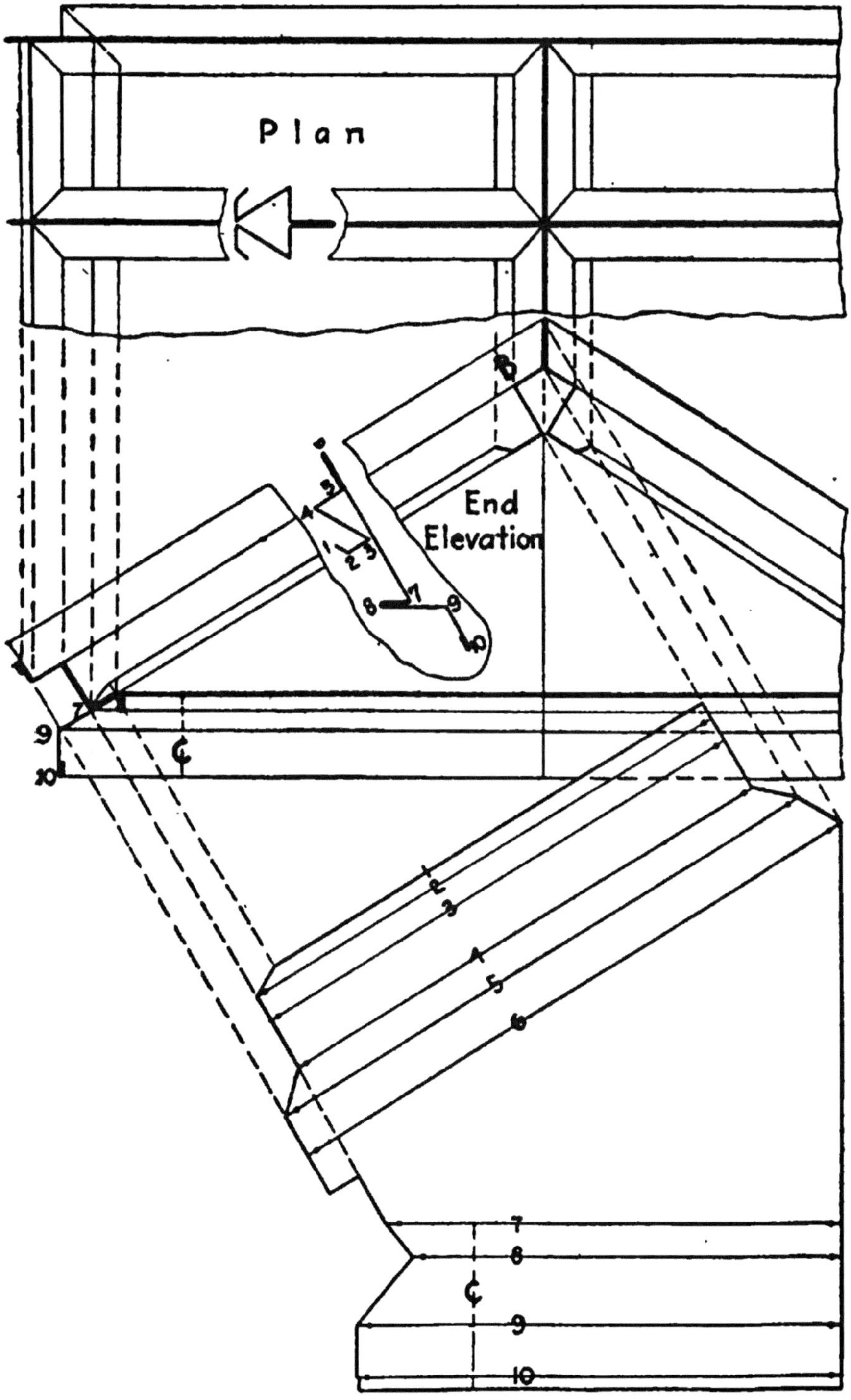

FIG. 157.—Details and Pattern of a Gable Skylight.

piece, but it is best to make them in two pieces, as then they can be cut out and formed-up on the

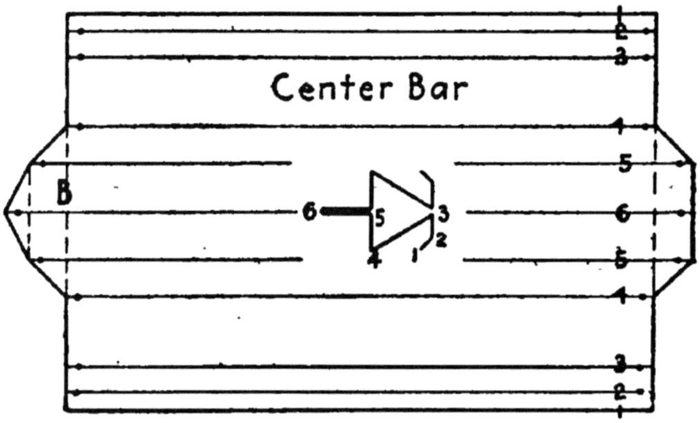

Fig. 158.—A Typical Pattern.

brake much more easily, also they cut out of the sheet with less waste.

The end elevation in Fig. 157 shows the section of a gable; the ridge bar, B, and the bottom curb.

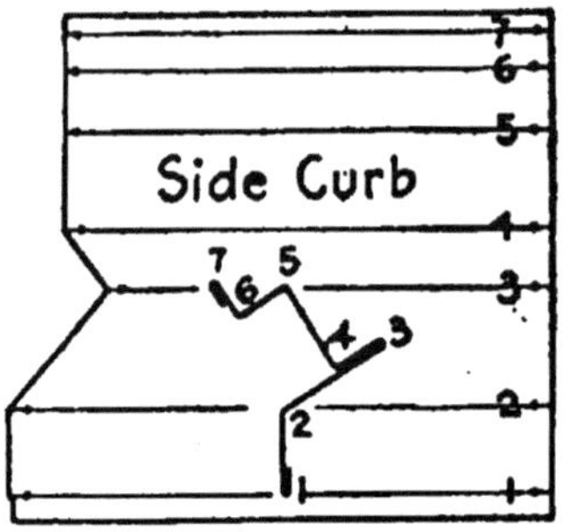

Fig. 159.—A Stub Pattern.

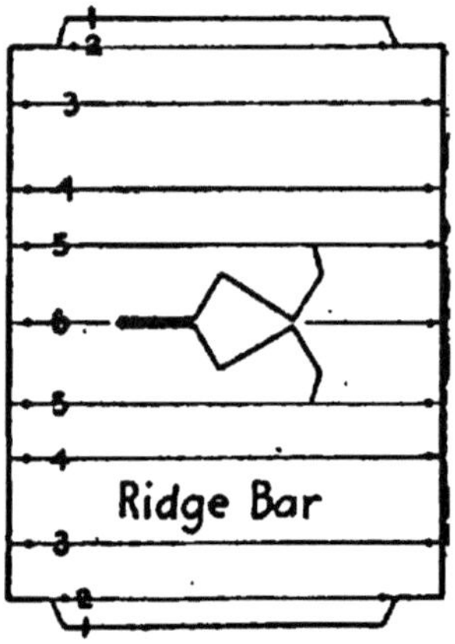

Fig. 160.—Another Stub Pattern.

Fig. 157 also shows a plan of the skylight to portray the various joints. A pattern of one-half the gable end is also given in this diagram and the method of obtaining this pattern should be apparent. Note particularly that part C is not developed by projecting lines but by carrying distances, measuring from line C in both elevation and pattern.

The center bar pattern is given in Fig. 158 and obtained in the usual manner; cut B being for the ridge end at B of Fig. 157. The curb pattern is given in Fig. 159 and the ridge bar in Fig. 160. The profiles are shown on each pattern, which is a good idea, as it instantly identifies the patterns. Laps should be allowed as required, as patterns are net.

Jack and Rafter Bar for a Hipped Skylight

Hipped skylights are one of the most important types made and a perspective view of such is given in Fig. 161. As a rule this type is set on a level roof curb for the four glazed sides provide the necessary inclination to shed snow and rain. Hip

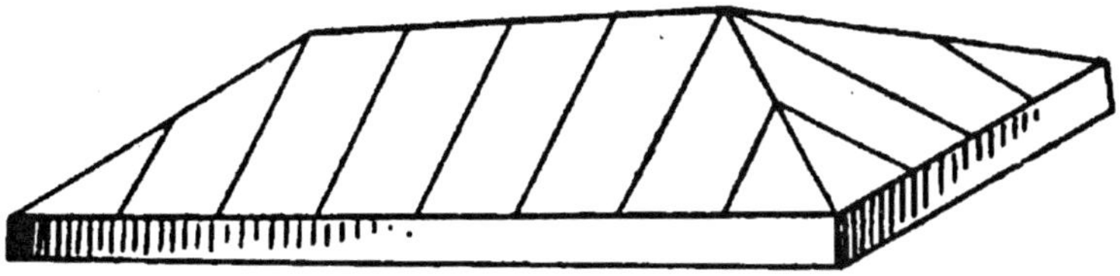

FIG. 161.—Perspective of a Hipped Skylight.

skylights are quite popular and many mechanics claim that they can be much more easily made than a gable skylight and are stronger.

As was stated before, the design is the essential requisite and in Fig. 162 is given a plan of a corner of a hipped skylight, showing the many joints in this type. A part elevation, or section, is also shown in this diagram. Note that the ridge bar can be changed to a ventilator neck, if that is wanted*; or, better still, for ventilation a ventilator can be placed directly over ridge bar.

Draw elevation of jack bar at 1-3 pitch, which is 8 inches in 12 inches; draw profile of the bar in

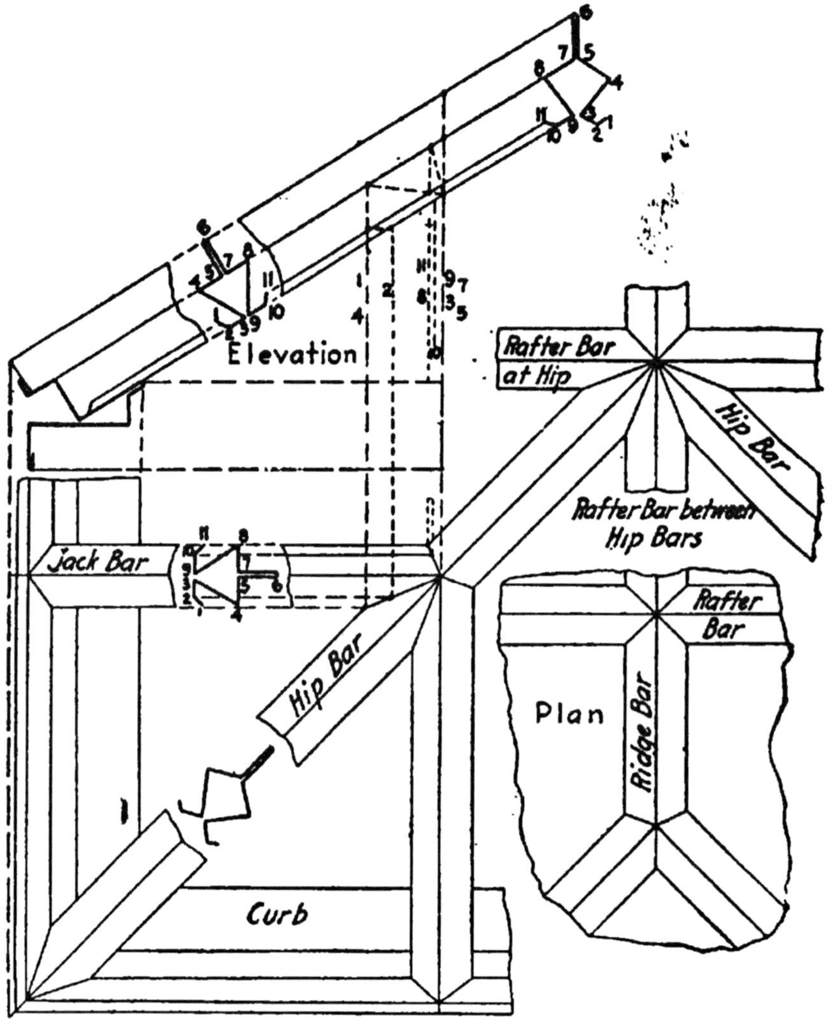

FIG. 162.—Preliminary Steps for Obtaining Patterns.

elevation and draw lines through all points in this profile indefinitely as shown in Fig. 162. Place T square at right angles to jack bar in plan, draw lines from all points in miter lines of hip intersecting lines of corresponding numbers in elevation. Drawing lines through the intersecting points will

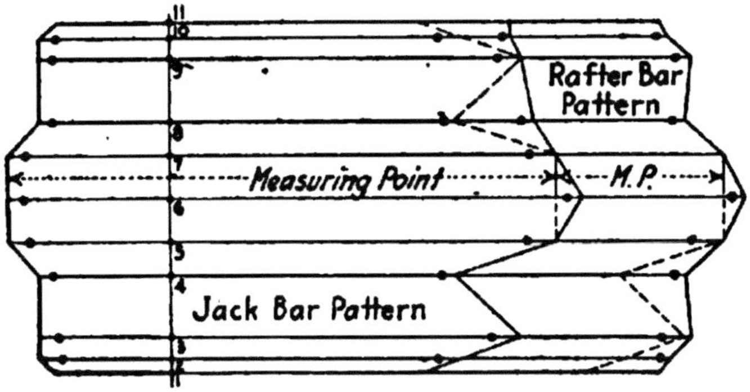

Fig. 163.—Composite Pattern.

give the miter lines in elevation. Draw stretchout line for jack bar at right angles to jack bar in elevation. Place T square at right angles to stretchout lines, draw lines from all points in miter lines of elevation intersecting lines of corresponding numbers in stretchout. Drawing lines through the intersecting points will give the pattern for jack bar. Or, as in Fig. 163, carry distances as explained before.

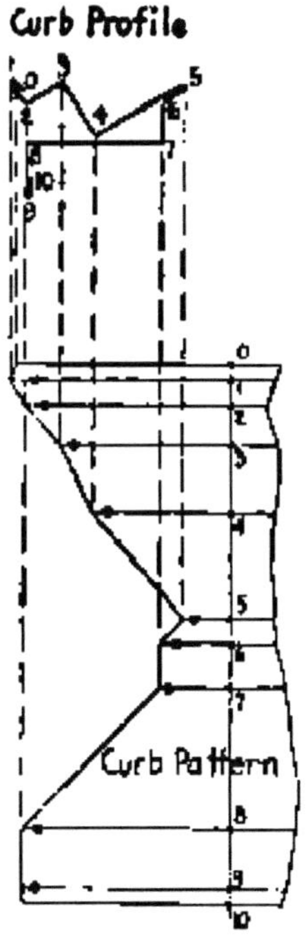

Fig. 164.—Developing Curb Pattern.

To make the pattern for jack bar it is not necessary to draw all the bars, as shown in plan. They are shown here more to clearly delineate how the many different bars should have their miters developed. The dotted lines in the jack bar pattern give the pattern for rafter bar between hip bars. The rafter bar pattern is developed on the same stretchout as jack bar. The dotted lines in the rafter bar pattern give the pattern for rafter bar against hip.

The developing of the curb pattern is as directed by Fig. 164. Owing to lack of space, the curb profile was transferred to avoid confusion. Divide and number the profile, as shown. Draw perpendicular lines to this stretchout and drop lines from points in the profile to like numbered lines of stretchout.

The measuring points should always be marked on the patterns to prevent error. It would also be a good idea to place a diagram of the profile on each pattern as was done in the patterns for the gable skylight. Laps should be allowed as required, for all these patterns are net.

Hip Bar for Hipped Skylight

In the article preceding this the developing of the curb, jack and rafter bar patterns, for a hipped skylight was explained. Now, there is another bar to have its pattern developed which is the important part of this type skylight and that is the hip bar.

To make the pattern for a hip bar: First draw the transverse section, which is a section showing half the width of skylight. Drop lines from curb and ridge bar, as shown in Fig. 165, which forms the plan of skylight. Draw plan of hip bar and place profile of bar A on hip bar as shown, draw lines from all points in profile A intersecting lines of corresponding numbers in curb and miter lines at ridge bar. Next draw elevation of hip bar at a convenient distance from hip bar in plan, first draw

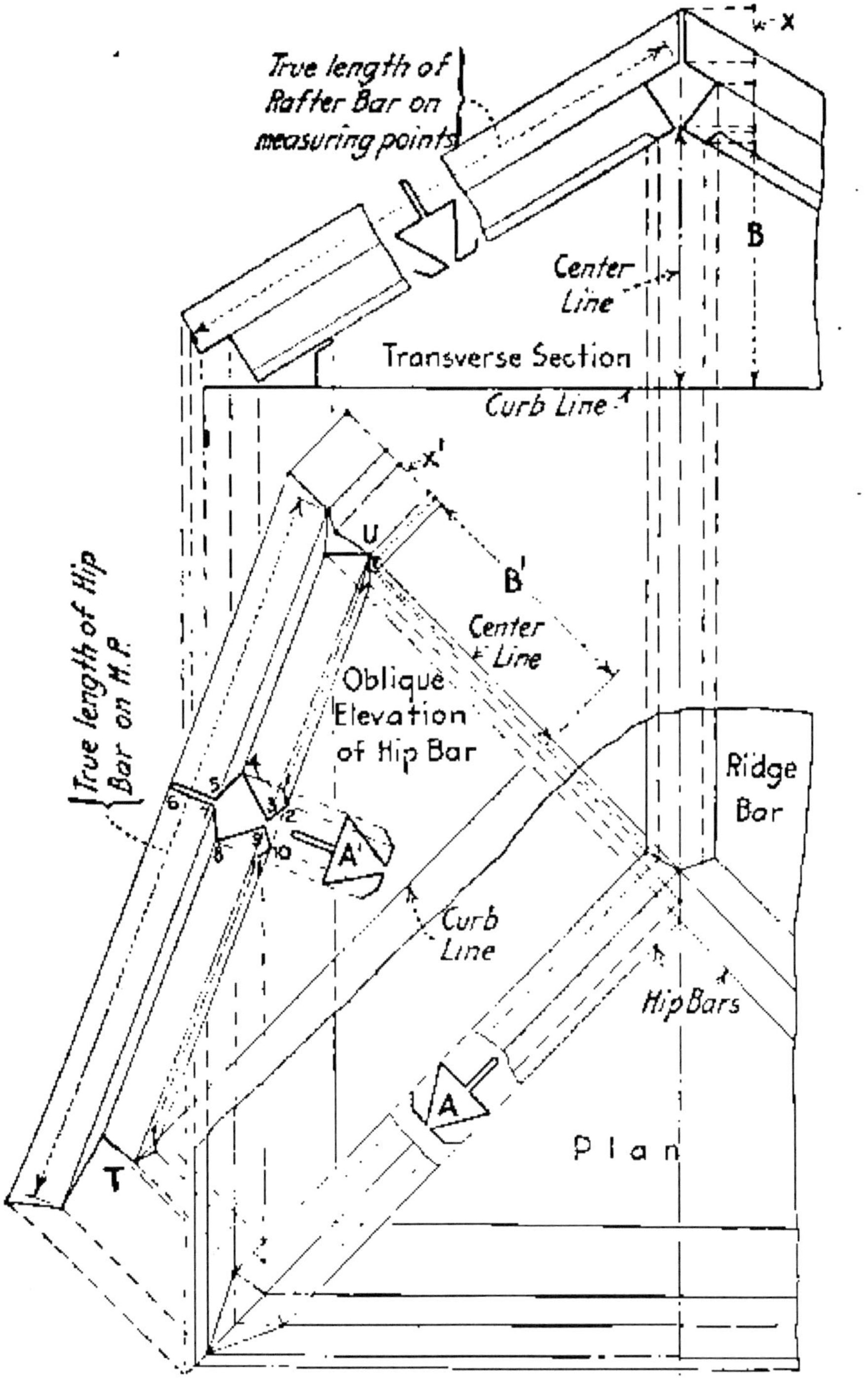

FIG. 165.—Developing Correct View of Hip Bar.

curb line parallel with hip bar of plan and erect center line the same length as center line in transverse section. Next draw line B in transverse section and from points 1 to 6 draw lines intersecting line B at right angles, erect line B′ in elevation of hip bar, and space it the same as line B in transverse section; place T square at right angles to line B′, draw lines from points 1 to 6 indefinitely. Place T square

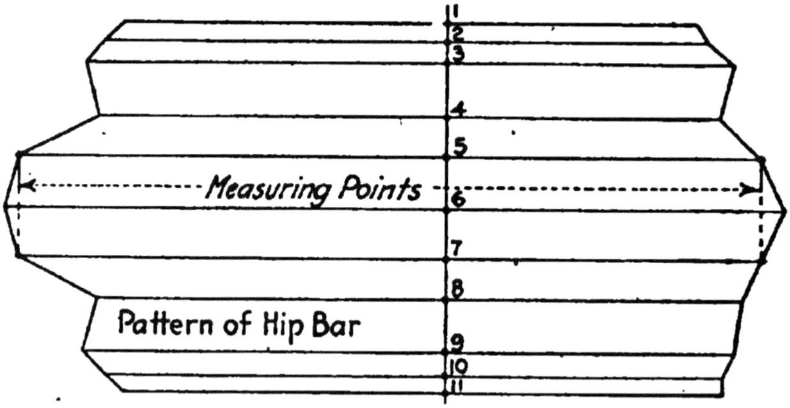

FIG. 166.—Developing the Hip Bar Pattern.

parallel with center line in elevation of hip bar, draw lines from points 1 to 11 in miter lines of hip bar in plan intersecting lines of corresponding numbers just drawn from line B′, draw lines through the intersecting points will give the miter lines in elevation of hip bar, with the T square in same position draw lines from all points at bottom of hip bar in plan intersecting lines drawn from A′, corresponding numbers in the miter lines in elevation of hip bar parellel to U T. Draw lines through the intersecting points gives the miter line at bottom of elevation of hip bar.

Draw profile A′ as shown in elevation of hip bar, being a duplicate of A in plan, erect lines from all points in profile A intersecting lines of corresponding numbers in elevation of hip bar; drawing lines through the intersecting points will give the profile of hip bar.

Draw stretchout line for pattern and place spacings on same 1 to 11 from profile of hip bar, draw lines from all points in stretchout line indefinitely, place T square parallel with stretchout line, draw lines from all points in miter lines of elevation of hip bar intersecting lines of corresponding numbers in stretchout, drawing lines through the intersecting points will give the pattern for the hip bar.

As was explained before, another way would be to draw a line and place thereon the stretchout of the hip bar as in Fig. 166. Through these points indefinite lines are drawn. Then, carrying the lengths from Fig. 165, to like numbered lines in Fig. 166, the two miter cuts are obtained. Measuring points should be marked on this pattern, also laps provided as wanted. And, too, if desired, the profile should be marked thereon. The ridge bar pattern is the same as shown in Fig. 160.

Finding Lengths of Bars

The first thing a cutter should do when he gets measurements for a skylight is to make a working plan, scaled 1 inch to the foot, marking the size of skylight; also lay out the bars to suit the glass which is to be used; then put down the measurements that all bars are to be cut. In this way the cutter has all measurements and is ready to go ahead and cut the skylight.

A typical layout like this is shown in Fig. 167,

which is for a four by five feet skylight. The lengths of these bars are found by a diagram of pitch or tables of lengths computed mathematically.

As was stated in the introduction to this chapter, there are books to give the lengths of skylight bars at a glance. It might be said that Gray's full-size working patterns have a chart accompanying them that gives the measurements for hip, jack and rafter bars, for any size skylight up to thirty feet wide for the pitch used for these patterns.

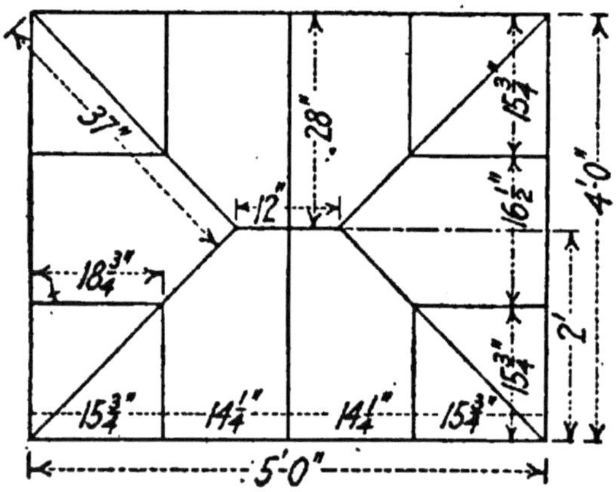

Fig. 167.—Layout of a Typical Size Hipped Skylight.

For those who do not wish to make a chart as suggested before, it can be mentioned that certain mathematical processes could be employed to determine lengths of bars. Without going into a lengthy explanation of these processes it will suffice to say that two factors are established, viz.: 1.2 inches for jack and rafter bars and 1.56 inches for hip bars, for one-third pitch used for the patterns given in this book. These computations will give very nearly the same results as developing triangles on a scale drawing, as was done for Fig. 164 as referring to charts.

To illustrate: In Fig. 167 the full width of the skylight from the length leaves 12 inches, which will be the length of the ridge bar. Now, one-half the width of the skylight is 24 inches and 24×1.2 gives $28.8 = 28\frac{13}{16}$ inches. The jack bar is spaced $15\frac{3}{4}$ inches, so $15\frac{3}{4} \times 1.2 = 18.9 = 18\frac{15}{16}$ inches. The hip bar length is found by the second factor, so one-half the width is 24 inches and $24 \times 1.56 = 37.44 = 37\frac{7}{16}$.

It will be observed that these bar lengths are a little bit full in comparison to those given in Fig. 167. This, however, is not of much consequence, inasmuch as so slight a difference would make no discernible variation in the pitch of the skylight. It would be serious, though, if the proportion of dimensions between jack or rafter bars and the hip bar was wrong, for then either the jack or rafter bars would not fit to the hip or else the hip would not suit the lengths of the jack or rafter bars, depending whether the hip bars were first set in or the rafter bars first when assembling. Now, as scaling from a diagram or calculating with factors takes as much labor it would seem best to use the factors.

For a detailed description for laying out all forms of skylights required in architectural building construction the reader is referred to Neubecker's "Home Instruction for Sheet Metal Workers."

CHAPTER IX

Seams, Joints and Processes

Provisions for Laps and Seams on Patterns

Very few writers of sheet metal subjects consider the importance of seams, joints, laps and similar essentials when demonstrating the development of sheet metal patterns. As a rule, they treat the problem in a geometrical sense, the object (for which the pattern is to be cut) being an imaginary body in space, so to speak. The final results or rather the desired pattern is then nct, which is to say, just the envelope or outer imaginary surface of the solid or body. The providing of laps and one thing or another is then dismissed with the remark to provide laps and edges for seams and so forth.

Special attention has been paid to this important phase of the subject in this volume. While it no doubt suffices to simply present an elucidation of the procedure to develop the net pattern, modern writers are beginning to realize the need of treating these expositions along more practical lines. That is to say, they bear in mind that the actual use for which the problem in hand is intended must be considered and spoken of, along with the geometrical demonstration of the problem. Take, for instance, the problem illustrated in Fig. 63; it not only shows how to cut the pattern but also gives as much information as possible about the laying out of the holes for the band iron supports, the providing of all edges, and even shows the swaging necessary to stiffen the object. This is just one example of the large number given herein.

Facts about Flat Seams

Flat seams are probably the most common of all the seams in sheet metal working. By flat seam is meant any seam in which the opposite edges to be joined lie in the same flat or curved plane and in

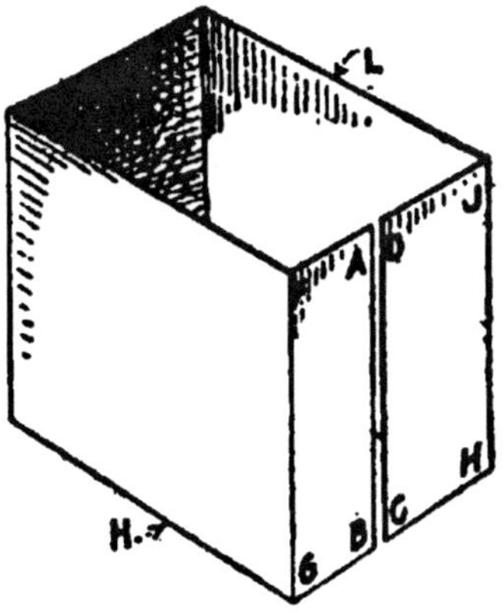

FIG. 168. A Body of Rectangular Contour.

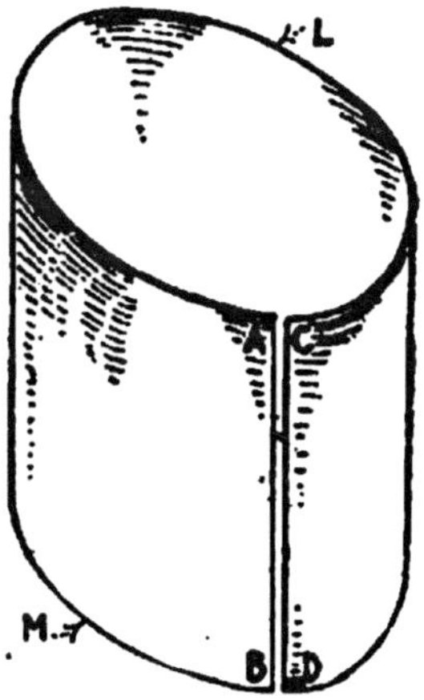

FIG. 169. A Body of Round Contour.

which said edges constitute a straight line. To illustrate, in Fig. 168, a sheet of metal has been shaped into a body of rectangular contour and edges A B and C D are to be joined together by a method depending on different circumstances. As should be apparent, edges A B and C D lie in the same flat plane, F G H and J; and edges A B and C D are truly straight lines, totally devoid of any curvature from A to B or C to D, and if a groove seam was to be used the edges could be bent in the brake or folder. Again, by referring to Fig. 169, it will be seen what is meant by the seam being also flat when employed for joining bodies which may be a cylinder, or a cone, or any irregular shaped body providing only that edges A B and C D—Fig. 169—are straight lines.

Facts about Butt Seams

When making seams the first thing that would come to mind is the butt seam, meaning a seam where edges A B and C D, of Figs. 168 and 169 are merely brought together as in Fig. 170, and connected by some of the usual methods in vogue. Probably the most popular method is by welding in which perhaps one of the edges would be slightly scarfed—thinned out—on both sides and the other

FIG. 170. A Butt Seam. FIG. 171. A Riveted Butt Seam.

edge is split (cleft weld) enough for the wedge of the other edge to enter. With these two edges held firmly together by clamps, or other means depending on circumstance and, after heating to a white heat and fluxing, with borax or some other flux, the joint is hammered and otherwise manipulated according to blacksmithing practice.

Such welds would be more usable for heavy plate work rather than tinsmithing, and would really be in the province of the blacksmith. Still, welding is rapidly displacing riveting and, indeed, even lock seaming on black iron goods up to as light as 26 gauge and is quite popular for gauges like number 16 or 14. It is to be understood though that such welding is not the old-fashioned method of the blacksmith, but the modern hot flame process, using the electric arc or oxy-acetylene torch. Spot welding by electricity is also rapidly being substituted for riveting and is now extensively used for joining structural shapes, like angle iron, to sheet iron; and the joining together of the various parts, like the ovens of French ranges, gas ranges and so on. For full seam welding the electric arc is often used, but not as extensively now as the highly developed oxy-acetylene process, known also as the hot flame method. This process has been brought to so high a point of perfection that modern sheet metal working shops employ it for making the seams on pieced elbows, ship ventilators, hotel kitchen goods, metal windows, doors, interior trim, and a host of articles heretofore riveted, double-seamed or otherwise joined. Were it not for this process the automobile sheet metal industry would not be so far advanced because sheet aluminum was a difficult material to use prior to the coming of this process; so it can readily be seen that it behooves the sheet metal worker to second his skill with seaming and riveting tools, with a knowledge of the hot flame process and spot welding.

A Discussion of Oxy-acetylene Welding

It may not be necessary for the owners of average sheet metal working shops to equip their plants with a complete welding outfit to meet this modern demand, for in most manufacturing centers there are concerns who specialize in welding for the trade. In that case all they would have to do is to get it shaped up and ready for welding. That is done as follows:

Taking a two-piece elbow to make of 14-gauge black iron as an example, the two pieces would be very accurately cut from the metal, especially at the miter cut. There would be no allowance for lap on the longitudinal seams as with the former riveted seams, but proper allowance should be made in the girth for the thickness of the metal—say an allowance of seven times the thickness of the metal added to the girth. This girth will be the same for both pieces, particularly along the miter line because the miter cuts of the two pieces are to butt and not lap into each other as for a riveted joint. Of course, a small and large end are to be provided depending on the manner of connecting the elbow to the round pipe, or whatever the elbow is to join.

The two pieces are now carefully rolled to true shape and a wire is bound about them to hold the longitudinal seam together. The two pieces are now held together on their miter cuts to see that they accurately butt, because if there are any openings it will be necessary for the welder to load up the holes with metal, as the welders charge extra for poor fits. The two parts can now be shipped to the welder and unless the welder is instructed not to, he will very likely smooth off the joints with a file and emery wheel. This adds to the cost, and if a little roughness (like the solder or any soldered seam) does not matter it could remain.

It should be plain that with this system much punching of holes and laborious flanging of the parts are obviated, and if quite a number of elbows are required the manufacturing cost is lessened to an appreciable extent. Even if these elbows were specified to be of galvanized iron they could be galvanized after welding and a splendid job acquired thereby. The use of the hot flame for cutting metal is also important enough to be worth the study of sheet metal workers.

Coming back to the usual sheet metal working procedure, it is to be said that for plate work a butt seam can only be riveted by employing another strip as in Fig. 171. This method is the fundamental of many more or less elaborate methods used in boiler work, but a discussion of such would be out of place here.

Making Lap Seams

From the butt seam the next step in flat seam methods is the lap seam. In plate work lap seams may be welded by the old blacksmith's method as mentioned before, welded by the hot flame process, or, as would be more likely, by riveting. An ordinary riveted lap seam for plate work would appear as shown in Fig. 172. These seams are made steam tight by caulking along edge A; the caulking being done by a chisel-like tool which cleaves the edge of the upper plate and forces a burr of metal down to the under plate.

For seams which are required to be flush on one side the upper plate would be offsetted as shown in Fig. 173, though it is also probable that then the strip method would be used as in Fig. 171; with countersunk head rivets instead of round head.

The seam that, without question, is the most used for sheet metal working is the soldered lap seam shown in Fig. 174. The articles or places where this seam is employed are so well known that it is needless to list them. It goes without dispute that inasmuch as the solder is the means of uniting the parts, the solder should be thoroughly soaked in as shown by the shaded lines.

A riveted lap seam is given in Fig. 175, and when these seams are to be water-tight they are also soldered as in Fig. 174, but need not be so

FIG. 172. A Riveted Lap Seam for Plate.

FIG. 173. Flush Riveted Lap Seam.

FIG. 174. Soldered Lap Seam.

thoroughly sweated in, because the rivets, rather than the solder, are depended on to hold the seam.

Lock and Groove Seams

Some clever genius invented the hook seam shown in Fig. 176 and thereby gave the trade a decidedly useful method of joining sheet metal. This lock seam, as some call it, is merely the turning of edges the opposite way for opposing sides to be joined and then hooking them together and flattening them tight with a mallet like in tin-roofing. These seams can be soldered; however, if positive assurance against unhooking is required, these seams should be grooved as in Fig. 177. The shoulder at A prevents B from slipping out.

There are many methods for making this groove—either by pounding the seam into a slot cut in a rail, or by grooving irons; or again, by grooving machines having a traveling revolving wheel with a groove in it. From the hook seam it is but a step to the standing seam shown in Fig. 178, which can be employed in a number of cases.

FIG. 175. Riveted Lap Seams for Sheet Metal.

FIG. 176. Common Lock Seam for Sheet Metal.

FIG. 177. Groove Seam for Sheet Metal.

FIG. 178. Common Standing Seam for Sheet Metal.

Double and Flange Seams

The seams and methods expounded in the foregoing pages are really the fundamentals of all seams. If a bottom was to be seamed 1 at M to the article shown in Figs. 168 and 169, a little different procedure would be necessary. In the case of Fig. 169, the hooks, flanges, etc., are similar, but the edge is curved and would require a modification of the flat seam method.

Fig. 179 shows how a bottom would be joined to the body in plate work, Fig. 180 being a reverse joint of the same. In the case of Fig. 168 the flanges (A) would be bent up in machines like a brake, but in the case of Fig. 169 the turned up edge would be done by what is termed flangeing. There are machines which do this work with precision, but more often a mechanic would be required to draw up the flange by hammering; an operation that requires the highest order of skill. The joints shown are the basis of many others, such as joining the branch to the pipe in a tee joint.

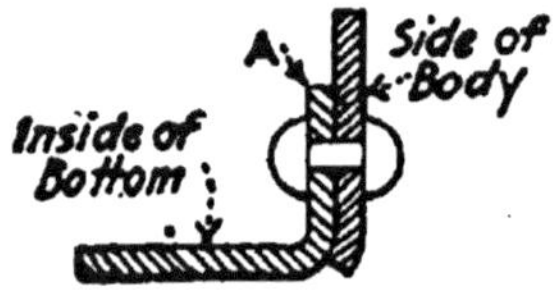

FIG. 179. Seaming a Bottom on in Plate Work.

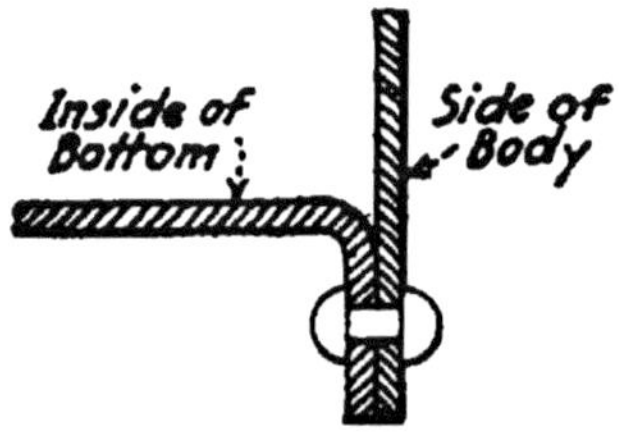

FIG. 180. A Reverse Seam for Bottoms in Plate Work.

In light gauge work a bottom could be simply hooked on as shown in Fig. 181. Often the seam is left that way, but it has nothing to prevent its being unhooked. This can be overcome by doubling over the edge, which gives the well-known double seam shown in Fig. 182. Fig. 183 is a reverse joint like Fig. 180, and is useful where the inside of the

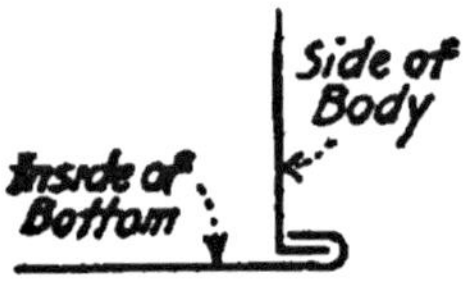

FIG. 181. Single Seam for Sheet Metal.

FIG. 182. Double Seam for Sheet Metal.

FIG. 183. Reverse Double Seam for Sheet Metal.

body is inaccessible for the holding of a dolly bar against the seam for throwing over the edges like, when there is a bottom at M and a head is to be placed at L, Fig. 168-169. Either the method of Fig. 181 or else the method of Fig. 183 would be used if a head was to be placed at L, Fig. 169. Fig. 183 is a seam made by power double seamers.

Stiffening Processes

Plate work, as a rule, has enough inherent stiffness without reinforcing bands. Should reinforcements be required, however, they most likely would be of structural steel shapes like angles, tees, channels and so on. Now, supposing the objects shown in Figs. 168 and 169 are made of plates, and it is required that they be stiffened at L. Usually an angle iron would be riveted there as shown in Fig. 184. This method would also be useful if two of

FIG. 184. Edge Stiffener for Plate.

FIG. 185. Hem Edge Stiffener for Sheet Metal.

FIG. 186. Double Hem for Sheet Metal.

FIG. 187. Band Iron Stiffener for Sheet Metal.

these objects were to be joined at L. Structural shapes would also be employed in a similar manner for ducts and other light gauge work.

It is more probable, though, if edge L is to be stiffened in light gauge work, that the ordinary hem edge shown in Fig. 185 would be used. This could be made stronger by doubling as in Fig. 186. A band iron stiffener shown in Fig. 187 is naturally the strongest of the three methods.

It would seem that the wiring scheme for stiffening should be so well known as to need no description. Still, it may be well to state that the customary method is to first let the edge stand out straight as in Fig. 188; said edge to be about three-quarters the circumference of the wire. Secondly, the edge is thrown over and tucked in, as in Fig. 189, by malleting and using the peen of the hammer. It may also be done on the machines made for that purpose.

Fig. 188. First Operation for Wiring.

Fig. 189. Final Operation for Wiring.

Fig. 190. Sheet Metal Body Stiffener.

Should it be required that a body, like Fig. 168, be stiffened somewhere between its top and bottom, many schemes are available. Structural shapes, band arms, or sheet metal could be bent, as in Fig. 190, and riveted or soldered to the object.

Fig. 191. Bead Swage and Slip Joint.

Fig. 192. Common Ogee Swage.

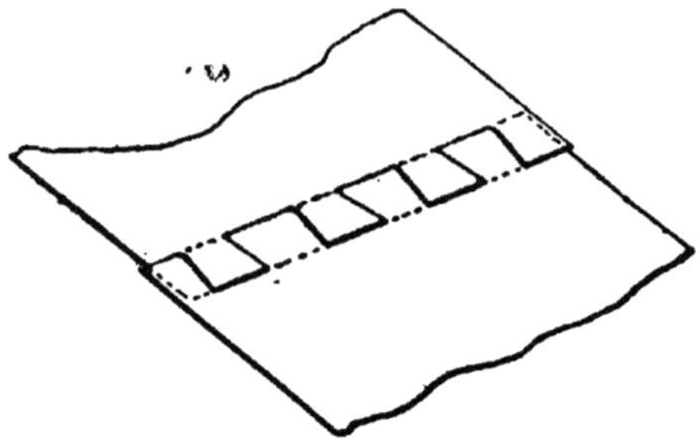

Fig. 193. Brazing Joint for Coppersmithing.

For such objects, as in Fig. 169, swaging is the most common procedure. Swaging is done on machines having two wheels grooved to the required profile of the swage. These wheels engage each other at these grooves and when the sheet metal object is caused to revolve between these wheels, the sheet metal is shaped according to these grooves.

Fig. 191 is a bead groove and Fig. 192 is an ogee groove. These two swages are very useful for joining two lengths of pipes, for they not only stiffen the pipe but also act as a stop, as shown at A in Fig. 191. In such cases edge B, Fig. 191, would probably be crimped by the same kind of a machine, only the wheels would have gear teeth.

Brazed Joint in Coppersmithing

All the methods just described apply to coppersmithing. There is a special method for brazing joints in flat seam work in coppersmithing, however, in which both edges are thinned out and then one edge is notched in to the length of the scarf. Both edges are brought together and the one notch is placed outside while the next is placed inside, about as shown in Fig. 193. Then, while the edges are firmly held together, the joint is brazed and completed by hammering out the joint and otherwise smoothing it off.

Flat Seam in Metal Roofing

The hook seam, shown in Fig. 176, is probably the most used method in metal or tin roofing, regardless of what general system is employed for laying the metal. The custom of nailing through the sheet in flat seam work, at the left of Fig. 194, is a serious error, and should never be done, particularly for copper, and cleats should be used as shown at the right of Fig. 194. The actual appearance of the seams in both of these diagrams is somewhat distorted inside to show the details mentioned.

When "knocking out" strips for flashing, gutters and for long strip, or standing seam roofing, the seam shown in Fig. 176 would be used ninety-nine times out of a hundred. However, a double-lock seam is sometimes used to avoid soldering or to allow for expansion and contraction. Such seams are decidedly difficult to make. The four successive

FIG. 194. Usual Flat Seam Method for Tin Roofing.

steps for making the seam are shown in Fig. 196. An adjustable folding machine is necessary to turn these edges because the first edge, No. 1, has to be turned, being considerably less in width than the second edge, No. 3. It should be clear, too, that in the turning operation of the second edge extreme care is requisite to prevent squashing of

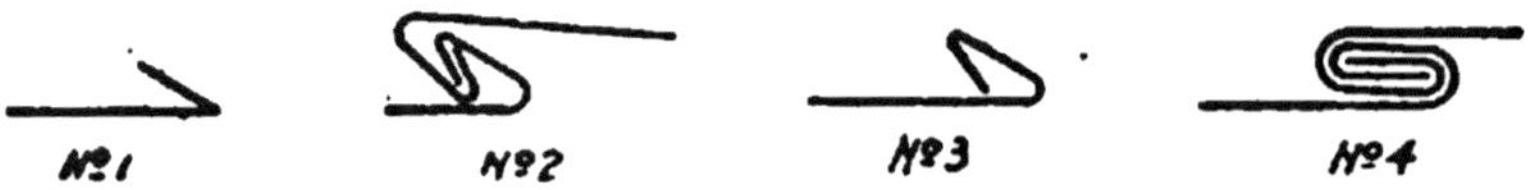

FIG. 195. Double-lock Seam for Tin Roofing.

the first edge. Diagram No. 2 shows the appearance of the seam after the two sheets have been slid together. This is then malleted down tight and will look as shown by diagram No. 4 when finished.

A Novel Flat Seam Procedure

In tin roofing it is often necessary to make a flat seam as the work progresses and sometimes the hook edge of the upper sheet can not be slipped into the lower sheet because the other side of the upper sheet is fast, or for some other reason. In that case, the edge of the upper sheet is not bent entirely over but almost square. Then, as in Fig. 196, the peen of the hammer is used to "peen in" the edge, after which it is flattened down with the mallet.

Fig. 196. Peening an Edge.

Another method would be to turn up square the edge of the lower sheet as at B in diagram No. 1 of Fig. 197. The edge A of the upper sheet is also turned up square, only this edge A should be double the height of edge B.

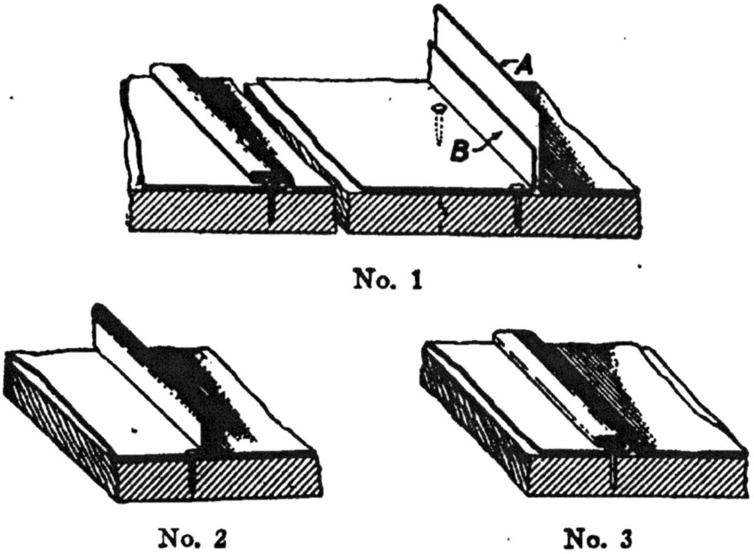

Fig. 197. An Ideal Method.

Edge A is then turned over edge B in any desired manner and appears as in diagram No. 2. This is malleted down and finished like diagram No. 3.

This method would be very handy for joining a new hanging gutter to an old tin roof. The tin should be cut to a straight line and enough left to turn up as high as A in No. 1 diagram and still

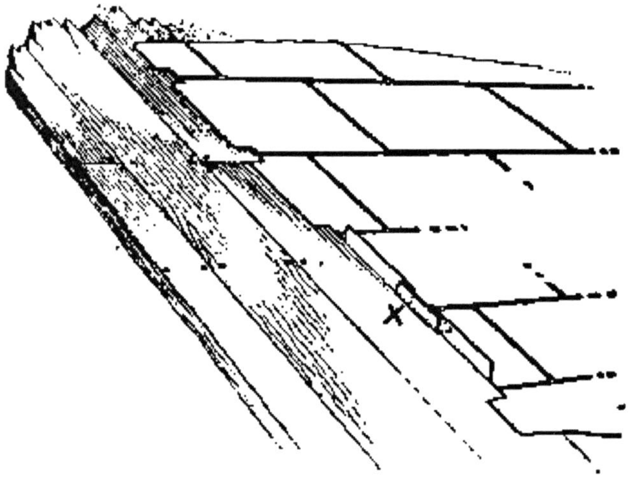

FIG. 198. Example of a Possible Situation.

leave enough to connect to the gutter roof flange. No attempt is made to turn up the cross seam locks of the tin, but they are cut away and a small piece of tin inserted, as at X of Fig. 198, and the rest of the seam made as described before.

Standing Seams for Roofing

Standing seams are used in tin roofing and often in copper roofing, for the long seams; that is, the seams running from the eaves to the ridge, the cross seams being the usual flat seam. The ordinary standing seam shown in Fig. 175 is often used but that does not give satisfaction unless the roof is very steep, or when it is used for siding.

The standing seam, which is doubled over at its top a couple of times, is the most used. The dimensions for opposing edges are shown in Fig. 199. Cleats are nailed to the roof and hooked onto the shortest edge, as in Fig. 200. Sometimes the cleat is placed on the high edge, depending on how the strips are laid, but that gives two turns to the cleat

FIG. 199. First Stage of Seam.

FIG. 200. Second Stage of Seam.

FIG. 201. First Edge Turned.

FIG. 202. Completed Standing Seam.

which is troublesome. With the cleat in place, the next strip is laid and the quarter-inch edge turned over, either with a mallet and roofing iron or with roofing double-seamers, and the seam will look as in Fig. 201. This edge is again turned over as in Fig. 202, which completes the seam which should be one inch high or three-quarters of an inch if

FIG. 203. Plain Sliding Cap.

FIG. 204. Ornamental Cap.

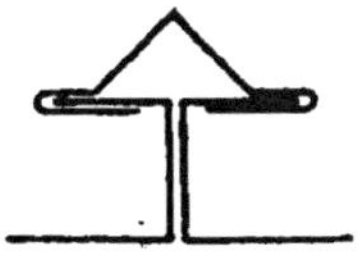

FIG. 205. Stiffer Ornamental Cap.

FIG. 206. Common Type of Sliding Cap.

one inch and one inch and a quarter edges are used.

There are different ways of finishing this seam at the eaves, hip and ridge; that which is most often used is to flatten the seam down for a short distance and seam it right in with the connecting edges to the gutter, hip or ridge.

The sliding cap type shown in Fig. 203 is sufficiently clear to be self-explanatory. By bending a

V in the cap an ornamental effect is obtained as in Fig. 204. In Fig. 205 is shown how a plain V cap gives a somewhat ornamental appearance and more strength to that of Fig. 203.

A common type of sliding cap is given in Fig. 206, and it goes without saying that all these seams must be carefully cut out, bent up and handled because it is not an easy matter to slide these caps onto the upstanding edges. As with the regular type of standing seam, Fig. 200, cleats are the means of fastening the sheets to the roof boards or, if there are no boards, to the roof purlins.

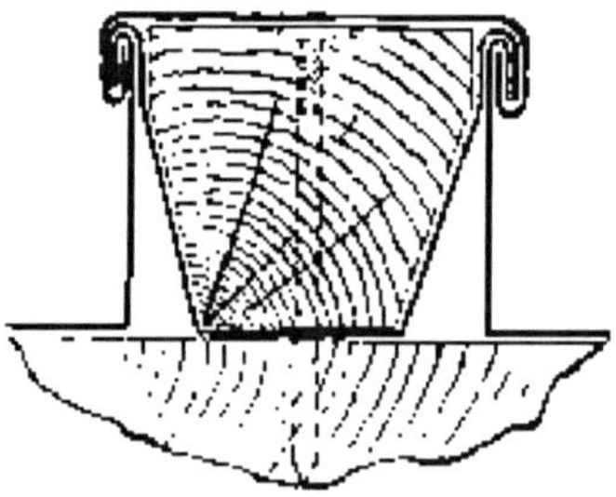

FIG. 207. Ideal Type of Batten Seam.

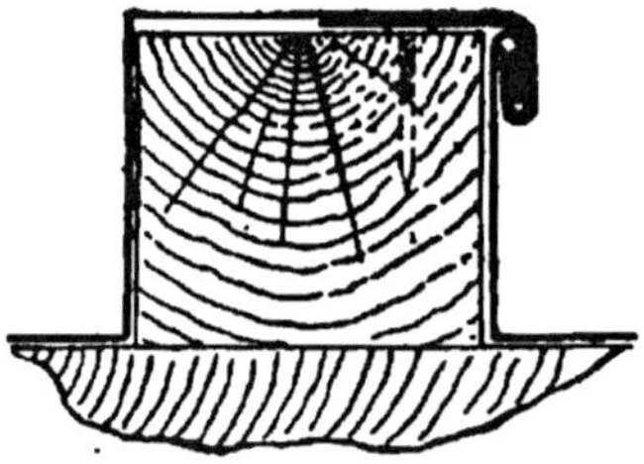

FIG. 208. Quicker Method for Batten Seams.

The wood batten type of roofing is also very common, especially for copper roofing, as it allows maximum provision for expansion and contraction. It is highly desirable when an ornamental and architectural effect is required for a tin roof. Fig. 207 shows the shape of the wood batten which allows movement of the pan in its expansion.

These caps are not slid on but are double-seamed by the customary operations. Fig. 208 shows how the cap can be eliminated and the pan formed to pass over the batten and seamed to the other pan. All the seams so far spoken of are adaptable for many kinds of roofing and the majority of the other types of seams for roofing are just a modification of these.

Seams in Duct Work

Duct work usually means pipe, elbows and other fittings which are rectangular in cross section, as illustrated in Fig. 168. In this class of work nearly all the seams so far discussed can be employed to advantage. The plain standing seam shown in Fig. 175 is frequently used, especially as it helps stiffen the duct. That seam, however, must be strongly

FIG. 209. A Shoulder Standing Seam.

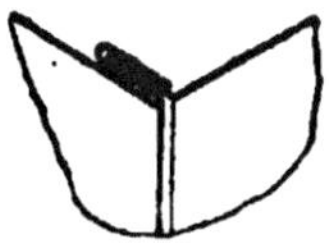

FIG. 210. A Pocket Seam.

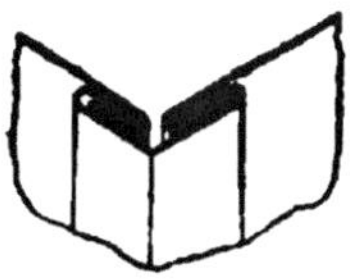

FIG. 211. A Sliding Corner Piece.

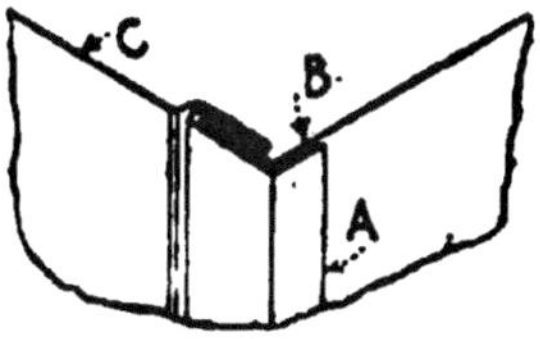

FIG. 212. The Pittsburg Seam or Hobo Seam.

riveted through its upstanding edges to hold together at all. The seam shown in Fig. 209 has a shoulder, A, bent under the opposite side as shown. After clinching edge B, seam cannot come apart.

Should it be desired to have the seam of the pipe at a corner instead of where it is in Fig. 168, many of the methods already mentioned could be used. Still, there are other ways like the pocket seam in Fig. 210—the edge is held in the pocket by soldering or riveting here and there.

A corner seam in which a slide piece is used is shown in Fig. 211. A slide piece like this, only without the square bend, is used at times for a flat seam, but it is not popular because the parts become undone too easily. This method is useful for joining the parts of a casing about a radiator in indirect steam heating.

A seam that is fast superseding the double seam to join the parts of rectangular elbows at their corners, is the Pittsburg or, as some term it, the hobo seam, which is shown in Fig. 212. The edge A is left standing out straight while forming this seam and when assembling the parts; the edge on part B

FIG. 213. Common S Slip.

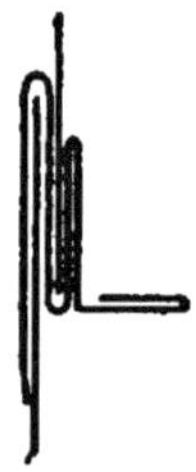

FIG. 214. Stiffened S Slip.

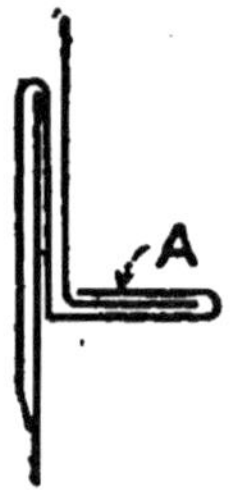

FIG. 215. Standing Edge Slip.

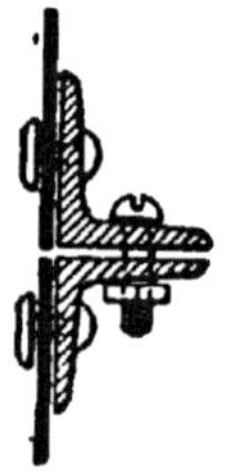

FIG. 216. Angle Connection.

is forced into the pocket of part C and then edge A is hammered over, locking parts C and B firmly together. Note particularly the shoulder on piece C which gives a flush surface and prevents distortion when closing edge A.

Horizontal Joints in Ducts

In all duct work it is necessary to join two or more lengths of pipe at their edges L, Fig. 168. The method generally used is the S slip shown at C in Fig. 213. Part A is the lower length of duct and part B the upper length. The slip is first placed on A and then B is slipped into it. Holes are then drilled through all wherever it is desired to fasten them together and metal screws are inserted.

As ducts are often very wide it is necessary to have a rigid slip and Fig. 214 shows how the hem edge of the S slip is carried down, bent out and then hemmed. This method is really the basis of many other styles used. Sometimes a band iron, or an angle iron or indeed furring strips of wood are encased in this slip to reinforce them.

The popular standing edge slip is shown in Fig. 215. With this method the slip is firmly riveted to the lower duct and the clinch edge A should be standing up square. The upper duct has a square edge bent out and when this is in place the clinch edge is malleted down.

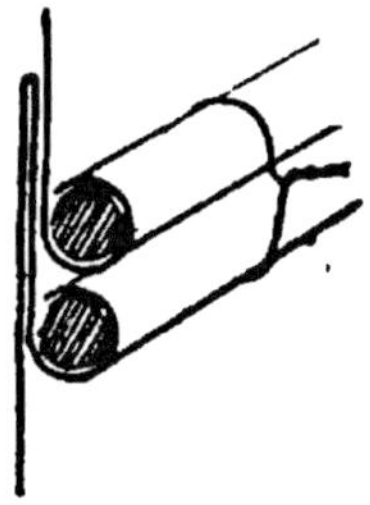

FIG. 217. Slip Joint for Furnace Work.

FIG. 218. Gutter Bead in Lieu of Wire.

FIG. 219. Tapped Band Iron Joint.

For heavy work structural shapes would be used as in Fig. 216. In Fig. 217 is shown the slip joint which is a familiar procedure to old furnace men and is used for cold air boxes. The ducts would be made in four parts, seaming the parts on the corners. Prior to doing this the wires are inserted and on the lower duct about two inches are folded over as shown. A wire drawn through holes in the ducts holds both securely together. Sometimes the gutter bead of Fig. 218 is used in lieu of a wire or rod of Fig. 217.

Quite frequently a joint is to be made where it is impossible to get at the inside for riveting, and it is required that the joint be easily unmade. A good method would be to rivet a band iron to the one part A, as in Fig. 219. Holes are then punched or drilled through the part and the band iron; after which the holes are tapped with a thread suitable for stove bolts. Holes are now accurately punched in the other part, B, to match those in part A, and then stove bolts screwed into the band iron hold all together.

Expansion Joints for Long Gutters

When a large roof is to be covered, and a long copper gutter is used, an expansion joint is constructed and placed at the highest point of the gutter, the water shedding either way to the leader. The method of constructing this joint is shown in Fig. 220. It makes no difference what shape the gutter may have, the same method is employed.

The gutters A and B meet at the highest point; two heads or bottoms C and D are flanged and soldered in the gutter, having an upper flange bent towards the inside of the gutter, as shown. On the roof part of the gutter a lock is bent as shown by E and F. Over these locks E and F and over the flanges on the heads a lock is slipped as shown by H, allowing it to run under the lock of the gutter as shown by J, the lock of the gutter being broken, to clearly show the slip. At the bottom the slip is allowed to project slightly over the front edge of the gutter, as shown by I.

The roof covering shown by L is locked to the gutter, overlapping the slip J as shown. Thus it will be seen that no soldering has been done, which allows the gutter to work as desired. To avoid the water from following the top of the slip H and dripping off over the front edge of the gutter, a V-shaped guard is soldered to the top of the slip

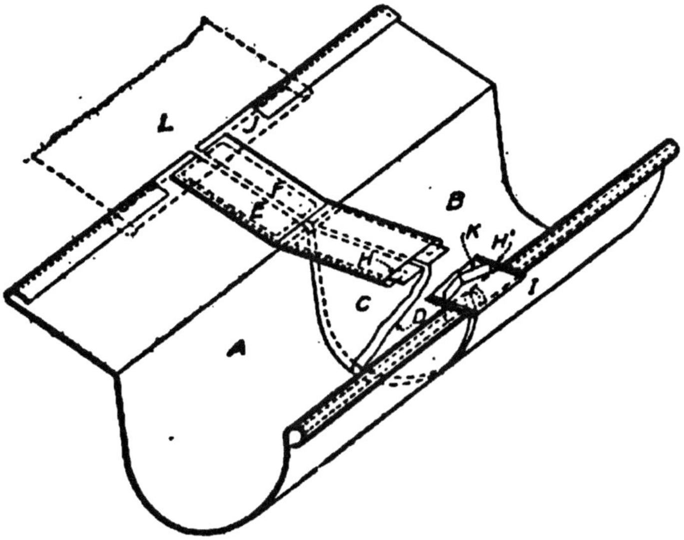

FIG. 220. Expansion Joint in Long Gutter.

H, as shown at K, which leads the water right and left into the gutter as at H^1.

Connecting Furnace Pipes to Furnace Tops

When furnace-warm-air pipes are to be connected to furnace hoods, as shown in A in Fig. 221, it is well to know the different methods which are used, so that the one best adapted can be employed in making the connections. As every collar in most cases has a different angle, the collars are usually trimmed at the job as follows: Run a line or spool wire from the register box on the first floor, or from the stacks leading to the upper floors, to the bonnet or hood, as indicated by the dotted lines *a, b* and *c*, which gives the proper angle at which the collars are to be cut to fit against the hood.

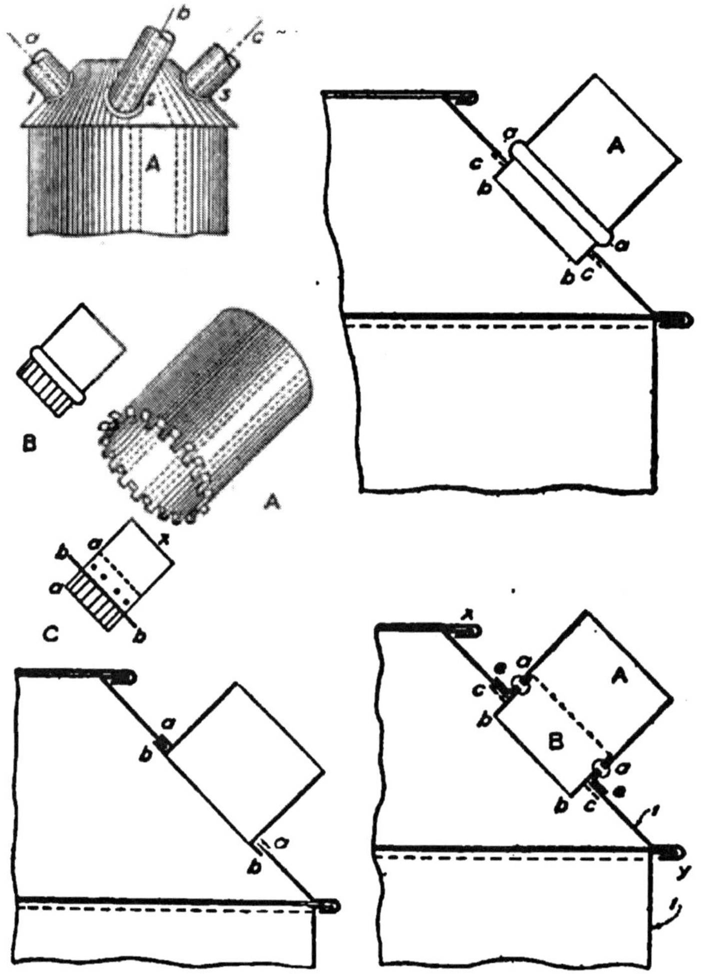

FIG. 221. Connecting Furnace Pipes to Tops.

After the collar has been fitted accurately it is held tightly against the hood and a pencil mark made on the hood and carefully cut out with the circular shears. Each collar is marked to correspond to the opening in the hood, as shown by

1, 2, 3, etc., as shown. The collars can now be joined to the hood by either one of the methods shown, A showing a notched or dove-tailed collar; B, a beaded notched collar and C, a flanged and notched collar.

Note in the collar A the alternate flanges are turned out at right angles, as shown, so that when the collar is joined to the hood, as shown in the diagram below C in the accompanying illustration, the edges just turned lie tight against the outside of the hood at *a a*, while the unturned edges are turned on the inside of the bonnet at *b b*. These edges are dressed down firmly, which secures the collar ready to connect with the warm-air pipe.

When the collar is beaded and notched, as shown by B, this collar is secured to the hood, as shown in the diagram in the upper right-hand corner of the illustration at A. The collar is set in the opening in the hood, with the bead snugly against the hood, as shown by *a a*, after which the flange *b b*, which is already notched, is turned over as shown by *c c*. The flanging and notching of the collar C is accomplished by first flanging the collar *x* at *b* and *b* until this flange fits snugly against the hood. A separate collar *a a* is now riveted to the main collar *x* as shown and notched at *a*.

When connecting this collar to the hood as shown in the diagram in the lower left-hand corner of the illustration, the main collar A is set tightly against the hood as shown by *e e* and the notched portion *b b* of the collar B which had previously been riveted to the collar A at *a* and *a* is then turned against the inside of the hood at *c* and *c*. Of course it is understood that the seaming at *x* and *y* is not done until the collars have been joined to the hood. After the collars were all fitted a mark was made at *1* on the hood and *1* on the casing as shown, after which the hood was removed from the casing, the collars secured and the hood set back again on the casing in its proper position as shown by the marks *1* and *1* and then seams *x* and *y* closed.

Connecting Collars to Register Boxes

Another method of seaming collars is shown in Fig. 222, where in diagram 1 it will be seen that

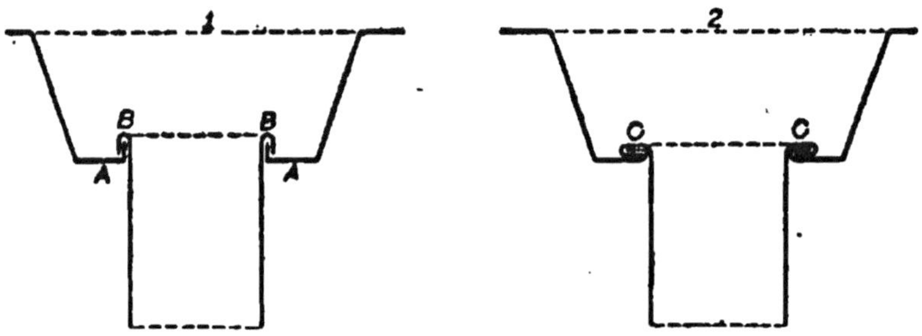

FIG. 222. First Method of Seaming Collars to Register Boxes.

the flange of the circular opening in the bottom is turned upward as shown at A, and the collar has a flange turned over and pressed tight with the flat pliers as shown by B. This seam B is now turned down as indicated in diagram 2 at C.

Fig. 223 shows the second method of securing the collar by means of flanging and notching. After the proper size circle has been cut in the bottom of the register box, the collar is prepared, around which another short collar about 2 inches high shown by *a* in diagram 1 is riveted at *b*, being careful to turn out a flange of about 1/4 inch on *a* before

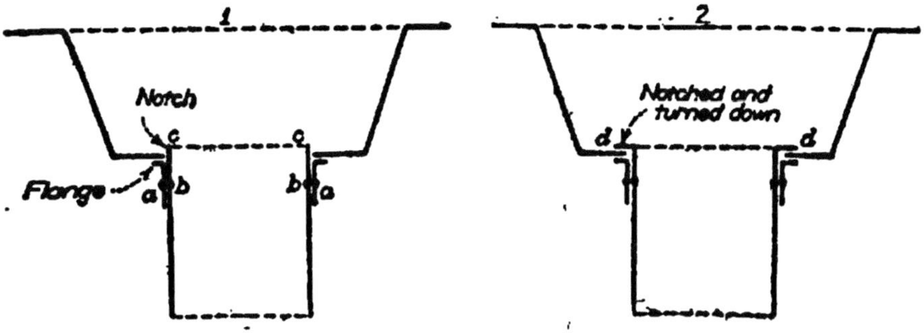

FIG. 223. Second Method of Seaming Collars.

riveting to the main collar *c*. Rivet this short collar *a* about 3/8 inch below the main collar as shown in the cut; then set the collar in the position as shown in diagram 1, notch with the snips the projecting flange *c* and dress down tightly on the stake as shown by *d* in diagram 2.

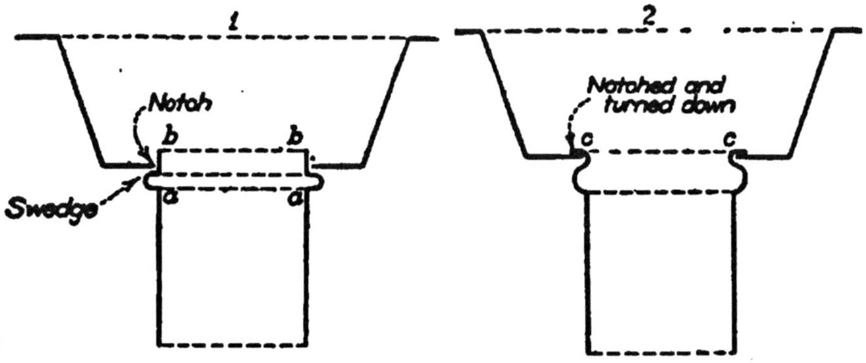

FIG. 224. Third Method of Fastening Collars.

The third method shown in Fig. 224 shows how the collar can be secured to the box by swaging and notching. Turn a swage or bead 1/8 or 1/4 inch deep on to the end of the collar, about 3/8 inch away from the ends as shown by *a a* in diagram 1. See that it fits snugly in the circular opening in the bottom of the register box, then notch the projecting flange *b* and dress it down tightly on the stake, so that when finished it will have the appearance shown by *c* in diagram 2.

While the last two methods are quick and simple, still either one of the first two methods are to be recommended as they are more rigid and tighter.

Expansion Joint of Skylight

Some large buildings, especially if they are built largely of steel or the more modern reinforced con-

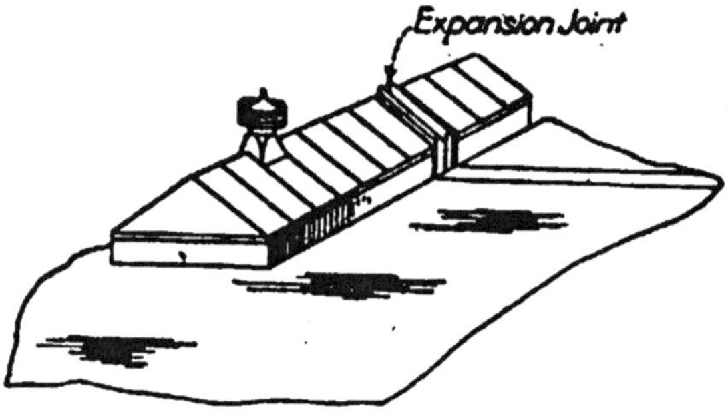

FIG. 225. Skylight with Expansion Joint.

crete type, have expansion joints, and often skylights or other work which sheet metal workers do come directly over these joints, and then the designers, as a rule, insist that that joint be also followed through this work.

The example given in Fig. 225 is for a skylight of the double pitch type and is about 20 feet wide at the curb line by some 600 feet in length. The skylight is directly over three expansion joints of the building transversing it. The expansion joints are in everything, the steel work, the walls, the concrete roof slabs, the gravel roofs, the curb, the flashing and the skylight.

In Fig. 226 is shown a rough idea of how the special bar is made. Spanning the space between two bars is a heavy sheet lead cap which is brass bolted to the bars and bent as shown for the obvious reason of allowing extension and compression and also to give the necessary rigidity. The

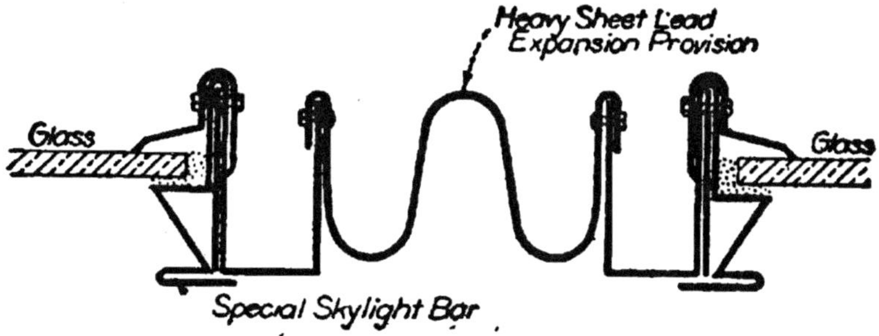

FIG. 226. Special Expansion Skylight Bar.

gravel roof and the curb flashing have a combination sheet metal and tar expansion joint, and the sheet lead cap mentioned and the apron of the skylight were made to fit loosely over this curb joint, for it would not do to miter and carry the sheet lead cap down the curb to form an apron over the joint inasmuch as said miter would be so stiff as to nullify the freedom of the cap. This applies to mitering the caps together at the ridge, and they were simply kept a short distance from each other and the opening covered with a sheet lead cap not fastened to the other caps but beneath to the ridge bar of one part of the skylight.

Joints for Corrugated Iron

Corrugated sheets may be had in many lengths and widths and corrugated in many styles and dimensions. A popular style is shown in Fig. 228.

Specifications for sheet metal enclosures usually call for a sheet like Fig. 227 for siding, as it gives one corrugation lap. For roofing the specifications prescribe sheets like that in Fig. 228, which give one and one-half corrugation.

Fig. 227. One Corrugation Lap.

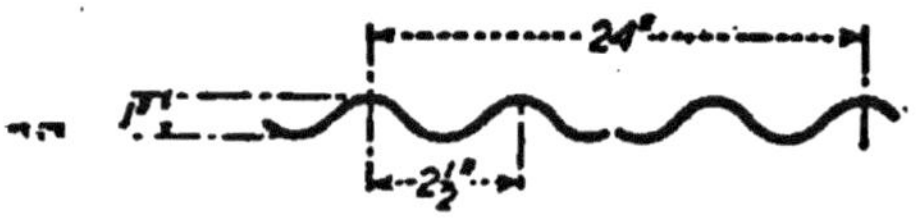

Fig. 228. One and One-Half Corrugation Lap.

When lapping sheets of Fig. 228 they would appear as in Fig. 229. Horizontal laps are merely lap seams and should lap at least six inches. Sheets should never be lapped as in Fig. 230, because the standing edge will show buckled and is therefore

Fig. 229. Proper Method of Lapping.

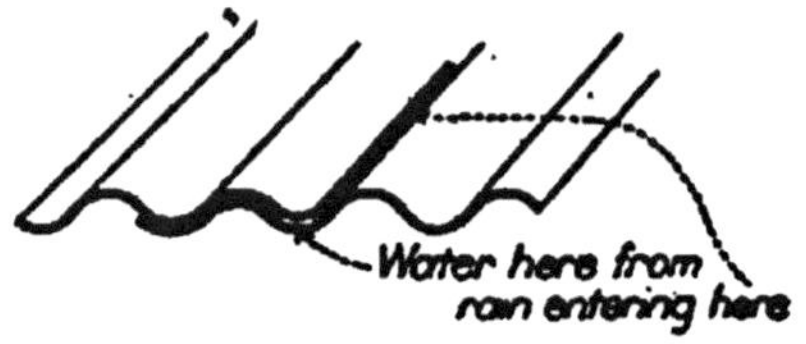

Fig. 230. Improper Method of Lapping.

unsightly. It will not leak, however, though water will get under the first lap and, having no chance to dry out, will eventually rot out the sheets. In the ideal method of Fig. 229 edge *a* should not go down into the corrugation because capillary attraction will draw water up under the edge *a*.

The method of finishing against the gable or sides of the structure is shown in Fig. 231; note how one or two corrugations are flattened out and then bent up to form a base flashing. At the eaves, of course, the sheets would lap over the roof flange of the gutter. Fig. 232 shows how a molding can be connected to the corrugated roofing. This is an ideal method and could also be used in a case like Fig. 231. A pocket in the foot of the molding is the means of finishing the molding to the siding.

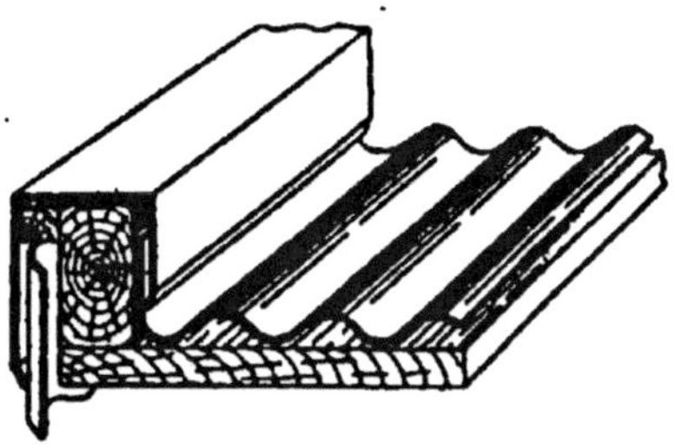

FIG. 231. Finish Against a Side Parapet.

The joints given in Figs. 231 and 232 are the basis for all other joints like window and door cas-

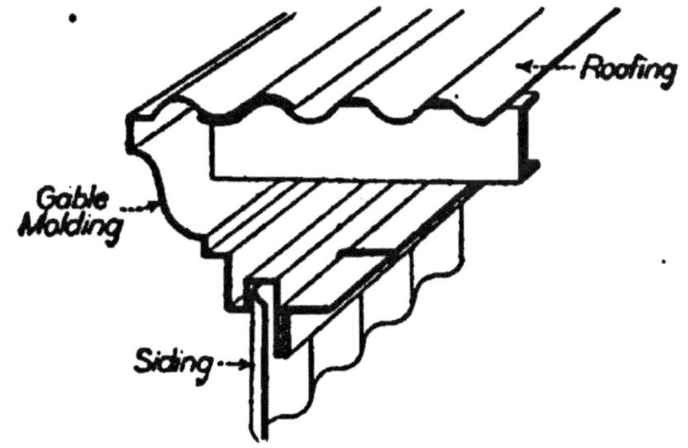

FIG. 232. Joining a Gable Molding to Corrugated Roof.

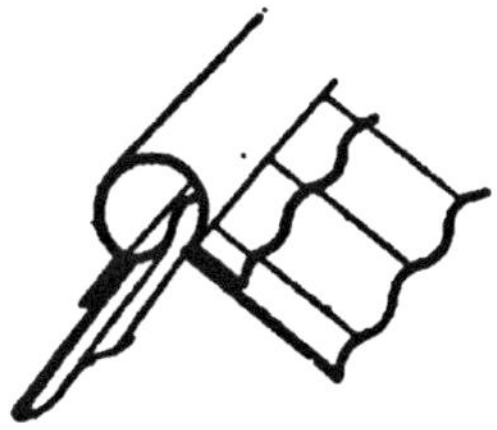

FIG. 233. Ridge Finish, Showing Ridge Roll.

ings. Fig. 233 shows the ridge finish, in which the apron of the ridge molding is corrugated to match the corrugated sheets. Pockets are not desirable at a ridge owing to the need of making them very deep to keep rain or snow from beating in the pocket and under the sheets into the building.

Straight Cornice Seams

Nearly all the common seams presented in this chapter can be used for architectural sheet metal work. As a rule, all vertical seams in straight cornices are the lap seam kind, soldered and riveted. The horizontal seams are also very often just lap seams soldered and riveted. The same is true of

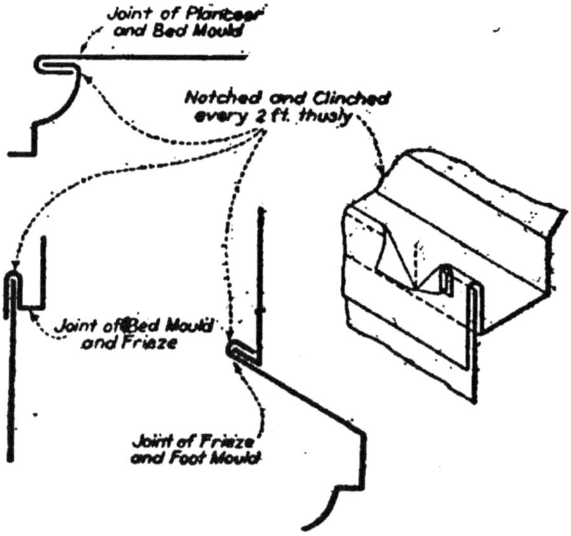

FIG. 234. Several Types of Joints for Straight Cornices.

the seams used for joining the different minor parts to the body of the cornice.

In Fig. 234 is shown a popular system for making the horizontal joints in cornices. These are all just clinched edge seams as shown. And while they are tacked with solder here and there, they are further strengthened and made fireproof by notching the standing edges and folding them over tightly as shown. The notching should not be done with a chisel as that mars the work, but with a special stubby point snips.

Seams in Circular Cornices

As in straight cornice work, the vertical seams in circular cornice work are lap seams soldered and riveted. In horizontal seams, however, the clinched hook edge is not practical and these must be lapped and then soldered and riveted as in

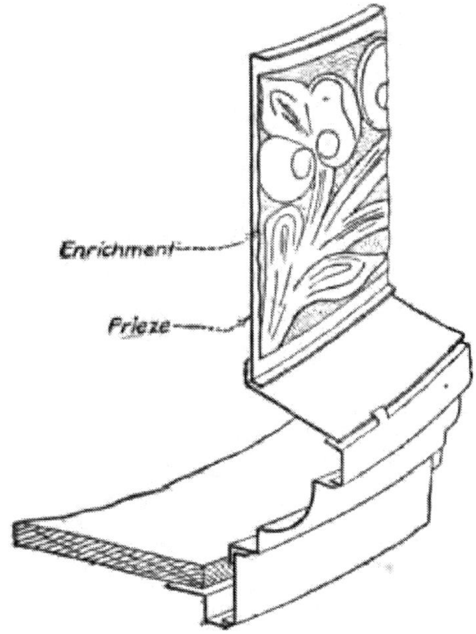

FIG. 235. Joining Frieze to Foot Mold Wash.

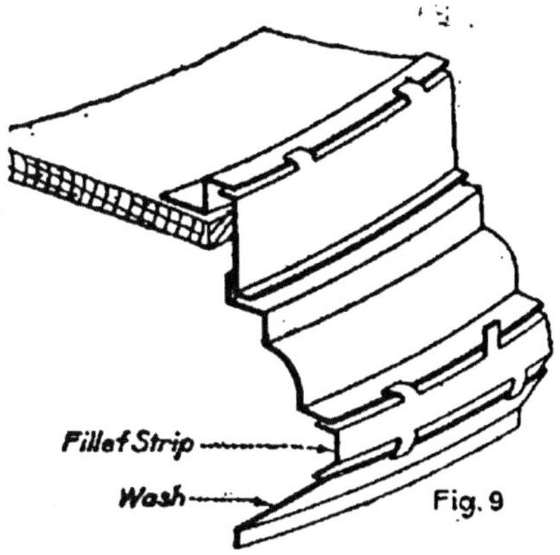

FIG. 236. Inverted Foot Mold Showing Joints.

Fig. 235. Many shops greatly strengthen these seams by first notching the edges and turning up small laps, about one-quarter of an inch wide and about six inches apart. Then as the parts of the cornice are gradually worked together, as in Fig. 236, these laps are hammered down and strongly soldered along the soldering of the edges.

The two diagrams do not show a complete cornice because the crown mold is not there; however, the same methods apply to that part of the cornice or rather entablature. Note how the parts are fastened to a circular wood template while assembling.

Sheet Metal Shingle Locks

Sheet metal shingles and tiles can be had from the manufacturers in single units or several on a sheet. There is not much difference in the procedure of laying sheet metal shingles or tiles from that of clay tiles or wooden shingles except that the joints are different.

The horizontal seams are always lap seams, the lower edge of the tile or shingle is slightly curled

FIG. 237.—Common Metal Shingle Joint.

FIG. 238.—High Grade Shingle Lock.

to stiffen it and the upper edge has a series of guide corrugations to both stiffen and act as a guide for laying the next course.

The vertical seams have special pocket features to obviate soldering and still have tight joints. These pockets vary with each manufacturer and are patented. They all follow, however, a basic idea as given in Fig. 237. It will be seen that a tile, or shingle, is laid and a couple of roofing nails are driven into the edge provided for these nails; the adjoining tile or shingle has its edge slipped into the pocket and its edge nailed and so on. Fig. 238 shows another style of side joint.

Joints in Automobiles

Modern automobile making is essentially quantity production and most work, such as forming, joining, etc., is done on special automatic machines. These joints, seams and so forth are adaptations of the old tinsmith's processes, even to the swaging, riveting and stiffening of the sheet metal.

FIG. 239.—Tube Stiffening for Sheet Edges.

FIG. 240.—Half Round Band Iron for Stiffening.

The average tinsmith is not concerned with these methods except for repairing and, in that case, he

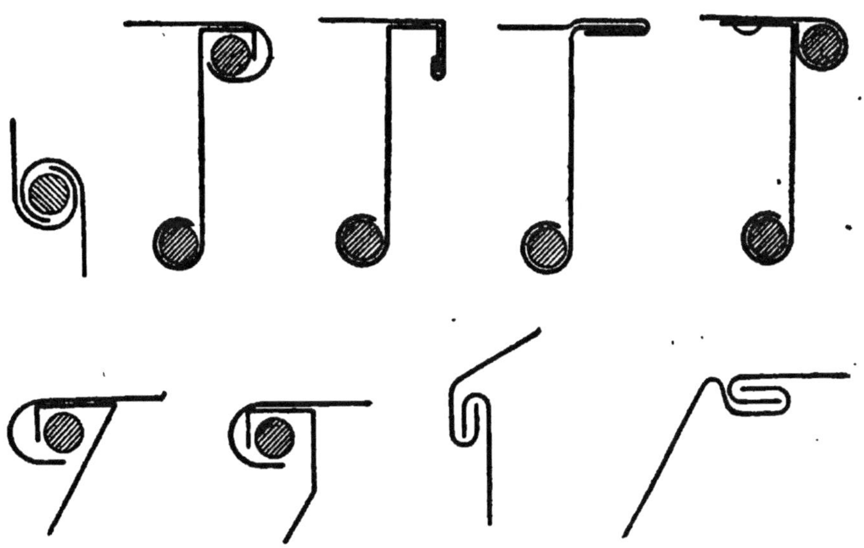

FIG. 241.

Diagrams Detailing Some of the Principal Automobile Joints.

would have the guidance of the article to be repaired.

Wood is seldom used now, but where it is, the joining of the metal to wood is by customary methods of pockets in the sheet metal and by screws or bolts.

One of the methods for stiffening edges is by splitting a tube longitudinally and slipping the sheet metal into the slot in the tube as in Fig. 239. These tubes are curved if necessary and are fastened to the sheet by welding or soldering. Another method is shown in Fig. 240, which is by a half-round band iron flush riveted to the sheet. Other joints for dash boards, mud guards, hinge joints and body seams are shown in Fig. 241.

Tin Clad Fire Doors—Joints and Seams

A sketch of a fire door is shown in Fig. 242. These doors are built up of two or more ply of

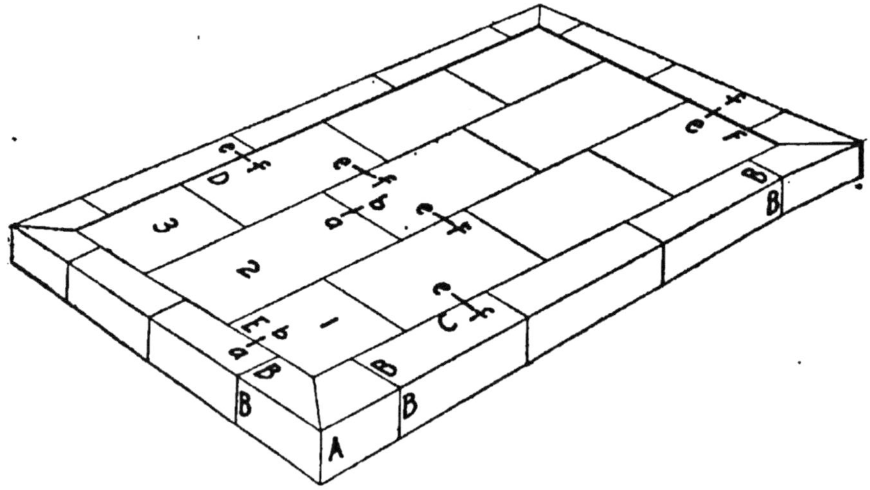

FIG. 242.—Tin Clad Fire Door.

seven-eighth boards firmly clinched-nailed together in accordance with the underwriter's specifications. They are then covered on both sides with tin plates of practically the same kind as for tin roofing. The seams, however, are not the same as in tin roofing.

The corner pieces A are made separate and are put on first. These are made in one piece and folded, much like the corners of a drip pan, as shown in Fig. 243. There are no nails placed in the folded miter so that it requires care to keep the miter from gaping. One or two roofing nails may be driven in under the hook edges at B, Fig. 242, to hold the pan in position.

The casing from B to B, Fig. 242, is made in one piece by knocking out a strip like that used for flashing. This is then bent to bind around the edge of the door, and two hook edges are also bent out. These casings are then seamed to the corner pans at B, and roofing nails may be driven in under C, here and there, to keep the casing in place and to a true line.

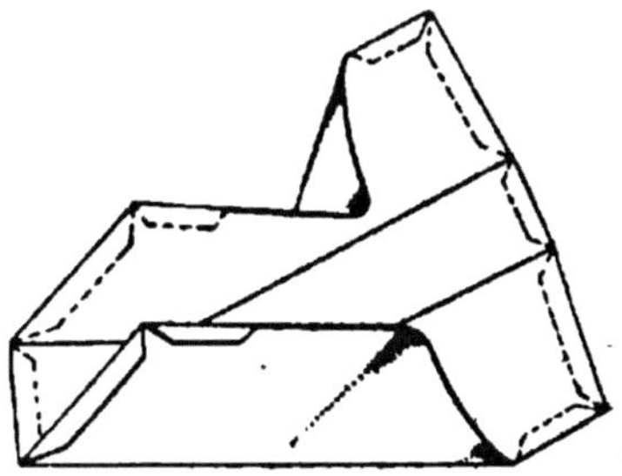

FIG. 243.—Corner Pan in One Piece.

The tin sheets are now notched and bent to look like Fig. 244, except those for the last course, at D, Fig. 242, which have the standing edge on both long sides. The sheets are laid by beginning at E, Fig. 242. The edge bent out square is inserted in the edge of pan and casing, as in Fig. 245, which is a section on line *a b* of Fig. 242. With the sheet standing up square, long barb wire nails are driven in in the edges as in Fig. 245. The

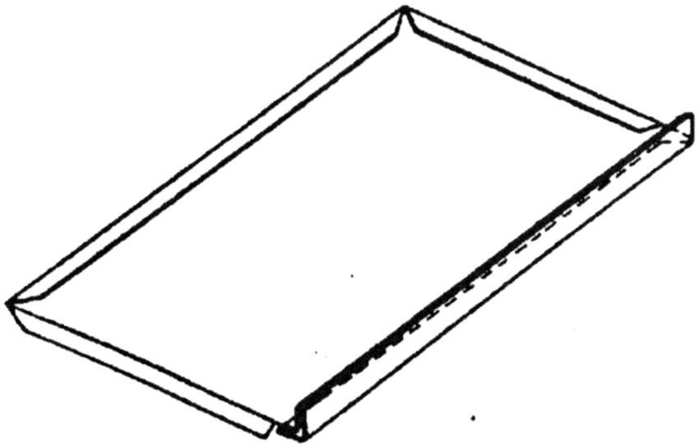

FIG. 244.—How Sheets Are Bent.

sheet is now carefully folded down over the nails like in Fig. 246, which is also a section of the pan and casing seams on line *a b*, Fig. 242.

FIG. 245.—The First Step in Laying the Sheets.

The turned under edge of the standing seams is now forced into the hook seam of the pan and casing as in Fig. 247. As before, long barb wire nails are driven in as shown. The next sheet is then put on in the same way and then the third finishing to the top pan and casing F, Fig. 242, with the standing edge seam.

FIG. 246.—The Flat-hooked Seams.

FIG. 248.—The Closed Down Seam on *e, f*, Fig. 210.

The next course, No. 2, is laid in the same manner, then No. 3 course, after which the standing edges are carefully malleted down, as in Fig. 248 to cover the nails which, by the way, should be three inches apart.

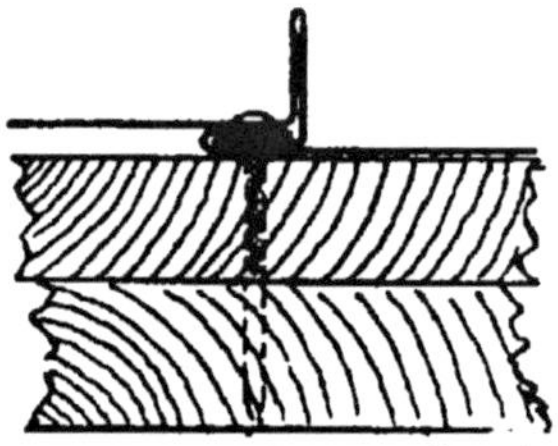

FIG. 247.—Cross Section on Line *e f* of Fig. 210.

The door is now turned over and the other side covered in a like manner. If labels are to be attached they should be riveted and soldered to one of the sheets before the sheet is laid. And, if the door is to be exposed to the weather, the upper seam at F would be a hooked flat seam on the exposed side of the door, so that the rain would flow over and not into the seam.

CHAPTER X

Roofing Slates and Tiles

One branch of tinsmithing is metal roofing using terne plates or copper or other sheet metal to cover the entire roof surface. There are, however, many other kinds of material used for roof covering; but, in most cases, it is necessary to use sheet metal in connection with this material. It is probably for this reason that the tinsmith is called upon to lay slate or vitrified tile roofing. It is always, therefore, a good idea for the tinsmith to know something about these materials, hence the presentation of this short chapter written by an expert in a well-known publication. Further information of all kinds of roofing is given in the series entitled "Practical Sheet Metal Worker and Demonstrated Patterns."

Laying Roofing-Tiles

Roofing-tiles have been laid directly on a porous book tile or concrete base or on a sheathed surface over such base, or they have been fastened to stripping over the sheathing or wooden or steel purlins by means of copper wires. When thus fastened by wires, the joints were usually pointed on the under side after they were laid, to prevent the entrance of dust or dry snow. Tiles of the older patterns were nailed to the sheathing, but later on this method was superseded by the practice of fastening with copper wires from pierced lugs near the lower ends of the tiles.

The best modern method, however, seems to be the one involving a solid continuous base for the roofing-tiles, whether or not purlins are used. "Such purlins should be filled in between either with book tiles or a concrete base and felt should be laid thereon. The book tiles, if used, should be of a porous quality. Instead of regarding the nailing of tiles as a defective method, it has been found that it is the only proper method of fastening tiles and has eliminated the stripping of sheathed roofs and the use of copper wires. Such methods would do in some portions of central Europe where the winds and other climatic conditions are not severe, but through a twenty-five years' experience in the varied climatic conditions of the United States it was found that the nailing of tiles with copper nails is the only satisfactory method of application. It was also found that a roof should be sheathed and covered with a good asphaltum-felt to prevent wind-suction and condensation.

Valuable information, of course, can be had in the literature furnished by makers of tiles. These remarks apply to the many types of tiles as flat tiles, pan and roll tiles and Spanish tiles. It is also of interest to state that tiles can be had transparent, like glass, for the admission of light to the interior of the structure. Tiles can also be had which are made of cement or cement and asbestos, also of sheet metal.

Best Sizes for Slate Roofing

The size of slates best adapted for plain roofs are the large wide slates, such as 12 x 16 inches, 18 x 12 inches, 20 x 12 inches, or 24 x 14 inches. Slates from 8 x 16 to 10 x 20 inches are popular sizes, 9 x 18-inch slates being probably used oftener than those of any other size. The 11 x 22 and 12 x 24-inch slates are used principally on very large high buildings. The lower grades of slate are used largely on warehouses and barns. The larger sizes make fewer joints in the roof, require fewer nails, and diminish the number of small pieces at hips and valleys. For roofs cut up into small sections the smaller sizes, such as 14 x 7 inches or 16 x 8 inches, look the best.

Measuring for Slates

Slates are sold by the square, by which is meant a sufficient number of slates of any size to cover 100 square feet of surface on a roof, with 3 inches of lap, over the head of those in the second course below. The square is also the basis on which the cost of laying is measured. Tables giving the weight and number of slate required per square of roof are given on page 297. Eaves, hips, valleys and cuttings against walls or dormers are measured extra; 1 foot wide of their whole length, the extra charge being made for waste material and the increased labor required in cutting and fitting. Openings less than 3 square feet are not deducted, and all cuttings around them are measured extra. Extra charges are also made for borders, figures, and any change of color of the work and for steeples, towers and perpendicular surfaces.

Slates from the quarry must be in carload lots to get the best freight rates. If a contract does not require a carload, it can be made up of various kinds of slates for stock in hand; it is good stock and can be realized on any time.

Laying Slates

Slates are laid either on a board sheathing (rough, or tongued and grooved) covered with tarred or water-proof paper or felt, or on roofing-laths from 2 to 3 inches wide and from 1 to 1¼ inches thick, nailed to the rafters at distances apart to suit the gauge of the slates. Each slate should lap the slate in the second course below, 3 inches. The slates are fastened with two threepenny or fourpenny nails, one near each upper corner. For slates 20 x 10 inches or larger, fourpenny nails should be used. Copper, composition, tinned, or galvanized nails should be used. Plain-iron nails are speedily weakened by rust, and they break and allow the slates to be blown off. On iron roofs slates are often placed directly on small iron purlins spaced at suitable distances apart to receive them, and fastened with wire or special forms of fasteners. The gauge of a slate is the portion exposed to the weather, which should be one-half the remainder obtained by subtracting 3 inches from the length of the slate. Roofs to be covered with slate should have a rise of not less than 6 inches to the foot for 20-inch or 24-inch slates, or 8 inches for smaller sizes. When driving the nails into the slates extreme care is to be used because, if nails are driven too tight the slate may crack, or if it does not while driving the nails, freezing weather, followed by a thaw, will crack them or burst the nail head through allowing the slate to fall down. If the nails are driven too loose the slates will not be held firmly to the sheathing and may break the slate above which is lying on it.

In first-class work the top course of slate on the ridge, and slate for from 2 to 4 feet from all gutters and 1 foot each way from all valleys and hips, should be bedded in elastic cement.

Counterflashings are of lead or zinc, and are laid between the courses in brick, and turned down over the flashings. In flashings against stonework, grooves or reglets often have to be cut to receive the counterflashings.

Close and Open Valleys

A close valley is one in which the slates are mitered and flashed in each course and laid in cement. In such valleys no metal can be seen. Close valleys should only be used for pitches above 45°. An open valley is one formed of sheets of copper or zinc 15 or 16 inches wide, over which the slates are laid.

Old English Method of Laying Slates

This method of laying slates involves the use of different shades of colored slates in graduated courses and in random widths beginning at the eaves, for example, with slates 28 inches long and

1¼ inches thick, and using the different thicknesses from 1¼ to ⅜ inch, in shorter lengths, in working upward on the roof. The use of this kind of work for roofs has increased in recent years and the method possesses vast possibilities for carrying out architects' ideas for varied artistic effects. The slates are made with rough-cut edges in all thicknesses from 3/16 to 1½ inches, in a combination of various shades carefully selected in such proportion as to produce the best possible harmony, when laid. As all of these colors and shades are unfading, the weathered effect is obtained at once and is permanent. These slates are made not only in usual sizes, but in the Old English style, to be laid in graduated courses of different lengths and in random widths. When graduated courses are desired, specifications should call for the number of courses to be laid in each length and thickness beginning at the eaves courses, where the thickest slates are used in the largest sizes, sometimes 30 or even 36 inches in length, and working upward on the roof with the shorter lengths and thinner slates to the ridges where the smallest sizes and thinnest slates are used. To secure a rough effect at minimum cost, use Old English color-combination, all slates fully ¼ inch thick with rough cut edges and graduated courses in sizes ranging from 24 by 16 to 12 by 6 inches, with nail-holes drilled and countersunk. To secure the best rough effect, use not less than ¾ inch thick for the eaves, and any desired number of courses in each length and thickness.

CHAPTER XI

Handy Receipts and Formulas

Aluminum Solders

The following aluminum solders have been successfully used:

Tin	Aluminum	Zinc	Copper	Bismuth	Lead	Phosphor-tin*	Silver	Antimony	Cadmium	Magnesium
95.00	.....	.....	.....	5.00	.....	.....	.....	.....	.....	.....
78.50	2.00	19.00	.....	.....	.....	0.50	.....	.....	.....	.....
.....	66.70	.....	.....	.....	.....	.....	33.30	.....	.....	.....
20.00	70.00	.....	.....	.....	.....	.....	10.00	.....	.....	.....
97.00	.....	.....	.....	3.00	.....	.....	.....	.....	.....	.....
.....	6.00	89.50	4.50	.....	.....	.....	.....	.....	.....	.....
71.25	2.25	26.00	.....	.....	.....	0.50	.....	.....	.....	.....
60.00	4.00	8.00	4.00	.....	12.00	.....	12.00	.....	.....	.....
37.50	.....	25.00	37.50	.....	.....	.....	.....	.....	.....	.....
.....	8.00	92.00	.....	.....	.....	.....	.....	.....	.....	.....
30.00	.....	20.00	.....	.....	.....	.....	.....	.....	50.00	.....
80.00	2.25	17.00	.....	.....	.....	0.75	.....	.....	.....	.....
66.00	15.50	.....	.....	9.00	.....	.....	.....	7.00		† 2.25
15.50	2.50	78.25	.....	.....	2.50	1.25	.....	.....	.....	.....
.....	20.00	65.00	15.00	.....	.....	.....	.....	.....	.....	.....
49.05	.....	20.31	1.15	.....	26.06	.....	.....	3.43	.....	.....
30.00	70.00	.....	.....	.....	.....	.....	.....	.....	.....	.....
.....	4.00	94.00	2.00	.....	.....	.....	.....	.....	.....	.....
85.10	10.80	.....	.....	.....	.....	.....	.....	.....	1.35	2.75
60.00	.....	15.00	.....	5.00	10.00	.....	.....	5.00	.....	‡
86.00	.....	.....	.....	14.00	.....	.....	.....	.....	.....	.....
98.00	1.00	.....	.....	1.00	.....	.....	.....	.....	.....	.....
20.00	70.00	.....	10.00	.....	.....	.....	.....	.....	.....	.....
48.00	2.00	27.00	.....	.....	23.00	.....	.....	.....	.....	.....
90.00	5.00	.....	.....	5.00	.....	.....	.....	.....	.....	.....
84.95	.....	.....	.....	15.05	.....	.....	.....	.....	.....	.....

* 10% phosphorous. † This solder also contains 0.25% vanadium. ‡ This solder also contains 5% chromium.

Novel's Solder for Aluminum Bronze

Tin, 900 parts, copper, 100, bismuth, 2 to 3.

It is claimed that this solder is also suitable for joining aluminum to copper, brass, zinc, iron or nickel.

Novel's Solders for Aluminum

Tin, 100 parts,	lead, 5;	melts at 536°	to 572° F.
" 100 "	zinc, 5;	" " 536	" 612
" 1000 "	copper, 10 to 15;	" " 662	" 842
" 1000 "	nickel, 10 to 15;	" " 662	" 842

Soldering and Welding Aluminum

Another authority states that aluminum can be readily electrically welded, but soldering is not altogether satisfactory. The high heat conductivity of the aluminum withdraws the heat of the molten solder so rapidly that it "freezes" before it can flow sufficiently. A German solder, said to give good results, is made of 80% tin to 20% zinc, using a flux composed of 80 parts stearic acid, 10 parts chloride of zinc, and 10 parts of chloride of tin. Pure tin, fusing at 250° C., has also been used as a solder. The use of chloride of silver as a flux has been patented, and used with ordinary soft solder has given some success. A pure nickel soldering-bit should be used, as it does not discolor aluminum as copper bits do.

Preparation and Application of Aluminum Solders

Tin, 95 to 99: Bismuth, 5 to 8.

This composition, which is an ordinary soft solder, is adapted for soldering aluminum by means of the common soldering iron.

No. 1		No. 2		No. 3	
Zinc	80 parts	Zinc	85 parts	Zinc	90 parts
Copper	8 parts	Copper	6 parts	Copper	4 parts
Aluminum	12 parts	Aluminum	5 parts	Aluminum	6 parts

In preparing aluminum solders the alloy of copper and aluminum is always made first and the zinc added. The zinc used should contain no iron as it will affect the fusibility and durability of the solder. In preparing the solder, first melt all the copper, then add the aluminum gradually. The two metals are of a very different density and the mixture should be stirred with an iron rod to unite them as far as possible. There is no solder which operates with aluminum in the same way as ordinary solder works with copper, tin, etc. This is due to the fact that aluminum will not alloy readily with solders with temperatures so low as the other metals require. Then, it is also covered with a thin coating of aluminum oxide, which is very refractory. All the surface to which it is intended that the solder shall adhere must first be tinned. This is accomplished by heating the metal to a temperature above the fusion point of the solder used and then rubbing the surface with a stick of the solder, thus rubbing the oxide off the surface with the solder itself and covering the exposed points with melted solder all in the same motion. After the edges to be united are thus tinned they may be sweated together with pure block tin with the aid either of a soldering iron or blast lamp. It is well to bear in mind that solder will not flow into an aluminum joint even when tinned, by capillary action, as it does into copper or tin joints, and it is therefore necessary to place on the surface of the metal all of the material necessary to sweat them together before the edges are brought into contact.

Black Solder No. 1

Copper	2 pounds
Zinc	3 pounds
Tin	2 ounces

Black Solder No. 2

Sheet brass	20 pounds
Zinc	1 pound
Tin	6 pounds

Yellow Solder for Brass or Copper No. 1

Copper	32 pounds
Zinc	29 pounds
Tin	1 pound

Yellow Solder for Copper or Brass No. 2

Copper	1 pound
Zinc	1 pound
Tin	....

The formula on the left is stronger than the other.

Best Soft Solder for Cast Britannia Ware

Tin	8 pounds	Lead	5 pounds

White Solder for Raised Britannia Ware

Tin	100 pounds	Copper	3 ounces

To make it free, add 3 ounces of lead.

Solder for Copper

Copper	10 pounds
Zinc	9 pounds
Nickel	....

German-silver Solder

Copper	38 parts
Zinc	54 parts
Nickel	8 parts

Gold Solder for 14-Carat Gold

Gold, 25 parts; silver, 25; brass, 12½; zinc, 1.

Soft Gold Solder

Is composed of 4 parts gold, 1 of silver and 1 of copper. It can be made softer by adding brass, but the solder becomes more liable to oxidize.

Gold Solder No. 1

Gold	14 parts
Silver	6 parts
Copper	4 parts

Gold Solder No. 2

Gold,	6 pennyweights
Silver,	1 pennyweight
Copper,	2 pennyweights

Hard Solder

Copper, 2; zinc, 1 part.

Pewterers' Solder

Tin, 2; lead, 1 part.

Plumbers' Solder

Lead	2 parts
Tin	1 part

Tinmen's Solder

Lead	1½ parts
Tin	1 part

Half and Half, Tinsmiths' Solder

Lead	1 part	Tin	1 part

Silver Solder No. 1

Yellow brass	70 parts
Zinc	7 parts
Tin	11½ parts

Silver Solder No. 2

Silver	145 parts
Brass (3 to 1)	73 parts
Zinc	4 parts

Solder for Silver, for the Use of Jewelers

Fine silver	19 pwts.	Sheet brass	10 pwts.
Copper,	1 pwt.		

White Solder for Silver

Silver	1 ounce	Tin	1 ounce

Silver Solder for Plated Metal

Fine silver	1 ounce	Brass	10 pwts.

Solder for Steel Joints

Silver	19 pwts.	Copper	1 pwt.
Brass	2 pwts.		

Melt these metals under a coat of charcoal dust.

Composition and Fusing Point of Soft Solders

Fusing point of tin-lead alloys (figures are approximate):

Tin, 1 to lead, 25	....558° F.	Tin, 1½ to lead, 1	....334° F.
" 1 " " 10	541	" 2 " " 1	340
" 1 " " 5	511	" 3 " " 1	356
" 1 " " 3	482	" 4 " " 1	365
" 1 " " 2	441	" 5 " " 1	378
" 1 " " 1	370	" 6 " " 1	381

The melting point of the tin-lead alloys decreases almost proportionately to the increase of tin, from 619° F., the melting point of pure lead, to 356° F., when the alloy contains 68% of tin, and then increases to 448° F., the melting point of pure tin. Alloys on either side of the 68% mixture begin to soften materially at 356° F., because at that temperature the eutectic alloy melts and permits the whole alloy to soften.

The relative hardness of the various tin and lead solders has been determined by Brinell's method. The results are as follows:

% Tin	0	10	20	30	40	50	60
Hardness	3.90	10.10	12.16	14.46	15.76	14.90	14.58
% Tin	66	67	68	70	80	90	100
Hardness	16.66	15.40	14.58	15.84	15.20	13.25	4.14

The hardest solder is the one composed of 2 parts of tin and 1 part of lead. It is the eutectic, or the one with the lowest melting point of all the mixtures given in the table.

Common Pewter

Common pewter contains 4 parts of lead to 1 part of tin.

Composition and Fusing Points of Hard Solders

Kind	Hard			Fusing-point
	Zinc	Copper	Silver	
Spelter, hardest	1	2	....	700°
" hard	2	3	....	550°
" soft	1	1	....	....
" fine	2	2	¼	....
Silver, hard	....	1	4	....
" medium	....	1	3	....
" soft	....	1	2	....

Coloring Solder to Match Copper Work

To color the solder on copper work to correspond in color with the copper, dissolve crystal sulphate of copper (blue vitriol) in water and apply with a brush or iron rod. The more coats of this solution that are applied, the deeper and nearer copper color is obtained.

For copper cornice work the exposed soldering may be concealed by first applying shellac dissolved in alcohol, and before it can dry freely sprinkle with powdered copper bronze; or the copper bronze can be placed in banana oil and applied where wanted with a brush. Do not make up more than needed because it dries up quickly.

Pattenizing or Ageing Copper Work

The weathering, that is to say, the beautiful greenish tint of aged and exposed copper, can be hastened by generously painting the copper with a solution of salt and vinegar or sal ammoniac and water. Some use a powerful acid solution. In all cases the operator must be careful not to get any on his clothes or person.

Cleaning Soldering Coppers

The modern method of cleaning soldering irons is to quickly dip them, while hot, into a cleaning liquid, which often is composed of just water and sal ammoniac. It has, however, been found that the coppers "smoke" excessively with this liquid so some workmen use water and boiled acid to the proportion of say one of acid to five of water; the objection to this liquid is that it soon eats small holes in the coppers, but it is to be remembered that eventually happens no matter what solution is used.

How to Judge Solder

The appearance of the solder when cold is what plumbers judge the quality by, and as plumber's solder is akin to that used by tinsmiths, only not so fine, it follows that this method will apply for tinsmith's solder; naturally, though, more tin is to be looked for. A small quantity is poured out on a level stone or brick and the color on setting is noted, also the number and size of bright spots on its surface. On a piece about the size of a silver dollar will appear, if the correct proportions are present, about four spots one-eighth inch or so in diameter. The side of the solder which was in contact with the stone will be bright. Adding lead to the solder will reduce the size or number of bright spots, and if continued will turn out solder of chalky appearance and coarse texture; adding more tin to the solder will brighten it.

The solder should be well stirred before a test is made or an incorrect impression of its quality will be received and the rate of cooling also affects its appearance. If cooled too quickly, as would happen when the solder is poured on an iron plate, the metal will appear much finer than it really is. If the appearance is chalky with numerous minute bright spots, there is probably a small percentage of zinc or antimony in it, which, of course, means that it is not as pure as it should be.

Doctoring Solder

A well known writer on plumbing states in one of his books how much plumber's solder may be refined and as tinsmith's solder is practically the same and they often remelt scrap solder, it would seem that this method is equally useful to both classes of workmen.

You may have spoiled your solder also by overheating it or you may have been tinning your brass couplings by dipping them. This should never be done owing to the risk of overheating the brass and releasing a proportion of the zinc. It may also have happened by pouring the solder when at too high a temperature over a brass ferrule in the process of wiping a joint, or in the case of tinsmiths much soldering in galvanized iron would permeate the scrap solder with an excess of zinc. Now for the cure.

Your solder should be made extra hot, almost twice the temperature it should be if all were right. Plumber's solder melts at 440° F. To clean it you want to raise it to 800° F. Why? Because zinc melts off at 773°. Do not make it red hot in the daylight or you will have reached a temperature of about 1,100° F. and you will spoil it. Throw in a lump of sulphur (rosin also helps) and this mixing with the zinc helps it to float. Stir up the contents and skim off the top, which will be a mixture of lead oxide, putty powder, sulphur and zinc. Then when it has cooled down to about the working point stir in tallow and some more rosin and skim again. Then add a little tin to replace what was burned out in raising the metal to such a high temperature, and it should be ready to wipe with again; or for tinsmithing add tin to a generous amount.

Another way to obtain the same result is to granulate the solder by pounding it. When it reaches the cooling point it will break up as fine as sawdust. Then put it into a dish and cover it with muriatic acid and allow it to stand over night. This will remove all traces of zinc.

If solder becomes overheated through inattention do not stir it until it has cooled to about the correct wiping temperature; otherwise more tin will oxidize on the surface and be lost. If you consider that tin forms putty powder at 428° F. and lead oxidizes at 612° F., the two together at 440° F., you will understand what happens when you allow it to become red hot in the daylight, for it is then about 700° hotter than it should be. Do not add fine or scrap solder to your pot unless you are certain of its purity.

Solder may be adulterated with antimony or bismuth to secure brightness and it will then be exceedingly difficult to wipe a joint that will not drop at the bottom and, too, for soldering purposes will not flow well. Be careful always to put paper below a joint to catch your surplus solder, never allow brass or zinc to mix with it and never melt zinc in a pot that is to be used again for solder. Refer to the tables on page 234 for information on the melting point of solder and its component parts and other useful information.

Common Soldering Fluxes

In tinsmithing, or rather sheet metal working, the common fluxes for soldering purposes are: Commercial muriatic acid used raw on galvanized iron work when the solder alone is the means of joining the parts together. Boiled acid, zinc chloride, for galvanized iron work when the solder is just to make a water or air-tight joint and rivets, or a groove or double seam hold the parts together.

Raw acid should be used for zinc work, but especial care is necessary so that the acid will not eat holes in the metal and all acid should be carefully cleaned away after soldering. If the zinc is very clean and bright boiled acid could be used.

Boiled acid is used for soft soldering copper or brass work, though if the copper is dirty it should first be cleaned with raw acid, which should be washed off before applying the boiled acid. Some workmen use rosin, but it is not as satisfactory as acid, especially for speedy work.

Rosin is used for tin roofing and tinware, though for rapid work on the latter boiled acid should be used and the article carefully cleaned in hot water after soldering. By "boiled" acid is meant muriatic acid to which small pieces of zinc have been fed until the acid ceases to boil, after which a large piece of zinc is placed in and the acid allowed to stand awhile before using; use a strong jar for a container and do not do this indoors because the fumes are disagreeable.

Flux for Soldering Tin Rocf

One part rosin and 2 parts binnacle oil mixed hot and used the same as rosin alone; or, cut with alcohol 1 pint as much rosin as possible and put on with a swab. Either, good when the wind blows. Or, saponified or red oil used with a swab along the seams. Solder flows more freely than with rosin alone as the flux.

Special Soldering Fluid or Flux

Prussiate of potash, borax and copperas, each 1 dram; sal ammoniac, ½ ounce, muriatic acid, 3½ ounces, well mixed, then add as much zinc as it will dissolve. Add 1 pint or more water according to strength required.

Flux of Sal Ammoniac, Borax and Zinc Chloride

Sal ammoniac and borax, each 1 dram; chloride of zinc, 1 ounce, water, 1 pint. It will not eat copper or tarnish tin. Use less water and it will be stronger.

Cleaning Brass

The articles to be cleaned must be warmed and then rubbed with a mixture of roche alum one part to water sixteen parts. Then finish with fine tripoli, according to requirements.

Case Hardening

Place the article to be case hardened in an iron box with horn, hoof, bone-dust or shreds of leather and heat blood red. Then dip the article in cold water.

Another method is to heat the article, after polishing, to a bright red and then rub the surface with prussiate of potash. Allow it to cool to a dull red and dip it in water.

Case Hardening Mixture No. 1

Prussiate of Potash	3 parts
Sal ammoniac	1 part

Case Hardening Mixture No. 2

Prussiate of Potash	1 part
Sal ammoniac	2 parts
Bone Dust	2 parts

Either mixture may be used with satisfactory results.

Ink for Marking Galvanized Iron Work

A marking fluid or ink that will not readily rub off when used on galvanized iron (or copper) is made by saving the filings from the soldering irons and depositing them in a glass receptacle which contains muriatic acid. After standing a short time this ink is ready for use and is applied as in ordinary writing or sketching, with a pointed hardwood stick. Remove the stick when not in use.

Ink for Marking Tinware

Tinware can be marked with an ink made by reducing asphalt or black varnish with turpentine to the desired consistency. It should be kept in a corked bottle and well shaken before using.

This ink can be used for marking any bright article and is easily removed by means of a cloth dipped in coal oil or turpentine. Another excellent ink for such articles is composed of shellac varnish and alcohol and colored with fine lamp black. This forms a jet black lusterless ink, insoluble in water, but removable with alcohol.

Rust-Proof Coating for Steel

Dissolve one part of caoutchouc and sixteen parts of turpentine with a low temperature. Then add eight parts of boiled oil. Mix them by bringing them to the boiling point. Apply to the steel with a brush just as you would in varnishing. The coating may be removed with turpentine.

Removing Rust from Steel

Brush with a paste compound of one-half ounce cyanide of potassium, one-half ounce castile soap, one ounce whiting and enough water to make a paste. The steel should then be washed with a solution of one-half ounce cyanide of potassium in two ounces of water.

Cement for Fastening Brass to Glass Vessels

Melt rosin 150 parts, wax 30, and add burnt ocher 30 and calcined plaster 2 parts. Apply warm.

A Cheap Cement

Melted brimstone, either alone or mixed with rosin and brick dust, forms a tolerably good and very cheap cement.

Cement for Fastening Blades, Files, Etc.

Shellac 2 parts, prepared chalk 1, powdered and mixed. The opening for the blade is filled with this powder, the lower end of the iron heated and pressed in.

China Cement

Take the curd of milk, dried and powdered, 10 ounces; quicklime, 1 ounce; camphor, 2 drams. Mix and keep in closely stoppered bottles. When used, a portion is to be mixed with a little water into a paste, to be applied quickly.

Cement to Render Cisterns and Casks Water Tight

An excellent cement for resisting moisture is made by incorporating thoroughly 8 parts of melted glue, of the consistence used by carpenters, with 4 parts of linseed oil, boiled into varnish with litharge. This cement hardens in about 48 hours and renders the joints of wooden cisterns and casks air and water tight. A compound of glue with one-quarter its weight of Venice turpentine, made as above, serves to cement glass, metal and wood to one another. Fresh made cheese curd and old skim milk cheese, boiled in water to a slimy consistency, dissolved in a solution of bicarbonate of potash are said to form a good cement for glass and porcelain. The gluten of wheat, well prepared, is also a good cement. White of eggs with flour and water, well mixed, and smeared over linen cloth, forms a ready lute for steam joints in small apparatus.

Cement for Holes in Castings

The best cement for this purpose is made by mixing 1 part of sulphur in powder, 2 parts of sal ammoniac and 80 parts of clean powdered iron turn-ings. Sufficient water must be added to make it into a thick paste, which should be pressed into the holes or seams which are to be filled up. The ingredients composing this cement should be kept separate and not mixed until required for use. It is to be applied cold, and the casting should not be used for two or three days afterward.

Cement for Coppersmiths and Engineers

Boiled linseed oil and red lead mixed together into a putty is often used by coppersmiths and engineers to secure joints. The washers of leather or cloth are smeared with this mixture in a pasty state.

Cement for Corks

The bituminous or black cement for bottle corks consists of pitch hardened by the addition of rosin and brick dust.

Cement for Mending Earthen and Glass Ware

1. Heat the article to be mended a little above boiling water heat, then apply a thin coating of gum shellac on both surfaces of the broken vessel, and when cold it will be as strong as it was originally. 2. Dissolve gum shellac in alcohol, apply the solution and bind the parts firmly together until the cement is perfectly dry.

Gas Fitters' Cement.

Mix together resin 4½ parts, wax 1 part, and Venetian red 3 parts.

Transparent Cement for Glass

Dissolve 1 part of India rubber in 64 of chloroform, then add gum mastic in powder 14 to 24 parts, and digest for two days with frequent shaking. Apply with camel's-hair brush.

Cement for Iron Pots and Pans

Take 2 parts of sulphur, and 1 part, by weight, of fine black lead; put the sulphur in an old iron pan, holding it over the fire until it begins to melt, then add the lead, stir well until all is mixed and melted, then pour out on an iron plate or smooth stone. When cool, break into small pieces. A sufficient quantity of this compound being placed upon the crack of the iron pot to be mended, can be soldered by a hot iron in the same way a tinsmith solders his sheets. If there is a small hole in the pot, drive a copper rivet in it and then solder over it with this cement.

Iron Rust Cement Nos. 1 and 2

Is made from 50 to 100 parts of iron borings, pounded and sifted, mixed with 1 part of sal ammoniac, and when it is to be applied, moistened with as much water as will give it a pasty consistency. Another composition of the same kind is made by mixing 4 parts of fine borings or filings of iron, 2 parts of potters' clay and 1 part of pounded potsherds, and making them into a paste with salt and water to the proportions required.

Rust Joint Cement No. 3		**Rust Joint Cement No. 4**	
Quick setting		Slow setting	
Sal ammoniac	1 part	Sal ammoniac	2 parts
Flour of sulphur	2 parts	Flour of sulphur	1 part
Iron borings	80 parts	Iron borings	200 parts

The slow setting is the best if the joint is not required for immediate use.

Cement for Iron Tubes, Boilers, etc.

Finely powdered iron, 66 parts; sal ammoniac, 1 part; water of a sufficient quantity to form a suitable paste, by mixing all thoroughly together.

Cement for Ivory, Mother of Pearl, etc.

Dissolve 1 part of isinglass and 2 of white glue in 30 of water, strain and evaporate to 6 parts. Add 1-30 part of gum mastic, dissolve in ½ part of alcohol and 1 part of white zinc. When this receipt is required for use warm it carefully in an apparatus like a glue pot, and then shake it up.

Cements for Leather

A mixture of India rubber and shellac varnish makes a very adhesive leather cement. A strong solution of common isinglass, with a little diluted alcohol added to it, makes another excellent cement for leather.

Marble Cement

Take plaster of Paris and soak it in a saturated solution of alum, then bake the two in an oven, the same as gypsum is baked to make it plaster of Paris;

after which they are ground to powder. It is then used as wanted, being mixed up with water like plaster and applied. It sets into a very hard composition capable of taking a very high polish. It may be fixed with various coloring minerals to produce a cement of any color capable of imitating marble.

Cement for Marble Workers and Coppersmiths

White of an egg alone, or mixed with finely sifted quicklime, will answer for uniting objects which are not exposed to moisture. The latter combination is very strong and is much employed for joining pieces of spar and marble ornaments. A similar composition is used by coppersmiths to secure the edges and rivets of boilers, only bullock's blood is the albuminous matter used instead of the white of an egg.

Cement for Joining Metals and Wood

Melt rosin and stir in calcined plaster until reduced to a paste, to which add boiled oil a sufficient quantity to bring it to the consistence of honey; apply warm. Or, melt rosin 180 parts and stir in burnt umber 30 parts, calcined plaster 15 parts and boiled oil 8 parts.

Non-Combustible and Waterproof Cement Paint

If hydraulic cement be mixed with oil, it forms a first rate anti-combustible and excellent water proof paint for roofs of buildings, walls, etc.

Plumbers' Cement

Black rosin, 1 part; brick dust, 2 parts; well incorporated by a melting heat.

Red Lead Cement for Face Joints

Mix one part of white lead and one part of red lead with linseed oil, using enough oil to give it the proper consistency.

Cement for Stone Ware

Another cement in which an analogous substance, the curd of milk, is employed, is made by boiling slices of skim milk cheese into a gluey consistence in a great quantity of water, and then incorporating it with quicklime on a slab with a muller, or in a marble mortar. When this compound is applied warm to broken edges of stone ware, it unites them very firmly after it is cold.

Waterproof Cement

Zinc white rubbed up with copal varnish to fill up the indentures; when dry, to be covered with the same mass somewhat thinner, and lastly with copal varnish alone.

Cement for Cracks in Wood

Make a paste of slaked lime 1 part, rye meal 2 parts, with a sufficient quantity of linseed oil. Or dissolve 1 part of glue in 16 parts of water, when almost cool stir in sawdust and prepared chalk a sufficient quantity. Or oil varnish thickened with a mixture of equal parts of white lead, red lead, litharge and chalk.

A Good General Cement

Shellac, dissolved in alcohol or in a solution of borax, forms a pretty good cement.

Cement for Repairing Fractured Bodies of All Kinds

White lead ground upon a slab with linseed oil varnish and kept out of contact of air affords a cement capable of repairing fractured bodies of all kinds. It requires a few weeks to harden. When stone and iron are to be cemented together, a compound of equal parts of sulphur with pitch answers very well.

Cement to Stop a Leaky Roof

Twenty-five pounds yellow ocher, 1 pound litharge, 6 pounds black lead, 1 pound fine salt; boil well in oil. Soak strips of cloth in the above and paste over the seams; first thoroughly cleaning the spot of all dirt and loose paint. Good where solder is not practicable.

Putty for Skylights

As a rule it is the cheapest in the end to buy your putty for skylight work. Each manufacturer has his own formula, but it is well to keep in mind that the cheapest putty is the dearest in the end. Only pure linseed oil putty should be used. If too soft thicken with whiting, and if too hard soften with linseed oil.

A good home-made putty is composed of fine white sand, litharge and rosin mixed in boiled linseed oil. Or just mix whiting in linseed oil to the consistency of dough.

Acid-proof Putty

1. Melt 1 part of gum elastic with 2 parts of linseed oil and mix with the necessary quantity of white bole by continued kneading to the desired consistency. Hydrochloric acid and nitric acid do not attack this putty, it softens somewhat when warm and does not dry readily on the surface. The drying and hardening is effected by an admixture of ½ part of litharge or red lead.

2. A putty which will even resist boiling sulphuric acid is prepared by melting caoutchouc at a moderate heat, then adding 8 per cent of tallow, stirring constantly, whereupon sufficiently slaked lime is added until the whole has the consistency of soft dough. Finally about 20 per cent of red lead is still added, which causes the mass to set immediately and to harden and dry. A solution of caoutchouc in double its weight of linseed oil, added by means of heat and with the like quantity (weight) of pipe clay, gives a plastic mass which likewise resists most acids.

Black Putty

Mix whiting and antimony sulphide, the latter finely powdered, with soluble glass. This putty, it is claimed, can be polished, after hardening, by means of a burnishing agate.

Glaziers' Putty

1. For puttying panes or looking glasses into picture frames a mixture prepared as follows is well adapted: Make a solution of gum elastic in ben-

zine, strong enough so that a syrup-like fluid results. If the solution be too thin, wait until the benzine evaporates. Then grind white lead in linseed-oil varnish to a stiff paste and add the gum solution. This putty may be used, besides the above purposes, for the tight puttying-in of window panes into their frames. The putty is applied on the glass lap of the frames and the panes are firmly pressed into it. The glass plates thereby obtain a good, firm support and stick to the wood, as the putty adheres both to the glass and to the wood.

2. A useful putty for mirrors, etc., is prepared by dissolving gummi elasticum (caoutchouc) in benzol to a syrupy solution, and incorporating this latter with a mixture of white lead and linseed oil to make a stiff pulp. The putty adheres strongly to both glass and wood, and may therefore be applied to the framework of the window, mirror, etc., to be glazed, the glass being then pressed firmly on the cementing layer thus formed. Surplus putty should be cleaned off.

3. Mix seventy pounds of whiting, thirty pounds of boiled oil and two gallons of water. If this is too thin, add more whiting. If too thick, add more oil until of suitable consistency.

To Soften Old Putty

To remove old putty from broken windows, dip a small brush in nitro-muriatic acid or caustic soda and apply it to the putty. In about an hour the putty will have become so soft that it may be easily removed with a glazier's putty knife.

To Soften Glaziers' Putty

1. Glaziers' putty which has become hard can be softened with the following mixture: Mix carefully equal parts of crude powdered potash and freshly burnt lime and make it into a paste with a little water. This dough, to which about 1/4 part of soft soap is still added, is applied on the putty to be softened, but care has to be taken not to cover other paint, as it would be surely destroyed thereby. After a few hours the hardest putty will be softened by caustic mass and can be removed from glass and wood.

2. A good way to make the putty soft and plastic enough in a few hours so that it can be taken off like fresh putty, is by the use of kerosene, which entirely dissolves the linseed oil of the putty, transformed into rosin, and quickly penetrates it.

Hard Putty

This is used by carriage painters and jewelers. Boil 4 pounds brown umber and 7 pounds linseed oil for 2 hours; stir in 2 ounces beeswax; take from the fire and mix in 5 1/2 pounds chalk and 11 pounds white lead; the mixing must be done very thoroughly by constantly stirring or kneading.

Painters' Putty and Rough Stuff

Gradually knead sifted dry chalk (whiting) or else rye flour, powdered white lead, zinc white, or lithopone white with good linseed-oil varnish. The best putty is produced from varnish with plenty of chalk and some zinc white. This mixture can be tinted with earth colors. These oil putties must be well kneaded together and rather compact (like glaziers' putty).

If flour paste is boiled (this is best produced by scalding with hot water, pouring in, gradually, the rye flour which has been previously dissolved in a little cold water and stirring constantly until the proper consistency is attained) and dry sifted chalk and a little varnish are added, a good stuff for wood or iron is obtained, which can be rubbed. This may also be produced from glaziers' oil putty by gradually kneading into it flour paste and a little more sifted dry chalk as may be required.

Waterproof Putties

1. Grind powdered white lead or minium (red lead) with thick linseed oil varnish to a stiff paste. This putty is used extensively for tightening wrought-iron gas pipes, for tightening rivet seams on gas meters, hot-water furnaces, cast-iron flange pipes for hot-water heating, etc. The putty made with minium dries very slowly, but becomes tight even before it is quite hard, and holds very firmly after solidification. Sometimes a little ground gypsum is added to it.

The two following putties are cheaper than the above-mentioned red lead putty:

2. One part white lead, 1 part manganese, one part white pipe clay, mix with linseed oil varnish.

3. Two parts red lead, 5 parts white lead, 4 parts clay, ground in or prepared with linseed oil varnish.

4. Excellent putty, which has been found invalu-

able where waterproof closing and permanent adhesion are desired, is made from litharge and glycerine. The litharge must be finely pulverized and the glycerine very concentrated, thickly liquid, and clear as water. Both substances are mixed into viscid, thickly liquid lumps. The pegs of kerosene lamps, for instance, can be fixed in so firmly with this putty that they can only be removed by chiseling it out. For putting in the glass panes of aquariums it is equally valuable. As it can withstand higher temperature it may be successfully used for fixing tools, curling irons, forks, etc., in the wooden handles. The thickish putty mass is rubbed into the hole, and the part to be fixed is inserted. As this putty hardens very quickly it cannot be prepared in large quantities, and only enough for immediate use must be compounded in each case.

5. Five parts of hydraulic lime, 0.3 parts of tar, 0.3 parts of rosin, 1 part of horn water (the decoction resulting from boiling horn in water and decanting the latter). The materials are to be mixed and boiled. After cooling, the putty is ready for use. This is an excellent cement for glass, and may be used also for reservoirs and any vessels for holding water, to cement the cracks; also for many other purposes. It will not give way, and is equally good for glass, wood, and metal.

6. This is especially recommended for boiler leaks: Mix well together 6 parts of powdered graphite, 3 parts of slaked lime, 8 parts of heavy spar (barytes), and 8 parts of thick linseed oil varnish, and apply in the ordinary way to the spots.

Concrete Mixtures

The right kind of concrete should have the voids completely filled so that one stone should not touch another, and one grain of sand should be separated from the next by the fine cement. Water will go through concrete male from ordinary mixtures, but 1 part cement, 1½ to 2 parts of sand and 4 parts of ¾-inch stone will be fairly watertight. Waterproofing of some kind is most always used.

The best proportions for ordinary work is: 1:3:6, for best work; 1:1½:4 is used for ordinary work—tanks, etc. The units are taken by measure and not by weight.

CHAPTER X

Useful Tables

Table I

Black Sheet Iron and Wire Gauge

Black Sheets are rolled to the following Standard Gauges adopted by the United States, taking effect July 1, 1893.

	Thickness		Weight	
Number of Gauge.	Approximate Thickness in Fractions of an Inch	Approximate Thickness in Decimal Parts of an Inch	Steel Weight Per Square Foot in Pounds	Iron Weight Per Square Foot in Pounds
8........		.1719	7.012	6.875
9........		.1563	6.375	6.250
10........	9-64	.140625	5.737	5.625
11........	1-8	.125	5.100	5.000
12........	7-64	.109375	4.462	4.375
13........	3-32	.09375	3.825	3.750
14........	5-64	.078125	3.157	3.125
15........	9-128	.0703125	2.869	2.8125
16........	1-16	.0625	2.550	2.500
17........	9-16	.05625	2.295	2.250
18........	1-20	.05	2.040	2.000
19........	7-16	.04375	1.785	1.750
20........	3-80	.0375	1.530	1.500
21........	11-32	.034375	1.402	1.375
22........	1-32	.03125	1.275	1.250
23........	9-32	.028125	1.147	1.125
24........	1-40	.025	1.020	1.000
25........	7-32	.02187	0.892	.875
26........	3-16	.01875	0.765	.750
27........	11-64	.0171875	0.701	.6875
28........	1-64	.015625	0.637	.625
29........	9-64	.0140625	0.574	.5625
30........	1-80	.0125	0.510	.500
31........	7-64	.0109375	0.446	.4375
32........	13-128	.01015625	0.414	.40625

A variation of 2½ per cent. either way is allowed

Weights of Plate Iron Per Lineal Foot in Pounds

Widths in Inches	Thickness in Inches															
	1/16	1/8	3/16	1/4	5/16	3/8	7/16	1/2	9/16	5/8	11/16	3/4	13/16	7/8	15/16	1
12	2.50	5.00	7.50	10.00	12.50	15.00	17.50	20.00	22.50	25.00	27.50	30.00	32.50	35.00	37.50	40.00
13	2.71	5.42	8.13	10.83	13.54	16.25	18.96	21.67	24.38	27.08	29.79	32.50	35.21	37.92	40.63	43.33
14	2.92	5.83	8.75	11.67	14.58	17.50	20.42	23.33	26.25	29.17	32.08	35.00	37.92	40.83	43.75	46.67
15	3.13	6.25	9.38	12.50	15.63	18.75	21.88	25.00	28.13	31.25	34.38	37.50	40.63	43.75	46.88	50.00
16	3.33	6.67	10.00	13.33	16.67	20.00	23.33	26.67	30.00	33.33	36.67	40.00	43.33	46.67	50.00	53.33
17	3.54	7.03	10.63	14.17	17.71	21.25	24.79	28.33	31.88	35.42	38.96	42.50	46.05	49.59	53.13	56.67
18	3.75	7.50	11.25	15.00	18.75	22.50	26.25	30.00	33.75	37.50	41.25	45.00	48.75	52.50	56.25	60.00
19	3.96	7.92	11.87	15.83	19.79	23.75	27.71	31.67	35.67	39.58	43.54	47.50	51.45	55.41	59.37	63.33
20	4.17	8.33	12.50	16.67	20.83	25.00	29.17	33.33	37.50	41.67	45.83	50.00	54.17	58.33	62.50	66.67
21	4.38	8.75	13.13	17.50	21.88	26.25	30.63	35.00	39.38	43.75	48.13	52.50	56.88	61.25	65.63	70.00
22	4.58	9.17	13.75	18.33	22.92	27.50	32.08	36.67	41.25	45.83	50.42	55.00	59.58	64.17	68.75	73.33
23	4.79	9.58	14.38	19.17	23.96	28.75	33.54	38.33	43.13	47.92	52.71	57.50	62.30	67.09	71.88	76.67
24	5.00	10.00	15.00	20.00	25.00	30.00	35.00	40.00	45.00	50.00	55.00	60.00	65.00	70.00	75.00	80.00
25	5.21	10.42	15.62	20.83	26.04	31.25	36.46	41.67	46.88	52.08	57.29	62.50	67.70	72.91	78.13	83.33
26	5.42	10.83	16.25	21.67	27.08	32.50	37.92	43.33	48.75	54.17	59.58	65.00	70.42	75.83	81.25	86.67
27	5.63	11.25	16.88	22.50	28.13	33.75	39.38	45.00	50.63	56.25	61.88	67.50	73.13	78.75	84.38	90.00
28	5.83	11.67	17.50	23.33	29.17	35.00	40.83	46.67	52.50	58.33	64.17	70.00	75.84	81.67	87.50	93.33
29	6.04	12.08	18.13	24.17	30.21	36.25	42.29	48.33	54.38	60.42	66.46	72.50	78.55	84.59	90.63	96.67
30	6.25	12.50	18.75	25.00	31.25	37.50	43.75	50.00	56.25	62.50	68.75	75.00	81.25	87.50	93.75	100.0
32	6.67	13.33	20.00	26.67	33.33	40.00	46.67	53.33	60.00	66.67	73.33	80.00	86.67	93.33	100.0	106.7
34	7.08	14.17	21.25	28.33	35.42	42.50	49.58	56.67	63.75	70.83	77.91	85.00	92.08	99.17	106.3	113.3
36	7.50	15.00	22.50	30.00	37.50	45.00	52.50	60.00	67.50	75.00	82.50	90.00	97.50	105.0	112.5	120.0
38	7.92	15.83	23.75	31.67	39.59	47.50	55.42	63.33	71.25	79.17	87.09	95.00	102.9	110.8	118.8	126.7
40	8.33	16.67	25.00	33.33	41.67	50.00	58.33	66.67	75.00	83.33	91.67	100.0	108.3	116.7	125.0	133.3
42	8.75	17.50	26.25	35.00	43.75	52.50	61.25	70.00	78.75	87.50	96.25	105.0	113.7	122.5	131.3	140.0
44	9.17	18.33	27.50	36.67	45.84	55.00	64.17	73.33	82.50	91.67	100.8	110.0	119.2	128.3	137.5	146.7
46	9.58	19.17	28.75	38.33	47.92	57.50	67.08	76.67	86.25	95.83	105.4	115.0	124.6	134.2	143.8	153.3
48	10.00	20.00	30.00	40.00	50.00	60.00	70.00	80.00	90.00	100.0	110.0	120.0	130.0	140.0	150.0	160.0

TABLE 3 Weights of Flat Rolled Iron Per Lineal Foot in Pounds

Thickness in Inches — Iron weighing 480 lbs. per cubic foot. For steel add 2 per cent.

Widths in Inches	1/16	1/8	3/16	1/4	5/16	3/8	7/16	1/2	9/16	5/8	11/16	3/4	13/16	7/8	15/16	1
1	0.208	0.417	0.625	0.833	1.04	1.25	1.46	1.67	1.88	2.08	2.29	2.50	2.71	2.92	3.13	3.33
1¼	.260	.521	.781	1.04	1.30	1.56	1.82	2.08	2.34	2.60	2.86	3.13	3.39	3.65	3.91	4.17
1½	.313	.625	.938	1.25	1.56	1.88	2.19	2.50	2.81	3.13	3.44	3.75	4.06	4.38	4.69	5.00
1¾	.365	.729	1.09	1.46	1.82	2.19	2.55	2.92	3.28	3.65	4.01	4.38	4.74	5.10	5.47	5.83
2	.417	.833	1.25	1.67	2.08	2.50	2.92	3.33	3.75	4.17	4.58	5.00	5.42	5.83	6.25	6.67
2¼	.469	.938	1.41	1.88	2.34	2.81	3.28	3.75	4.22	4.69	5.16	5.63	6.09	6.56	7.03	7.50
2½	.521	1.04	1.56	2.08	2.60	3.13	3.65	4.17	4.69	5.21	5.73	6.25	6.77	7.29	7.81	8.33
2¾	.573	1.15	1.72	2.29	2.86	3.44	4.01	4.58	5.16	5.73	6.30	6.88	7.45	8.02	8.59	9.17
3	.625	1.25	1.88	2.50	3.13	3.75	4.38	5.00	5.63	6.25	6.88	7.50	8.13	8.75	9.38	10.00
3¼	.677	1.35	2.03	2.71	3.39	4.06	4.74	5.42	6.09	6.77	7.45	8.13	8.80	9.48	10.16	10.83
3½	.729	1.46	2.19	2.92	3.65	4.38	5.10	5.83	6.56	7.29	8.02	8.75	9.48	10.21	10.94	11.67
3¾	.781	1.56	2.34	3.13	3.91	4.69	5.47	6.25	7.03	7.81	8.59	9.38	10.16	10.94	11.72	12.50
4	.833	1.67	2.50	3.33	4.17	5.00	5.83	6.67	7.50	8.33	9.17	10.00	10.83	11.67	12.50	13.33
4¼	.885	1.77	2.66	3.54	4.43	5.31	6.20	7.08	7.97	8.85	9.74	10.63	11.51	12.40	13.28	14.17
4½	.938	1.88	2.81	3.75	4.69	5.63	6.56	7.50	8.44	9.38	10.31	11.25	12.19	13.13	14.06	15.00
4¾	.990	1.98	2.97	3.96	4.95	5.94	6.93	7.92	8.91	9.90	10.89	11.88	12.86	13.85	14.84	15.83
5	1.04	2.08	3.13	4.17	5.21	6.25	7.29	8.33	9.38	10.42	11.46	12.50	13.54	14.58	15.63	16.67
5¼	1.09	2.19	3.28	4.38	5.47	6.56	7.66	8.75	9.84	10.94	12.03	13.13	14.22	15.31	16.41	17.50
5½	1.15	2.29	3.44	4.58	5.73	6.88	8.02	9.17	10.31	11.46	12.60	13.75	14.90	16.04	17.19	18.33
5¾	1.20	2.40	3.59	4.79	5.99	7.19	8.39	9.58	10.78	11.98	13.18	14.38	15.57	16.77	17.97	19.17
6	1.25	2.50	3.75	5.00	6.25	7.50	8.75	10.00	11.25	12.50	13.75	15.00	16.25	17.50	18.75	20.00
6¼	1.30	2.60	3.91	5.21	6.51	7.81	9.11	10.42	11.72	13.02	14.32	15.63	16.93	18.23	19.53	20.83
6½	1.35	2.71	4.06	5.42	6.77	8.13	9.48	10.83	12.19	13.54	14.90	16.25	17.60	18.96	20.31	21.67
6¾	1.41	2.81	4.22	5.63	7.03	8.44	9.84	11.25	12.56	14.06	15.47	16.88	18.28	19.69	21.09	22.50
7	1.46	2.92	4.38	5.83	7.29	8.75	10.21	11.67	13.13	14.58	16.04	17.50	18.96	20.42	21.88	23.33
7½	1.56	3.13	4.69	6.25	7.81	9.38	10.94	12.50	14.06	15.63	17.19	18.75	20.31	21.88	23.44	25.00
8	1.67	3.33	5.00	6.67	8.33	10.00	11.67	13.33	15.00	16.67	18.33	20.00	21.67	23.33	25.00	26.67
8½	1.77	3.54	5.31	7.08	8.85	10.63	12.41	14.17	15.94	17.71	19.48	21.25	23.02	24.79	26.56	28.33
9	1.88	3.75	5.63	7.50	9.38	11.25	13.13	15.00	16.88	18.75	20.63	22.50	24.38	26.25	28.13	30.00
10	2.08	4.17	6.25	8.33	10.42	12.50	14.58	16.67	18.75	20.83	22.92	25.00	27.08	29.17	31.25	33.33
11	2.29	4.58	6.88	9.17	11.46	13.75	16.04	18.33	20.63	22.92	25.21	27.50	29.79	32.08	34.38	36.67
12	2.50	5.00	7.50	10.00	12.50	15.00	17.51	20.00	22.50	25.00	27.50	30.00	32.50	35.00	37.50	40.00

TABLE 3 (Continued) **Weights of Flat Rolled Iron Per Lineal Foot in Pounds**

Widths in Inches	Thickness in Inches															
	1 1/16	1 1/8	1 2/16	1 1/4	1 5/16	1 3/8	1 7/16	1 1/2	1 9/16	1 5/8	1 11/16	1 3/4	1 13/16	1 7/8	1 15/16	2
1	3.54	3.75	3.96	4.17	4.37	4.58	4.70	5.00	5.21	5.42	5.63	5.83	6.04	6.25	6.46	6.67
1¼	4.43	4.69	4.95	5.21	5.47	5.73	5.99	6.25	6.51	6.77	7.03	7.29	7.55	7.81	8.07	8.33
1½	5.31	5.63	5.94	6.25	6.56	6.88	7.19	7.50	7.81	8.13	8.44	8.75	9.06	9.38	9.69	10.00
1¾	6.20	6.56	6.93	7.29	7.66	8.02	8.39	8.75	9.11	9.48	9.84	10.21	10.57	10.94	11.30	11.67
2	7.08	7.50	7.92	8.33	8.75	9.17	9.58	10.00	10.42	10.83	11.25	11.67	12.08	12.50	12.92	13.33
2¼	7.97	8.44	8.91	9.38	9.84	10.31	10.78	11.25	11.72	12.19	12.66	13.13	13.59	14.06	14.53	15.00
2½	8.85	9.38	9.90	10.42	10.94	11.46	11.98	12.50	13.02	13.54	14.06	14.58	15.10	15.63	16.15	16.67
2¾	9.74	10.31	10.89	11.46	12.03	12.60	13.18	13.75	14.32	14.90	15.47	16.04	16.61	17.19	17.76	18.33
3	10.63	11.25	11.88	12.50	13.13	13.75	14.38	15.00	15.63	16.25	16.88	17.50	18.13	18.75	19.38	20.00
3¼	11.51	12.19	12.86	13.54	14.22	14.90	15.57	16.25	16.93	17.60	18.28	18.96	19.64	20.31	20.99	21.67
3½	12.40	13.13	13.85	14.58	15.31	16.04	16.77	17.50	18.23	18.96	19.69	20.42	21.15	21.88	22.60	23.33
3¾	13.28	14.06	14.84	15.63	16.41	17.19	17.97	19.73	19.53	20.31	21.09	21.88	22.66	23.44	24.22	25.00
4	14.17	15.00	15.83	16.67	17.50	18.33	19.17	20.00	20.83	21.67	22.50	23.33	24.17	25.00	25.83	26.67
4¼	15.05	15.94	16.82	17.71	18.59	19.48	20.36	21.25	22.14	23.02	23.91	24.79	25.68	26.56	27.45	28.33
4½	15.94	16.88	17.81	18.75	19.69	20.63	21.56	22.50	23.44	24.38	25.31	26.25	27.19	28.13	29.06	30.00
4¾	16.82	17.81	18.80	19.79	20.78	21.77	22.76	23.75	24.74	25.73	26.72	27.71	28.70	29.69	30.68	31.67
5	.....	18.75	.....	20.83	.....	22.92	.....	25.00	.....	27.08	.....	29.17	.....	31.25	.....	33.33
5¼	.....	19.69	.....	21.88	.....	24.06	.....	26.25	.....	28.44	.....	30.63	.....	32.81	.....	35.00
5½	.....	20.63	.....	22.92	.....	25.21	.....	27.50	.....	29.79	.....	32.08	.....	34.38	.....	36.67
5¾	.....	21.56	.....	23.96	.....	26.35	.....	28.75	.....	31.15	.....	33.54	.....	35.94	.....	38.33
6	.....	22.50	.....	25.00	.....	27.50	.....	30.00	.....	32.50	.....	35.00	.....	37.50	.....	40.00
6¼	.....	23.44	.....	26.04	.....	28.65	.....	31.25	.....	33.85	.....	36.46	.....	39.06	.....	41.67
6½	.....	24.38	.....	27.08	.....	29.79	.....	32.50	.....	35.21	.....	37.92	.....	40.63	.....	43.33
6¾	.....	25.31	.....	28.13	.....	30.94	.....	33.75	.....	36.56	.....	39.38	.....	42.19	.....	45.00
7	.....	26.25	.....	29.17	.....	32.08	.....	35.00	.....	37.92	.....	40.83	.....	43.75	.....	46.67
7½	.....	28.13	.....	31.25	.....	34.38	.....	37.50	.....	40.63	.....	43.75	.....	46.88	.....	50.00
8	.....	30.00	.....	33.33	.....	36.67	.....	40.00	.....	43.33	.....	46.67	.....	50.00	.....	53.33
8½	.....	31.88	.....	35.42	.....	33.96	.....	42.50	.....	46.04	.....	49.58	.....	53.13	.....	56.67
9	.....	33.75	.....	37.50	.....	41.25	.....	45.00	.....	48.75	.....	52.50	.....	56.25	.....	60.00
10	.....	37.50	.....	41.67	.....	45.83	.....	50.00	.....	54.17	.....	58.33	.....	62.50	.....	66.67
11	.....	41.25	.....	45.83	.....	50.42	.....	55.00	.....	59.58	.....	64.17	.....	68.75	.....	73.33
12	.....	45.00	.....	50.00	.....	55.00	.....	60.00	.....	65.00	.....	70.00	.....	75.00	.....	80.00

TABLE 4

Plate Iron

The following table gives the weight per square foot for iron plates 1/16 inch up to 2 inches thick.

Thickness	Weight in Lbs.	Thickness	Weight in Lbs.
1/16	2.5	1 1/16	42.5
1/8	5.0	1 1/8	45.0
3/16	7.5	1 3/16	47.5
1/4	10.0	1 1/4	50.0
5/16	12.5	1 5/16	52.5
3/8	15.0	1 3/8	55.0
7/16	17.5	1 7/16	57.5
1/2	20.0	1 1/2	60.0
9/16	22.5	1 9/16	62.5
5/8	25.0	1 5/8	65.0
11/16	27.5	1 11/16	67.5
3/4	30.0	1 3/4	70.0
13/16	32.5	1 13/16	72.5
7/8	35.0	1 7/8	75.0
15/16	37.5	1 15/16	77.5
1	40.0	2	80.0

TABLE 5

Weight of Russia Sheet Iron with Approximate U. S. Guage Number

Russian Gauge Number	U. S. Gauge Number (Approx.)	Weight Per Sheet (28" = 56") Pounds
16	21	14 1/2
15	22 3/8	13 1/2
14	23 1/2	12 1/2
13	23	12
12	24	11
11	25	10
10	26	9
9	27	8
8	28	7 1/4
7	29	6 1/4

Average net weight per bundle is about 225 pounds.

TABLE 6

Weight Per Sheet of Wood's Patent-Planished Iron in Pounds and Equivalent Russian Gauge

Gauges,	18	20	22	Sq. Ft. per Sheet
Approx. Russian Gauge	—	—	14	
28 × 45	16.25 to 17	12 to 12.5	10 to 10.25	8.75
28 × 48	17.25 to 18	13 to 13.5	10.5 to 10.75	9.33
28 × 56	20.25 to 21	14.75 to 15.25	12.25 to 12.5	10.89
28 × 60	21.5 to 21.75	16.25 to 16.75	13.25 to 13.5	11.66
28 × 72	26 to 27	18.5 to 19	16 to 16.25	14
28 × 84	30.5 to 31.25	22.75 to 23.5	18.75 to 19	16.33
30 × 45	17.25 to 18	13 to 13.75	10.25 to 10.75	9.37
30 × 48	18.25 to 19	14 to 14.75	11.25 to 11.75	10
30 × 56	21.25 to 22	16.25 to 16.75	13.25 to 13.75	11.66
30 × 60	23 to 23.75	17.25 to 17.75	14.25 to 14.75	12.5
30 × 72	27.5 to 28.25	20.75 to 21.25	17 to 17.75	15
30 × 84	32.25 to 33	24.5 to 25	19.75 to 20.25	17.5

Gauges,	23	24	25	Sq. Ft. per Sheet
Approx. Russian Gauge	13	12	11	
28 × 45	9.25 to 9.5	8.25 to 8.5	7.25 to 7.5	8.75
28 × 48	10 to 10.25	8.75 to 9	7.75 to 8	9.33
28 × 56	11.25 to 11.5	10.25 to 10.5	9 to 9.5	10.89
28 × 60	12.5 to 12.75	10.75 to 10.25	9.75 to 10.25	11.66
28 × 72	15.25 to 15.5	13.25 to 13.5	11.75 to 12.25	14
28 × 84	17.25 to 17.5	15.5 to 16	13.75 to 14.25	16.33
30 × 45	10.25 to 10.5	8.5 to 9	7.5 to 8	9.37
30 × 48	10.75 to 11.25	9.25 to 9.75	8.25 to 8.75	10
30 × 56	12.5 to 13	11.25 to 11.75	9.5 to 9.75	11.66
30 × 60	13.5 to 14	12 to 12.5	10.25 to 10.75	12.5
30 × 72	16.25 to 16.75	14 to 14.75	12.25 to 12.75	15
30 × 84	19 to 19.5	16.25 to 16.75	14.25 to 14.75	17.5

Gauges,	26	27	28	Sq. Ft. per Sheet
Approx. Russian Gauge	10	9	8	
28 × 45	6.5 to 6.75	6.25 to 6.5	5.5 to 5.75	8.75
28 × 48	7 to 7.25	6.75 to 7.25	6 to 6.25	9.33
28 × 56	8.25 to 8.5	7.75 to 8.25	6.75 to 7.25	10.89
28 × 60	8.75 to 9.25	8 to 8.5	7.5 to 8	11.66
28 × 72	10.75 to 11	10 to 10.5	9 to 9.5	14
28 × 84	12.75 to 13	11.5 to 12	10.5 to 11	16.33
30 × 45	7 to 7.25	6.5 to 6.75	6 to 6.25	9.37
30 × 48	7.5 to 8	7 to 7.5	6.5 to 6.75	10
30 × 56	9 to 9.25	8.25 to 8.5	7.25 to 7.5	11.66
30 × 60	9.5 to 9.75	9 to 9.25	8 to 8.25	12.5
30 × 72	11.5 to 11.75	10.25 to 10.75	9.5 to 9.75	15
30 × 84	13.5 to 13.75	12.25 to 12.75	11.25 to 11.5	17.5

Table 7 Weights and Areas of Square and Round Steel Bars *

Thickness or Diameter in Inches	Weight of □ Bar 1 Ft. Long in Lbs.	Weight of ○ Bar 1 Ft. Long in Lbs.	Area of □ Bar in Sq. Ins.	Area of ○ Bar in Sq. Ins.	Circum. of ○ Bar in Ins.	Thickness or Diameter in Inches	Area of □ Bar in Sq. Inches	Weight of □ Bar per Ft. in Lbs.	Area of ○ Bar in Sq. Inches	Weight of ○ Bar per Ft. in Lbs.
1/16	0.013	0.010	0.0039	0.0031	0.1963	1	1.000	3.400	0.785	2.670
5/64	0.021	0.016	0.0061	0.0048	0.2454	1 1/16	1.129	3.838	0.887	3.014
3/32	0.030	0.023	0.0088	0.0069	0.2945	1 1/8	1.266	3.303	0.994	3.379
7/64	0.041	0.032	0.0120	0.0094	0.3436	1 3/16	1.410	4.795	1.108	3.766
1/8	0.053	0.042	0.0156	0.0123	0.3927	1 1/4	1.563	5.312	1.227	4.173
9/64	0.067	0.053	0.0198	0.0155	0.4418	1 5/16	1.723	5.847	1.353	4.600
5/32	0.083	0.065	0.0244	0.0192	0.4909	1 3/8	1.891	6.428	1.485	5.049
11/64	0.100	0.079	0.0295	0.0232	0.5400	1 7/16	2.066	7.026	1.623	5.518
3/16	0.120	0.094	0.0352	0.0276	0.5890	1-1/2	2.250	7.650	1.767	6.008
13/64	0.140	0.110	0.0413	0.0324	0.6381	1 9/16	2.441	8.301	1.918	6.520
7/32	0.163	0.128	0.0479	0.0376	0.6872	1 5/8	2.641	8.978	2.074	7.051
15/64	0.187	0.147	0.0549	0.0431	0.7363	1 11/16	2.848	9.682	2.237	7.604
1/4	0.213	0.167	0.0625	0.0491	0.7854	1 3/4	3.063	10.41	2.405	8.178
17/64	0.240	0.188	0.0706	0.0554	0.8345	1 13/16	3.285	11.17	2.580	8.773
9/32	0.269	0.211	0.0791	0.0621	0.8836	1 7/8	3.516	11.95	2.761	9.388
19/64	0.300	0.235	0.0881	0.0692	0.9327	1 15/16	3.754	12.76	2.948	10.02
5/16	0.332	0.261	0.0977	0.0767	0.9817	2	4.000	13.60	3.142	10.68
11/32	0.402	0.316	0.1182	0.0928	1.0799	2 1/16	4.254	14.46	3.341	11.36
3/8	0.478	0.376	0.1406	0.1104	1.1781	2 1/8	4.516	15.35	3.547	12.06
13/32	0.561	0.441	0.1650	0.1296	1.2763	2 3/16	4.785	16.27	3.758	12.78
7/16	0.651	0.511	0.1914	0.1503	1.3744	2 1/4	5.063	17.22	3.976	13.52
15/32	0.747	0.587	0.2197	0.1726	1.4726	2 5/16	5.348	18.19	4.200	14.28
1/2	0.850	0.668	0.2500	0.1963	1.5708	2 3/8	5.641	19.18	4.430	15.07
17/32	0.960	0.754	0.2822	0.2217	1.6690	2 7/16	5.941	20.20	4.666	15.86
9/16	1.076	0.845	0.3164	0.2485	1.7671	2-1/2	6.250	21.25	4.909	16.69
19/32	1.199	0.941	0.3525	0.2769	1.8653	2 9/16	6.566	22.33	5.157	17.53
5/8	1.328	1.043	0.3906	0.3068	1.9635	2 5/8	6.891	23.43	5.412	18.40
11/16	1.607	1.262	0.4727	0.3712	2.1598	2 11/16	7.223	24.56	5.673	19.29
3/4	1.913	1.502	0.5625	0.4418	2.3562	2 3/4	7.563	25.71	5.940	20.20
13/16	2.245	1.763	0.6602	0.5185	2.5525	2 13/16	7.910	26.90	6.213	21.12
7/8	2.603	2.044	0.7656	0.6013	2.7489	2 7/8	8.266	28.10	6.492	22.07
15/16	2.989	2.347	0.8789	0.6903	2.9452	2 15/16	8.629	29.34	6.777	23.04

Thickness or Diameter in Inches	Area of □ Bar in Sq. Inches	Weight of □ Bar per Ft. in Lbs.	Area of ○ Bar in Sq. inches	Weight of ○ Bar per Ft. in Lbs.
3	9.000	30.60	7.069	24.03
3 1/16	9.379	31.89	7.366	25.04
3 1/8	9.766	33.20	7.670	26.08
3 3/16	10.16	34.55	7.980	27.13
3 1/4	10.56	35.92	8.296	28.20
3 5/16	10.97	37.31	8.618	29.30
3 3/8	11.39	38.73	8.946	30.42
3 7/16	11.82	40.18	9.281	31.56
3-1/2	12.25	41.65	9.621	32.71
3 9/16	12.69	43.14	9.968	33.90
3 5/8	13.14	44.68	10.32	35.09
3 11/16	13.60	46.24	10.68	36.31
3 3/4	14.06	47.82	11.05	37.56
3 13/16	14.54	49.42	11.42	38.81
3 7/8	15.02	51.05	11.79	40.10
3 15/16	15.50	52.71	12.18	41.40
4	16.00	54.40	12.57	42.73
4 1/16	16.50	56.11	12.96	44.07
4 1/8	17.02	57.85	13.36	45.44
4 3/16	17.54	59.62	13.77	46.83
4 1/4	18.06	61.41	14.19	48.24
4 5/16	18.60	63.23	14.61	49.66
4 3/8	19.14	65.08	15.03	51.11
4 7/16	19.69	66.95	15.47	52.58
4-1/2	20.25	68.85	15.90	54.07
4 9/16	20.82	70.78	16.35	55.59
4 5/8	21.39	72.73	16.80	57.12
4 11/16	21.97	74.70	17.26	58.67
4 3/4	22.56	76.71	17.72	60.25
4 13/16	23.16	78.74	18.19	61.84
4 7/8	23.77	80.81	18.67	63.46
4 15/16	24.38	82.89	19.15	65.10
5	25.00	85.00	19.64	66.76
5 1/16	25.63	87.14	20.13	68.44
5 1/8	26.27	89.30	20.63	70.14
5 3/16	26.91	91.49	21.14	71.86
5 1/4	27.56	93.72	21.65	73.60
5 5/16	28.22	95.96	22.17	75.37
5 3/8	28.89	98.23	22.69	77.15
5 7/16	29.57	100.5	23.22	78.95
5 1/2	30.25	102.8	23.76	80.77
5 9/16	30.94	105.2	24.30	82.62
5 5/8	31.64	107.6	24.85	84.49
5 11/16	32.35	110.0	25.41	86.38
5 3/4	33.06	112.4	25.97	88.29
5 13/16	33.79	114.9	26.54	90.22
5 7/8	34.52	117.4	27.11	92.17
5 15/16	35.25	119.9	27.69	94.14
6	36.00	122.4	28.27	96.14
6 1/8	37.52	127.6	29.47	100.2
6 1/4	39.06	132.8	30.68	104.3
6 3/8	40.64	138.2	31.92	108.5
6 1/2	42.25	143.6	33.18	112.8
6 5/8	43.89	149.2	34.47	117.2
6 3/4	45.56	154.9	35.79	121.7
6 7/8	47.27	160.8	37.12	126.2
7	49.00	166.6	38.49	130.9
7 1/4	52.56	178.7	41.28	140.4
7 1/2	56.25	191.3	44.18	150.2
7 3/4	60.06	204.2	47.17	160.3
8	64.00	217.6	50.27	171.0
8 1/4	68.06	231.4	53.46	181.8
8 1/2	72.25	245.6	56.75	193.0
8 3/4	76.56	260.3	60.13	204.4

* Weights are for steel at 489.6 lbs. per cubic foot. Adapted from the 1912 edition of the Cambria Steel Co. Hand Book.

Table 8

Weights and Safe Loads of Carnegie Angles

Unequal Legs Size of Angle, Inches	Thickness, Inches	Weight Per Foot, Lbs.	Safe Load Short Leg	Safe Load Long Leg	Equal Legs Size of Angle, Inches	Thickness, Inches	Weight Per Foot, Lbs.	Safe Load 1-Foot Span
4½ × 3	13/16	18.5	18.24	38.61	8 × 8	1 1/8	56.9	186.99
	9/16	13.3	13.33	28.16		13/16	42.0	139.84
	5/16	7.7	8.00	16.43		1/2	26.4	89.28
4 × 3½	13/16	18.5	24.53	31.15	6 × 6	1	37.4	91.41
	9/16	13.3	17.92	20.93		11/16	26.5	65.81
	5/16	7.7	10.67	13.44		3/8	14.9	37.65
4 × 3	13/16	17.1	17.92	30.61	5 × 5	1	30.6	61.87
	9/16	12.4	13.12	22.40		11/16	21.8	44.80
	1/4	5.8	6.40	10.67		3/8	12.3	25.81
3½ × 3	13/16	15.8	17.60	23.47	4 × 4	13/16	19.9	32.11
	9/16	11.4	12.91	17.17		9/16	14.3	23.36
	1/4	5.4	6.19	8.32		1/4	6.6	11.20
3½ × 2½	11/16	12.5	10.56	19.73	3½ × 3½	13/16	17.1	24.00
	1/2	9.4	8.11	15.04		9/16	12.4	17.60
	1/4	4.9	4.37	8.00		1/4	5.8	8.43
3 × 2½	9/16	9.5	8.75	12.27	3 × 3	5/8	11.5	13.87
	7/16	7.6	7.04	9.92		7/16	8.3	10.13
	1/4	4.5	4.27	5.97		1/4	4.9	6.19
3 × 2	1/2	7.7	5.01	10.67	2½ × 2½	1/2	7.7	7.79
	3/8	5.9	3.95	8.32		5/16	5.0	5.12
	1/4	4.1	2.77	5.76		1/8	2.08	2.13
2½ × 2	1/2	6.8	4.91	7.47	2 × 2	7/16	5.3	4.27
	5/16	4.5	3.31	5.01		1/4	3.19	2.67
	1/8	1.86	1.49	2.13		1/8	1.65	1.39
2½ × 1½	5/16	3.92	1.81	4.69	1¾ × 1¾	7/16	4.6	3.20
	3/16	2.44	1.17	2.99		5/16	3.39	2.45
2¼ × 1½	1/2	5.6	2.77	5.76		1/8	1.44	1.07
	3/16	2.28	1.17	2.45	1½ × 1½	3/8	3.35	2.03
2 × 1½	3/8	3.99	2.13	3.63		1/4	2.34	1.39
	1/8	1.44	0.80	1.39		1/8	1.23	0.77
2 × 1¼	1/4	2.55	1.04	2.45	1¼ × 1¼	5/16	2.33	1.17
	3/16	1.96	0.80	1.92		3/16	1.48	0.76
1¾ × 1¼	1/4	2.34	1.01	1.92		1/8	1.01	0.52
	1/8	1.23	0.56	1.00	1 × 1	1/4	1.49	0.60
1½ × 1¼	5/16	2.59	1.17	1.71		3/16	1.16	0.47
	3/16	1.64	0.78	1.07		1/8	0.80	0.33

Safe loads are given in thousands of pounds for one foot span.

Table 9

Weights and Safe Loads of Carnegie Channels

Depth of Channel Inches	Weight per Foot Lbs.	Area of Section Sq. In.	Thickness of Web Inches	Width of Flange Inches	Maximum Safe Load in Thousands of Lbs.
5.............	11½	3.38	0.48	2.04	44.4
5.............	9.	2.65	0.33	1.89	33.0
5.............	6½	1.95	0.19	1.75	+19.0
4.............	7¼	2.13	0.33	1.73	24.4
4.............	6¼	1.84	0.25	1.65	20.2
4.............	5¼	1.55	0.18	1.58	+14.4
3.............	6.	1.76	0.36	1.60	14.7
3.............	5.	1.47	0.26	1.50	13.1
3.............	4.	1.19	0.17	1.41	−10.2

TABLE 10

Weights and Safe Loads of Carnegie T-Shapes

Size, Flange by Stem. Inches	Minimum Thickness, Inches: Flange	Minimum Thickness, Inches: Stem.	Weight per Foot, Lb.	1 Ft. Span, Safe Load
5 × 3	½	—	13.4	11.41
5 × 2½	⅜	7/16	10.9	8.96
4½ × 3½	7/16	11/16	15.7	22.72
4½ × 3	⅜	⅜	9.8	9.71
4½ × 3	5/16	5/16	8.4	8.32
4½ × 2½	⅜	⅜	9.2	6.72
4½ × 2½	5/16	5/16	7.8	5.76
4 × 5	½	½	15.3	33.39
4 × 5	⅜	⅜	11.9	25.92
4 × 4½	½	½	14.4	27.09
4 × 4½	⅜	⅜	11.2	21.12
4 × 4	½	½	13.5	21.55
4 × 4	⅜	⅜	10.5	16.85
4 × 3	⅜	⅜	9.2	9.60
4 × 3	5/16	5/16	7.8	8.21
4 × 2½	⅜	⅜	8.5	6.61
4 × 2½	5/16	5/16	7.2	5.65
4 × 2	⅜	⅜	7.8	4.27
4 × 2	5/16	5/16	6.7	3.63
3½ × 4	½	½	12.6	21.12
3½ × 4	⅜	⅜	9.8	16.53
3½ × 3½	½	½	11.7	16.32
3½ × 3½	⅜	⅜	9.2	12.69
3½ × 3	½	½	10.8	12.05
3½ × 3	⅜	⅜	8.5	9.49
3½ × 3	5/16	⅜	7.5	9.07
3 × 4	½	½	11.7	20.69
3 × 4	7/16	7/16	10.5	18.35
3 × 4	⅜	⅜	9.2	16.11
3 × 3½	½	½	10.8	15.89
3 × 3½	7/16	7/16	9.7	14.19
3 × 3½	⅜	⅜	8.5	12.37
3 × 3	½	½	9.9	11.73
3 × 3	7/16	7/16	8.9	10.45
3 × 3	⅜	⅜	7.8	9.17
3 × 3	5/16	5/16	6.7	7.89
3 × 2½	⅜	⅜	7.1	6.40
3 × 2½	5/16	5/16	6.1	5.55
3 × 2½	¼	¼	5.0	4.59
2½ × 3	⅜	⅜	7.1	8.96
2½ × 3	5/16	5/16	6.1	7.68
2½ × 2½	⅜	⅜	6.4	6.29
2½ × 1¼	3/16	3/16	2.87	0.93
2¼ × 2¼	5/16	5/16	4.9	4.37
2 × 2	5/16	5/16	4.3	3.31
2 × 1½	¼	¼	3.09	1.60
1¾ × 1¾	¼	¼	3.09	2.03
1½ × 1½	¼	¼	2.47	1.49
1¼ × 1¼	¼	¼	2.02	1.01
1 × 1	3/16	3/16	1.25	0.49

How to Estimate on Quantity and Cost of Corrugated Sheets

First, select the best lengths of sheets that will fit the space you intend covering, not forgetting the end laps.

On siding, a one-inch or two-inch end lap is sufficient, but on roofing it varies from three to six inches, according to pitch of roof.

Our common 2½-inch corrugated sheets will lay 24 inches wide with a side lap of one corrugation, but the selling measurement is 26 inches wide.

A	6-foot	sheet	will	measure	13	sq. ft.	and	lay	12	sq. ft.
"	7 "	"	"	"	15⅙	"	"	"	14	"
"	8 "	"	"	"	17⅓	"	"	"	16	"
"	9 "	"	"	"	19½	"	"	"	18	"
"	10 "	"	"	"	21⅔	"	"	"	20	"

In the above table, end laps are not considered.

You make your own allowance for end laps.

The extreme length of corrugated sheets is 10 feet.

TABLE 11

Measurements of Corrugated Sheets

Kind of Corrugation, Inches	Width of Corrugation, Inches	Depth of Corrugation, Inches	Number of Corrugations to the Sheet	Covering Width Lapped One Corrugation, Inches	Width of Sheet Corrugated, Inches	Length of Longest Sheets Furnished, Feet
5	5	1	6	24	27	10
2½	2½	½ to ⅝	10	24	26	10
1¼	1¼	⅜ to ½	19½	24	26	10
¾	¾	¼	34½	25	26	8

TABLE 12

Weight of Corrugated Sheets Per Square for Sheets 30½ Inches Wide Before Corrugating

Number by Birmingham Gauge	Thickness, Inches	Weight per Sq. Ft. Flat, Lbs.	Weight per Sq. Ft. Corrugated, Lbs.	Weight per Square of 100 Square Feet, when Laid, Allowing 6 Inches Lap in Length and 2½ Inches or One Corrugation in Width of Sheet for Sheet Lengths of						Weight per Sq. Ft. Flat Galvanized
				5 Feet	6 Feet	7 Feet	8 Feet	9 Feet	10 Feet	
16	.065	2.61	3.28	365	358	353	350	348	346	2.95
18	.049	1.97	2.48	275	270	267	264	262	261	2.31
20	.035	1.40	1.76	196	192	190	188	186	185	1.74
22	.028	1.12	1.41	156	154	152	150	149	148	1.46
24	.022	.88	1.11	123	121	119	118	117	117	1.22
26	.018	.72	.91	101	99	97	97	96	95	1.06

TABLE 13

Weight of Corrugated Sheets Per 100 Square Feet in Pounds

Corrugations,	5/8 in.		1 1/4 in.		2 in.		2 1/2 in. 26 in. Wide		2 1/2 in. 27 1/2 in. Wide		3 in.		5 in.	
U. S. Std. Sheet Metal Gauge	Painted	Galvanized	Painted	Galvanized	Painted	Galvanized	Painted	Galvanized	Painted	Galvanized	Painted	Galvanized	Painted	Galvanized
29	...	81	...	81	...	77	...	77	...	78	...	77	...	77
28	71	88	71	88	68	84	68	84	69	85	68	84	68	84
27	78	95	78	95	75	91	75	91	76	92	75	91	75	91
26	85	102	85	102	82	98	82	98	83	99	82	98	81	97
25	99	116	99	116	95	111	95	111	97	113	95	111	95	111
24	113	130	113	130	109	125	109	125	110	126	109	125	108	124
23	...	...	127	144	122	138	122	138	124	140	122	138	122	137
22	...	...	141	158	136	151	136	151	137	153	136	151	135	151
21	...	...	155	172	149	165	149	165	151	167	149	165	148	164
20	...	...	169	186	163	178	163	178	165	181	163	178	162	178
18	...	...	...	...	216	232	216	232	219	235	216	232	215	231
16	...	...	...	...	270	286	270	286	274	290	270	286	269	285
14	...	...	...	...	...	...	338	353	342	358	338	353	336	352
12	...	...	...	...	...	...	472	488	478	494	472	488	470	486
10	...	...	...	...	...	...	607	623	615	631	...	...	...	...

TABLE 14

Number of Corrugated Iron and Steel Sheets in One Square (100 Square Feet)

Length of Sheet, Inches	3-Inch Corrugations. Width (flat) 28 Inches. Width (after corrugating) 26 Inches	2 1/2-Inch Corrugations. Width (flat) 28 Inches. Width (after corrugating) 26 Inches	1 1/4-Inch Corrugations. Width (flat) 28 Inches. Width (after corrugating) 25 Inches.
72	7.692	7.692	8.000
84	6.593	6.593	6.857
96	5.769	5.769	6.000
108	5.128	5.128	5.333
120	4.616	4.616	4.800

TABLE 15

Spacing of Supports for Corrugated Sheets

Nos. 16 and 18	6 to 7 feet apart
Nos. 20 and 22	4 to 5 feet apart
No. 24	2 to 4 feet apart
No. 28	2 feet apart

TABLE 16

Comparison of Standard Gauges for Wire and Sheet Metal

Diameter or Thickness in Decimals of an Inch

Number of Gauge	United States Gauge for Sheet and Plate Iron and Steel	American or Brown & Sharpe Wire-Gauge	Birmingham or Stubs Iron Wire-Gauge	John A. Roebling's Sons Co. Wire-Gauge	British Imperial or English Standard Wire-Gauge	Trenton Iron Co. Wire-Gauge	American Screw Co. Wire-Gauge
0000000	0.5	....	......	0.4900	0.500	....	....
000000	0.46875	0.580000	......	0.4615	0.464	....	....
00000	0.4375	0.516500	0.500	0.4305	0.432	0.450	....
0000	0.40625	0.460000	0.454	0.3938	0.400	0.400	....
000	0.375	0.409642	0.425	0.3625	0.372	0.360	0.0315
00	0.34375	0.364796	0.380	0.3310	0.348	0.330	0.0447
0	0.3125	0.324861	0.340	0.3065	0.324	0.305	0.0578
1	0.2825	0.289297	0.300	0.2830	0.300	0.285	0.0710
2	0.265625	0.257627	0.284	0.2625	0.276	0.265	0.0842
3	0.25	0.229423	0.259	0.2437	0.252	0.245	0.0973
4	0.234375	0.204307	0.238	0.2253	0.232	0.225	0.1105
5	0.21875	0.181940	0.220	0.2070	0.212	0.205	0.1236
6	0.203125	0.162023	0.203	0.1920	0.192	0.190	0.1368
7	0.1875	0.144285	0.180	0.1770	0.176	0.175	0.1500
8	0.171875	0.128490	0.165	0.1620	0.160	0.160	0.1631
9	0.15625	0.114423	0.148	0.1433	0.144	0.145	0.1763
10	0.140625	0.101897	0.134	0.1350	0.128	0.130	0.1894
11	0.125	0.090742	0.120	0.1205	0.116	0.1175	0.2026
12	0.109375	0.080808	0.109	0.1055	0.104	0.105	0.2158
13	0.09375	0.071962	0.095	0.0915	0.092	0.0925	0.2289
14	0.078125	0.064084	0.083	0.0800	0.080	0.0806	0.2421
15	0.0703125	0.057068	0.072	0.0720	0.072	0.070	0.2552
16	0.0625	0.050821	0.065	0.0625	0.064	0.061	0.2684
17	0.05625	0.045257	0.058	0.0540	0.056	0.0525	0.2816
18	0.05	0.040303	0.049	0.0475	0.048	0.045	0.2947
19	0.04375	0.035890	0.042	0.0410	0.040	0.040	0.3079
20	0.0375	0.031961	0.035	0.0348	0.036	0.035	0.3210
21	0.034375	0.028462	0.032	0.03175	0.032	0.031	0.3342
22	0.03125	0.025346	0.028	0.0286	0.028	0.028	0.3474
23	0.028125	0.022572	0.025	0.0258	0.024	0.025	0.3605
24	0.025	0.020101	0.022	0.230	0.022	0.0225	0.3737
25	0.021875	0.017900	0.020	0.0204	0.020	0.020	0.3868
26	0.01875	0.015941	0.018	0.0181	0.018	0.018	0.4000
27	0.0171875	0.014195	0.016	0.0173	0.0164	0.017	0.4132
28	0.015625	0.012641	0.014	0.0162	0.0148	0.016	0.4263
29	0.0140625	0.011257	0.013	0.0150	0.0136	0.015	0.4395
30	0.0125	0.010025	0.012	0.0140	0.0124	0.014	0.4526
31	0.0109375	0.008928	0.010	0.0132	0.0116	0.013	0.4658
32	0.01015625	0.007950	0.009	0.0128	0.0108	0.012	0.4790
33	0.009375	0.007080	0.008	0.0118	0.0100	0.011	0.4921
34	0.00859375	0.006305	0.007	0.0104	0.0092	0.010	0.5053
35	0.0078125	0.005615	0.005	0.0095	0.0084	0.0095	0.5184
36	0.00703125	0.005000	0.004	0.0090	0.0076	0.009	0.5316
37	0.006640625	0.004453	......	0.0085	0.0068	0.0085	0.5448
38	0.00625	0.003965	......	0.0080	0.0060	0.008	0.5579
39	....	0.003531	......	0.0075	0.0052	0.0075	0.5711
40	....	0.003144	......	0.0070	0.0048	0.007	0.5842

As there are many gauges in use differing from each other, and even the thicknesses of a certain specified gauge, as the Birmingham, are not assumed the same by all manufacturers, orders for sheets and wires should always state the weight per square foot, or the thickness in thousandths of an inch.

TABLE 17

Weight of Sheets of Wrought Iron, Steel, Copper and Brass Per Square Foot in Pounds

American or B. & S. Gauge	Thickness in Inches	Iron	Steel	Copper	Brass
0000	.46	18.46	18.70	20.84	19.69
000	.4096	16.44	16.66	18.56	17.53
00	.3648	14.64	14.83	16.53	15.61
0	.3249	13.04	13.21	14.72	13.90
1	.2893	11.61	11.76	13.11	12.38
2	.2576	10.34	10.48	11.67	11.03
3	.2294	9.21	9.33	10.39	9.82
4	.2043	8.20	8.31	9.26	8.74
5	.1319	7.30	7.40	8.24	7.79
6	.1620	6.50	6.59	7.34	6.93
7	.1443	5.79	5.87	6.54	6.18
8	.1285	5.16	5.22	5.82	5.50
9	.1144	4.59	4.65	5.18	4.90
10	.1019	4.09	4.14	4.62	4.36
11	.0907	3.64	3.69	4.11	3.88
12	.0808	3.24	3.29	3.66	3.46
13	.0720	2.89	2.93	3.26	3.08
14	.0641	2.57	2.61	2.90	2.74
15	.0571	2.29	2.32	2.59	2.44
16	.0508	2.04	2.07	2.30	2.18
17	.0453	1.82	1.84	2.05	1.94
18	.0403	1.62	1.64	1.83	1.73
19	.0359	1.44	1.46	1.63	1.54
20	.0320	1.28	1.30	1.45	1.37
21	.0285	1.14	1.16	1.29	1.22
22	.0253	1.02	1.03	1.15	1.08
23	.0226	.906	.918	1.02	.966
24	.0201	.807	.817	.911	.860
25	.0179	.718	.728	.811	.766
26	.0159	.640	.648	.722	.682
27	.0142	.570	.577	.643	.608
28	.0126	.507	.514	.573	.541
29	.0113	.452	.458	.510	.482
30	.0100	.402	.408	.454	.429
31	.0089	.358	.363	.404	.382
32	.0080	.319	.323	.360	.340
33	.0071	.284	.288	.321	.303
34	.0063	.253	.256	.286	.270
35	.0056	.225	.228	.254	.240

Table 18

Weights of Steel, Wrought Iron, Brass and Copper Plates

Number of Gauge	Thickness in Inches	Birmingham or Stubs' Gauge Weights in Lbs. per Foot			
		Steel	Iron	Brass	Copper
0000	.454	18.52	18.16	19.431	20.556
000	.425	17.34	17.00	18.190	19.253
00	.380	15.30	15.20	16.264	17.214
0	.340	13.87	13.60	14.552	15.402
1	.300	12.24	12.00	12.840	13.590
2	.284	11.59	11.36	12.155	12.865
3	.259	10.57	10.36	11.085	11.733
4	.238	9.71	9.52	10.186	10.781
5	.220	8.98	8.80	9.416	9.966
6	.203	8.28	8.12	8.689	9.196
7	.180	7.34	7.20	7.704	8.154
8	.165	6.73	6.60	7.062	7.475
9	.148	6.04	5.92	6.334	6.704
10	.134	5.47	5.36	5.735	6.070
11	.120	4.90	4.80	5.137	5.436
12	.109	5.45	4.36	4.667	4.938
13	.095	3.88	3.80	4.066	4.303
14	.083	3.39	3.32	3.552	3.769
15	.072	2.94	2.88	3.081	3.262
16	.065	2.65	2.60	2.782	2.945
17	.058	2.37	2.32	2.482	2.627
18	.049	2.00	1.96	2.097	2.220
19	.042	1.71	1.68	1.797	1.902
20	.035	1.43	1.40	1.498	1.585
21	.032	1.31	1.28	1.369	1.450
22	.028	1.14	1.12	1.198	1.270
23	.025	1.02	1.10	1.070	1.132
24	.022	.898	.88	.941	.997
25	.020	.816	.80	.856	.906
26	.018	.734	.72	.770	.815
27	.016	.653	.64	.685	.725
28	.014	.571	.56	.599	.634
29	.013	.530	.52	.556	.589
30	.012	.490	.48	.514	.544
31	.010	.408	.40	.428	.453
32	.009	.367	.36	.385	.408
33	.008	.326	.32	.342	.362
34	.007	.286	.28	.2996	.317
35	.005	.204	.20	.214	.227
36	.004	.163	.16	.171	.181

TABLE 19 Net Weight Per Box Bright Tin Plates in Pounds

Basis 10 x 14, 225 sheets; or, 14 x 20, 112 sheets.

Trade term		80 lb.	85 lb.	90 lb.	95 lb.	100 lb.	IC	IXL	IX	IXX	IXXX	IXXXX
Stubs Iron Wire gauge No.		34	33	32	31½	31	30	28½	28	27	26	25
Size of Sheets.	Sheets per Box.	Weight per Box of Sizes Specified in Pounds										
10 x 14	225	80	85	90	95	100	107	128	135	156	176	196
14 x 20	112	80	85	90	95	100	107	128	135	156	176	196
20 x 28	112	160	170	180	190	200	214	256	270	312	352	392
10 x 20	225	114	121	129	136	143	153	183	193	223	251	280
11 x 11	225	69	73	78	82	86	92	111	117	135	152	169
11 x 22	225	138	147	156	164	172	184	222	234	270	304	339
11½ x 23	225	151	161	170	179	189	202	242	255	295	333	370
12 x 12	225	82	87	93	98	103	110	132	139	160	181	202
12 x 24	112	82	87	93	98	103	110	132	139	160	181	202
13 x 13	225	97	103	109	115	121	129	154	163	188	212	236
13 x 26	112	97	103	109	115	121	129	154	163	188	212	236
14 x 14	225	112	119	126	133	140	150	179	189	218	246	274
14 x 28	112	112	119	126	133	140	150	179	189	218	246	274
15 x 15	225	129	137	145	153	161	172	206	217	251	283	315
16 x 16	225	146	155	165	174	183	196	234	247	285	322	358
17 x 17	225	165	175	186	196	206	221	264	279	322	363	405
18 x 18	112	93	98	104	110	116	124	148	156	180	204	227
19 x 19	112	103	110	116	122	129	138	165	174	201	227	253
20 x 20	112	114	121	129	136	143	153	183	193	223	251	280
21 x 21	112	126	134	142	150	158	169	202	213	246	277	309
22 x 22	112	138	147	156	164	172	184	221	234	270	304	339

TABLE 19 (Continued) **Net Weight Per Box Bright Tin Plates in Pounds**

Basis 10 x 14, 225 sheets; or, 14 x 20, 112 sheets.

Weight per box, pounds		80	85	90	95	100	107	128	135	156	176	196
Size of Sheets.	Sheets per Box.	Weight per Box of Sizes Specified in Pounds										
23 x 23	112	151	161	170	179	189	202	242	255	295	333	370
24 x 24	112	164	175	185	195	204	220	263	278	321	362	404
26 x 26	112	193	205	217	229	241	258	309	326	377	424	472
13½ x 19½	112	75	80	85	89	94	100	120	127	147	165	183
14 x 18¾	124	83	88	93	98	103	110	132	139	161	182	202
14 x 19¼	120	83	88	93	98	103	110	132	139	161	182	202
14 x 21	112	84	89	95	100	105	112	134	142	164	185	206
14 x 22	112	88	94	99	105	110	118	141	149	172	194	216
15 x 21	112	80	95	101	107	113	120	144	152	176	197	220
16 x 20	112	91	97	103	109	114	122	146	154	178	201	224
14 x 31	112	124	132	140	147	155	166	198	209	242	273	304
Approximate Wire Gauge D Plates							No. 28		No. 25	No. 24	No. 23	No. 22
12½ x 17D	100						94		122	142	162	182
17 x 25D	50						94		122	142	162	182
15 x 21D	100						140		181	211	241	271

	10 x 14		14 x 20		20 x 28		20 x 40	
Taggers Iron and Tin.	Sheets per box.	Pounds per box.	Sheets per box.	Pounds per box.	Sheets per box.	Pounds per box.	Sheets per box.	Pounds per box.
No. 30 W G			112	107	112	214	79	224
No. 32 W G			128	112	128	224	79	180
No. 34 W G	300	112	150	112	150	224	79	160
No. 36 W G	360	112	180	112	180	224		
No. 38 W G	450	112	225	112	225	224		

TABLE 20

Weights of Standard Galvanized Sheets

Gauge	Oz. Per Sq. Ft.	Lb. Per Sq. Ft.	Gauge	Oz. Per Sq. Ft.	Lb. Per Sq. Ft.	Gauge	Oz. Per Sq. Ft.	Lb. Per Sq. Ft.	Gauge	Oz. Per Sq. Ft.	Lb. Per Sq. Ft.
8	112.5	7.031	15	47.5	2.969	22	22.5	1.406	29	11.5	0.719
9	102.5	6.406	16	42.5	2.656	23	20.5	1.281	30	10.5	.656
10	92.5	5.781	17	38.5	2.406	24	18.5	1.156	31	9.5	.594
11	82.5	5.156	18	34.5	2.156	25	16.5	1.031	32	9.0	.563
12	72.5	4.531	19	30.5	1.906	26	14.5	0.906	33	8.5	.531
13	62.5	3.906	20	26.5	1.656	27	13.5	.844	34	8.0	.500
14	52.5	3.281	21	24.5	1.531	28	12.5	.781	..	....	.....

TABLE 21

Ordinary Dimensions of Galvanized Sheets

Widths.........	40	38	36	34	32	30	28	26	24	22	20
Gauges.						Lengths.					
No. 14.........	...	...	96	96	96	96	96	96	96	96	96
Nos. 16 to 22....	120	120	120	120	120	120	120	120	120	120	120
Nos. 23 and 24..	96	96	96	96	108	120	120	120	120	108	108
Nos. 25 to 28....	...	...	96	96	108	120	120	120	120	108	108
Nos. 29 and 30..	...	...	...	...	...	96	96	96	96	...	...

TABLE 22

Weights and Sizes of Sheet Lead

The thickness of lead is in common determined or understood by the weight, the unit being that of a square or superficial foot; a square foot 1/16 of an inch thick weighs four pounds.

12	Ounce	Lead	is	.013	Inch	Thick	8	Pound	Lead	is	1/8	Inch	Thick
1	Pound	"	"	1/64	"	"	10	"	"	"	5/32	"	"
1½	"	"	"	1/43	"	"	12	"	"	"	3/16	"	"
2	"	"	"	1/32	"	"	14	"	"	"	7/32	"	"
2½	"	"	"	1/24	"	"	16	"	"	"	1/4	"	"
3	"	"	"	3/64	"	"	20	"	"	"	5/16	"	"
4	"	"	"	1/16	"	"	24	"	"	"	3/8	"	"
5	"	"	"	5/64	"	"	32	"	"	"	1/2	"	"
6	"	"	"	3/32	"	"	60	"	"	"	1	"	"
7	"	"	"	7/64	"	"							

TABLE 23

Standard Weights and Gauges of Tin Plate

Trade Term	Nearest Wire Gauge No.	Wt. Per Sq. Ft. Lbs.	Wt. of Box 14 × 20 in., Lbs.	Trade Term	Nearest Wire Gauge No.	Wt. Per Sq. Ft. Lbs.	Wt. of Box 14 × 20 in., Lbs.	Trade Term	Nearest Wire Gauge No.	Wt. Per Sq. Ft. Lbs.	Wt. of Box 14 × 20 in, Lbs.
55 lb.	38	0.252	55	100 lb.	30½	0.459	100	3XL	26	0.771	168
60 "	37	.275	60	IC	30	.491	107	DX	26	.826	180
65 "	36	.298	65	118 lb.	29	.542	118	4X	25	.895	195
70 "	35	.321	70	IX	28	.619	135	4XL	25	.863	188
75 "	34	.344	75	IXL	28	.588	128	D2X	24	.964	210
80 "	33	.367	80	DC	28	.638	139	D3X	23	1.102	240
85 "	32	.390	85	2X	27	.711	155	D4X	22	1.239	270
90 "	31	.413	90	2XL	27	.679	148	....	....	.....	....
95 "	31	.436	95	3X	26	.803	175	....	....	.....	....

TABLE 24

Specifications for Tin and Terne Plate

	Material Desired			Rejected if Less Than		
	Tin Plate	No. 1 Terne	No. 2 Terne	Tin Plate	No. 1 Terne	No. 2 Terne
Coating:						
Tin, per cent......	100	26	16	......	......	.....
Lead, per cent.....	0	74	84	......	......	.....
Amount per sq. ft. lb.	0.023	0.046	0.023	0.0183	0.0413	0.083
Weight, lb. per sq. ft. of						
Grade IC.........	0.496	0.519	0.496	0.468	0.490	0.468
Grade IX.........	.625	.648	.625	.590	.612	.590
Grade IXX.......	.716	.739	.716	.676	.699	.676
Grade IXXX.....	.808	.831	.808	.763	.787	.763
Grade IXXXX...	.900	.925	.900	.850	.874	.850

TABLE 25

Weight of Terne Plates

TERNE PLATES, or Roofing Tin, are coated with an alloy of tin and lead. In the "U. S. Eagle, N.M." brand the alloy is 32% tin, 68% lead. The weight per 112 sheets of this brand before and after coating is as follows:

	IC 14 x 20	IC 20 x 28	IX 14 x 20	IX 20 x 28
Black plates	95 to 100 lb.	190 to 200 lb.	125 to 130 lb.	250 to 260 lb.
After coating	115 to 120	230 to 240	145 to 150	290 to 300

Terne plates are made in two thicknesses: 1C, in which the iron body weighs about 50 lb. per 100 sq. ft., and IX, in which it weighs 62½ lb. per 100 sq. ft. The IC grade is preferred for roofing, while the IX grade is used for spouts, valleys, gutters, and flashings. The standard weight of 14 x 20 in. IC plates is 107 lb. per base-box, and of 14 x 20 in. IX plate 135 lb.

Long terne sheets are made in gauges, Nos. 14 to 32, from 10 to 40 in. wide and up to 12 in. long. They are made in five grades with coatings of 8, 12, 15, 20, and 25 lb.

A box of 112 sheets 14 x 20 in. will cover approximately 192 sq. ft. of roof, flat seam, or 583 sheets 1,000 sq. ft. For standing seam roofing a sheet 20 x 28 in. will cover 475 sq. in. or 303 sheets per 1,000 sq. ft. A box of 112 sheets 20 x 28 in. will cover approximately 366 sq. ft.

The common sizes of tin plates are 10 x 14 in. and multiples of that measure. The sizes most generally used are 14 x 20 and 20 x 28 in.

TABLE 26

Thickness and Weight Per Sq. Foot of Sheet Tin

1	lb. tin is 1/40 inch thick	3½	lb. tin is 1/11 inch thick
1½	lb. tin is 1/21 inch thick	4	lb. tin is 1/10 inch thick
2	lb. tin is 1/20 inch thick	4½	lb. tin is 1/9 inch thick
2½	lb. tin is 1/16 inch thick	5	lb. tin is ⅛ inch thick
3	lb. tin is 1/13 inch thick	10	lb. tin is ¼ inch thick

20 lb. tin is ½ inch thick

TABLE 27

Pure Block-Tin Pipe

Calibre	Weight Per Ft. Oz.	Calibre	Weight per Ft. Lbs.	Oz.
⅛ inch strong............	2½	½ inch double extra strong..		15
¼ " extra strong.......	5	⅝ " extra strong........		9
¼ " double extra strong.	6	⅝ " double extra strong..		14
5/16 " double extra strong.	6½	¾ " extra strong........		11
⅜ " extra strong.......	6	¾ " double extra strong..	1	..
⅜ " double extra strong.	8	1 " extra strong........		14
½ " strong............	6½	1 " double extra strong..	1	4
½ " extra strong.......	10			

TABLE 28

Weight of Round Zinc Rods Per Lineal Foot

3/8 inch diameter	....	.33 pounds
1/2 " "	....	.58 "
5/8 " "	....	.90 "
3/4 " "	....	1.30 "
7/8 " "	....	1.78 "
1 " "	....	2.32 "

TABLE 29

Weights of Aluminum Sheets

Stubs' Gauge (Nearest) No.	Thickness in Decimal Parts of 1 Inch	Weight in Pounds of Aluminum of Same Thickness				
		Sheets 14 x 48	Sheets 24 x 48	Sheets 30 x 60	Sheets 36 x 72	Sheets 48 x 72
35	.00537	0.35	0.61	0.96	1.38	1.83
33	.00806	0.53	0.92	1.43	2.06	2.75
31	.0107	0.71	1.22	1.91	2.75	3.66
29	.0134	0.89	1.53	2.38	3.43	4.57
27	.0161	1.07	1.83	2.86	4.12	5.49
26	.0188	1.25	2.14	3.33	4.80	6.40
24	.0215	1.42	2.44	3.81	5.49	7.32
23	.0242	1.60	2.75	4.29	6.17	8.23
22	.0269	1.78	3.05	4.76	6.86	9.14
21	.0322	2.14	3.66	5.72	8.23	11.00
19	.0430	2.85	4.88	7.62	11.00	14.70
18	.0538	3.56	6.10	9.52	13.75	18.30
16	.0645	4.27	7.32	11.45	16.50	22.00
15	.0754	4.98	8.53	13.35	19.20	25.60
14	.0860	5.69	9.75	15.30	21.95	29.30
13	.095	.....	10.70	16.80	24.10	32.00
12	.109	.....	12.40	19.20	27.75	37.20
11	.120	.....	13.60	21.35	30.50	40.85
10	.134	.....	15.30	23.80	34.20	45.70
9	.148	.....	16.80	26.20	37.80	50.30
8	.165	.....	18.60	29.30	42.10	56.10
7	.180	.....	20.40	32.00	46.00	61.30
6	.203	.....	23.00	36.00	51.80	69.20
5	.220	.....	25.00	39.00	56.10	75.00
4	.238	.....	27.00	42.10	60.70	81.10
3	.259	.....	29.30	46.00	66.10	88.10
2	.284	.....	32.20	50.30	72.50	96.60
1	.300	.....	34.00	53.10	76.50	102.20
0	.340	.....	38.60	60.40	86.90	116.00

One ounce per square foot aluminum sheet is 0.0044 inch thick and corresponds to about No. 37 B. & S. gauge.

Rolled Aluminum has a specific gravity of 2.72. One cubic foot weighs $196^{510}/_{1000}$ pounds. One square foot of one inch thick weighs $14^{126}/_{1000}$ pounds.

TABLE 30

Thickness and Weights of Sheet Zinc

M & H Gauge No.		4	5	6	7	8	9	10	11	12	13	14	15	16	17	18	19	20	21	22
Weight per Sq. Ft. in Lbs.		.30	.37	.45	.52	.60	.67	.75	.90	1.05	1.20	1.35	1.50	1.68	1.87	2.06	2.25	2.62	3.00	3.37
Thickness in Ins. Approx.		.008	.010	.012	.014	.016	.018	.020	.024	.028	.032	.036	.040	.045	.050	.055	.060	.070	.080	.090
Size of Sheet	Sq. Ft. per Sheet	APPROXIMATE WEIGHT PER SHEET Sizes 8 to 15 are the same as U. S. Standard Ncs. 20 to 28.																		
24 x 84	14.	4.2	5.2	6.3	7.3	8.4	9.4	10.5	12.6	14.7	16.8	18.9	21.	23.5	26.2	28.9	31.5	36.7	42.	47.2
26 x 84	15.2	4.6	5.6	6.9	7.9	9.1	10.2	11.4	13.7	16.	18.3	20.5	22.8	25.6	28.4	31.3	34.2	39.9	45.6	51.2
28 x 84	16.3	4.9	6.	7.4	8.5	9.8	10.9	12.2	14.7	17.1	19.6	22.	24.5	27.4	30.5	33.6	36.7	42.7	48.9	54.9
30 x 84	17.5	5.3	6.5	7.9	9.1	10.5	11.8	13.2	15.8	18.4	21.	23.6	26.2	29.4	32.8	36.1	39.4	45.8	52.5	59.
32 x 84	18.7	5.6	6.9	8.4	9.7	11.2	12.6	14.1	16.9	19.7	22.5	25.3	32.8	31.4	35.	38.5	42.	49.	56.1	63.
34 x 84	19.9	6.0	7.4	9.	10.4	12.	13.4	15.	18.	20.9	23.9	26.9	29.9	33.4	37.2	41.	44.8	52.2	59.7	67.
36 x 84	21.	6.3	7.8	9.5	10.9	12.6	14.1	15.8	18.9	22.	25.2	28.4	31.5	35.3	39.3	43.3	47.2	55.	63.	70.8
36 x 96	24.	7.2	8.9	10.8	12.5	14.4	16.1	18.	21.6	25.2	28.8	32.4	36.	40.3	44.9	49.5	54.	62.8	72.	80.9
36 x 108	27.	8.1	10.	12.2	14.1	16.2	18.1	20.3	24.3	28.4	32.4	36.5	40.5	45.4	50.5	55.6	60.7	70.7	81.	91.
40 x 84	23.4	7.	8.7	10.6	12.2	14.1	15.7	17.6	21.	24.6	28.1	31.6	35.1	39.3	43.8	48.2	52.6	61.3	70.2	78.8
40 x 96	26.8	8.	9.9	12.1	14.	16.1	18.	20.1	24.1	28.1	32.2	36.2	40.2	45.	50.1	55.2	60.3	70.2	80.4	90.3
44 x 84	25.7	7.7	9.5	11.6	13.4	15.4	17.2	19.3	23.1	27.	30.8	34.7	38.6	43.2	48.1	53.	57.8	67.4	77.1	86.6
46 x 90	28.7	8.6	10.6	12.9	14.9	17.2	19.2	21.5	25.8	30.1	34.4	38.7	43.	48.2	53.7	59.1	64.6	75.2	86.1	96.7
48 x 84	28.	8.4	10.4	12.6	14.6	16.8	18.8	21.	25.2	29.4	33.6	37.8	42.	47.	52.4	57.7	63.	73.4	84.	94.4
48 x 96	32.	9.6	11.9	14.4	16.7	19.2	21.5	24.	28.8	33.6	38.4	43.2	48.	53.8	59.9	65.9	72.	83.9	96.	107.8
50 x 108	37.5	11.3	13.9	16.9	19.5	22.5	25.1	28.2	33.8	39.3	45.	50.7	56.3	63.	70.1	77.3	84.4	98.3	112.5	126.4
52 x 84	30.4	9.1	11.3	13.7	15.8	18.3	20.4	22.8	27.4	31.9	36.5	41.	45.6	51.	56.9	62.6	68.4	79.6	91.2	102.5

Casks average about 600 pounds each. No. 4 to No. 17. Boxes average about 500 pounds. No. 18 and heavier.

TABLE 31

Weight of Aluminum Sheets

B. & S. Gauge No.	B. & S. Gauge Decimal Parts of an Inch	Corresponding Fractional Part of an Inch	Weight Per Sq. Ft. Aluminum, Lbs.	B. & S. Gauge No.	B. & S. Gauge Decimal Parts of an Inch	Corresponding Fractional Part of an Inch	Weight Per Sq. Ft. Aluminum, Lbs.
0000	.460	15/32	6.406	20	.032	1/32	.445
000	.410	..	5.704	21	.028	..	.396
00	.365	3/8	5.080	22	.025	..	.353
0	.325	21/64	4.524	23	.023	..	.314
1	.289	9/32	4.029	24	.020	..	.280
2	.258	1/4	3.588	25	.018	..	.249
3	.229	15/64	3.195	26	.016	1/64	.222
4	.204	13/64	2.845	27	.014	..	.197
5	.182	3/16	2.534	28	.013	..	.176
6	.162	5/32	2.256	29	.011	..	.157
7	.144	9/64	2.009	30	.010	..	.140
8	.128	1/8	1.789	31	.009	..	.124
9	.114	7/64	1.594	32	.00795	..	.1107
10	.102	..	1.418	33	.00708	..	.0985
11	.091	3/32	1.264	34	.0063	..	.0877
12	.081	5/64	1.126	35	.0056	..	.0782
13	.072	..	1.002	36	.005	..	.0696
14	.064	1/16	.892	37	.00445	..	.0620
15	.057	..	.795	38	.00396	..	.0052
16	.051	..	.708	39	.00353	..	.0491
17	.045	3/64	.630	40	.00314	..	.0438
18	.040	..	.561	41	.0028	..	.....
19	.036	..	.500	42	.00249	..	.....

To obtain the weight of aluminum in bars, sheets, etc., divide the weight of similar pieces of copper by 3.3, brass by 3.1 and steel by 2.9.

TABLE 32

Weights of Aluminum and Brass Sheets

Stubs' Gauge Nearest No.	Weight Per Sq. Ft. in Ounces		Stubs' Gauge Nearest No.	Weight Per Sq. Ft. in Ounces	
	Brass	Aluminum		Brass	Aluminum
35	3.424	1.22	13	65.05	21.35
33	5.472	1.83	12	74.67	24.70
31	6.846	2.44	11	82.19	27.15
29	8.896	3.05	10	91.76	30.50
27	10.96	3.60	9	101.34	33.55
26	12.32	4.27	8	112.09	37.50
24	15.05	4.88	7	123.26	40.85
23	17.12	5.49	6	139.02	46.00
22	19.20	6.10	5	150.65	50.00
21	21.92	7.32	4	163.04	53.95
19	28.80	9.75	3	177.44	64.30
18	33.60	12.20	2	194.48	67.95
16	44.48	14.65	1	205.44	77.10
15	49.28	17.10	0	232.83	.....
14	56.83	19.50			

Table 33

Weight of Square and Round Aluminum Bars

Thickness, Side, or Dia.	Square Bars, 1 Ft. Long	Round Bars, 1 Ft. Long	Thickness, Side, or Dia.	Square Bars, 1 Ft. Long	Round Bars, 1 Ft. Long	Thickness, Side, or Dia.	Square Bars, 1 Ft. Long	Round Bars, 1 Ft. Long
In.	Lb.	Lb.	In.	Lb.	Lb.	In.	Lb.	Lb.
1/16	0.004	0.003	3/4	0.652	0.516	1 7/16	2.396	1.882
1/8	.018	.014	13/16	.766	.601	1 1/2	2.609	2.049
3/16	.041	.032	7/8	.888	.697	1 9/16	2.831	2.223
1/4	.072	.057	15/16	1.019	.800	1 5/8	3.062	2.405
5/16	.114	.089	1	1.159	.911	1 11/16	3.302	2.593
3/8	.163	.128	1 1/16	1.309	1.028	1 3/4	3.550	2.789
7/16	.222	.174	1 1/8	1.467	1.152	1 13/16	3.810	2.992
1/2	.290	.227	1 3/16	1.635	1.284	1 7/8	4.075	3.202
9/16	.367	.288	1 1/4	1.812	1.423	1 15/16	4.352	3.417
5/8	.453	.356	1 5/16	1.997	1.569	2	4.638	3.642
11/16	.548	.430	1 3/8	2.192	1.722			

Table 34

Weight of Sheet Copper

Stubs' Gauge Nearest No.	Thickness in Decimal Parts of 1 Inch	Oz. Per Sq. Ft.	Sheets 14 x 48, Weight in Lbs.	Sheets 24 x 48, Weight in Lbs.	Sheets 30 x 60, Weight in Lbs.	Sheets 36 x 72, Weight in Lbs.	Sheets 48 x 72, Weight in Lbs.
35	.00537	4	1.16	2	3.12	4.50	6
33	.00806	6	1.75	3	4.68	6.75	9
31	.0107	8	2.03	4	6.25	9	12
29	.0134	10	2.91	5	7.81	11.25	15
27	.0161	12	3.50	6	9.37	13.50	18
26	.0188	14	4.08	7	10.93	15.75	21
24	.0215	16	4.66	8	12.50	18	24
23	.0242	18	5.25	9	14.06	20.25	27
22	.0269	20	5.83	10	15.62	22.50	30
21	.0322	24	7	12	18.75	27	36
19	.0430	32	9.33	16	25	36	48
18	.0538	40	11.66	20	31.25	45	60
16	.0645	48	14	24	37.50	54	72
15	.0754	56	16.33	28	43.75	63	84
14	.0860	64	18.66	32	50	72	96
13	.095	70	.....	35	55	79	105
12	.109	81	.....	40 1/2	63	91	122
11	.120	89	.....	44 1/2	70	100	134
10	.134	100	.....	50	78	112	150
9	.148	110	.....	55	86	124	165
8	.165	123	.....	61	96	138	184
7	.180	134	.....	67	105	151	201
6	.203	151	.....	75 1/2	118	170	227
5	.220	164	.....	82	128	184	246
4	.238	177	.....	88 1/2	138	199	266
3	.259	193	.....	96	151	217	289
2	.284	211	.....	105 1/2	165	238	317
1	.300	223	.....	111 1/2	174	251	335
0	.340	253	.....	126 1/2	198	285	380

Official table adopted by the Association of Copper Manufacturers of the United States.

Rolled copper has specific gravity of 8.93. One cubic foot weighs 558$^{125}/_{1000}$ pounds. One square foot, of 1 inch thick, weighs 46$^{51}/_{100}$ pounds.

TABLE 35 **Weights of Sheets and Bars of Lead, Copper and Brass**

Thickness or Diameter, Inches	Lead: Sheets Per Sq. Ft. Lb.	Lead: Square Bars 1 Ft. Long, Lb.	Lead: Round Bars 1 Ft. Long, Lb.	Copper: Sheets Per Sq. Ft. Lb.	Copper: Square Bars 1 Ft. Long, Lb.	Copper: Round Bars 1 Ft. Long, Lb.	Brass: Sheets Per Sq. Ft. Lb.	Brass: Square Bars 1 Ft. Long, Lb.	Brass: Round Bars 1 Ft. Long, Lb.	Thickness or Diameter, Inches
1/32	1.86	0.005	0.004	1.44	0.004	0.003	1.36	0.004	0.003	1/32
1/16	3.72	0.019	0.015	2.89	0.015	0.012	2.71	0.014	0.011	1/16
3/32	5.58	0.044	0.034	4.33	0.034	0.027	4.06	0.032	0.025	3/32
1/8	7.44	0.078	0.061	5.77	0.060	0.047	5.42	0.056	0.044	1/8
5/32	9.30	0.121	0.095	7.20	0.094	0.074	6.75	0.088	0.069	5/32
3/16	11.20	0.174	0.137	8.66	0.135	0.106	8.13	0.127	0.100	3/16
7/32	13.00	0.237	0.187	10.10	0.184	0.144	9.50	0.173	0.136	7/32
1/4	14.90	0.310	0.244	11.50	0.240	0.189	10.80	0.226	0.177	1/4
5/16	18.60	0.485	0.381	14.40	0.376	0.295	13.50	0.353	0.277	5/16
3/8	22.30	0.698	0.548	17.30	0.541	0.425	16.30	0.508	0.399	3/8
7/16	26.00	0.950	0.746	20.30	0.736	0.578	19.00	0.691	0.543	7/16
1/2	29.80	1.240	0.974	23.10	0.962	0.755	21.70	0.903	0.709	1/2
9/16	33.50	1.570	1.230	26.00	1.220	0.955	24.30	1.140	0.900	9/16
5/8	37.20	1.940	1.520	28.90	1.500	1.180	27.10	1.410	1.110	5/8
11/16	40.90	2.340	1.840	31.70	1.820	1.430	29.80	1.700	1.340	11/16
3/4	44.60	2.790	2.190	34.60	2.160	1.700	32.50	2.030	1.600	3/4
13/16	48.30	3.270	2.570	37.50	2.550	1.990	35.20	2.380	1.870	13/16
7/8	52.10	3.800	2.980	40.40	2.940	2.310	37.90	2.760	2.170	7/8
15/16	56.00	4.370	3.420	43.30	3.380	2.650	40.60	3.180	2.490	15/16
1	59.50	4.960	3.900	46.20	3.850	3.020	43.30	3.610	2.840	1
1 1/8	66.90	6.270	4.920	52.00	4.870	3.820	48.70	4.570	3.600	1 1/8
1 1/4	74.40	7.750	6.090	57.70	6.010	4.720	54.20	5.640	4.430	1 1/4
1 3/8	81.80	9.370	7.370	63.50	7.280	5.720	59.60	6.820	5.370	1 3/8
1 1/2	89.30	11.200	8.770	69.30	8.650	6.800	65.00	8.120	6.380	1 1/2
1 5/8	96.70	13.100	10.30	75.10	10.200	7.980	70.40	9.530	7.490	1 5/8
1 3/4	104.00	15.200	11.90	80.80	11.800	9.250	75.90	11.100	8.680	1 3/4
1 7/8	112.00	17.500	13.70	86.60	13.500	10.600	81.30	12.700	9.970	1 7/8
2	119.00	19.800	15.60	92.30	15.400	12.100	86.70	14.400	11.300	2

To find the weight of octagon rod, take weight of round rod of a given size and multiply by 1.084.
To find the weight of hexagon rod, take the weight of round rod of a given size and multiply by 1.12.

TABLE 36

Approximate Weight Per Lineal Foot of Rectangular or Flat Copper and Brass Bars

Size, Inch	Copper Lbs.	Brass Lbs.	Size, Inch	Copper Lbs.	Brass Lbs.
1/16 × 1/2	.12	.114	3/16 × 2	1.44	1.368
1/16 × 5/8	.15	.142	1/4 × 1/2	.48	.450
1/16 × 3/4	.18	.171	1/4 × 5/8	.60	.570
1/16 × 7/8	.21	.199	1/4 × 3/4	.72	.684
1/16 × 1	.24	.228	1/4 × 7/8	.84	.798
1/16 × 1 1/4	.30	.285	1/4 × 1	.97	.921
1/16 × 1 1/2	.36	.342	1/4 × 1 1/4	1.20	1.140
1/8 × 1/2	.24	.228	1/4 × 1 1/2	1.44	1.368
1/8 × 5/8	.30	.285	1/4 × 1 3/4	1.68	1.596
1/8 × 3/4	.36	.342	1/4 × 2	1.93	1.833
1/8 × 7/8	.42	.399	3/8 × 1	1.44	1.368
1/8 × 1	.48	.456	3/8 × 1 1/4	1.80	1.710
1/8 × 1 1/4	.60	.570	3/8 × 1 1/2	2.16	2.052
1/8 × 1 1/2	.72	.684	3/8 × 1 3/4	2.52	2.394
1/8 × 1 3/4	.84	.798	3/8 × 2	2.88	2.736
1/8 × 2	.96	.912	3/8 × 2 1/4	3.24	3.078
3/16 × 1/2	.36	.342	3/8 × 2 1/2	3.60	3.420
3/16 × 5/8	.45	.427	1/2 × 1	1.93	1.833
3/16 × 3/4	.54	.513	1/2 × 1 1/4	2.41	2.289
3/16 × 7/8	.63	.598	1/2 × 1 1/2	2.89	2.745
3/16 × 1	.72	.684	1/2 × 1 3/4	3.37	3.201
3/16 × 1 1/4	.90	.855	1/2 × 2	3.86	3.667
3/16 × 1 1/2	1.08	1.026	1/2 × 2 1/4	4.34	4.123
3/16 × 1 3/4	1.26	1.197	1/2 × 2 1/2	4.82	4.579

TABLE 37

Weight Per Foot of Lead Pipe

Inside Diameter, Inches	AAA Brooklyn Lb.	AAA Brooklyn Oz.	AA Ex. Strong Lb.	AA Ex. Strong Oz.	A Strong Lb.	A Strong Oz.	B Medium Lb.	B Medium Oz.	C Light Lb.	C Light Oz.	D Ex. Light Lb.	D Ex. Light Oz.	E Fountain Lb.	E Fountain Oz.
3/8	1	12	1	8	1	4	1	0	0	12	0	10	1	7
7/16	..	..	..	..	..	..	1	0	0	13	..	..	..	..
1/2	3	0	2	0	1	12	1	4	1	0	0	12	0	9
5/8	3	8	2	12	2	8	2	0	1	8	1	0	0	12
3/4	4	12	3	8	3	0	2	4	1	12	1	4	1	0
1	6	0	4	12	4	0	3	4	2	8	2	0	1	8
1 1/4	6	12	5	12	4	12	3	12	3	0	2	8	2	0
1 1/2	8	8	7	8	6	8	5	0	4	4	3	8	3	0
1 3/4	10	0	8	8	7	0	6	0	5	0	4	0	0	0
2	11	12	9	0	8	0	7	0	6	0	4	12	..	..

TABLE 38

Weight Per Foot of Seamless Brass Tubes

A.W.G.	2	4	6	8	10	12	14	16	18	20	22	24
Wall.*	.2576	.2043	.1620	.1285	.1019	.0808	.0641	.0508	.0403	.0320	.0253	.0201
Diam.†												
1/8	.....	.....	.....	.....	.....	.....	.....	0.044	0.039	0.034	0.0290	.024
3/16	.....	.....	.....	.....	.....	.....	0.092	.080	.069	.058	.048	.039
1/4	.....	.....	.....	.....	0.175	0.158	.138	.117	.098	.081	.066	.053
5/16	.....	.....	.....	.....	.248	.217	.184	.154	.127	.104	.084	.068
3/8	.....	.....	.....	0.376	.322	.275	.231	.191	.156	.127	.103	.083
1/2	.....	.....	0.634	.562	.469	.392	.323	.264	214	.173	.139	.112
5/8	1.10	0.994	.863	.748	.617	.509	.416	.338	.273	.219	.176	.141
3/4	1.47	1.29	1.10	.934	.764	.626	.509	.411	.331	.266	.213	.170
7/8	1.84	1.59	1.34	1.12	.911	.743	.601	.485	.389	.312	.249	.199
1	2.21	1.88	1.57	1.31	1.06	.859	.694	.558	.448	.358	.286	.228
1 1/8	2.59	2.18	1.81	1.49	1.21	.976	.787	.632	.506	.404	.322	.257
1 1/4	2.96	2.47	2.04	1.68	1.35	1.09	.879	.705	.564	.450	.359	.286
1 3/8	3.33	2.77	2.27	1.86	1.50	1.21	.972	.779	.622	.497	.396	.315
1 1/2	3.70	3.06	2.51	2.05	1.65	1.33	1.06	.852	.681	.543	.432	.344
1 3/4	4.45	3.65	2.98	2.42	1.94	1.56	1.25	.999	.797	.635	.506	.402
2	5.19	4.24	3.45	2.79	2.24	1:79	1.44	1.15	.914	.728	.579	.460
2 1/4	5.94	4.84	3.91	3.16	2.53	2.03	1.62	1.29	1.03	.820	.652	.519
2 1/2	6.68	5.43	4.38	3.54	2.83	2.26	1.81	1.44	1.15	.913	.722	.577
2 3/4	7.43	6.02	4.85	3.91	3.12	2.50	1.99	1.59	1.26	1.01	.799	.635
3	8.17	6.61	5.32	4.28	3.42	2.73	2.18	1.73	1.38	1.10	.872	.693
3 1/4	8.92	7.20	5.79	4.65	3.71	2.96	2.36	1.88	1.50	1.19	.946	.751
3 1/2	9.66	7.79	6.26	5.02	4.01	3.20	2.55	2.03	1.61	1.28	1.02	.809
3 3/4	10.4	8.38	6.73	5.39	4.30	3.43	2.73	2.18	1.73	1.37	1.09	.867
4	11.2	8.97	7.19	5.77	4.60	3.66	2.92	2.32	1.85	1.47	1.17	.926
4 1/4	11.9	9.56	7.66	6.14	4.89	3.90	3.10	2.47	1.96	1.56	1.24	.984
4 1/2	12.6	10.2	8.13	6.51	5.19	4.13	3.29	2.62	2.08	1.65	1.31	1.04
4 3/4	13.4	10.7	8.60	6.88	5.48	4.37	3.47	2.76	2.20	1.74	1.39	1.10
5	14.1	11.3	9.07	7.25	5.78	4.60	3.66	2.91	2.31	1.84	1.46	1.16
5 1/4	14.9	11.9	9.54	7.62	6.07	4.83	3.85	3.06	2.43	1.93	....	....
5 1/2	15.6	12.5	10.0	8.00	6.36	5.07	4.03	3.20	2.55	2.02	....	....
5 3/4	16.4	13.1	10 5	8 37	6.66	5.30	4.22	3.35	2.66	2.11	....	....
6	17.1	13.7	10.9	8 74	6.95	5.58	4.40	3.50	2.78	2.21	....	....
6 1/4	17.9	14.3	11.4	9.11	7.25	5.77	4.59	3.65	2.90	....	....	....
6 1/2	18.6	14.9	11.9	9.48	7.54	6.00	4.77	3.79	3.01	....	....	....
6 3/4	19.4	15.5	12.3	9 85	7.84	6.24	4.96	3.94	....	....	....	....
7	20.1	16.1	12.8	10 2	8.13	6.47	5.14	4.09	....	....	....	....
7 1/4	20.8	16 7	13 3	10 6	8.43	6 70	5.33	4.23	....	....	....	....
7 1/2	21.6	17.2	13.8	11.0	8.72	6.94	5 51	4.38	....	....	....	....
7 3/4	22.3	17.8	14 2	11.3	9.02	7.17	5 70	4.53	....	....	....	....
8	23.1	18.4	14.7	11.7	9.31	7.40	5.88	4.67	....	....	....	....
8 1/4	23.8	19 0	15.2	12 1	9.61	7.64	6 07	4.82	....	....	....	....
8 1/2	24 6	19 6	15.6	12.5	9.90	7.87	6.25	4.97	....	....	....	....
8 3/4	25.3	20 2	16.1	12.8	10 2	8.11	6 44	5.12	....	....	....	....
9	26.1	20 8	16.6	13.2	10.5	8 34	6.63	5.26	....	....	....	....

* Thickness in inches. † Outside diameter, inches.

Seamless brass tubes are made from 1/8 in. to 1 in. outside diameter, varying by 1/16 in., and from 1 1/8 in. to 10 in. outside diameter, varying by 1/8 in., and in all gauges from No. 2 to No. 24 A.W.G. within the limits of the above table. To determine the weight per foot of a tube of a given inside diameter, add to the weights given above, the weights given below, under the corresponding gauge numbers.

A.W.G.	2	4	6	8	10	12	14	16	18	20	22	24	26
Lb. per ft.	1.54	.966	6 07	3.82	.240	.151	.095	.060	.038	.024	.015	.009	.0059

For copper tubing add 5% to the weights given above.

TABLE 39

Weight of Lead Wire Per Lineal Foot in Pounds

Diameter in Brown & Sharpe Gauge	Corresponding Decimal Equivalent	Corresponding Fractional Equivalent	Approximate Number of Feet to Pound
No. 6	.16202	$\frac{5}{32}$ (F)	10
No. 8	.12849	$\frac{1}{8}$ (F)	$15\frac{1}{2}$
No. 10	.10189	$\frac{7}{64}$ (S)	25
No. 11	.09074	$\frac{3}{32}$ (S)	31
No. 12	.08081	$\frac{5}{64}$ (F)	40
No. 13	.07196	$\frac{5}{64}$ (S)	50
No. 14	.06408	$\frac{1}{16}$ (F)	$62\frac{1}{2}$
No. 15	.05706	$\frac{1}{16}$ (S)	77
No. 16	.05082	$\frac{3}{64}$ (F)	100
No. 17	.04525	$\frac{3}{64}$ (S)	125
No. 18	.0403	$\frac{3}{64}$ (S)	166
No. 19	.03589	$\frac{1}{32}$ (F)	200
No. 20	.03196	$\frac{1}{32}$	250
No. 21	.02846	$\frac{1}{36}$	332
No. 22	.02535	$\frac{1}{40}$	400
No. 23	.02257	$\frac{1}{44}$	510

NOTE.—Sizes above No. 6 B. & S. gauge increase by $\frac{1}{32}$ of an inch. (F) = Full. (S) = Scant.

TABLE 40

Weights of Wrought Iron, Copper and Lead Pipe

Thick. Inch.	Wrought Iron	Copper	Lead	Thick. Inch	Wrought Iron	Copper	Lead
1-32	.326	.38	.483	5-32	1.627	1.90	2.417
1-16	.653	.76	.967	3-16	1.950	2.28	2.900
3-32	.976	1.14	1.450	7-32	2.277	2.66	3.383
1-8	1.300	1.52	1.933	1-40	2.600	3.04	3.867

Rule: *To the interior diameter of the pipe, in inches, add the thickness of the metal; multiply the sum by the decimal number opposite the required thickness and under the metal's name; also by the length of the pipe in feet; and the product is the weight of the pipe in pounds.*

1. Required the weight of a copper pipe whose interior diameter is $2\frac{1}{2}$ in., its length 20 ft., and the metal $\frac{1}{8}$ in. in thickness.

$$2.25 + .125 = 2.375 \times 1.52 \times 20 = 72.2 \text{ lbs.}$$

TABLE 41

Quantity of Tin for Roofs

Surface of Roof to be Covered	Flat Seam				Standing Seam							
	Edged ¼ In.		Edged ⅜ In.		Single Lock				Double Lock			
					¾-In. Seam		1-In. Seam		¾-In. Seam		1-In. Seam	
	14 x 20	20 x 28	14 x 20	20 x 28	14 x 20	20 x 28	14 x 20	20 x 28	14 x 20	20 x 28	14 x 20	20 x 28
Sq. Ft.	S	S	S	S	S	S	S	S	S	S	S	S
10	6	3	6	3	7	4	7	4	7	4	7	4
11	7	4	7	4	7	4	8	4	8	4	8	4
12	7	4	8	4	8	4	8	4	8	4	8	4
13	8	4	8	4	9	4	9	5	9	4	9	5
14	9	4	9	4	9	5	10	5	10	5	10	5
15	9	5	9	5	10	5	10	5	10	5	10	5
16	10	5	10	5	11	5	11	5	11	5	11	6
17	10	5	11	5	11	6	12	6	11	6	12	6
18	11	6	11	6	12	6	12	6	12	6	12	6
19	12	6	12	6	12	6	13	6	13	6	13	6
20	12	6	12	6	13	7	13	7	13	7	14	7
21	13	6	13	6	14	7	14	7	14	7	14	7
22	13	7	14	7	14	7	15	7	15	7	15	7
23	14	7	14	7	15	7	15	8	15	8	16	8
24	14	7	15	7	16	8	16	8	16	8	16	8
25	15	8	15	8	16	8	17	8	17	8	17	8
26	16	8	16	8	17	8	17	9	17	8	18	9
27	16	8	16	8	18	9	18	9	18	9	18	9
28	17	8	17	8	18	9	19	9	19	9	19	9
29	17	9	18	9	19	9	19	10	19	9	20	10
30	18	9	18	9	19	10	20	10	20	10	20	10
31	19	9	19	9	20	10	21	10	21	10	21	10
32	19	9	19	10	21	10	21	10	21	10	22	11
33	20	10	20	10	21	10	22	11	22	11	22	11
34	20	10	21	10	22	11	23	11	22	11	23	11
35	21	10	21	10	23	11	23	11	23	11	24	11
36	21	11	22	11	23	11	24	12	24	11	24	12
37	22	11	22	11	24	12	24	12	24	12	25	12
38	23	11	23	11	24	12	25	12	25	12	26	12
39	23	11	24	12	25	12	26	13	26	12	26	13
40	24	12	24	12	26	13	26	13	26	13	27	13
41	24	12	25	12	26	13	27	13	27	13	28	13
42	25	12	25	12	27	13	28	14	28	13	28	14
43	26	13	26	13	28	13	28	14	28	14	29	14
44	26	13	27	13	28	14	29	14	29	14	30	14
45	27	13	27	13	29	14	30	14	30	14	30	15
46	27	13	28	14	29	14	30	15	30	15	31	15
47	28	14	28	14	30	15	31	15	31	15	32	15
48	28	14	29	14	31	15	32	15	31	15	32	16
49	29	14	30	14	31	15	32	16	32	15	33	16
50	30	15	30	15	32	16	33	16	33	16	34	16
51	30	15	31	15	33	16	34	16	33	16	34	17
52	31	15	31	15	33	16	34	17	34	16	35	17
53	31	15	32	16	34	16	35	17	35	17	36	17
54	32	16	32	16	35	17	36	17	35	17	33	17

Table 41 (Continued)

Quantity of Tin for Roofs

Surface of Roof to be Covered	Flat Seam				Standing Seam							
	Edged ¼ In.		Edged ⅜ In.		Single Lock				Double Lock			
					¾-In. Seam		1-In. Seam		¾-In. Seam		1-In. Seam	
	14 x 20	20 x 28	14 x 20	20 x 28	14 x 20	20 x 28	14 x 20	20 x 28	14 x 20	20 x 28	14 x 20	20 x 28
Sq. Ft.	S	S	S	S	S	S	S	S	S	S	S	S
55	33	16	33	16	35	17	36	18	36	17	37	18
56	33	16	34	16	36	17	37	18	37	18	38	18
57	34	16	34	17	36	18	37	18	37	18	38	18
58	34	17	35	17	37	18	38	19	38	18	39	19
59	35	17	35	17	38	18	39	19	39	19	40	19
60	35	17	36	18	38	19	39	19	39	19	40	19
61	36	18	37	18	39	19	40	19	40	19	41	20
62	37	18	37	18	40	19	41	20	41	19	42	20
63	37	18	38	18	40	20	41	20	41	20	42	20
64	38	18	38	19	41	20	42	20	42	20	43	21
65	38	19	39	19	41	20	43	21	42	20	44	21
66	39	19	40	19	42	20	43	21	43	21	44	21
67	40	19	40	20	43	21	44	21	44	21	45	22
68	40	20	41	20	43	21	45	22	44	21	46	22
69	41	20	41	20	44	21	45	22	45	22	46	22
70	41	20	42	20	45	22	46	22	46	22	47	22
71	42	20	43	21	45	22	47	23	46	22	48	23
72	42	21	43	21	46	22	47	23	47	22	48	23
73	43	21	44	21	46	23	48	23	48	23	49	23
74	44	21	44	22	47	23	48	23	48	23	50	24
75	44	22	45	22	48	23	49	24	49	23	50	24
76	45	22	46	22	48	23	50	24	50	24	51	24
77	45	22	46	22	49	24	50	24	50	24	52	25
78	46	22	47	23	50	24	51	25	51	24	52	25
79	47	23	47	23	50	24	52	25	52	25	53	25
80	47	23	48	23	51	25	52	25	52	25	54	26
81	48	23	48	23	52	25	53	26	53	25	54	26
82	48	24	49	24	52	25	54	26	53	26	55	26
83	49	24	50	24	53	26	54	26	54	26	56	27
84	49	24	50	24	53	26	55	27	55	26	56	27
85	50	24	51	25	54	26	56	27	55	26	57	27
86	51	25	51	25	55	26	56	27	56	27	58	28
87	51	25	52	25	55	27	57	28	57	27	58	28
88	52	25	53	25	56	27	58	28	57	27	59	28
89	52	26	53	26	57	27	58	28	58	28	60	28
90	53	26	54	26	57	28	59	28	59	28	60	29
91	54	26	54	26	58	28	60	29	59	28	61	29
92	54	26	55	27	58	28	60	29	60	29	62	29
93	55	27	56	27	59	29	61	29	61	29	62	30
94	55	27	56	27	60	29	61	30	61	29	63	30
95	56	27	57	27	60	29	62	30	62	30	64	30
96	56	27	57	28	61	29	63	30	62	30	64	31
97	57	28	58	28	62	30	63	31	63	30	65	31
98	58	28	59	28	62	30	64	31	64	30	66	31
99	58	28	59	29	63	30	65	31	64	31	66	32

TABLE 41 (Continued)

Quantity of Tin for Roofs

Surface of Roof to be Covered	Flat Seam, Edged ¼ In., 14 x 20		Flat Seam, Edged ¼ In., 20 x 28		Flat Seam, Edged ⅜ In., 14 x 20		Flat Seam, Edged ⅜ In., 20 x 28		Standing Seam, Single Lock ¾-In. Seam, 14 x 20		Standing Seam, Single Lock ¾-In. Seam, 20 x 28	
Sq. Ft.	B.	S.	B.	S.	B.	S.	B.	S.	B.	S.	B.	S.
100	0	59	0	29	0	60	0	29	0	64	0	31
200	1	5	0	57	1	7	0	57	1	15	0	61
300	1	63	0	85	1	66	0	86	1	78	0	91
400	2	10	1	1	2	14	1	2	2	29	1	9
500	2	68	1	29	2	73	1	30	2	92	1	39
600	3	14	1	57	3	20	1	59	3	43	1	70
700	3	73	1	85	3	79	1	87	3	106	1	100
800	4	19	2	1	4	27	2	3	4	57	2	18
900	4	77	2	29	4	86	2	32	5	8	2	48
1000	5	23	2	57	5	33	2	60	5	71	2	78
1100	5	82	2	85	5	92	2	89	6	22	2	109
1200	6	28	3	1	6	40	3	5	6	85	3	27
1300	6	86	3	29	6	99	3	34	7	36	3	57
1400	7	33	3	57	7	46	3	62	7	99	3	87
1500	7	91	3	86	7	105	3	90	8	50	4	5
1600	8	37	4	2	8	53	4	7	9	1	4	35
1700	8	96	4	30	9	0	4	35	9	64	4	66
1800	9	42	4	58	9	59	4	63	10	15	4	96
1900	9	100	4	86	10	6	4	92	10	78	5	14
2000	10	46	5	2	10	66	5	8	11	29	5	44
2100	10	105	5	30	11	13	5	37	11	92	5	74
2200	11	52	5	58	11	72	5	65	12	43	5	105
2300	11	110	5	86	12	19	5	93	12	106	6	23
2400	12	36	6	2	12	79	6	10	13	57	6	53
2500	13	2	6	30	13	26	6	38	14	8	6	83
2600	13	60	6	58	13	85	6	67	14	71	7	1
2700	14	7	6	86	14	32	6	95	15	22	7	32
2800	14	65	7	2	14	92	7	11	15	85	7	62
2900	15	11	7	31	15	39	7	40	16	36	7	92
3000	15	69	7	59	15	98	7	68	16	99	8	10
3100	16	16	7	87	16	45	7	97	17	50	8	40
3200	16	74	8	3	16	105	8	13	18	1	8	70
3300	17	20	8	31	17	52	8	41	18	64	8	101
3400	17	78	8	59	17	111	8	70	19	15	9	19
3500	18	25	8	87	18	58	8	98	19	78	9	49
3600	18	83	9	3	19	6	9	14	20	29	9	79
3700	19	30	9	31	19	65	9	43	20	92	9	109
3800	19	88	9	59	20	12	9	71	21	43	10	28
3900	20	35	9	87	20	71	9	100	21	106	10	58
4000	20	92	10	3	21	19	10	16	22	57	10	88
4100	21	39	10	31	21	78	10	44	23	8	11	6
4200	21	97	10	59	22	25	10	73	23	71	11	36
4300	22	44	10	88	22	85	10	101	24	22	11	67
4400	22	102	11	4	23	32	11	18	24	85	11	97
4500	23	48	11	32	23	91	11	46	25	36	12	15
4600	23	107	11	60	24	38	11	74	25	99	12	45
4700	24	53	11	85	24	98	11	103	26	50	12	75
4800	24	111	12	4	25	45	12	19	27	1	12	105
4900	25	57	12	37	25	104	12	48	27	64	13	24
5000	26	4	12	60	26	51	12	76	28	15	13	54
6000	31	27	15	5	31	84	15	24	33	85	16	20
7000	36	50	17	62	37	4	17	84	39	43	18	98
8000	41	73	20	7	42	37	20	32	45	1	21	63
9000	46	95	22	65	47	70	22	91	50	72	24	29
10000	52	6	25	8	52	102	25	39	56	30	26	107

Table 41 (Continued)

Quantity of Tin for Roofs

Standing Sean

Surface of Roof to be Covered	Single Lock				Double Lock							
	1-In. Seam				¾-In. Seam				1-In. Seam			
	14 x 20		20 x 28		14 x 20		20 x 28		14 x 20		20 x 28	
Sq. Ft.	B.	S.	B.	S.	B.	S.	B.	S.	B.	S.	B.	S.
100	0	65	0	32	0	65	0	31	0	67	0	32
200	1	18	0	63	1	18	0	62	1	21	0	63
300	1	83	0	94	1	82	0	92	1	88	0	95
400	2	36	1	13	2	35	1	11	2	42	1	14
500	2	101	1	44	2	99	1	41	2	109	1	46
600	2	54	1	75	3	52	1	72	3	63	1	77
700	4	6	1	106	4	5	1	102	4	18	1	108
800	4	71	2	25	4	69	2	21	4	84	2	28
900	5	24	2	56	5	22	2	51	5	39	2	59
1000	5	89	2	87	5	86	2	82	5	105	2	91
1100	6	42	3	6	6	39	3	0	6	59	3	10
1200	6	107	3	37	6	103	3	31	7	14	3	42
1300	7	59	3	68	7	56	3	62	7	80	3	73
1400	8	12	3	99	8	9	3	92	8	39	3	104
1500	8	77	4	18	8	73	4	11	8	101	4	24
1600	9	30	4	49	9	26	4	41	9	56	4	55
1700	9	95	4	81	9	90	4	72	10	10	4	87
1800	10	48	5	0	10	43	4	102	10	77	5	6
1900	11	0	5	31	10	108	5	21	11	31	5	38
2000	11	65	5	62	11	60	5	51	11	97	5	69
2100	12	18	5	93	12	13	5	82	12	52	5	100
2200	12	83	6	12	12	77	6	0	13	6	6	20
2300	13	36	6	43	13	30	6	31	13	73	6	51
2400	13	101	6	74	13	94	6	61	14	27	6	83
2500	14	53	6	105	14	47	6	92	14	94	7	2
2600	15	6	7	24	15	0	7	11	15	48	7	34
2700	15	71	7	55	15	64	7	41	16	3	7	65
2800	16	24	7	86	16	17	7	72	16	69	7	96
2900	16	89	8	5	16	81	7	102	17	24	8	16
3000	17	42	8	36	17	34	8	21	17	90	8	47
3100	17	106	8	67	17	98	8	51	18	44	8	79
3200	18	59	8	98	18	51	8	82	18	111	8	110
3300	19	12	9	18	19	4	9	0	19	65	9	30
3400	19	77	9	49	19	68	9	31	20	20	9	61
3500	20	30	9	80	20	21	9	61	20	86	9	92
3600	20	95	9	111	20	85	9	92	21	41	10	12
3700	21	48	10	30	21	38	10	11	21	107	10	43
3800	22	0	10	61	21	103	10	41	22	62	10	75
3900	22	65	10	92	22	55	10	72	23	16	10	106
4000	23	18	11	11	23	8	10	102	23	82	11	26
4100	23	83	11	42	23	72	11	21	24	37	11	57
4200	24	36	11	73	24	25	11	51	24	103	11	88
4300	24	101	11	104	24	89	11	82	25	58	12	8
4400	25	53	12	23	25	42	12	0	26	12	12	39
4500	26	6	12	54	25	107	12	31	26	79	12	71
4600	26	71	12	85	26	59	12	61	27	33	12	102
4700	27	24	13	4	27	12	12	92	27	100	13	22
4800	27	89	13	35	27	76	13	10	28	54	13	53
4900	28	42	13	67	28	29	13	41	29	9	13	84
5000	28	106	13	98	28	93	13	72	29	75	14	4
6000	34	83	16	72	34	67	16	41	35	67	16	94
7000	40	59	19	47	40	41	19	10	41	60	19	72
8000	46	36	22	21	46	15	21	92	47	52	22	51
9000	52	12	24	108	51	101	24	61	53	45	25	29
10000	57	100	27	83	57	74	27	31	59	37	28	7

Basis of Calculation

Flat Seams

One table is calculated on a basis of ¼-inch edges on 14 x 20 and 20 x 28 sheets, consuming about 1 inch, covering a space 13 x 19 and 19 x 27 inches and exposing a surface of 247 and 513 square inches respectively.

The other table is calculated on a basis of ⅜-inch edges on 14 x 20 and 20 x 28 sheets, consuming 1⅛ inches, covering a space 12⅞ x 18⅞ and 18⅞ x 26⅞ inches and exposing a surface of 243 1/64 and 507 17/64 square inches respectively.

Standing Seam, Single Lock

This table is calculated on the basis of ⅜-inch single lock cross seams, consuming 1⅛ inches of tin and covering 228 17/32 square inches when edged 1 and 1¼ inches and giving a finished seam ¾-inch high, and covering 222 3/32 square inches when edged 1¼ and 1½ inches and giving a finished seam 1 inch high, with 14 x 20 tin. With 20 x 28 tin edged in the same way with a ¾-inch finished seam 477 1/32 square inches are covered, and with a 1-inch finished seam 463 19/32 square inches are covered.

Standing Seam, Double Lock

This table is calculated on the basis of the amount of tin consumed by double lock machines, which is 1 7/16 inches by measurement for cross seams and covering 222 63/64 square inches when edged 1 and 1¼ inches and giving a finished seam ¾ inch high, and covering 216-45/64 square inches when edged 1¼ and 1½ inches, giving a finished seam 1 inch high, with 14 x 20 tin. With 20 x 28 tin edged in the same way with a ¾-inch finished seam 471 31/64 square inches are covered, and with a 1-inch finished seam 458 13/64 square inches are covered.

Directions for Use

Look for the number of squares nearest the required surface. Note the quantity of tin opposite in the column for the kind of roof to be put on, whether it be 1/4 inch or 3/8 inch Flat Seam or 3/4 inch or 1 inch Standing Seam, Single Lock or Double Lock, and set down the amount. Then, in the same manner, determine the quantity of tin for the odd feet and add this to the former amount. Reduce the sheets to boxes by dividing by 112.

Flat Seam Example

How much 14 x 20 tin edged 1/4 inch covering 13 x 19 will be required to cover a roof of 4,665 square feet Flat Seam?

First look for 4,600 square feet (=46 squares) and set down the quantity opposite, thus:

	23 boxes 107 sheets
Then for 65 square feet and set down..	38 sheets
Making a total of....................	23 boxes 145 sheets

which is equal to 24 boxes 33 sheets.

Single Lock Standing Seam Example

How much 14 x 20 tin will be required to cover a roof of 3,752 square feet with single lock cross seams and 1-inch standing seams?

First look for 3,700 square feet (=37 squares) and set down the quantity opposite, thus:

	21 boxes 48 sheets
Then for 52 square feet and set down..	34 sheets
Making a total of....................	21 boxes 82 sheets

Double Lock Standing Seam Example

How much 20 x 28 tin will be required to cover a roof of 2,987 square feet with double lock cross seams and 3/4-inch standing seams?

First look for 2,900 square feet (=29 squares) and set down the quantity opposite, thus:

	7 boxes 102 sheets
Then look for 87 square feet and set down	27 sheets
Making a total of	7 boxes 129 sheets

Dividing 129 by 112, they are found to be equal to 1 box and 17 sheets, which added to 7 boxes give a total of .... 8 boxes 17 sheets

Table 42

Weight of Skylight Glass

The glass used in the majority of cases for skylight work is either rough or ribbed skylight glass and can be had with or without the wire mesh. No two lists agree on the weights of this material, but the following table of Kidder's is as correct as possible to make a table of weights, and will be found useful in computing the loads on skylight bars and the like.

Thickness in inches.	1/8	3/16	1/4	3/8	1/2	5/8	3/4	1
Weight in pounds..	2	2½	3½	5	7	8½	10	12½

Table 43

Skylight Glass Required for One Square of Roof

Dimensions, inches.........	12 × 48	15 × 60	20 × 100	94 × 156
Thickness, inches..........	3/16	1/4	3/8	1/2
Area, square feet...........	3.997	6.246	13.880	101.768
Weight per square, lb......	250	350	500	700

No allowance has been made in the above figures for lap. If ordinary window-glass is used, single thick glass (about 1/16 inch) will weigh about 82 lb. per square, and double thick glass (about 1/8 inch) will weigh about 164 lb. per square, *no allowance being made for lap.* A box of ordinary window-glass contains as nearly 50 square feet as the size of the panes will admit. Panes of any size are made to order by the manufacturers, but a great variety of sizes are usually kept in stock, ranging from 6 × 8 inches to 36 × 60 inches.

TABLE 44

Tin in Rolls, or Gutter-Strips

Number of sheets required per linear foot for 20 and 28-inch widths

Feet	Widths 20	Widths 28	Feet	Widths 20	Widths 28	Feet	Widths 20	Widths 28	Feet	Widths 20	Widths 28
1	1	1	35	16	23	69	31	44	200	89	128
2	1	2	36	16	23	70	32	45	300	134	192
3	2	2	37	17	24	71	32	45	400	178	256
4	2	3	38	17	24	72	32	46	500	223	320
5	3	4	39	18	25	73	33	47	600	267	384
6	3	4	40	18	26	74	33	47	700	312	444
7	4	5	41	19	27	75	34	48	800	356	512
8	4	5	42	19	27	76	34	48	900	401	576
9	4	6	43	20	28	77	35	49	1,000	445	640
10	5	7	44	20	28	78	35	50	1,100	495	704
11	5	7	45	20	29	79	36	50	1,200	540	768
12	6	8	46	21	29	80	36	51	1,300	585	832
13	6	9	47	21	30	81	36	52	1,400	630	896
14	7	9	48	22	31	82	37	52	1,500	675	960
15	7	10	49	22	31	83	37	53	1,600	720	1,024
16	8	11	50	23	32	84	38	54	1,700	765	1,088
17	8	11	51	23	33	85	38	54	1,800	810	1,152
18	8	12	52	24	33	86	39	55	1,900	855	1,216
19	9	12	53	24	34	87	39	55	2,000	900	1,280
20	9	13	54	24	34	88	40	56	2,100	945	1,344
21	10	14	55	25	35	89	40	57	2,200	900	1,408
22	10	14	56	25	36	90	40	57	2,300	1,035	1,472
23	11	15	57	26	36	91	41	58	2,400	1,080	1,536
24	11	16	58	26	37	92	41	59	2,500	1,135	1,600
25	12	16	59	27	38	93	42	59	2,600	1,170	1,664
26	12	17	60	27	38	94	42	60	2,700	1,215	1,738
27	12	18	61	28	39	95	43	61	2,800	1,260	1,792
28	13	18	62	28	40	96	43	62	2,900	1,305	1,856
29	13	19	63	28	40	97	44	62	3,000	1,350	1,920
30	14	19	64	29	41	98	44	63	3,100	1,395	1,984
31	14	20	65	29	41	99	44	64	3,200	1,440	2,048
32	15	21	66	30	42	100	45	64	3,300	1,485	2,112
33	15	21	67	30	43	..	..	..	3,400	1,530	2,176
34	16	22	68	31	43	..	..	..	3,500	1,575	2,240

112 sheets in 28-in. roll cover 175 lin. ft.
112 sheets in 20-in. roll cover 248 lin. ft.
112 sheets in 14-in. roll cover 350 lin. ft.
112 sheets in 10-in. roll cover 496 lin. ft.

This table enables tin roofers to tell how many sheets to lock together to cover any desired length. For example: How many 20 x 28-inch sheets shall be locked together to "knock out" a gutter strip 65 feet long, 28 inches wide.

Now, if the strip is to be 28 inches wide it means that the sheets are to be edged on the 28-inch sides so that from turned edge to turned edge will be approximately 19 inches and it will then take 41 times this dimension to make 65 feet; so referring to first column locate 65 feet, read across to column under 28-inch width and find 41, meaning 41 sheets are required. Supposing the strip is to be 20 inches wide, which would mean that the edges are to be turned on the 20-inch sides, so that there will be about 27 inches from turned edge to turned edge and the 20-inch wide column directs that 29 sheets be locked together for 65 feet length.

TABLE 45

Angles of Roofs as Commonly Used

Proportion of Rise to Span	Angle Deg.	Angle Min.	Length of Rafter to Rise	Proportion of Rise to Span	Angle Deg.	Angle Min.	Length of Rafter to Rise
½	45	..	1.4142	¼	26	34	2.2361
⅓	33	41	1.8028	1/5	21	48	2.6926
$\frac{1}{2\sqrt{3}}$	30	..	2.0000	1/6	18	26	3.1623

TABLE 46

Number of Flat Head Copper Rivets to Pound

Diameter of Shank	Length Measured Under Head ¾	1	1¼	1⅜	1½	2
¼	48	36	32	30	..	..
5/16	26	24	21	17	..	..
⅜	..	17	15	13	12	10
½	..	9	8	7	6	5

TABLE 47

Number and Weight of Cedar and Pine Shingles Per Square of One Hundred Square Feet

Length, In.	Assumed width, In.	Weather or Gauge, In.	Number of Shingles Per Square	Weight Per Square Cedar, Lb.	Weight Per Square Pine, Lb.	Number of Nails Per Square	Weight of Nails Per Square, Lb.
14	4	4	900	210	233	1,800	4.50
15	4	4½	800	200	222	1,600	4.00
16	4	5	720	192	213	1,440	3.60
18	4	5½	655	197	218	1,310	3.28
20	4	6	600	200	222	1,200	3.00
22	4	6½	554	203	226	1,108	2.77
24	4	7	515	206	229	1,030	2.58

TABLE 48

Weights of Hot Air Pipe in Pounds

Sizes in Inches	7 In.	8 In.	9 In.	10 In.	12 In.	14 In.	16 In.	18 In.	20 In.
Hot air pipe per foot,—									
IC	$\frac{31}{34}$	$\frac{33}{34}$	$1\frac{3}{19}$	$1\frac{5}{17}$	$1\frac{9}{17}$	...	...	...	...
IX	$1\frac{3}{34}$	$1\frac{4}{17}$	$1\frac{7}{17}$	$1\frac{10}{17}$	$1\frac{16}{17}$	$2\frac{5}{14}$	$2\frac{4}{7}$	$2\frac{29}{34}$	3
Hot air elbows,—									
3 piece, IC	¾	⅞	1¼	1⅜	2⅛	...	...	...	...
4 piece, IC	⅞	1⅛	1¼	1½	2	...	...	...	...
4 piece, IX	1	1¼	1⅝	1⅞	2½	3¼	3⅞	5½	6½
Hot air angles,—									
45° IC	½	$\frac{9}{16}$	⅝	¾	...	...	...	...	...
45° IX	...	¾	$1\frac{3}{16}$	1	1½	1⅞	2¾	3	3⅝
22½° IC	½	½	½	⅝	1	...	...	...	...
22½° IX	...	$\frac{9}{16}$	⅝	¾	1⅛	1¼	1¾	2	2¼
Hot air dampers, style "A"	$\frac{7}{16}$	½	½	⅝	⅞	1⅛	1⅜	2	2½
Galvanized iron pipe,—									
Per foot	1¾	1⅞	2	2¼	2⅝	3¼	3⅝	$4\frac{5}{16}$	$4\frac{13}{16}$
Elbows	1½	1⅞	2⅜	2¾	3⅝	4½	5⅞	7½	9
Angles, 45°	1	1⅛	1⅜	1½	2½	3	3¾	4½	5½
Angles, 22½°	$\frac{13}{16}$	$\frac{15}{16}$	$1\frac{1}{16}$	1	1¾	2	2⅝	3¼	3½
Smoke pipe dampers	2½	3⅛	4	5	6	...	...	...	...
Safety thimbles	1⅛	1⅜	$1\frac{7}{16}$	1½	1¾	...	...	...	...
Top bonnet collars	⅜	$\frac{7}{16}$	½	½	$\frac{9}{16}$	...	...	...	...
Side bonnet collars	½	½	⅝	¾	1¼	1¾	2	2¾	3⅛
Pitch bonnet collars	⅝	⅝	$1\frac{11}{16}$	¾	1	...	...	...	...
Cold air collars	...	...	...	...	...	1½	2	2¼	2⅝

TABLE 49

Table Showing Number of Star Brand Brass Escutcheon Pins to the Pound

Length Measured under the Head

No.	1/4	3/8	1/2	5/8	3/4	7/8	1	1 1/4	1 1/2	1 3/4	2
12	...	720	650	460	416	400	336	272	212	192	170
13	...	1120	948	672	528	480	400	380	320	229	220
14	1875	1312	1100	950	830	692	600	432	378	320	272
15	2440	1820	1376	1152	960	888	720	576	580	432	400
16	3100	2240	1720	1460	1275	1130	980	720	592	578	464
17	3540	2700	2076	1812	1500	1185	1051	928	800	640	...
18	4972	3175	2550	2450	2200	1740	1520	1216	960	...	...
19	7303	5140	4130	3565	2900	...	...	...	...	...	...
20	9932	8419	6374	5500	4155	...	...	...	...	...	...

TABLE 50

Oval Head Copper Braziers' Rivets

Length Measured under the Head

Numbers	00	0	1	2	3	4	5	6	7	8	9	10
Diameter of shank	5/32	3/16	1/4	17/64	9/32	5/16	23/64	3/8	7/16	17/32	5/8	21/32
Length, inches	5/16	3/8	1/2	1/2	5/8	11/16	3/4	11/16	11/16	1 1/8	1 1/4	1 1/4
Number to pound	160	148	66	49	37	28	23	19	13	8	6	5

TABLE 51

Approximate Dimensions of Tinners' Rivets

Size	Length	Diameter, Wire Gauge	Size	Length	Diameter, Wire Gauge
8 oz.	5/32	No. 13 1/4	3 1/2 lbs.	21/64	No. 8
10 "	11/64	" 13	4 "	11/32	" 7 1/4
12 "	3/16	" 12 1/4	5 "	3/8	" 6 3/4
14 "	3/16	" 12	6 "	25/64	" 6
1 lb.	13/64	" 11 3/4	7 "	13/32	" 5 1/4
1 1/4 "	7/32	" 11	8 "	7/16	" 4 3/4
1 1/2 "	15/64	" 10 1/4	9 "	29/64	" 4 1/4
1 3/4 "	1/4	" 10	10 "	15/32	" 4
2 "	17/64	" 9 1/4	12 "	1/2	" 3
2 1/2 "	9/32	" 9	14 "	33/64	" 2
3 "	5/16	" 8 1/4	16 "	17/32	" 1

TABLE 52

Oval Head Rivets and Burs to the Pound

Length Measured under the Head

No.	1/4	5/16	3/8	7/16	1/2	9/16	5/8	3/4	7/8	1	1 1/8	1 1/4	Burs.
9	317	270	254	220	206	193	189	163	138	116	107	101	600

TABLE 53

Size of Conductor Pipes

3½	in.	Trough,	up to 12	ft.	long;	use	2	in.	Conductor	Pipe
3½	"	"	12 to 25	"	"	"	3	"	"	"
4	"	"	25 to 35	"	"	"	3	"	"	"
5	"	"	35 to 45	"	"	"	4	"	"	"
6	"	"	45 to 55	"	"	"	5	"	"	"
7	"	"	55 to 65	"	"	"	6	"	"	"
8	"	"	65 to 75	"	"	"	7	"	"	"

TABLE 54

Weight of Tiles

Flat tiles 6¼ × 10½ × ⅝ in. weigh from 1,480 to 1,850 lb. per square of roof (100 square feet), the lap being one-half the length of the tile.

Tiles with grooves and fillets weigh from 740 to 925 lbs. per square of roof.

Pan-tiles 14½ × 10½ laid 10 in. to the weather weigh 850 lbs. per square.

Sheet-Metal Tiles. Roofing-tiles stamped from sheet steel, plain or galvanized, and also from sheet copper, in imitation of clay tiles, are made by several manufacturers and have been extensively used for factories and buildings of secondary importance. The first cost of these tiles, except those made of copper, is much less than that of clay tiles and they do not require as heavy roof-framing. Tin or galvanized-iron tiles, however, must be painted every few years, so that for a long period of years they probably cost as much as clay tiles and more than slate.

TABLE 55

Approximate Weight of Roof Coverings Per Square in Pounds

Material	Weight in Lbs. per Square of Roof
Ash sheathing, 1 inch thick	500
Chestnut sheathing, 1 inch thick	400
Copper, 16 ounce, standing seam	150
Felt and asphalt, without sheathing	150
Felt and gravel, without sheathing	800 to 1000
Glass with skylight frame $\frac{3}{16}$ inch to ½ inch thick	250 to 700
Hemlock sheathing, 1 inch thick	200
Iron, corrugated, No. 20, without sheathing	250
Iron, galvanized, flat	100 to 350
Lath and plaster ceiling (ordinary)	600 to 800
Lead, about ⅛ inch thick	600 to 800
Maple sheathing, 1 inch thick	400
Mackite, 1 inch thick, with plaster	1000
Neponset roofing felt, 2 layers	50
Oak sheathing, 1 inch thick	500
Slate, ¼ inch thick	900
Slate, $\frac{3}{16}$ inch thick	675
Slate, ⅛ inch thick	450
Shingles, 6 inches × 18 inches, 6 inches to the weather	200
Sheet iron, $\frac{1}{16}$ inch thick	300
Sheet iron, $\frac{1}{16}$ inch thick, with laths	400
Spruce sheathing, 1 inch thick	250
Slag roofing, four-ply	400
Tiles (plain) 10½ inches × 6¼ inches × ⅝ inches, 5½ inches to weather	1800
Tiles (Spanish) 14½ inches × 10½ inches, 7½ inches to weather	850
Tiles, plain with mortar	2000 to 3000
Terne plate (tin), IC, without sheathing	50
Terne plate (tin), IX, without sheathing	65
White pine sheathing, 1 inch thick	250
Yellow pine sheathing, 1 inch thick	400

TABLE 56

Weight of Metal Shingles

Metal shingles weigh from 80 to 90 pounds per square of 100 feet, depending on the shape of the shingle and the weight of the metal.

TABLE 57

Number of Slates, and Pounds of Nails to 100 Square Feet of Roof 3-inch Lap

Sizes of Slates	Exposed When Laid	Number to a Square		Weights of Galvanized Nails	
Inches	Inches			Lb.	Oz.
14 × 24	10½	98	4d	1	6
12 × 24	10½	115		1	10
12 × 22	9½	126		1	12
11 × 22	9½	138		1	15
11 × 20	8½	155		2	0
10 × 20	8½	170		2	6
12 × 18	7½	160	3d	1	13
10 × 18	7½	192		2	3
9 × 18	7½	214		2	7
12 × 16	6½	185		2	2
10 × 16	6½	222		2	8
9 × 16	6½	247		3	0
8 × 16	6½	277		3	2
10 × 14	5½	262		3	0
8 × 14	5½	328		3	12
7 × 14	5½	375		4	4
8 × 12	4½	400		4	9
7 × 12	4½	457		5	3
6 × 12	4½	534		6	1

TABLE 58

Weight of Slate Per Square of Roof in Pounds

Length of Slate, In.	Thickness of Slate, Inches							
	$\frac{1}{8}$	$\frac{3}{16}$	$\frac{1}{4}$	$\frac{3}{8}$	$\frac{1}{2}$	$\frac{5}{8}$	$\frac{3}{4}$	1
12	483	724	967	1450	1936	2419	2902	3872
14	430	688	920	1379	1842	2301	2760	3683
16	445	667	890	1336	1784	2229	2670	3567
18	434	650	869	1303	1740	2174	2607	3480
20	425	637	851	1276	1704	2129	2553	3408
22	418	626	836	1254	1675	2093	2508	3350
24	412	617	825	1238	1653	2066	2478	3306
26	407	610	815	1222	1631	2039	2445	3263

(1 cu. ft. slate = 175 lbs.) The cost of slate varies with the size, color and quality. The medium sizes cost the most, and those of the larger and smaller sizes the least. Special prices are quoted for special sizes. The larger sizes make the cheapest roofs. Red slates cost from 60 to 150% more than black slates. The green slates are more expensive than the black with the exception of the Maine and Peach Bottom varieties.

Table 59

Sizes of Tinware in the Form of Frustum of a Cone

Pans

Size	Diam. of Top	Diam. of Bot.	Height
20 qt.	19½ in.	13 in.	8 in.
16 "	18 "	11¼ "	6¼ "
14 "	15¼ "	9¼ "	6¼ "
10 "	14¾ "	11 "	4⅛ "
6 "	12¾ "	9 "	4 "
2 "	9 "	6 "	3¾ "
3 pt.	8¼ "	5¾ "	2¾ "
1 "	6¼ "	4 "	2¾ "
Pie	9 "	7½ "	1¾ "

Druggists' and Liquor Dealers' Measures

Size	Diam. of Top	Diam. of Bot.	Height
5 gal.	8 in.	13½ in.	12⅜ in.
3 "	7 "	11½ "	10⅛ "
2 "	6 "	10½ "	3⅜ "
1 "	3¾ "	8¾ "	7½ "
½ "	3⅛ "	6⅝ "	6 "
1 qt.	2½ "	5⅛ "	4⅞ "
1 pt.	2 "	4 "	4 "
½ "	1¾ "	3¾ "	3½ "

Dish Kettles and Pails

Size	Diam. of Top	Diam. of Bot.	Height
14 qt.	13 in.	9 in.	9 in.
10 "	11½ "	7 "	8 "
6 "	9¼ "	5½ "	6½ "
2 "	6¼ "	4 "	4 "

Measures

Size	Diam. of Top	Diam. of Bot.	Height
1 gal.	5½ in.	6⅛ in.	9¼ in.
½ "	4 "	4⅞ "	8 "
1 qt.	3½ "	4 "	5¾ "
1 pt.	2⅛ "	3¾ "	4¼ "
½ "	2⅜ "	2⅞ "	3⅛ "

Coffee Pots

Size	Diam. of Top	Diam. of Bot.	Height
1 gal.	4 in.	7 in.	8½ in.
3 qt.	3½ "	6 "	8½ "

Dippers

Size	Diam. of Top	Diam. of Bot.	Height
½ gal.	6½ in.	4 in.	4 in.
1 pt.	4¼ "	3¾ "	2¾ "

Wash Bowls

Size	Diam. of Top	Diam. of Bot.	Height
Large wash bowl....................	11 in.	5¾ in.	5 in.
Cullender..........................	11 "	5¾ "	5 "
Small wash bowl....................	9½ "	5½ "	3¾ "
Milk strainer......................	9½ "	5½ "	3¾ "

Table 60

Dimensions for Liquid Measures

	1 Pint	1 Quart	1 Gallon	2 Gallon	3 Gallon	5 Gallon
Diam. of top, inches...	2	2½	3¾	6	7	8
Diam. of bottom, inches	4	5⅛	8¾	10½	11½	13½
Height, inches........	4	4⅞	7½	8⅜	10⅛	12⅜

A gill contains 7.22 cu. in.
A quart contains 57.75 cu. in.
A pint contains 28.87 cu. in.
A gallon contains 231 cu. in.

TABLE 61

Pine Shingles

The figures below give the weight of shingles required to cover one square of a common gable roof. For hip roofs add 5 per cent.

Inches exposed to weather	4	4½	5	5½	6
Number of shingles per square of roof	900	800	720	655	600
Weight of shingles per square, lb	216	192	173	157	144

TABLE 62

Capacity of Cans One Inch Deep in U. S. Gallons

Diam.		1/10	2/10	3/10	4/10	5/10	6/10	7/10	8/10	9/10
3	.03	.03	.03	.03	.03	.04	.04	.04	.04	.05
4	.05	.05	.05	.05	.06	.06	.07	.07	.07	.08
5	.08	.08	.08	.08	.09	.10	.10	.11	.11	.11
6	.12	.12	.12	.13	.13	.14	.14	.15	.15	.15
7	.16	.17	.17	.18	.18	.19	.19	.20	.20	.21
8	.21	.22	.22	.23	.23	.24	.25	.25	.26	.26
9	.27	.28	.28	.29	.30	.30	.31	.31	.32	.33
10	.34	.34	.35	.36	.36	.37	.38	.38	.39	.40
11	.41	.41	.42	.43	.44	.44	.45	.46	.47	.48
12	.48	.49	.50	.51	.52	.53	.53	.54	.55	.56
13	.57	.58	.59	.60	.60	.61	.62	.63	.64	.65
14	.66	.67	.68	.69	.70	.71	.72	.73	.74	.75
15	.76	.77	.78	.79	.80	.81	.82	.83	.84	.85
16	.87	.88	.89	.90	.91	.92	.93	.94	.95	.97
17	.98	.99	1.005	1.017	1.028	1.040	1.051	1.063	1.075	1.086
18	1.101	1.113	1.125	1.138	1.150	1.162	1.170	1.187	1.200	1.211
19	1.227	1.240	1.253	1.266	1.279	1.292	1.304	1.317	1.330	1.343
20	1.360	1.373	1.385	1.400	1.414	1.428	1.441	1.455	1.478	1.482
21	1.499	1.513	1.527	1.542	1.556	1.570	1.585	1.600	1.612	1.630
22	1.645	1.660	1.675	1.696	1.705	1.720	1.735	1.750	1.770	1.780
23	1.798	1.814	1.830	1.845	1.861	1.876	1.892	1.908	1.923	1.940
24	1.958	1.974	1.991	2.007	2.023	2.040	2.056	2.072	2.096	2.105
25	2.125	2.142	2.159	2.176	2.193	2.120	2.227	2.244	2.261	2.280
26	2.298	2.316	2.333	2.351	2.369	2.386	2.404	2.422	2.440	2.460
27	2.478	2.496	2.515	2.533	2.552	2.570	2.588	2.607	2.625	2.643
28	2.665	2.684	2.703	2.722	2.741	2.764	2.780	2.800	2.820	2.836
29	2.859	2.879	2.898	2.918	2.938	2.958	2.977	2.997	3.017	3.036
30	3.060	3.080	3.100	3.121	3.141	3.162	3.182	3.202	3.223	3.245
31	3.267	3.288	3.309	3.330	3.351	3.372	3.393	3.414	3.436	3.457
32	3.481	3.503	3.524	3.543	3.568	3.590	3.612	3.633	3.655	3.589
33	3.702	3.725	3.747	3.773	3.795	3.814	3.837	3.860	3.882	3.904
34	3.930	3.953	3.976	4.003	4.022	4.046	4.070	4.092	4.115	4.140
35	4.165	4.188	4.212	4.236	4.260	4.284	4.307	4.331	4.355	4.380
36	4.406	4.430	4.455	4.483	4.503	4.528	4.553	4.577	4.602	4.626
37	4.654	4.679	4.704	4.730	4.755	4.780	4.805	4.834	4.855	4.880
38	4.909	4.935	4.961	4.987	5.012	5.038	5.064	5.090	5.120	5.142
39	5.171	5.197	5.224	5.250	5.277	5.304	5.330	5.357	5.383	5.410
40	5.440	5.467	5.491	5.521	5.548	5.576	5.603	5.630	5.657	5.684

Use of the Table

Required the contents of a vessel, diameter $6^7/_{10}$ inches, depth 10 inches.

By the table a vessel 1 inch deep and $6^7/_{10}$ inches diameter contains .15 (hundredths) gallon, then $.15 \times 10 = 1.50$, or 1 gallon and 2 quarts.

Required the contents of a can, diameter $19^8/_{10}$ inches, depth 30 inches.

By the table a vessel 1 inch deep and $19^8/_{10}$ inches diameter contains 1 gallon and .33 (hundredths), then $1.33 \times 30 = 39.90$, or nearly 40 gallons.

Required the depth of a can whose diameter is $12^2/_{10}$ inches, to contain 16 gallons.

By the table a vessel 1 inch deep and $12^2/_{10}$ inches diameter contains .50 (hundredths) gallon, then $16 \div .50 = 32$ inches, the depth required.

Number of Barrels in Cisterns and Tanks

The following table shows the number of barrels (31½ gallons) contained in cisterns of various diameters, from 5 to 30 feet, and of depths ranging from 5 to 20 feet.

To use the table, find the required depth in the side column, and then follow along the line to the column which has the required diameter at the top. Thus, with a cistern 6 feet deep and 16 feet in diameter, we find 6 in the second line, and then follow along until column 16 is reached, when we find that the contents is 286.5 barrels.

For tanks that are tapering the diameter may be measured four-tenths from large end.

TABLE 63

Capacity of Cisterns and Tanks in Barrels

Depth in Feet	Diameter in Feet 5	6	7	8	9	10	11	12	13
5	23.3	33.6	45.7	59.7	75.5	93.2	112.8	134.3	157.6
6	28.0	40.3	54.8	71.7	90.6	111.9	135.4	161.1	189.1
7	32.7	47.0	64.0	83.6	105.7	130.6	158.0	188.0	220.6
8	37.3	53.7	73.1	95.5	120.9	149.2	180.5	214.8	252.1
9	42.0	60.4	82.2	107.4	136.0	167.9	203.1	241.7	283.7
10	46.7	67.1	91.4	119.4	151.1	186.5	225.7	268.6	315.2
11	51.3	73.9	100.5	131.3	166.2	205.1	248.2	295.4	346.7
12	56.0	80.6	109.7	143.2	181.3	223.8	270.8	322.3	378.2
13	60.7	87.3	118.8	155.2	196.4	242.4	293.4	349.1	409.7
14	65.3	94.0	127.9	167.1	211.5	261.1	315.9	376.0	441.3
15	70.0	100.7	137.1	179.0	226.6	289.8	338.5	402.8	472.8
16	74.7	107.4	146.2	191.0	241.7	298.4	361.1	429.7	504.3
17	79.3	114.1	155.4	202.9	256.8	317.0	383.6	456.6	535.8
18	84.0	120.9	164.5	214.8	272.0	335.7	406.2	483.4	567.3
19	88.7	127.6	173.6	226.8	287.0	354.3	428.8	510.3	598.0
20	93.3	134.3	182.8	238.7	302.1	373.0	451.3	537.1	630.4

Depth in Feet	Diameter in Feet 14	15	16	17	18	19	20	21	22
5	182.8	209.8	238.7	269.5	302.1	336.6	373.0	411.2	451.3
6	219.3	251.8	286.5	323.4	362.6	404.0	447.6	493.5	541.6
7	255.9	293.7	334.2	377.3	423.0	471.3	522.2	575.7	631.9
8	292.4	335.7	382.0	431.2	483.4	538.6	396.8	658.0	722.1
9	329.0	377.7	429.7	485.1	543.8	605.9	671.4	740.2	812.4
10	365.5	419.6	477.4	539.0	604.3	673.3	746.0	822.5	902.7
11	402.1	461.6	525.2	592.9	667.7	740.6	820.6	904.7	992.9
12	438.6	503.5	572.9	646.8	725.1	807.9	895.2	987.0	1083.2
13	475.2	545.5	620.7	700.7	785.5	875.2	969.8	1069.2	1173.5
14	511.8	587.5	668.2	751.6	846.6	942.6	1044.4	1151.5	1263.7
15	548.3	629.4	716.2	808.5	906.0	1009.9	1119.0	1233.7	1354.0
16	584.9	671.4	773.9	862.4	966.8	1077.2	1193.6	1315.9	1444.3
17	621.4	713.4	811.6	916.3	1027.2	1144.6	1268.2	1398.2	1534.5
18	658.0	755.3	859.4	970.2	1087.7	1211.9	1342.8	1480.4	1624.8
19	694.5	797.3	907.1	1024.1	1148.1	1279.2	1417.4	1562.7	1715.1
20	731.1	839.3	954.9	1078.0	1208.5	1346.5	1492.0	1644.9	1805.3

Depth in Feet	Diameter in Feet 23	24	25	26	27	28	29	30
5	493.3	537.1	532.8	630.4	679.8	731.1	784.2	839.3
6	592.0	644.5	699.4	756.5	815.8	877.3	941.1	1007.1
7	690.6	752.0	815.9	882.5	951.7	1023.5	1097.9	1175.0
8	789.3	859.4	932.5	1008.6	1087.7	1169.7	1254.8	1342.8
9	887.9	966.8	1049.1	1134.7	1223.6	1316.0	1411.6	1510.7
10	986.6	1074.2	1165.6	1260.8	1359.6	1462.2	1568.2	1678.5
11	1085.2	1181.7	1282.2	1386.8	1495.6	1608.7	1723.0	1846.4
12	1183.9	1289.1	1398.7	1512.9	1631.5	1754.6	1882.2	2014.2
13	1282.6	1396.5	1515.3	1639.0	1767.5	1900.8	2039.0	2182.0
14	1381.2	1503.9	1631.9	1765.1	1903.4	2047.1	2195.9	2343.9
15	1479.9	1611.4	1748.4	1891.1	2039.4	2193.3	2352.7	2517.8
16	1578.5	1718.8	1865.0	2017.2	2175.4	2339.5	2509.6	2685.6
17	1677.2	1826.2	1981.6	2143.3	2311.3	2485.7	2666.4	2853.5
18	1775.9	1933.6	2098.1	2269.4	2447.3	2631.9	2823.3	3021.3
19	1874.5	2041.1	2214.7	2395.4	2583.2	2778.1	2980.1	3189.2
20	1973.2	2148.5	2321.2	2521.5	2719.2	2924.4	3137.0	3357.0

Capacity of Cylinders in United States Gallons

Table 65 gives the capacity in United States gallons (231 cubic inches) of cylindrical vessels from 1 to 72 inches in depth and from 4 to 72 inches in diameter. Table 64 will be found useful in reducing the decimal parts of a gallon to gills, pints and quarts. A very few words will suffice to explain the use of the tables, and perhaps the simplest method of doing so is to apply it to a practical case. Suppose, for instance, it is desired to find the dimensions of a cylinder holding 27 gallons. Running down the column headed 19, we find the number 27.0028, and following the line across, we come to the number 22; hence a cylinder 19 inches in diameter and 22 inches deep will hold 27 gallons and .0028 gallon. Turning to Table 64 we find a gill is equal to .03125 gallon, so that the capacity of the cylinder in question is about $^1/_{10}$ gill more than 27 gallons.

Again, if it is desired to find the depth of a 15-inch cylinder that shall hold 27 gallons, we run down the column headed 15 till we come to the number 27.54, and following the line across we find the depth to be 36 inches. The decimal .54 we find, on consulting Table 64, is equivalent to between 1 and 2 pints; therefore a 15-inch cylinder 36 inches deep will hold between 1 and 2 pints more than 27 gallons. Similarly, to find the diameter of a cylinder 15 inches deep that shall hold 27 gallons, we run across the line opposite 15 till we come to the number 26.976, under the column headed 23. The decimal part, according to Table 64, is equivalent to between 31 gills and 1 gallon, so the capacity of a cylinder 15 inches deep and 23 inches diameter is about ½ gill less than 27 gallons. Where it is desired to find the capacity of a cylinder both dimensions of which are given, it is only necessary to run down the column headed with the diameter till we come to the line across from the given depth, where the number found will be the capacity of the cylinder in gallons. To illustrate: What is the capacity of a cylinder 29 inches deep and 32 inches in diameter? Consulting Table 65 in the manner described, we find the number 100.966, the decimal part of which, according to Table 64, is about 31 gills, or 3 quarts, 1 pint and 3 gills; the given cylinder, therefore, holding 100 gallons, 3 quarts, 1 pint and 3 gills. These examples, we think, fully illustrate the uses of the tables, and serve to show their wide application to the determination of the capacities and dimensions of cylindrical vessels.

TABLE 64

The Decimal Equivalents of the Fractional Parts of a Gallon

0.03125 of a gallon	= 1	gill	0.53125 of a gallon	= 17	gills
0.06250 of a gallon	= ½	pint	0.56250 of a gallon	= 4½	pints
0.09375 of a gallon	= 3	gills	0.59375 of a gallon	= 19	gills
0.12500 of a gallon	= 1	pint	0.62500 of a gallon	= 5	pints
0.15625 of a gallon	= 5	gills	0.65625 of a gallon	= 21	gills
0.18750 of a gallon	= 1½	pints	0.68750 of a gallon	= 5½	pints
0.21875 of a gallon	= 7	gills	0.71875 of a gallon	= 23	gills
0.25000 of a gallon	= 1	quart	0.75000 of a gallon	= 3	quarts
0.28125 of a gallon	= 9	gills	0.78125 of a gallon	= 25	gills
0.31250 of a gallon	= 2½	pints	0.81250 of a gallon	= 6½	pints
0.34375 of a gallon	= 11	gills	0.84375 of a gallon	= 27	gills
0.37500 of a gallon	= 3	pints	0.87500 of a gallon	= 7	pints
0.40625 of a gallon	= 13	gills	0.90625 of a gallon	= 29	gills
0.43750 of a gallon	= 3½	pints	0.93750 of a gallon	= 7½	pints
0.43875 of a gallon	= 15	gills	0.96875 of a gallon	= 31	gills
0.50000 of a gallon	= ½	gallon	1.00000 of a gallon	= 1	gallon

Table 65

Capacity of Cylinders in United States Gallons

Depth, Inches	Diameter in Inches 4	5	6	7	8	9
1	.0544	.085	.1224	.1666	.2176	.2754
2	.1088	.170	.2448	.3332	.4352	.5508
3	.1632	.255	.3672	.4998	.6528	.8262
4	.2176	.340	.4896	.6664	.8704	1.1016
5	.2720	.425	.6120	.8330	1.0880	1.3770
6	.3264	.510	.7344	.9996	1.3056	1.6524
7	.3808	.595	.8568	1.1662	1.5232	1.9278
8	.4352	.680	.9792	1.3328	1.7408	2.2023
9	.4896	.765	1.1016	1.4994	1.9584	2.4780
10	.5440	.850	1.2240	1.6660	2.1760	2.7546
11	.5984	.935	1.3464	1.8326	2.3936	3.0294
12	.6528	1.020	1.4688	1.9992	2.6112	3.3048
13	.7072	1.105	1.5912	2.1658	2.8288	3.5802
14	.7616	1.190	1.7136	2.3324	3.0464	3.8556
15	.8160	1.275	1.8360	2.4990	3.2640	4.1310
16	.8704	1.360	1.9584	2.6656	3.4816	4.4064
17	.9248	1.445	2.0808	2.8322	3.6992	4.6818
18	.9792	1.530	2.2032	2.9988	3.9168	4.9572
19	1.0336	1.615	2.3256	3.1654	4.1344	5.2326
20	1.0880	1.707	2.4480	3.3320	4.3520	5.5080
21	1.1424	1.785	2.5704	3.4986	4.5696	5.7834
22	1.1968	1.870	2.6928	3.6652	4.7872	6.0588
23	1.2512	1.955	2.8152	3.8318	5.0048	6.3342
24	1.3056	2.040	2.9376	3.9984	5.2224	6.6096
25	1.3600	2.125	3.0600	4.1650	5.4400	6.8850
26	1.4144	2.210	3.1824	4.3316	5.6576	7.1604
27	1.4688	2.295	3.3048	4.4982	5.8752	7.4358
28	1.5232	2.380	3.4272	4.6648	6.0928	7.7112
29	1.5776	2.465	3.5496	4.8314	6.3104	7.9866
30	1.6320	2.550	3.6720	4.9980	6.5280	8.2620
31	1.6864	2.635	3.7944	5.1646	6.7456	8.5374
32	1.7408	2.720	3.9168	5.3312	6.9632	8.8128
33	1.7952	2.805	4.0392	5.4978	7.1808	9.0882
34	1.8496	2.890	4.1616	5.6644	7.3984	9.3636
35	1.9040	2.975	4.2840	5.8310	7.6160	9.0390
36	1.9584	3.060	4.4064	5.9976	7.8336	9.9144
40	2.1760	3.400	4.8960	6.6640	8.7040	11.0160
44	2.3936	3.740	5.3856	7.3304	9.5744	12.1176
48	2.6112	4.080	5.8752	7.9968	10.4448	13.2192
54	2.9376	4.590	6.6096	8.9964	11.7504	14.8716
60	3.2640	5.100	7.3440	9.9960	13.0560	16.5240
72	3.9168	6.120	8.8128	11.9952	15.6672	19.8288

Note.—This table on heavy cardboard 11 × 14 ins., eyeletted, $0.25.

TABLE 65 (Continued)

Capacity of Cylinders in United States Gallons

Depth, Inches	Diameter in Inches 10	11	12	13	14	15
1	.34	.4114	.4896	.5746	.6664	.765
2	.68	.8228	.9792	1.1492	1.3328	1.530
3	1.02	1.2342	1.4688	1.7238	1.9992	2.295
4	1.36	1.6456	1.9584	2.2984	2.6656	3.060
5	1.70	2.0570	2.4480	2.8730	3.3320	3.825
6	2.04	2.4684	2.9376	3.4476	3.9984	4.590
7	2.38	2.8798	3.4272	4.0222	4.6648	5.355
8	2.72	3.2912	3.9168	4.5968	5.3312	6.120
9	3.06	3.7026	4.4064	5.1714	5.9976	6.885
10	3.40	4.1140	4.8960	5.7460	6.6640	7.650
11	3.74	4.5254	5.3856	6.3206	7.3304	8.415
12	4.08	4.9368	5.8752	6.8952	7.9968	9.180
13	4.42	5.3482	6.3648	7.4698	8.6632	9.945
14	4.76	5.7596	6.8544	8.0444	9.3296	10.710
15	5.10	6.1710	7.3440	8.6190	9.9960	11.475
16	5.44	6.5824	7.8336	9.1936	10.6624	12.240
17	5.78	6.9938	8.3232	9.7682	11.3288	13.005
18	6.12	7.4052	8.8128	10.3428	11.9952	13.770
19	6.46	7.8166	9.3024	10.9174	12.6616	14.535
20	6.80	8.2280	9.7920	11.4920	13.3280	15.300
21	7.14	8.6394	10.2816	12.0666	13.9944	16.065
22	7.48	9.0508	10.7712	12.6412	14.6608	16.830
23	7.82	9.4622	11.2608	13.2158	15.3272	17.595
24	8.16	9.8736	11.7504	13.7904	15.9936	18.360
25	8.50	10.2850	12.2400	14.3650	16.6600	19.125
26	8.84	10.6964	12.7296	14.9396	17.3264	19.890
27	9.18	11.1078	13.2192	15.5142	17.9928	20.655
28	9.52	11.5192	13.7088	16.0888	18.6592	21.420
29	9.86	11.8306	14.1984	16.6634	19.3256	22.185
30	10.20	12.3420	14.6880	17.2380	19.9920	22.950
31	10.54	12.7534	15.1776	17.8126	20.6584	23.715
32	10.88	13.1648	15.6672	18.3872	21.3248	24.480
33	11.22	13.5762	16.1568	18.9618	21.9912	25.245
34	11.56	13.9876	16.6464	19.5364	22.6576	26.010
35	11.90	14.3998	17.1360	20.1110	23.3240	26.775
36	12.24	14.8104	17.6256	20.6856	23.9904	27.540
40	13.60	16.4560	19.5840	22.9840	26.6560	30.600
44	14.96	18.1016	21.5424	25.2824	29.3216	33.660
48	16.32	19.7472	23.5008	27.5808	31.9872	36.720
54	18.36	22.2156	26.4384	31.0284	35.9856	41.310
60	20.40	24.6840	29.3760	34.4760	39.9840	45.900
72	24.48	29.6208	35.2512	41.3712	47.9808	55.080

NOTE.—This table on heavy cardboard 11 × 14 ins., eyeletted, $0.25.

Table 65 (Continued)

Capacity of Cylinders in United States Gallons

Depth, Inches	Diameter in Inches					
	16	17	18	19	20	21
1	.8704	.9826	1.1016	1.2274	1.36	1.4994
2	1.7408	1.9652	2.2032	2.4548	2.72	2.9988
3	2.6112	2.9478	3.3048	3.6822	4.08	4.4982
4	3.4816	3.9304	4.4064	4.9096	5.44	5.9976
5	4.3520	4.9130	5.5080	6.1370	6.80	7.4970
6	5.2224	5.8956	6.6096	7.3644	8.16	8.9964
7	6.0928	6.8782	7.7112	8.5918	9.52	10.4958
8	6.9632	7.8608	8.8128	9.8192	10.88	11.9952
9	7.8336	8.8434	9.9144	11.0466	12.24	13.4946
10	8.7040	9.8260	11.0160	12.2740	13.60	14.9940
11	9.5744	10.8086	12.1176	13.5014	14.96	16.4934
12	10.4448	11.7912	13.2192	14.7288	16.32	17.9928
13	11.3152	12.7738	14.3208	15.9562	17.68	19.4922
14	12.1856	13.7564	15.4224	17.1636	19.04	20.9916
15	13.0560	14.7390	16.5240	18.4110	20.40	22.4910
16	13.9264	15.7216	17.6256	19.6384	21.76	23.9904
17	14.7968	16.7042	18.7272	20.8658	23.12	25.4898
18	15.6672	17.6868	19.8288	22.0932	24.48	26.9892
19	16.5376	18.6694	20.9304	23.3206	25.84	28.4886
20	17.4080	19.6520	22.0320	24.5480	27.20	29.9880
21	18.2784	20.6346	23.1336	25.7754	28.56	31.4874
22	19.1488	21.6172	24.2352	27.0028	29 92	32.9868
23	20.0192	22.5998	25.3368	28.2302	31.28	34.4862
24	20.8806	23.5824	26.4384	29.4576	32.64	35.9856
25	21.7600	24.5650	27.5400	30.6850	34.00	37.4850
26	22.6304	25.5476	28.6416	31.9124	35.36	38.9844
27	23.5008	26.5302	29.7432	33.1398	36.72	40.4838
28	24.3712	27.5128	30.8448	34.3672	38.08	41.9832
29	25.2416	28.4954	31.9464	35.5946	39.44	43.4826
30	26.1120	29.4780	33.0480	40.8220	40.80	44.9820
31	26.9824	30.4606	34.1496	38.0494	42.16	46.4814
32	27.8528	31.4432	35.2512	39.2768	43.52	47.9808
33	28.7232	32.4258	36.3528	40.5042	44.88	49.4802
34	29.5936	33.4084	37.4544	41.7316	46.14	50.9796
35	30.4640	34.3910	38.5560	42.9590	47.60	52.4790
36	31.3344	35.3736	39.6576	44.1864	48.96	53.9784
40	34.8160	39.3040	44.0640	49.0960	54.40	59.9760
44	38.2976	43.2344	48.4704	54.0056	59.84	65.9736
48	41.7792	47.1648	52.8768	58.9152	65.28	71.9712
54	47.0016	53.0604	59.4864	66.4796	73.44	80.9676
60	52.2240	58.9560	66.0960	73.6440	81.60	89.9640
72	62.6688	70.7472	79.3151	88.3728	97.92	107.9570

Note.—This table on heavy cardboard 11 × 14 ins., eyeletted, $0.25.

TABLE 65 (Continued)

Capacity of Cylinders in United States Gallons

Depth, Inches	Diameter in Inches 22	23	24	26	28
1	1.6456	1.7986	1.9584	2.2984	2.6656
2	3.2912	3.5972	3.9168	4.5968	5.3312
3	4.9368	5.3958	5.8752	6.8952	7.9968
4	6.5824	7.1944	7.8336	9.1936	10.6624
5	8.2280	8.9930	9.7920	11.4920	13.3280
6	9.8736	10.7916	11.7504	13.7904	15.9936
7	11.5192	12.5902	13.7089	16.0888	18.6592
8	13.1648	14.3888	15.6672	18.3872	21.3248
9	14.8104	16.1874	17.6256	20.6856	23.9904
10	16.4560	17.9860	19.5840	22.9840	26.6560
11	18.1016	19.7846	21.5424	25.2824	29.3216
12	19.7472	21.5832	23.5008	27.5808	31.9872
13	21.3928	23.3818	25.4592	29.8792	34.6528
14	23.0384	25.1804	27.4176	32.1776	37.3184
15	24.6840	26.9790	29.3760	34.4760	39.9840
16	26.3296	28.7776	31.3344	36.7741	42.6596
17	27.9752	30.5762	33.2928	39.0728	45.3152
18	29.6208	32.3748	35.2512	41.3712	47.9808
19	31.2664	34.1734	37.2096	43.6696	50.6464
20	32.9120	35.9720	39.1680	45.9680	53.3120
21	34.5576	37.7706	41.1264	48.2664	55.9776
22	36.2032	39.5692	43.0848	50.5648	58.6432
23	37.8488	41.3678	45.0432	52.8832	61.3088
24	39.4944	43.1664	47.0016	55.1616	63.9744
25	41.1400	44.9650	48.9600	57.4600	66.6400
26	42.7856	46.7636	50.9184	59.8584	69.3056
27	44.4312	48.5622	52.8768	62.0568	71.9712
28	46.0768	50.3608	54.8352	64.3552	74.6368
29	47.7224	52.1594	56.7936	66.6536	77.3024
30	49.3680	53.9580	58.7520	68.9520	79.9680
31	51.0136	55.7566	60.7104	71.2504	82.6336
32	52.6592	57.5552	62.6688	73.5488	85.2992
33	54.3048	59.3538	64.6272	75.8472	87.9648
34	55.9504	61.1524	66.5856	78.1456	90.6304
35	57.5960	62.9510	68.5440	80.4440	93.2960
36	59.2416	64.7496	70.5024	82.7424	95.9616
40	65.8240	71.9440	78.3360	91.9360	106.6240
44	72.4064	79.1384	86.1696	101.1300	117.2860
48	78.9888	86.3328	94.0032	110.3230	127.9490
54	88.8624	97.1244	105.7540	124.1140	143.9420
60	98.7360	107.9160	117.5040	137.9040	159.9360
72	118.4830	129.4990	141.0050	165.4850	191.9230

NOTE.—This table on heavy cardboard 11 × 14 ins., eyeletted, $0.25.

TABLE 65 (Continued)

Capacity of Cylinders in United States Gallons

Depth, Inches	Diameter in Inches 30	32	34	36	40
1	3.06	3.4816	3.9304	4.4064	5.44
2	6.12	6.9632	7.8608	8.8128	10.88
3	9.18	10.4448	11.7912	13.2192	16.32
4	12.24	13.9264	15.7216	17.6256	21.76
5	15.30	17.4080	19.6520	22.5320	27.20
6	18.36	20.8896	23.5824	26.4384	32.64
7	21.42	24.3712	27.5128	30.8448	38.08
8	24.48	27.8528	31.4432	35.2512	43.52
9	27.54	31.3344	35.3736	39.6576	48.96
10	30.60	34.8160	39.3040	44.0640	54.40
11	33.66	38.2976	43.2344	48.4704	59.84
12	36.72	41.7792	47.1648	52.8768	65.28
13	39.78	45.2608	51.0952	57.2832	70.72
14	42.84	48.7424	55.0256	61.6896	76.16
15	45.90	52.2240	58.9560	66.0960	81.60
16	48.96	55.7056	62.8864	70.5024	87.04
17	52.02	59.1872	66.8168	74.9088	92.48
18	55.08	62.6688	70.7472	79.3152	97.92
19	58.14	66.1504	74.6776	83.7216	103.36
20	61.20	69.6320	78.6080	88.1280	108.80
21	64.26	73.1136	82.5384	92.5344	114.24
22	67.32	76.5952	86.4688	96.9408	119.68
23	70.38	80.0768	90.3902	101.3470	125.12
24	73.44	83.5584	94.3296	105.7540	130.56
25	76.50	87.0400	98.2600	110.1600	136.00
26	79.53	90.5213	102.1900	114.5660	141.44
27	82.62	94.0032	103.1210	118.9730	146.88
28	85.68	97.4848	110.0510	123.3790	152.32
29	88 74	100.9660	113.9320	127.7860	157.76
30	91.80	100.4480	117.9120	132.1920	163.20
31	94.86	107.9300	121.8420	136.5980	168.64
32	97.92	111.4110	125.7730	141.0050	174.08
33	100.98	114.8930	129.7030	145.4110	179.52
34	104.04	118.3740	133.6440	149.8180	184.96
35	107.10	121.8560	137.5640	154.2240	190.40
36	110.16	125.3380	141.4944	158.6300	195.84
40	122.04	139.2640	157.2160	176.2560	217.60
44	134.64	153.1900	172.9380	193.8820	239.36
48	146.88	167.1170	188.6590	211.5070	261.12
54	165.24	188.0060	212.2420	237.9460	293.76
60	183.60	208.8960	235.8240	264.3840	326.40
72	220.32	250.6750	282.9890	317.2610	391.68

NOTE.—This table on heavy cardboard 11 × 14 ins., eyeletted, $0.25.

TABLE 65 (Continued)

Capacity of Cylinders in United States Gallons

Depth, Inches	Diameter in Inches 44	48	54	60	72
1	6.5824	7.8336	9.9144	12.24	17.6256
2	13.1648	15.6672	19.8288	24.48	35.2512
3	19.7472	23.5008	29.7432	36.72	52.8768
4	26.3296	31.3344	39.6576	44.96	70.5024
5	32.9120	39.1680	49.5720	61.20	88.1280
6	39.4944	47.0016	59.4864	73.44	105.7540
7	46.0768	54.8352	69.4008	85.68	123.3790
8	52.6592	62.6688	79.3152	97.92	141.0050
9	59.2416	70.5024	89.2296	110.16	158.6300
10	65.8240	78.3360	99.1440	122.40	176.2560
11	72.4034	86.1696	109.0580	134.64	193.8820
12	78.9888	94.0032	118.9730	146.88	211.5070
13	85.5712	101.8370	128.8870	159.12	229.1330
14	92.1536	109.6700	138.8020	171.36	246.7580
15	98.7360	117.5040	148.7160	183.60	264.3840
16	105.3180	125.3380	158.6300	195.84	282.0100
17	111.9010	133.1710	168.5450	208.08	299.6350
18	118.1830	141.0050	178.4590	220.32	317.2610
19	125.0660	148.8380	188.3740	232.56	334.8860
20	131.6480	156.6720	198.2880	244.80	352.5120
21	138.2300	164.5060	208.2020	257.04	370.1380
22	144.8130	172.3390	218.1170	269.28	387.7630
23	151.3950	180.1730	228.0310	281.52	405.3890
24	157.9780	188.0060	237.9460	293.76	423.0140
25	164.5600	195.8400	247.8600	306.00	440.6400
26	171.1420	203.6740	257.7740	318.24	458.2660
27	177.7250	211.5070	267.6890	330.48	475.8910
28	184.3070	219.3410	277.6030	342.72	493.5170
29	190.8900	227.1740	287.5180	354.96	511.1420
30	197.4720	235.0080	297.4320	367.20	528.7680
31	204.0540	242.8420	307.3460	379.44	546.3940
32	210.6370	250.6750	317.2610	391.68	564.0190
33	217.2190	258.5090	327.1750	403.92	581.6450
34	223.8020	266.3420	337.0900	416.16	599.2700
35	230.3840	274.1760	347.0040	428.40	616.8930
36	236.9660	282.0100	356.9180	440.64	634.5220
40	263.2960	313.3440	396.5760	489.60	705.0240
44	289.6260	344.6780	436.2340	538.56	775.5260
48	315.9550	376.0130	475.8910	587.52	846.0290
54	355.4500	423.0140	535.3780	660.96	951.7820
60	394.9440	470.0160	594.8640	734.40	1057.5400
72	473.9330	564.0190	713.8370	881.28	1269.0400

NOTE.—This table on heavy cardboard 11 × 14 ins., eyeletted, $0.25.

Table 65 (Continued)

Capacity of Cylinders in United States Gallons

Depth in Feet	Diameter in Feet 5	6	7	8	9	10	11	12
5	735	1,060	1,440	1,875	2,380	2,925	3,550	4,237
6	881	1,270	1,728	2,250	2,855	3,510	4,260	5,084
7	1,028	1,480	2,016	2,625	3,330	4,095	4,970	5,931
8	1,175	1,690	2,304	3,000	3,805	4,680	5,680	6,778
9	1,322	1,900	2,592	3,375	4,280	5,265	6,390	7,625
10	1,469	2,110	2,880	3,750	4,755	5,850	7,100	8,472
11	1,616	2,320	3,168	4,125	5,250	6,435	7,810	9,319
12	1,762	2,530	3,456	4,500	5,705	7,020	8,520	10,166
13	1,909	2,740	3,744	4,875	6,180	7,605	9,230	11,013
14	2,056	2,950	4,032	5,250	6,655	8,190	9,940	11,860
15	2,203	3,160	4,320	5,625	7,130	8,775	10,650	12,707
16	2,356	3,370	4,608	6,000	7,605	9,360	11,360	13,554
17	2,497	3,580	4,896	6,375	8,080	9,945	12,070	14,401
18	2,644	3,790	5,184	6,750	8,535	10,530	12,780	15,245
19	2,791	4,000	5,472	7,125	9,010	11,115	13,490	16,098
20	2,938	4,210	5,760	7,500	9,490	11,700	14,200	16,942

Depth in Feet	Diameter in Feet 13	14	15	16	18	20	22	24
5	4,960	5,765	6,698	7,520	9,516	11,750	14,215	16,918
6	5,952	6,918	8,038	9,024	11,419	14,100	17,059	20,302
7	6,944	8,071	9,378	10,528	13,322	16,450	19,902	23,680
8	7,936	9,224	10,718	12,032	15,225	18,800	22,745	27,070
9	8,928	10,377	12,058	13,536	17,128	21,150	25,588	30,454
10	9,920	11,530	13,398	15,050	19,031	23,500	28,431	33,838
11	10,913	12,683	14,738	16,544	20,934	25,850	31,274	37,222
12	11,904	13,836	16,078	18,048	22,837	28,200	34,117	40,606
13	12,896	14,989	17,418	19,552	24,740	30,550	36,960	43,990
14	13,888	16,142	18,758	21,056	26,643	32,900	39,803	47,374
15	14,880	17,295	20,098	22,260	28,546	35,250	42,646	50,758
16	15,872	18,448	21,438	26,064	30,449	37,600	45,489	54,142
17	16,864	19,601	22,778	25,568	32,352	39,950	48,332	57,520
18	17,856	20,754	24,118	27,072	34,255	42,300	51,175	60,910
19	18,848	21,907	25,458	28,576	36,158	44,650	54,018	64,294
20	19,840	23,060	26,798	30,080	38,062	47,000	56,861	67,678

To find the number of gallons in a tank of unequal diameter multiply the inside bottom diameter in inches by the inside top diameter in inches, then this product by 34: point off four figures and the result will be the average number of gallons to one inch in depth of the tank.

TABLE 66

Number of U. S. Gallons in Rectangular Tanks One Foot in Depth

Width in Feet	Length of Tank in Feet										
	2	2.5	3	3.5	4	4.5	5	5.5	6	6.5	7
2	29.92	37.40	44.88	52.36	59.84	67.32	74.81	82.29	89.77	97.25	104.73
2.5	.....	46.75	56.10	65.45	74.80	84.16	93.51	102.86	112.21	121.56	130.91
3	.....	.....	67.32	78.54	89.77	100.99	112.21	123.43	134.65	145.87	157.09
3.5	.....	.....	.....	91.64	104.73	117.82	130.91	144.00	157.09	170.18	183.27
4	.....	.....	.....	.....	119.69	134.65	149.61	164.57	179.53	194.49	209.45
4.5	.....	.....	.....	.....	......	151.48	168.31	185.14	201.97	218.80	235.63
5	.....	.....	.....	.....	......	......	187.01	205.71	224.41	243.11	261.82
5.5	.....	.....	.....	.....	......	......	......	226.28	246.86	267.43	288.00
6	.....	.....	.....	.....	......	......	......	......	269.30	291.74	314.18
6.5	.....	.....	.....	.....	......	......	......	......	......	316.05	340.36
7	.....	.....	.....	.....	......	......	......	......	......	......	366.54

Width in Feet	Length of Tank in Feet									
	7.5	8	8.5	9	9.5	10	10.5	11	11.5	12
2	112 21	119.69	127.17	134.65	142.13	149.61	157.09	161.57	172.05	179.53
2.5	140.26	149.61	158.96	168.31	177.66	187.01	196.36	205.71	215.06	224.41
3	168.31	179.53	190.75	202.97	213.19	224.41	235.63	246.86	258.07	269.30
3.5	196.36	209.45	222.54	235.63	248.73	261.82	274.90	288.00	301.09	314.18
4	224.41	239.37	254.34	269.30	284.26	299.22	314.18	329.14	344.10	359.06
4 5	252.47	269.30	286.13	302.96	319.79	336.62	353.45	370.28	387.11	403.94
5	280.52	299.22	317.92	336.62	355.32	374.03	392.72	411.43	430.13	448.83
5.5	308.57	329.14	349.71	370.28	390.85	411.43	432.00	452.57	473.14	493.71
6	336.62	359.06	381.50	403.94	426.39	448.83	471.27	493.71	516.15	538.59
6.5	364.67	388.98	413.30	437.60	461.92	486.23	510.54	534.85	559.16	583.47
7	392.72	418.91	445.09	471.27	497.45	523.64	549.81	575.99	602.18	628.36
7.5	420.78	448.83	476.88	504.93	532.98	561.04	589.08	617.14	645.19	673.24
8	......	478.75	508.67	538.59	568.51	598.44	628.36	658.28	688.20	718.12
8.5	......	......	540.46	572.25	604.05	635.84	667.63	699.42	731.21	763.00
9	......	......	......	605.92	639.58	673.25	706.90	740.56	774.23	807.89
9.5	......	......	......	......	675.11	710.65	746.17	781.71	817.24	852.77
10	......	......	......	......	......	748.05	785.45	822.86	860.26	897.66
10.5	......	......	......	......	......	......	824.73	864.00	903.23	942.56
11	......	......	......	......	......	......	......	905.44	946.27	937.43
11.5	......	......	......	......	......	......	......	......	989.29	1032.3
12	......	......	......	......	......	......	......	......	......	1077.2

Example.—To find number of gallons in a rectangular tank that is 7.5 feet by 10 feet, the water being 4 feet deep: Look in extreme left-hand column for 7.5, and opposite to this in column headed 10 read 561.04, which being multiplied by 4, the depth of water in the tank, gives 2244.2, the number of gallons required.

TABLE 67

Capacity of Cylinders in Imperial Gallons

Depth, Inches	Diameter in Inches 4	5	6	7	8	9	10
1	.0453	.0708	.102	.1388	.1814	.2295	.2833
2	.0906	.1416	.204	.2776	.3628	.4590	.5666
3	.1359	.2124	.306	.4164	.5442	.6885	.8499
4	.1812	.2832	.408	.5552	.7256	.9180	1.1332
5	.2265	.3540	.510	.6940	.9070	1.1475	1.4165
6	.2718	.4248	.612	.8328	1.0884	1.3770	1.6998
7	.3171	.4956	.714	.9716	1.1698	1.6065	1.9831
8	.3624	.5664	.816	1.1104	1.4512	1.8360	2.2664
9	.4077	.6372	.918	1.2492	1.6326	2.0655	2.5497
10	.4530	.7080	1.020	1.3880	1.8140	2.2950	2.8330
11	.4983	.7788	1.122	1.5268	1.9954	2.5245	3.1163
12	.5436	.8496	1.224	1.6656	2.1768	2.7540	3.3996
13	.5889	.9204	1.326	1.8044	2.3582	2.9835	3.6829
14	.6342	.9912	1.428	1.9432	2.3396	3.2130	3.9662
15	.6795	1.0620	1.530	2.0820	2.7210	3.4425	4.2495
16	.7248	1.1328	1.632	2.2208	2.9024	3.6720	4.5328
17	.7701	1.2036	1.734	2.3596	3.0838	3.9015	4.8161
18	.8154	1.2744	1.836	2.4984	3.2652	4.1310	5.0994
19	.8607	1.3452	1.938	2.6372	3.4466	4.3605	5.3827
20	.9060	1.4160	2.040	2.7760	3.6280	4.5900	5.6660
21	.9513	1.48[illegible]8	2.142	2.9148	3.5094	4.8195	5.9493
22	.9966	1.5576	2.244	3.0536	3.9908	5.0490	6.2326
23	1.0419	1.6284	2.346	3.1924	4.1722	5.2785	6.5159
24	1.0872	1.6992	2.448	3.3312	4.3536	5.5080	6.7992
25	1.1325	1.7700	2.550	3.4700	4.5350	5.7375	7.0825
26	1.1778	1.8408	2.652	3.6088	4.7164	5.9670	7.3658
27	1.2231	1.9116	2.754	3.7476	4.8978	6.1965	7.6491
28	1.2684	1.9824	2.856	3.8864	4.6792	6.4260	7.9324
29	1.3137	2.0532	2.958	4.0252	5.2606	6.6555	8.3057
30	1.3590	2.1240	3.060	4.1640	5.4420	6.8850	8.4990
31	1.4043	2.1948	3.162	4.3028	5.6234	7.1145	8.7823
32	1.4496	2.2656	3.264	4.4416	5.8048	7.3440	9.0656
33	1.4949	2.3364	3.366	4.5804	5.9862	7.5735	9.3489
34	1.5402	2.4072	3.468	4.7192	6.1676	7.8030	9.6322
35	1.5855	2.4780	3.570	4.8580	6.3490	8.0325	9.9155
36	1.6308	2.5488	3.672	4.9968	6.5304	8.2620	10.1988
40	1.8120	2.8320	4.080	5.5520	7.2560	9.1800	11.3320
44	1.9932	3.1152	4.489	6.1072	7.9816	10.0980	12.4652
48	2.1744	3.3984	4.896	6.6624	8.7072	11.0160	13.5984
54	2.4462	3.8232	5.508	7.4952	9.7956	12.3930	15.2982
60	2.7180	4.2480	6.120	8.3280	10.8840	13.7700	16.2980
72	3.2616	5.0976	7.344	9.9936	13.0608	16.5240	20.3976

This table gives number of Imperial gallons (277.274 inches) in cylindrical vessels from 1 to 72 inches in depth and from 4 to 72 inches in diameter.

Table 67 (Continued)

Capacity of Cylinders in Imperial Gallons

Depth, Inches	Diameter in Inches 11	12	13	14	15	16
1	.3428	.4080	.4788	.5553	.6375	.7253
2	.6856	.8160	.9576	1.1106	1.2750	1.4506
3	1.0284	1.2240	1.4364	1.6659	2.0125	2.1759
4	1.3712	1.6320	1.9152	2.2212	2.5500	2.9012
5	1.7140	2.0400	2.3940	2.7765	3.1875	3.6265
6	2.0568	2.4480	2.8728	3.3318	3.8250	4.3518
7	2.3996	2.8560	3.3516	3.8871	4.3625	5.0771
8	2.7424	3.2640	3.8304	4.4424	5.1000	5.8024
9	3.0852	3.6720	4.3092	4.9977	5.7375	6.5277
10	3.4280	4.0800	4.7880	5.5530	6.3750	7.2530
11	3.7708	4.4880	5.2668	6.1083	7.0125	7.9783
12	4.1136	4.8960	5.7456	6.6636	7.6500	8.7036
13	4.4564	5.3040	6.2244	7.2189	8.2875	9.4289
14	4.7992	5.7120	6.7032	7.7742	8.7250	10.1542
15	5.1420	6.1200	7.1820	8.3295	9.5625	10.8795
16	5.4848	6.5280	7.6608	8.8848	10.2000	11.6048
17	5.8276	6.9360	8.1396	9.4401	10.8375	12.3301
18	6.1704	7.3440	8.6184	9.9954	11.4750	13.0554
19	6.5132	7.7520	9.0972	10.5507	12.1125	13.7807
20	6.8560	8.1600	9.5760	11.1060	12.7500	14.5060
21	7.1988	8.5680	10.0548	11.6613	13.0875	15.2313
22	7.5416	8.9760	10.5336	12.2166	14.0250	15.9566
23	7.8844	9.3840	11.0124	12.7719	14.6625	16.6819
24	8.2272	9.7920	11.4912	13.3272	15.3000	17.4072
25	8.5700	10.2000	11.9700	13.8825	15.9375	18.1325
26	8.9128	10.6080	12.4488	14.4378	16.5750	18.8578
27	9.2556	11.0160	12.9276	14.9931	17.2125	19.5831
28	9.5984	11.4240	13.4064	15.5484	17.4500	20.3084
29	9.9412	11.8320	13.8852	16.1037	18.4875	21.0337
30	10.2840	12.2400	14.3640	16.6590	20.1250	21.7590
31	10.6268	12.6480	14.8428	17.2143	19.7625	22.4843
32	10.9696	13.0560	15.3216	17.7696	20.4000	23.2096
33	11.3124	13.4640	15.8004	18.3249	21.0375	23.9349
34	11.6552	13.8720	16.2792	18.8802	21.6750	24.6602
35	11.9980	14.2800	16.7580	19.4355	21.8125	25.3855
36	12.3408	14.6880	17.2368	19.9908	22.9500	26.1108
40	13.7120	16.3200	19.1520	22.2120	25.5000	29.0120
44	15.0832	17.9520	21.0672	24.4332	28.0500	31.9132
48	16.4544	19.5840	22.9824	26.6544	30.6000	34.8144
54	18.5112	22.0320	25.8552	29.9862	34.4250	39.1702
60	20.5680	24.4800	28.7280	33.3180	38.2500	43.5180
72	24.6816	29.3760	34.4736	39.9816	45.9000	52.2216

This table gives the number of Imperial gallons (277.274 inches) in cylindrical vessels from 1 to 62 inches in depth and from 4 to 72 inches in diameter.

TABLE 67 (Continued)

Capacity of Cylinders in Imperial Gallons

Depth, Inches	Diameter in Inches 17	18	19	20	21	24
1	.8188	.9180	1.0228	1.1333	1.2495	1.632
2	1.6376	1.8360	2.0456	2.2666	2.4990	3.264
3	2.4564	2.7540	3.0684	3.3999	3.7485	4.986
4	3.2752	3.6720	4.0912	4.5332	4.9980	6.528
5	4.0940	4.5900	5.1140	5.6665	6.2475	8.160
6	4.9128	5.5080	6.1368	6.7998	7.4970	9.792
7	5.7316	6.4260	7.1596	7.9331	8.7465	11.424
8	6.5504	7.3440	8.1824	9.0664	9.9960	13.056
9	7.3692	8.2620	9.2052	10.1997	11.2455	14.688
10	8.1880	9.1800	10.2280	11.3330	12.4950	16.320
11	9.0068	10.0980	11.2518	12.4663	13.7445	17.952
12	9.8256	11.0160	12.2736	13.5996	14.9940	19.584
13	10.6444	11.9340	13.2964	14.7329	16.2435	21.216
14	11.4632	12.8520	14.3192	15.8662	17.4930	22.848
15	12.2820	13.7700	15.3420	16.9995	18.7425	24.480
16	13.1008	14.6880	16.3648	18.1328	19.9920	26.112
17	13.9196	15.6060	17.3876	19.2661	21.2415	27.744
18	14.7384	16.5240	18.4104	20.3994	22.4910	29.376
19	15.5572	17.4420	19.4332	21.5327	23.7405	31.008
20	16.3760	18.3600	20.4560	22.6660	24.9900	32.640
21	17.1948	19.2780	21.4788	23.7993	26.2395	34.272
22	18.0136	20.1960	22.5036	24 9326	27.4890	35.904
23	18.8324	21.1140	23.5244	26.0659	28.7385	37.536
24	19.6512	22.0320	24.5472	27.1992	29.9880	39.168
25	20.4700	22.9500	25.5700	28.3325	31.2375	40.800
26	21.2888	23.8680	26.5928	29.4658	32.4870	42.432
27	22.1076	24.7860	27.6156	30.5991	33.7365	44.064
28	22.9264	25.7040	28.6384	31.7324	34.9860	45.696
29	23.7452	26.6220	29 6612	32.8657	36.2355	47.328
30	24.5640	27.5400	30.6840	33.9990	37.4850	48.960
31	25.3828	28.4580	31.7068	35.1323	38.7345	50.592
32	26 2016	29.3760	32.7296	36.2656	39.9840	52.224
33	27.0204	30.2940	33 7554	37.3989	41.2335	53.856
34	27.8392	31.2120	34.7752	38.5322	42.4830	55.488
35	28.6580	32.1300	35.7980	39.6655	43.7325	57.120
36	29.4768	33.0480	36 8208	40.7988	44.9820	58.752
40	32.7520	36.7200	40 9120	45.3320	49.9800	65.280
44	36.0272	40.3920	45.0072	49.8652	54.9780	71.808
48	39.3024	44.0640	45.0944	54.6384	59.9760	78.336
54	44.2152	49.5720	55.2312	61.1982	67.4730	88.128
60	49.1280	55.0800	61.3680	67.9980	74.9700	97.920
72	58.9536	66.0960	73.6416	81.5976	89.9640	117.504

This table gives the number of Imperial gallons (277.274 inches) in cylindrical vessels from 1 to 72 inches in depth and from 4 to 72 inches in diameter.

Table 67 (Continued)

Capacity of Cylinders in Imperial Gallons

Depth, Inches	Diameter in Inches 30	36	40	48	60	72
1	2.55	3.672	4.5333	6.528	10.2	14.688
2	5.10	7.344	9.0366	13.056	20.4	29.376
3	7.65	11.016	13.5999	19.584	30.6	44.064
4	10.20	14.688	18.1332	26.112	40.8	58.752
5	12.75	18.360	22.6665	32.640	51.0	73.440
6	15.30	22.032	27.1998	39.168	61.2	88.128
7	17.85	25.704	31.7331	45.696	71.4	102.816
8	20.40	29.376	36.2664	52.224	81.6	117.504
9	22.95	33.048	40.7997	58.752	91.8	132.192
10	25.50	36.720	45.3330	65.280	102.0	146.880
11	28.05	40.392	49.8663	71.808	112.2	161.568
12	30.60	44.064	54.3996	78.336	122.4	176.256
13	33.15	47.736	58.9329	84.864	132.6	190.944
14	35.70	51.408	63.4662	91.382	142.8	205.632
15	38.25	55.080	67.9995	97.920	153.0	220.320
16	40.80	58.752	72.5328	104.448	163.2	235.008
17	43.35	62.424	77.0661	110.976	173.4	249.696
18	45.90	66.096	81.5994	117.504	183.6	264.384
19	48.45	69.768	86.1327	124.032	193.8	279.072
20	51.00	73.440	90.6660	130.560	204.0	293.760
21	53.55	77.112	95.1999	137.088	214.2	308.448
22	56.10	80.784	99.7326	143.616	224.4	323.136
23	58.65	84.456	104.2659	150.144	234.6	337.824
24	61.20	88.128	108.7992	156.672	244.8	352.512
25	63.75	91.800	113.3325	163.200	255.0	367.200
26	66.30	95.472	117.8658	169.728	265.2	381.888
27	68.85	99.144	122.3091	176.256	275.4	396.576
28	71.40	102.816	126.9324	182.784	285.6	411.264
29	73.95	106.488	131.4657	189.312	295.8	425.952
30	76.50	110.160	135.9000	195.840	306.0	440.640
31	79.05	113.832	140.5326	202.368	316.2	455.328
32	81.60	117.504	145.0656	208.896	326.4	470.016
33	84.15	121.176	149.5989	215.424	336.6	484.704
34	86.70	124.848	154.1322	221.952	346.8	499.392
35	89.25	128.520	158.6655	228.480	357.0	514.080
36	91.80	132.192	163.1988	235.008	367.2	528.768
40	102.00	146.880	181.3320	261.120	408.0	587.520
44	112.20	161.568	199.4652	287.232	448.8	646.272
48	122.40	176.256	217.5984	313.344	489.6	705.024
54	137.70	198.288	244.2982	352.512	550.0	793.152
60	153.00	220.320	271.9980	391.680	612.0	881.280
72	183.60	264.384	326.3976	470.016	734.4	1057.536

This table gives the number of Imperial gallons (277.274 inches) in cylindrical vessels from 1 to 72 inches in depth and from 4 to 72 inches in diameter.

TABLE 68

Diameters, Areas and Circumferences of Circles

To find the capacity of any cylindrical measure, from 1 inch diameter to 30 inches, take the inside diameter of the measure in inches, and multiply the area in the table which corresponds to the diameter by the depth in inches, and divide the products, if gills are required, by 7.2135; if pints, by 28.875; if quarts, by 57.75; if gallons, by 231.

If bushels are required (say in a tierce or barrel, after the mean diameter is obtained), multiply as above, and divide the product by 2150.42.

Calling the diameters feet the areas are feet,—then, if a ship's water tank, steam boiler, etc., is 5⅛, or any number of feet and parts of feet in diameter, find the area in the table which corresponds in inches, multiply it by the length in feet, and multiply this result by the number of gallons in a cubic foot (7.4805), and the product is the answer in gallons. In any case where there are more figures in the divisor than in the dividend, add ciphers.

Any of the areas in inches, multiplied by .052, or the areas in feet multiplied by 7.48, the product is the numbers of gallons at 1 foot in depth.

Any of the areas in feet, multiplied by .03704, the product equals the number of cubic yards at 1 foot in depth.

Diam., Ins.	Circum., Ins.	Area, Sq. Ins.	Diam., Ins.	Circum., Ins.	Area, Sq. Ins.	Diam., Ins.	Circum., Ins.	Area, Sq. Ins.
1/16	7/32	.0030	7/8	2 3/4	.6013	2 3/8	7 3/8	4.430
1/8	13/32	.0122	15/16	2 15/16	.6903	2 1/2	7 3/4	4.908
3/16	19/32	.0276	1	3 1/8	.7854	2 5/8	8 1/4	5.412
1/4	25/32	.0490	1 1/8	3 1/2	.9940	2 3/4	8 5/8	5.939
5/16	31/32	.0767	1 1/4	3 7/8	1.227	2 7/8	9	6.491
3/8	1 3/16	.1104	1 3/8	4 1/4	1.484	3	9 3/8	7.068
7/16	1 3/8	.1503	1 1/2	4 5/8	1.767	3 1/8	9 3/4	7.669
1/2	1 9/16	.1963	1 5/8	5 1/8	2.074	3 1/4	10 1/4	8.295
9/16	1 25/32	.2485	1 3/4	5 1/2	2.405	3 3/8	10 5/8	8.946
5/8	1 31/32	.3068	1 7/8	5 7/8	2.761	3 1/2	11	9.621
11/16	2 5/32	.3712	2	6 1/4	3.141	3 5/8	11 3/8	10.320
3/4	2 11/32	.4417	2 1/8	6 5/8	3 546	3 3/4	11 3/4	11.044
13/16	2 9/16	.5185	2 1/4	7	3.976	3 7/8	12 1/8	11.793

Table 68 (Continued)

Diameters, Areas and Circumferences of Circles

Diam., Ins.	Cir., Ft.	Cir., Ins.	Area, Sq. Ins.	Area, Sq. Ft.	Diam., Ins.	Cir., Ft.	Cir., Ins.	Area, Sq. Ins.	Area, Sq. Ft.
4 in.	1	0½	12.566	.0879	10½	2	8⅞	86.590	.6061
4⅛	1	0⅞	13.364	.0935	10⅝	2	9⅜	88.664	.6206
4¼	1	1⅜	14.186	.0993	10¾	2	9¾	90.762	.6353
4⅜	1	1¾	15.033	.1052	10⅞	2	10⅛	92.855	.6499
4½	1	2⅛	15.904	.1113	11 in.	2	10½	95.033	.6652
4⅝	1	2½	16.800	.1176	11⅛	2	10⅞	97.205	.6874
4¾	1	2⅞	17.720	.1240	11¼	2	11¼	99.402	.6958
4⅞	1	3¼	18.665	.1306	11⅜	2	11¾	101.623	.7143
5 in.	1	3⅝	19.635	.1374	11½	3	0⅛	103.869	.7290
5⅛	1	4⅛	20.629	.1444	11⅝	3	0½	106.139	.7429
5¼	1	4½	21.647	.1515	11¾	3	0⅞	108.434	.7590
5⅜	1	4⅞	22.690	.1588	11⅞	3	1¼	110.753	.7752
5½	1	5¼	23.758	.1663	12 in.	3	1⅝	113.097	.7916
5⅝	1	5⅝	24.850	.1739	12⅛	3	2	115.466	.8082
5¾	1	6	25.967	.1817	12¼	3	2½	117.859	.8250
5⅞	1	6⅜	27.108	.1897	12⅜	3	2⅞	120.276	.8419
6 in.	1	6¾	28.274	.1979	12½	3	3¼	122.718	.8590
6⅛	1	7¼	29.464	.2062	12⅝	3	3¾	125.185	.8762
6¼	1	7⅝	30.679	.2147	12¾	3	4	127.676	.8937
6⅜	1	8	31.919	.2234	12⅞	3	4⅜	130.192	.9113
6½	1	8⅜	33.183	.2322	13 in.	3	4¾	132.732	.0291
6⅝	1	8¾	34.471	.2412	13⅛	3	5¼	135.297	.9470
6¾	1	9⅛	35.784	.2504	13¼	3	5⅝	137.886	.9642
6⅞	1	9½	37.122	.2598	13⅜	3	6	140.500	.9835
7 in.	1	10	38.484	.2603	13½	3	6⅜	143.139	1.0019
7⅛	1	10⅜	39.871	.2791	13⅝	3	6¾	145.802	1.0206
7¼	1	10¾	41.232	.2839	13¾	3	7⅛	148.489	1.0294
7⅜	1	11⅛	42.718	.2900	13⅞	3	7½	151.201	1.0584
7½	1	11½	44.178	.3002	14 in.	3	7⅞	153.938	1.0775
7⅝	1	11⅞	45.663	.3196	14⅛	3	8⅜	156.699	1.0968
7¾	2	0⅜	47.173	.3299	14¼	3	8¾	159.485	1.1193
7⅞	2	0¾	47.707	.3409	14⅜	3	9⅛	162.295	1.1360
8 in.	2	1⅛	50.265	.3518	14½	3	9½	165.130	1.1569
8⅛	2	1½	51.848	.3629	14⅝	3	9⅞	167.989	1.1749
8¼	2	1⅞	53.456	.3741	14¾	3	10¼	170.873	1.1961
8⅜	2	2¼	55.088	.3856	14⅞	3	10¾	173.782	1.2164
8½	2	2⅝	56.745	.3072	15 in.	3	11⅛	176.715	1.2370
8⅝	2	3	58.426	.4089	15⅛	3	11½	179.672	1.2577
8¾	2	3⅜	60.132	.4209	15¼	3	11⅞	182.654	1.2785
8⅞	2	3⅞	61.862	.4330	15⅜	4	0¼	185.661	1.2996
9 in.	2	4¼	63.617	.4453	15½	4	0⅝	188.692	1.3208
9⅛	2	4⅝	65.306	.4517	15⅝	4	1	191.748	1.3422
9¼	2	5	67.200	.4704	15¾	4	1½	194.828	1.3637
9⅜	2	5⅜	69.029	.4832	15⅞	4	1⅞	197.933	1.3855
9½	2	5¾	70.882	.4061	16 in.	4	2¼	201.062	1.4074
9⅝	2	6¼	72.759	.5003	16⅛	4	2⅝	204.216	1.4295
9¾	2	6⅞	74.662	.5226	16¼	4	3	207.394	1.4517
9⅞	2	7	76.588	.5301	16⅜	4	3⅜	210.597	1.4741
10 in.	2	7⅜	78.540	.5407	16½	4	3¾	213.825	1.4967
10⅛	2	7¾	80.515	.5636	16⅝	4	4¼	217.077	1.5195
10¼	2	8⅛	82.516	.5776	16¾	4	4⅝	220.353	1.5424
10⅜	2	8½	84.540	.5917	16⅞	4	5	223.654	1.5655

Note.—This table on heavy cardboard 11 × 14 ins., eyeletted, $0.25.

Table 68 (Continued)

Diameters, Areas and Circumferences of Circles

Diam., Ins.	Cir., Ft.	Cir., Ins.	Area, Sq. Ins.	Area, Sq. Ft.	Diam., Ft.	Diam., Ins.	Cir., Ft.	Cir., Ins.	Area, Sq. Ins.	Area, Sq. Ft.
17 in.	4	5⅜	226.980	1.5888	2	0	6	3⅜	452.290	3.1418
17⅛	4	5¾	230.330	1.6123	2	0¼	6	4⅛	461.864	3.2075
17¼	4	6⅛	233.705	1.6359	2	0½	6	4⅞	471.436	3.2731
17⅜	4	6½	237.104	1.6597	2	0¾	6	5¾	481.106	3.3410
17½	4	6⅞	240.528	1.6836	2	1	6	6½	490.875	3.4081
17⅝	4	7⅜	243.977	1.7078	2	1¼	6	7¼	500.741	3.4775
17¾	4	7¾	247.450	1.7321	2	1½	6	8⅛	510.706	3.5468
17⅞	4	8⅛	250.947	1.7566	2	1¾	6	8⅞	520.769	3.6101
18 in.	4	8½	254.469	1.7812	2	2	6	9⅝	530.930	3.6870
18⅛	4	8⅞	258.016	1.8061	2	2¼	6	10½	541.189	3.7583
18¼	4	9¼	261.587	1.8311	2	2½	6	11¼	551.547	3.8302
18⅜	4	9¾	265.182	1.8562	2	2¾	7	0	562.002	3.9042
18½	4	10⅛	268.803	1.8816	2	3	7	0¾	572.556	3.9761
18⅝	4	10½	272.447	1.9071	2	3¼	7	1⅝	583.208	4.0500
18¾	4	10⅞	276.117	1.9328	2	3½	7	2⅜	593.958	4.1241
18⅞	4	11¼	279.811	1.9586	2	3¾	7	3⅛	604.807	4.2000
19 in.	4	11⅝	283.529	1.9847	2	4	7	3⅞	615.753	4.2760
19⅛	5	0	287.272	1.9941	2	4¼	7	4¾	626.798	4.3521
19¼	5	0½	291.039	2.0371	2	4½	7	5½	637.941	4.4302
19⅜	5	0⅞	294.831	2.0637	2	4¾	7	6¼	649.182	4.5083
19½	5	1¼	298.648	2.0904	2	5	7	7	660.521	4.5861
19⅝	5	1⅝	302.489	2.1172	2	5¼	7	7⅛	671.958	4.6665
19¾	5	2	306.355	2.1443	2	5½	7	8⅝	683.494	4.7467
19⅞	5	2⅜	310.245	2.1716	2	5¾	7	9½	695.128	4.8274
20 in.	5	2⅞	314.160	2.1990	2	6	7	10¼	706.860	4.9081
20⅛	5	3¼	318.099	2.2265	2	6¼	7	11	718.690	4.9901
20¼	5	3⅝	322.063	2.2543	2	6½	7	11¾	730.618	5.0731
20⅜	5	4	326.051	2.2822	2	6¾	8	0⅝	742.644	5.1573
20½	5	4⅜	330.064	2.3103	2	7	8	1⅜	754.769	5.2278
20⅝	5	4¾	334.101	2.3386	2	7¼	8	2⅛	766.992	5.3264
20¾	5	5⅛	338.163	2.3670	2	7½	8	2⅞	779.313	5.4112
20⅞	5	5½	342.250	2.3956	2	7¾	8	3¾	791.732	5.4982
21 in.	5	5⅞	346.361	2.4244	2	8	8	4½	804.249	5.5850
21⅛	5	6⅜	350.497	2.4533	2	8¼	8	5⅜	816.865	5.6729
21¼	5	6¾	354.657	2.4824	2	8½	8	6⅛	829.578	5.7601
21⅜	5	7⅛	358.841	2.5117	2	8¾	8	6⅞	842.390	5.8491
21½	5	7½	363.051	2.5412	2	9	8	7⅝	855.300	5.9398
21⅝	5	7⅞	367.284	2.5708	2	9¼	8	8½	868.308	6.0291
21¾	5	8¼	371.543	2.6007	2	9½	8	9¼	881.415	6.1201
21⅞	5	8¾	375.826	2.6306	2	9¾	8	10	894.619	6.2129
22 in.	5	9⅛	380.133	2.6608	2	10	8	10¾	907.922	6.3051
22⅛	5	9½	384.465	2.6691	2	10¼	8	11½	921.323	6.3981
22¼	5	9⅞	388.822	2.7016	2	10½	9	0⅜	934.822	6.4911
22⅜	5	10¼	393.203	2.7224	2	10¾	9	1⅛	948.419	6.5863
22½	5	10⅝	397.608	2.7632	2	11	9	1⅞	962.115	6.6815
22⅝	5	11	402.038	2.7980	2	11¼	9	2¾	975.908	6.7772
22¾	5	11½	406.493	2.8054	2	11½	9	3½	989.800	6.8738
22⅞	5	11⅞	410.972	2.8658	2	11¾	9	4¼	1003.79	6.9701
23 in.	6	0¼	415.476	2.8903	3	0	9	5	1017.87	7.0688
23⅛	6	0⅝	420.004	2.9100	3	0¼	9	5⅞	1032.06	7.1671
23¼	6	1	424.557	2.9518	3	0½	9	6⅝	1046.35	7.2664
23⅜	6	1⅜	429.135	2.9937	3	0¾	9	7½	1060.73	7.3662
23½	6	1¾	433.737	3.0129	3	1	9	8¼	1075.21	7.4661
23⅝	6	2¼	438.363	3.0261	3	1¼	9	9	1089.79	7.5671
23¾	6	2⅝	443.014	3.0722	3	1½	9	9⅞	1104.46	7.6601
23⅞	6	3	447.690	3.1081	3	1¾	9	10½	1119.24	7.7791

NOTE.—This table on heavy cardboard 11 × 14 ins., eyeletted, $0.25.

TABLE 68 (Continued)

Diameters, Areas and Circumferences of Circles

Diam., Ft.	Diam., Ins.	Cir., Ft.	Cir., Ins.	Area, Sq. Ins.	Area, Sq. Ft.	Diam., Ft.	Diam., Ins.	Cir., Ft.	Cir., Ins.	Area, Sq. Ins.	Area, Sq. Ft.
3	2	9	11⅜	1134.12	7.8681	4	4	13	7⅜	2123.72	14.748
3	2¼	10	0⅛	1149.09	7.9791	4	4¼	13	8⅛	2144.19	14.890
3	2½	10	0⅞	1164.16	8.0846	4	4½	13	8⅞	2164.75	15.033
3	2¾	10	1¾	1179.32	8.1891	4	4¾	13	9¾	2185.42	15.176
3	3	10	2½	1194.59	8.2951	4	5	13	10½	2206.18	15.320
3	3¼	10	3¼	1209.95	8.4026	4	5	13	11¼	2227.05	15.465
3	3½	10	4	1225.42	8.5091	4	5½	14	0	2248.01	15.611
3	3¾	10	4⅞	1240.98	8.6171	4	5¾	14	0⅞	2269.06	15.757
3	4	10	5⅝	1256.64	8.7269	4	6	14	1⅝	2290.22	15.904
3	4¼	10	6⅜	1272.39	8.8361	4	6¼	14	2⅜	2311.48	16.051
3	4½	10	7¼	1288.25	8.9462	4	6½	14	3¼	2332.83	16.200
3	4¾	10	8	1304.20	9.0561	4	6¾	14	4	2354.28	16.349
3	5	10	8¾	1320.25	9.1686	4	7	14	4¾	2375.83	16.498
3	5¼	10	9½	1336.40	9.2112	4	7¼	14	5½	2397.48	16.649
3	5½	10	10⅜	1352.65	9.3936	4	7½	14	6⅜	2419.22	16.800
3	5¾	10	11⅛	1369.00	9.5061	4	7¾	14	7⅛	2441.07	16.951
3	6	10	11⅞	1385.44	9.6212	4	8	14	7⅞	2463.01	17.104
3	6¼	11	0¾	1401.98	9.7364	4	8¼	14	8⅝	2485.05	17.256
3	6½	11	1½	1418.62	9.8518	4	8½	14	9½	2507.19	17.411
3	6¾	11	2¼	1435.36	9.9671	4	8¾	14	10¼	2529.42	17.565
3	7	11	3	1452.20	10.084	4	9	14	11	2551.76	17.720
3	7¼	11	3⅞	1469.14	10.202	4	9¼	14	11⅞	2574.19	17.876
3	7½	11	4⅝	1486.17	10.320	4	9½	15	0⅝	2596.72	18.033
3	7¾	11	5⅜	1503.30	10.439	4	9¾	15	1⅜	2619.35	18.189
3	8	11	6¼	1530.53	10.559	4	10	15	2¼	2642.08	18.347
3	8¼	11	7	1537.86	10.679	4	10¼	15	2⅞	2664.91	18.506
3	8½	11	7¾	1555.28	10.800	4	10½	15	3¾	2687.83	18.665
3	8¾	11	8½	1572.81	10.922	4	10¾	15	4½	2710.85	18.825
3	9	11	9⅜	1590.43	11.044	4	11	15	5¼	2733.97	18.965
3	9¼	11	10⅛	1608.15	11.167	4	11¼	15	6⅛	2757.19	19.147
3	9½	11	10⅞	1625.97	11.291	4	11½	15	6⅞	2780.51	19.309
3	9¾	11	11¾	1643.89	11.415	4	11¾	15	7¾	2803.92	19.471
3	10	12	0½	1661.90	11.534	5	0	15	8½	2827.44	19.635
3	10¼	12	1¼	1680.02	11.666	5	0¼	15	9¼	2851.05	19.798
3	10½	12	2	1698.23	11.793	5	0½	15	10	2874.76	19.963
3	10¾	12	2⅝	1716.54	11.920	6	0¾	15	10¾	2898.56	20.128
3	11	12	3⅛	1734.94	12.048	5	1	15	11⅝	2922.47	20.294
3	11¼	12	4⅝	1753.45	12.176	5	1¼	16	0⅜	2946.47	20.461
3	11½	12	5¼	1772.05	12.305	5	1½	16	1¼	2970.57	20.629
3	11¾	12	6	1790.76	12.435	5	1¾	16	1⅞	2994.77	20.797
4	0	12	6¾	1809.56	12.566	5	2	16	2¾	3019.07	20.965
4	0¼	12	7½	1828.46	12.697	5	2¼	16	3½	3043.47	21.135
4	0½	12	8⅜	1847.45	12.829	5	2½	16	4¼	3067.96	21.305
4	0¾	12	9⅛	1866.55	12.962	5	2¾	16	5⅛	3092.56	21.476
4	1	12	9⅞	1885.74	13.095	5	3	16	5⅞	3117.25	21.647
4	1¼	12	10⅝	1905.03	13.229	5	3¼	16	6¼	3142.04	21.819
4	1½	12	11½	1924.42	13.304	5	3½	16	7½	3166.92	21.992
4	1¾	13	0¼	1943.91	13.499	5	3¾	16	8¼	3191.91	22.166
4	2	13	1	1963.50	13.635	5	4	16	9	3216.99	22.333
4	2¼	13	1⅞	1983.18	13.772	5	4¼	16	9¾	3242.17	22.515
4	2½	13	2½	2002.96	13.909	5	4½	16	10⅝	3267.46	22.621
4	2¾	13	3⅜	2022.84	14.047	5	4¾	16	11⅜	3292.83	22.866
4	3	13	4¼	2042.82	14.186	5	5	17	0⅛	3318.31	23.043
4	3¼	13	5	2062.90	14.325	5	5¼	17	0⅞	3343.88	23.221
4	3½	13	5¾	2083.07	14.465	5	5½	17	1¾	3369.56	23.330
4	3¾	13	6½	2103.35	14.606	5	5¾	17	2½	3395.33	23.578

NOTE.—This table on heavy cardboard 11 × 14 ins., eyeletted, $0.25.

Table 68 (Continued)

Diameters, Areas and Circumferences of Circles

Diam., Ft.	Diam., Ins.	Cir., Ft.	Cir., Ins.	Area, Sq. Ins.	Area, Sq. Ft.	Diam., Ft.	Diam., Ins.	Cir., Ft.	Cir., Ins.	Area, Sq. Ins.	Area, Sq. Ft.
5	6	17	3⅝	3421.20	23.758	6	8	20	11¼	5026.26	34.900
5	6¼	17	4⅛	3447.16	23.938	6	8¼	21	0⅛	5058.02	35.125
5	6½	17	4⅜	3473.23	24.119	6	8½	21	0⅞	5089.58	35.344
5	6¾	17	5⅞	3499.39	24.301	6	8¾	21	1⅝	5121.24	35.564
5	7	17	6½	3525.26	24.483	6	9	21	2⅜	5153.00	35.784
5	7¼	17	7¼	3552.01	24.606	6	9¼	21	3¼	5184.86	36.006
5	7½	17	8	3578.47	24.850	6	9½	21	4	5216.82	36.227
5	7¾	17	8¾	3605.03	25.034	6	9¾	21	4¾	5248.87	36.450
5	8	17	9⅝	3631.68	25.220	6	10	21	5½	5281.02	36.674
5	8¼	17	10⅜	3658.44	25.405	6	10¼	21	6⅜	5313.27	36.897
5	8½	17	11⅛	3685.29	25.592	6	10½	21	7⅛	5345.62	37.122
5	8¾	17	11⅞	3712.24	25.779	6	10¾	21	7⅞	5378.07	37.347
5	9	18	0¾	3730.28	25.964	6	11	21	8¾	5410.62	37.573
5	9¼	18	1½	3766.43	26.155	6	11¼	21	9½	5443.26	37.700
5	9½	18	2¼	3793.67	20.344	6	11½	21	10¼	5476.00	38.027
5	9¾	18	3⅛	3821.02	26.534	6	11¾	21	11	5508.84	38.256
5	10	18	3⅞	3848.46	26.725	7	0	21	11⅞	......	38.4846
5	10¼	18	4⅜	3875.99	26.916	7	1	22	3	......	39.4060
5	10½	18	5½	3903.63	27.108	7	2	22	6⅛	......	40.3388
5	10¾	18	6¼	3931.36	27.301	7	3	22	9¼	......	41.2825
5	11	18	7	3959.20	27.494	7	4	23	0⅜	......	42.2367
5	11¼	18	7¾	3987.13	27.688	7	5	23	2⅛	......	43.2022
5	11½	18	8⅝	4015.16	27.883	7	6	23	6¾	......	44.1787
5	11¾	18	9⅜	4043.28	28.078	7	7	23	11	......	45.1656
6	0	18	10⅛	4071.51	28.274	7	8	24	1⅛	......	46.1638
6	0¼	18	10⅞	4099.83	28.471	7	9	24	4⅛	......	47.1730
6	0½	18	11¾	4128.25	28.663	7	10	24	7¼	......	48.1926
6	0¾	19	0½	4156.77	28.866	7	11	24	10⅜	......	49.2236
6	1	19	1¼	4185.39	29.064	8	0	25	1½	......	50.2656
6	1¼	19	2⅛	4214.11	29.264	8	1	25	4⅝	......	51.6178
6	1½	19	2⅞	4242.92	29.466	8	2	25	7⅞	......	52.3816
6	1¾	19	3⅝	4271.83	29.665	8	3	25	11	......	53.4562
6	2	19	4½	4300.85	29.867	8	4	26	2⅛	......	54.5412
6	2¼	19	5¼	4329.95	30.069	8	5	26	5¼	......	55.6377
6	2½	19	6	4359.16	30.271	8	6	26	8⅜	......	56.7451
6	2¾	19	6¾	4388.47	30.475	8	7	26	11½	......	57.8628
6	3	19	7⅝	4417.87	30.619	8	8	27	2¾	......	58.9920
6	3¼	19	8⅜	4447.37	30.884	8	9	27	5¾	......	60.1321
6	3½	19	9⅛	4476.97	31.000	8	10	27	9	......	61.2826
6	3¾	19	9⅞	4506.67	31.296	8	11	28	0⅛	......	62.4445
6	4	19	10¾	4536.47	31.503	9	0	28	3¼	......	63.6174
6	4¼	19	11½	4566.36	31.710	9	1	28	6⅜	......	64.8006
6	4½	20	0¼	4596.35	31.919	9	2	28	9½	......	65.9951
6	4¾	20	1⅛	4626.44	32.114	9	3	29	0⅝	......	67.2007
6	5	20	1⅞	4656.63	32.337	9	4	29	3¾	......	68.4166
6	5¼	20	2⅝	4686.92	32.548	9	5	29	7	......	69.6440
6	5½	20	3⅛	4717.30	32.759	9	6	29	10⅛	......	70.8823
6	5¾	20	4¼	4747.79	32.970	9	7	30	1¼	......	72.1309
6	6	20	5	4778.37	33.183	9	8	30	4⅜	......	73.3910
6	6¼	20	5¾	4809.05	33.396	9	9	30	7½	......	74.6620
6	6½	20	6½	4839.83	33.619	9	10	30	11⅝	......	75.9433
6	6¾	20	7⅜	4870.70	33.824	9	11	31	1¾	......	77.2362
6	7	20	8⅛	4901.68	34.039	10	0	31	5	......	78.5400
6	7¼	20	8⅞	4932.75	34.255	10	1	31	8⅛	......	79.8540
6	7½	20	9¾	4963.92	34.471	10	2	31	11¼	......	81.1795
6	7¾	20	10½	4995.19	34.688	10	3	32	2⅜	......	82.5190

NOTE.—This table on heavy cardboard 11 × 14 ins., eyeletted, $0.25.

TABLE 68 (Continued)

Diameters, Areas and Circumferences of Circles

Diam., Ft.	Diam., Ins.	Cir., Ft.	Cir., Ins.	Area., Sq. Ft.	Diam., Ft.	Diam., Ins.	Cir., Ft.	Cir., Ins.	Area, Sq. Ft.
10	4	32	5½	83.8627	15	3	47	10⅞	182.6545
10	5	32	8⅝	85.2211	15	4	48	2½	184.6555
10	6	32	11¾	86.5903	15	5	48	5⅛	186.6684
10	7	33	2⅞	87.9697	15	6	48	8¼	188.6923
10	8	33	6⅛	89.3668	15	7	48	11⅜	190.7260
10	9	33	9¼	90.7627	15	8	49	2⅝	192 7716
10	10	34	0⅜	92.1749	15	9	49	5¾	194.8282
10	11	34	3½	93.5986	15	10	49	8⅞	196.8946
11	0	34	6⅝	95.0334	15	11	50	0	198.9730
11	1	34	9¾	96.4783	16	0	50	3⅛	201.0624
11	2	35	0⅞	97.9347	16	1	50	6¼	203.1615
11	3	35	4⅛	99.4021	16	2	50	9⅝	205.2726
11	4	35	7¼	100.8797	16	3	51	0½	207.3946
11	5	35	10⅝	102.3689	16	4	51	3¾	209.5264
11	6	36	1½	103.8601	16	5	51	6½	211.6703
11	7	36	4½	105.3794	16	6	51	10	213.8251
11	8	36	7¾	106.9013	16	7	52	1⅛	215.9896
11	9	36	10⅞	108.4342	16	8	52	4¼	218.1662
11	10	37	2¼	109.9772	16	9	52	7⅜	220.3537
11	11	37	5¼	111.5319	16	10	52	10½	222.5510
12	0	37	8⅜	113.0976	16	11	53	1⅝	224.7608
12	1	37	11½	114.6732	17	0	53	4⅞	226.9806
12	2	38	2⅝	116.2607	17	1	53	8	229.2105
12	3	38	5¾	117.8590	17	2	53	11⅛	231.4625
12	4	38	8⅞	119.4674	17	3	54	2⅛	233.7055
12	5	39	0	121.0876	17	4	54	5⅜	235.9682
12	6	39	3¼	122.7187	17	5	54	8½	238.2430
12	7	39	6⅜	124.3593	17	6	54	11⅝	240.5287
12	8	39	9½	126.0127	17	7	55	2⅞	242.8241
12	9	40	0⅝	127.6765	17	8	55	6	245.1316
12	10	40	3¾	129.3504	17	9	55	9⅛	247.4500
12	11	40	6⅞	131.0369	17	10	56	0¼	249.7781
13	0	40	10	132.7326	17	11	56	3½	252.1184
13	1	41	1⅛	134.4391	18	0	56	6½	254.4696
13	2	41	4⅜	136.1574	18	1	56	9⅝	256.8303
13	3	41	7½	137.8867	18	2	57	0⅞	259.2033
13	4	41	10⅝	139.6260	18	3	57	4	261.5872
13	5	42	1⅝	141.3771	18	4	57	7⅛	263.9807
13	6	42	4⅞	143.1391	18	5	57	10¼	266.3864
13	7	42	8	144.9111	18	6	58	1⅜	268.8031
13	8	42	11⅛	146.6949	18	7	58	4½	271.2293
13	9	43	2¼	148.4896	18	8	58	7⅝	273.6678
13	10	43	5½	150.2943	18	9	58	10¾	276.1171
13	11	43	8⅝	152.1109	18	10	59	2	278.5761
14	0	43	11¾	153.9484	18	11	59	5⅛	281.0472
14	1	44	2⅞	155.7758	19	0	59	8¼	283.5294
14	2	44	6	157.6250	19	1	59	11⅜	286.0210
14	3	44	9⅛	159.4852	19	2	60	2½	288 5249
14	4	45	0¼	161.3553	19	3	60	5⅝	291 3970
14	5	45	3½	163.2373	19	4	60	8¾	293.5641
14	6	45	6⅝	165.1303	19	5	60	11⅞	296.1107
14	7	45	9¾	167.0331	19	6	61	3⅛	298.6483
14	8	46	0⅞	168.9479	19	7	61	6¼	301.2054
14	9	46	4	170.8735	19	8	61	9½	303.7747
14	10	46	7⅛	172.8091	19	9	62	0½	306.3550
14	11	46	11¼	174.7565	19	10	62	3⅝	308.9448
15	0	47	1½	176.7150	19	11	62	6¾	311.5469
15	1	47	4⅝	178.6832	20	0	62	9⅞	314.1600
15	2	47	7¾	180.6624					

NOTE.—This table on heavy cardboard 11 × 14 ins., eyeletted, $0.25.

Table 69

Long or Linear Measure

12	inches		= 1 foot
3	feet,	or 36 inches	= 1 yard
5½	yards,	or 198 ins., or 16½ ft.	= 1 rod
40	rods,	or 7,920 ins., or 660 ft., or 220 yds.	= 1 furlong
8	furlongs,	or 6,330 ins., or 5,280 ft., or 1,760 yds. or 320 rods	= 1 mile

Measures in Occasional Use

1,000	mils	= 1 inch	9	ins.	= 1 span
3	ins.	= 1 palm	2½	ft.	= 1 military pace
4	ins.	= 1 hand	2	yds., or 6 ft.	= 1 fathom

Table 70

Square Measure for Surface

1	sq. in.		= 1.2732 circular inches
144	sq. ins.,	or 183.35 cir ins.	= 1 square foot
9	sq. ft.,	or 1,296 sq. ins.	= 1 square yard
100	sq. ft.		= 1 square
30¼	sq. yds.,	or 272¼ sq. ft.	= 1 square rod
40	sq. rods,	or 1,210 sq. yds.	= 1 square rood
4	sq. roods,	or 10 sq. chains, or 160 sq. rods or 4,840 sq. yds., or 43,560 sq. ft.	= 1 acre
640	acres,	one section, or 27,878,400 sq. ft.	= 1 square mile

One square inch = 1.2732 circular inches. An acre = a square whose side is 208.71 feet.

Table 71

Liquid Measure

4	gills	or 16 fluid ounces	= 1 pint
2	pints	or 8 gills	= 1 quart
4	quarts,	or 128 fluid ounces	= 1 gallon
31½	gallons		= 1 barrel
42	gallons		= 1 tierce
63	gallons,	or 2 barrels	= 1 hogshead
84	gallons,	or 2 tierces	= 1 puncheon
126	gallons	or 2 hogsheads	= 1 pipe or butt
2	pipes,	or 3 puncheons	= 1 tun

A gallon of water at 62° F. weighs 8.3356 pounds. The U. S. gallon contains 231 cubic inches. A measure six inches high and seven inches in diameter will hold almost a gallon, or one 6 inches high by 3½ inches in diameter one quart; or one three inches high and three and one-half inches in diameter will hold one pint. The British Imperial gallon contains 277.274 cubic inches or 1.20032 U. S. gallons.

Table 72

Dry Measure

2 pints,	or 67.2 cu. ins.	= 1 quart
4 quarts,	or 268.8 cu. ins.	= 1 gallon
2 gallons,	or 8 quarts	= 1 peck
4 pecks,	or 2,150.42 cu. ins.	= 1 bushel

The standard U. S. bushel is the Winchester bushel which is in cylinder form 18½ inches diameter and 8 inches deep. The British Imperial bushel equals 8 Imperial gallons or 2218.192 cubic inches. Eight Imperial bushels equal one British quarter.

The following measures are sanctioned by custom or law:

32 lbs. oats	= 1 bushel	56 lbs. butter	= 1 firkin
45 lbs. timothy seed	= 1 "	100 lbs. meal or flour	= 1 sack
48 lbs. barley	= 1 "	100 lbs. grain or flour	= 1 cental
50 lbs. indian meal	= 1 "	100 lbs. dry fish	= 1 quintal
56 lbs. rye	= 1 "	100 lbs. nails	= 1 cask
56 lbs. Indian corn	= 1 "	196 lbs. flour	= 1 barrel
60 lbs. wheat	= 1 "	200 lbs. beef or pork	= 1 "
60 lbs. potatoes	= 1 "	280 lbs. salt N. Y.	= 1 "
60 lbs. clover seed	= 1 "	280 lbs. lime	= 1 "
80 lbs. lime	= 1 "	400 lbs. Portland cement	= 1 "

Table 73

Cubic Measure—Measures of Volume

1,728	cu. ins.	= 1 cubic foot
27	cu. ft.	= 1 cubic yard
128	cu. ft. (a pile, 4 × 4 × 8 ft.)	= 1 cord of wood
24¾	cu. ft. (16½ × 1½ × 1 ft.)	= 1 perch of masonry
16	cu. ft.	= 1 cord foot

Table 74

Apothecaries' Fluid Measure

60 minims (m) or drops (gtt)	= 1 fluid drachm	ƒʒ
8 drachms	= 1 fluid ounce	ƒ℥
16 fluid ounces	= 1 pint	O
8 pints	= 1 gallon	(Cong)

In the U. S. a fluid ounce is the 128th part of a U. S. gallon, or 1.805 cubic inches. It contains 456.3 grains of water at 39° F. In Great Britain the fluid ounce is 1.732 cubic inches and contains 1 ounce avoirdupois, or 437.5 grains of water at 62° F.

TABLE 75

Avoirdupois or Commercial Weight

27.343 grains		= 1 drachm
16 drachms,	or 437.5 grains	= 1 ounce, oz.
16 ounces,	or 7,000 grains	= 1 pound, lb.
28 pounds		= 1 quarter, qr.
4 quarters,	or 112 pounds	= 1 hundredweight, cwt.
20 hundredweight,	or 2,240 lb.	= 1 gross or long ton
2,000 pounds		= 1 net or short ton
2,204.6 pounds		= 1 metric ton
14 pounds		= 1 stone
100 pounds		= 1 quintal

The drachm, quarter, hundredweight, stone and quintal are now seldom used in the United States.

TABLE 76

Troy Weight

24 grains		= 1 pennyweight, dwt.
20 pennyweights,	or 480 grains	= 1 ounce, oz.
12 ounces,	or 5,760 grains	= 1 pound, lb.
1 U. S. cent		= 48 T. grains
1 U. S. nickel		= 77.16 T. grains
1 U. S. dime,	silver	= 38.58 T. grains
1 U. S. quarter dollar,	silver	= 96.45 T. grains
1 U. S. half dollar,	silver	= 192 T. grains
1 U. S. dollar,	silver	= 412.5 T. grains
1 U. S. dollar,	gold	= 25.8 T. grains
1 U. S. quarter eagle,	$2.50, gold	= 64.5 T. grains
1 U. S. half eagle,	$5, gold	= 129 T. grains
1 U. S. eagle,	$10, gold	= 258 T. grains
1 U. S. double eagle,	$20, gold	= 516 T. grains

Troy weight is used for weighing gold and silver. The grain is the same as Avoirdupois, Troy, and Apothecaries' weights. A carat, for weighing diamonds = 3.168 grains = 0.200 gramme. In gold it indicates the fineness and means 1/24 part: Thus 18 carats fine is 18/24 gold and 6/24 alloy.

TABLE 77

Apothecaries' Weight

20 grains		= 1 scruple	℈
3 scruples,	or 60 grains	= 1 drachm	ʒ
8 drachms,	or 480 grains	= 1 ounce, oz.	℥
12 ounces,	or 5,760 grains	= 1 pound, lb.	

TABLE 78

Metric and U. S. Equivalent Measures

Measures of Length

French	British and U. S.
1 meter	= 39.37 inches, or 3.28083 feet, or 1.09361 yds.
0.3048 meter	= 1 foot
1 centimeter	= 0.3937 inch
2.54 centimeters	= 1 inch
1 millimeter	= 0.03937 inch, or about 1/25 inch
25.4 millimeters	= 1 inch
1 kilometer	= 1,093.61 yards, or 0.62137 mile
1.60935 kilometers	= 1 mile
1 myriameter	= 6.2137 miles

TABLE 79

Square or Surface Measure

French	British and U. S.
1 sq. meter	= 10.7639 sq. feet, or 1.196 sq. yards
0.836 sq. meter	= 1 sq. yard
0.0920 sq. meter	= 1 sq. foot
1 sq. centimeter	= 0.15500 sq. inch
6.452 sq. centimeters	= 1 sq. inch
1 sq. cemtimeter	= 0.00155 sq. inch = 1,973 circ. mils
645.2 sq. cemtimeters	= 1 sq. inch
1 centiare = 1 sq. meter	= 10.734 sq. feet, or 1.196 sq. yards
1 are, or 1 sq. decameter	= 1,076.41 sq. feet, or 119.6 sq. yards
1 hectare, or 100 ares	= 107,641 sq. feet = 2.4711 acres
1 sq. kilometer	= 0.386109 sq. miles = 247.11 acres
1 sq. myriameter	= 38.6109 sq. miles

TABLE 80

Cubic or Volume Measure

French	British and U. S.
1 cu. meter	= 35.314 cu. feet, or 1.308 cu. yards
0.7645 cu. meter	= 1 cu. yard
0.02832 cu. meter	= 1 cu. foot
1 cu. decimeter	= 61.0234 cu. inches, or 0.035314 cu. foot
28.32 cu. decimeters	= 1 cu. foot
1 cu. centimeter	= 0.061 cu. inch
16.387 cu. centimeters	= 1 cu. inch
1 cu. centimeter = 1 milliliter	= 0.061 cu. inch
1 deciliter	= 6.102 cu. inches
1 liter = 1 cu. decimeter	= 61.0234 cu. inches = 1.05671 qts, U. S.
1 hectoliter or decistere	= 3.5314 cu. feet = 2.8375 bu., U. S.
1 stere, kiloliter, or cu. meter	= 1.308 cu. yards = 28.37 bu., U. S.

TABLE 81

Liquid and Dry Measures

The liter is the primary unit of measures of capacity, and is a cube, each of whose edges is a tenth of a meter in length.

The hectoliter is the unit in measuring large quantities of grain, fruits, roots and liquids.

10 milliliters (ml)	= 1 centiliter (cl)	= 0.338 fluid ounce
10 centiliters	= 1 deciliter	= 0.845 liquid gill
10 deciliters	= 1 liter (l)	= 1.0567 liquid quarts
10 liters	= 1 decaliter	= 2.6417 gallons
10 decaliters	= 1 hectoliter (hl)	= 2 bushels, 3.35 pecks
10 hectoliters	= 1 kiloliter	= 28 bushels, 1½ pecks

A centiliter is about ⅓ of a fluid ounce; a liter is about 1 1/18 liquid quarts, or 9/10 of a dry quart; a hectoliter is about 2⅚ bushels; and a kiloliter is one cubic meter, or stere.

TABLE 82

Weights

The gram is the primary unit of weights, and is the weight in a vacuum of a cubic centimeter of distilled water at the temperature of 39.2° F.

10 milligrams (mg)	= 1 centigram (cg)	= 0.1543 troy grain
10 centigrams	= 1 decigram (dg)	= 1.543 troy grains
10 decigrams	= 1 gram (g)	= 15.432 troy grains
10 grams	= 1 decagram	= 0.3527 avoirdupois ounce
10 decagrams	= 1 hectogram	= 3.5274 avoirdupois ounces
10 hectograms	= 1 kilogram (kg)	= 2.2046 avoirdupois pounds
10 kilograms	= 1 myriagram	= 22.046 avoirdupois pounds
10 myriagrams	= 1 quintal (q)	= 220.46 avoirdupois pounds
10 quintals	= 1 tonneau (t)	= 2204.6 avoirdupois pounds
1 kilogram per kilometer		= 0.67195 pound per 1,000 feet
1 pound per thousand feet		= 1.4882 kilograms per kilometer
1 kilogram per sq. millimeter		= 1,423 pounds per sq. inch
1 pound per sq. inch		= 0.000743 kilogram per sq. millimeter

The gram is used in weighing gold, jewels, letters and small quantities of things. The kilogram, or, for brevity, kilo, is used by grocers; and the tonneau, or metric ton, is used in finding the weight of very heavy articles.

A gram is about 15½ grains troy; the kilo about 2⅕ pounds avoirdupois; and the metric ton, about 2,205 pounds.

A kilo is the weight of a liter of water at its greatest density; and the metric ton, of a cubic meter of water.

Metric numbers are written with the decimal point (.) at the right of the figures denoting the unit; thus the expression, 15 meters 3 centimeters, is written, 15.03 m.

When metric numbers are expressed by figures, the part of the expression at the left of the decimal point is read as the number of the unit, and the part at the right, if any, as a number of the lowest denomination indicated, or as a decimal part of the unit; thus, 46.525 m is read 46 meters and 525 millimeters, or 46 and 525 thousandths meters.

In writing and reading metric numbers, according as the scale is 10, 100 or 1,000, each denomination should be allowed one, two or three orders of figures.

TABLE 83

Comparison of U. S. and Foreign Weights and Measures

	Avoirdupois Weights		Liquid Measures		Dry Measures	
Country	Name	U.S. Lbs.	Name	U.S. Gals.	Name	U.S. Bush.
Austria	Pfund	1.234	Eimer	14.95	Nutze	1.745
Bremen	Pfund	1.009	Stubchen	.851	Scheffel	2.103
Buenos Ay's	Libra	1.0127	Frasco	.627	Fanega	3.894
China	Catty	1.3333			Sei	3.472
Cuba	Libra	1.0119	Arroba	4.1	Fanega	3.124
Denmark	Pund	1.1025	Pott	.255	Fonda	3.948
England	Pound	1.	Imp. Gall.	1.2003	Imp. Bush.	1.0315
France	Kilo	2.2046	Liter	.2642	Hectoliter	2.838
Hamburg	Pfund	1.0633	Ohm	48.278	Fass	1.56
Japan	Monme	3.858	Masa	.459		
Mexico	Libra	1.0119	Frasco	.4	Fanega	1.547
Nor. & Swdn.	Skalpund	.937	Kamea	.662		
Papal States	Libra	.7475	Barile (w'e)	15.412	Rubblio	.836
Portugal	Libra	1.0119	Almude	4.422	Alqueire	.393
Russia	Fuat	1.097	Vedro	3.249	Chetviert	5.956
Turkey	Oke	2.834			Kilo	1.001

TABLE 84

Decimal Equivalents of the Fractional Parts of an Inch

Fractions		Decimals	Millimeter	Fractions		Decimals	Millimeter
1/64	inch =	0.015625	0.3968	33/64	inch =	0.515625	13.0966
2/64	" =	0.03125	0.7937	34/64	" =	0.53125	13.4934
3/64	" =	0.046875	1.1906	35/64	" =	0.546875	13.8903
1/16	" =	0.0625	1.5875	**9/16**	" =	0.5625	14.2872
5/64	" =	0.078125	1.9843	37/64	" =	0.578125	14.6841
6/64	" =	0.09375	2.3812	38/64	" =	0.59375	15.0809
7/64	" =	0.109375	2.7780	39/64	" =	0.609375	15.4778
1/8	" =	0.125	3.1749	**5/8**	" =	0.625	15.8747
9/64	" =	0.14625	3.5718	41/64	" =	0.640625	16.2715
10/64	" =	0.15625	3.9686	42/64	" =	0.65625	16.6684
11/64	" =	0.171875	4.3655	43/64	" =	0.671875	17.0653
3/16	" =	0.1875	4.7624	**11/16**	" =	0.6875	17.4621
13/64	" =	0.203125	5.1592	45/64	" =	0.703125	17.8590
14/64	" =	0.21875	5.5561	46/64	" =	0.71875	18.2559
15/64	" =	0.234375	5.9530	47/64	" =	0.734375	18.6527
1/4	" =	0.250	6.3498	**3/4**	" =	0.750	19.0496
17/64	" =	0.265625	6.7467	49/64	" =	0.765625	19.4465
18/64	" =	0.28125	7.1436	50/64	" =	0.78125	19.8433
19/64	" =	0.296875	7.5404	51/64	" =	0.796875	20.2402
5/16	" =	0.3125	7.9373	**13/16**	" =	0.8125	20.6371
21/64	" =	0.328125	8.3342	53/64	" =	0.828125	21.0339
22/64	" =	0.35375	8.7310	54/64	" =	0.84375	21.4308
23/64	" =	0.359375	9.1279	55/64	" =	0.859375	21.8277
3/8	" =	0.375	9.5248	**7/8**	" =	0.875	22.2245
25/64	" =	0.390625	9.9216	57/64	" =	0.890625	22.6214
26/64	" =	0.40625	10.3185	58/64	" =	0.90625	23.0183
27/64	" =	0.421875	10.7154	59/64	" =	0.921875	23.4151
7/16	" =	0.4375	11.1122	**15/16**	" =	0.9375	23.8120
29/64	" =	0.453125	11.5091	61/64	" =	0.953125	24.2089
30/64	" =	0.46875	11.9060	62/64	" =	0.96875	24.6057
31/64	" =	0.484375	12.3029	63/64	" =	0.983275	25.0057
1/2	" =	0.500	12.6997	**1**	" =	1.000	25.3995

TABLE 85

Inches and Fractions Expressed in Decimals of One Foot

Inches	0	1	2	3	4	5	6	7	8	9	10	11
0	....	0833	1667	2500	3833	4167	5000	5833	6667	7500	8333	9167
1/8	0104	0938	1771	2604	3438	4271	5104	5938	6771	7604	8438	9271
1/4	0208	1042	1875	2708	3542	4375	5208	6042	6875	7708	8542	9375
3/8	0313	1146	1979	2813	3646	4479	5313	6146	6979	7813	8646	9479
1/2	0417	1250	2083	2917	3750	4583	5417	6250	7083	7917	8750	9583
5/8	0521	1354	2188	3021	3854	4688	5521	6354	7188	8021	8854	9688
3/4	0625	1458	2292	3125	3958	4792	5625	6458	7292	8125	8958	9792
7/8	0729	1563	2396	3229	4063	4896	5729	6563	7396	8229	9063	9896

Table 86

Weights of Various Substances Per Cubic Foot in Pounds

Material	Weight per Cubic Foot, Lbs.
Aluminum	162 to 166.5
Antimony	421.6
Ashes	37 to 43.
Asphaltum	87.
Bismuth	612.4
Brass:	
Cast	504
Copper + Zinc	
80 20	536.3
70 30	523.8
60 40	521.3
50 50	511.4
Brick:	
Soft	100.
Common	112.
Hard	125.
Pressed	135 to 150.
Fire	140 to 150.
Sand-lime	136.
Brickwork in—	
Mortar	100.
Cement	112.
Bronze:	
Cop., 95 to 80; Tin 5 to 20	552
Cadmium	539.
Calcium	98.5
Cement:	
American, Rosendale	56.
Louisville, Portland	50.
loose	90 to 92.
in barrel	115.
Chromium	311.8
Clay	120 to 150.
Cobalt	533.1
Concrete	120 to 155.
Copper	552.
Earth:	
Loose	72 to 80.
Rammed	90 to 110.
Emery	250.
Glass	156 to 172.
" flint	180 to 196.
Gneiss, Granite	160 to 170.
Gold, pure:	
Cast	1200.9 to 1204
Hammered	1217
Gravel	100 to 120.
Gypsum	130 to 150.
Hornblende	200 to 220.
Ice	55 to 57.
Iridium	1393.
Iron:	
Cast	450.
Wrought	480.
Lead	709.7
Lime, quick, in bulk	50 to 60.
Limestone	140 to 185.
Magnesia, Carbonate	150.
Magnesium	109.
Manganese	499.
Marble	160 to 180.
Masonry:	
Dry rubble	140 to 160.
Dressed	140 to 180.
Mercury 32°	848.6
Mercury 60°	846.8
Mercury 212°	834.4
Mica	175 to 183.
Mortar	90 to 100.
Mud, soft flowing	104 to 120.
Nickel	548.7
Pitch	72.
Plaster of Paris	93 to 113.
Platinum	1347.0
Potassium	53.9
Quartz	165.
Rosin	69.
Salt:	
Coarse, N. Y.	45.
Fine, Liverpool	49
Sand	90 to 110.
" wet	118 to 129.
Sandstone	140 to 150.
Silver	655.1
Slate	170 to 180.
Snow:	
Freshly fallen	5 to 12.
Moistened	15 to 50.
Soapstone	166 to 175.
Sodium	60.5
Steel	489.6
Stone:	
Various	135 to 200.
Crushed	100.
Tar	62.
Tile	110 to 120.
Tin	458.3
Titanium	330.5
Trap Rock	170 to 200.
Tungsten	1078.7
Water:	
Distilled at 60° F.	62.35
Sea	64.08
Zinc	436.5

TABLE 87

Weight of Liquids Per Gallon

1 Gallon	Lbs.	1 Gallon	Lbs.
Acid, Nitric	10.58	Oil of Turpentine	7.25
Acid, Sulphuric	15.42	Oil, Whale	7.25
Acid, Muriatic	10.	Petroleum	7.35
Alcohol, Commerce	6.74	Vinegar	8.43
Alcohol, Proof Spirit	7.94	Salt Water	8.59
Naphtha	7.08	Tar	8.43
Oil, Linseed	7.75	Distilled Water	8.34

TABLE 88

Weight of Water

1	cubic inch	is equal to	.03617	pound.
12	cubic inches	is equal to	.434	pound.
1	cubic foot	is equal to	62.5	pounds.
1	cubic foot	is equal to	7.50	U. S. gallons.
1.8	cubic feet	is equal to	112.00	pounds.
35.84	cubic feet	is equal to	2240.00	pounds.
1	cylindrical in.	is equal to	.02842	pound.
12	cylindrical ins.	is equal to	.341	pound.
1	cylindrical ft.	is equal to	49.10	pounds.
1	cylindrical ft.	is equal to	6.00	U. S. gallons.
2.282	cylindrical ft.	is equal to	112.00	pounds.
45.64	cylindrical ft.	is equal to	2240.00	pounds.
13.43	U. S. gallons	is equal to	112.00	pounds.
268.8	U. S. gallons	is equal to	2240.00	pounds.

Center of pressure is at two-thirds depth from surface.

TABLE 89

Pressure of Water Per Square Inch, Due to Different Heads, from 1 to 250 Feet

Head	Pressure in Lbs.	Head	Pressure in Lbs.	Head	Pressure in Lbs.
1	.4335	19	8.237	37	16.04
2	.8670	20	8.670	38	16.47
3	1.300	21	9.104	39	16.91
4	1.734	22	9.537	40	17.34
5	2.167	23	9.971	50	21.67
6	2.601	24	10.40	100	43.35
7	3.035	25	10.84	110	47.68
8	3.408	26	11.27	120	52.02
9	3.902	27	11.70	130	56.36
10	4.335	28	12.14	140	60.69
11	4.768	29	12.57	150	65.03
12	5.202	30	13.00	160	69.36
13	5.636	31	13.44	170	73.70
14	6.069	32	13.87	180	78.03
15	6.503	33	14.31	190	82.36
16	6.936	34	14.74	200	86.70
17	7.370	35	15.17	225	97.41
18	7.803	36	15.60	250	108.37

TABLE 90

Strength and Weight of Rope

Specifications of the United States Navy, June, 1910

Circumferences in	Diameters in	Manila hemp, plain laid		American hemp, tarred, plain laid, three stands	
		Weights lbs. per ft.	Breaking-loads lb.	Weights lbs. per ft.	Breaking-loads lb.
¾	0.24	0.02	700	0.051	750
1	0.32	0.033	1,000	0.06	1,060
1¼	0.40	0.05	1,800	0.067	1,670
1½	0.48	0.083	2,500	0.083	2,340
1¾	0.56	0.10	3,000	0.105	3,325
2	0.64	0.14	4,000	0.16	3,955
2¼	0.72	0.17	5,000	0.21	4,720
2½	0.80	0.21	5,500	0.26	5,770
2¾	0.87	0.26	6,600	0.32	7,000
3	0.95	0.305	7,800	0.37	8,400
3¼	1.03	0.36	9,200	0.44	9,800
3½	1.16	0.42	10,500	0.51	11,200
3¾	1.19	0.47	12,200	0.59	13,000
4	1.27	0.54	13,700	0.67	14,550
4½	1.43	0.67	17,400	.....	.....
5	1.59	0.83	21,800	.....	.....
5½	1.75	1.00	27,700	.....	.....
6	1.90	1.21	31,000	.....	.....
7	2.22	1.63	36,200	.....	.....
8	2.54	2.17	47,300	.....	.....
9	2.87	2.70	60,000	.....	.....
10	3.14	3.33	74,200	.....	.....

Manila-hemp rope is made in three strands and in sizes up to 3 inches in circumference; four strands are used for sizes larger than 3 inches in circumference.

Working-Load

The *Working-Load* for slow-speed derrick and hoisting-service is usually taken at one-seventh the *Breaking-Load.* This makes some allowance for the loss of strength at splices and connections. The deterioration of rope exposed to the weather is very rapid.

TABLE 91

Boiling Point of Acid, Oil, Water, Etc., at Atmospheric Pressure 14.7 lb. Per Sq. Inch

	Degrees F.		Degrees F.
Alcohol	173	Mercury	676
Aniline	363	Naphthaline	428
Aqua ammonia, sp. gr. 0.95	146	Nitric acid	248
Average sea-water	213.2	Oil of turpentine	315
Benzine	176	Phosphorus	554
Bromine	145	Saturated brine	226
Carbon bisulphide	118	Sulphur	800
Chloroform	140	Sulphuric acid	590
Ether, sulphuric	100	Water	212
Linseed oil	597	Wood spirit	150

The boiling-points of liquids increase as the pressure increases.

TABLE 92

Melting Points of Various Materials

	Degrees F.		Degrees F.
Acetic acid	113	Palladium	2732*
Alloy, 1½ tin, 1 lead	334, 367†	Platinum	3227*, 3110†
Aluminum	1157*, 1214†	Phosphorus	112
Antimony	1150, 1169†	Potassium	136 to 144
Bismuth	504 to 507	Potassium sulphate	1859*, 1958†
Brass melts at	1873	Rhodium	3578
Bronze	1692	Silver	1733*, 1751†
Bromine	− 9.5	Sodium	194 to 208
Cadmium	442	Spermaceti	120
Calcium	Full red heat.	Stearic acid	158
Carbonic acid	−108	Stearine	109 to 120
Cast iron: White	1922, 2075†	Steel	2372 to 2532*
Gray	2012 to 2786, 2228*	hard	2570*; mild, 2687
Copper	1929*, 1943†	Sulphur	239
Gold	1913*, 1947†	Sulphurous acid	−148
Hyponitric acid	16	Tallow	92
Ice	32	Tin	446, 449†
Iodine	225	Tin and lead, equal parts, melt at	418
Iridium	4280	Tin 2 parts, bismuth 5 and lead 3, melt at	199
Lead	618*, 620†	Tungsten	5252
Magnesium	1200	Turpentine	14
Margaric acid	131 to 140	Vanadium	3110
Mercury	−39, 38†	Wax	142 to 154
Molybdenum	4622	Wrought iron	2732 to 2912, 2737*
NaCl, common salt	1472†	Zinc	779*, 786†
Nickel	2600†		
Nitro-glycerine	45		

The figures given above are by Clark (on the authority of Pouillet, Claudel, and Wilson), except those marked *, which are given by Prof. Roberts-Austen, those marked −, which are from H. von Wartenberg, and those marked †, which are given by Dr. J. A. Harker.

INDEX

C

D

E

S

U

V

W

Y

Z

LaVergne, TN USA
26 July 2010
191012LV00003B/89/P

9 781146 094832